MARXISM: AN AMERICAN
CHRISTIAN PERSPECTIVE

MARXISM: AN AMERICAN CHRISTIAN PERSPECTIVE

Arthur F. McGovern

ORBIS BOOKS

Maryknoll, New York 10545

The Catholic Foreign Mission Society of America (Maryknoll) recruits and trains people for overseas missionary service. Through Orbis Books Maryknoll aims to foster the international dialogue that is essential to mission. The books published, however, reflect the opinions of their authors and are not meant to represent the official position of the society.

Library of Congress Cataloging in Publication Data

McGovern, Arthur F
  Marxism, an American Christian perspective.

  Includes bibliographical references and index.
  1. Communism and Christianity. I. Title.
HX536.M29   261.8   79-27257
ISBN 0-88344-301-5

Contents

PART II
The Impact of Marxism on Christian Social Thought and Action

Introduction

For more than a century Christianity and Marxism confronted each other as hostile, diametrically opposed ideologies. For most Christians in the world, this opposition remains strong. But in recent years, and in many parts of the world, a very different attitude toward Marxism has developed. Many Christians now espouse Marxism; some even call themselves "Christian Marxists."

The first two countries which Pope John Paul II chose to visit, after his surprising election in the fall of 1978, symbolized the two very different ways in which the issue of Marxism and Christianity is being contested in the Church. When he returned in triumph to his native Poland, in May of 1979, the pontiff visited a country where Catholicism stands steadfast in its resistance to absorption by an atheistic Marxist ideology. But when he flew earlier in the year to Puebla, Mexico, to address Latin American bishops assembled there, the pope found a Church deeply troubled by problems of poverty and oppression which have led many within the Church to espouse Marxist analysis and strategies as the only solution. How such very different attitudes toward Marxism could occur in the same epoch of history requires some explanation, an explanation which this book attempts to provide.

The adversary relationship between Marxism and Christianity is far more familiar. Since its inception Marxism has appeared to be the very antithesis of Christianity. It seemed clear that its atheism scorned God and religion. Its materialism denied the soul and after-life. Its determinism negated free will. Its revolutionary strategy promoted class antagonisms and violent overthrow of the state. Its socialism would take away the right to private property, and with it, all incentive to work.

A Stalinist Russia seemed clearly to prove how destructive these ideas were in practice. Marxist theory had become Communist reality; the terms became identified. Pope Pius XI denounced Communism as "intrinsically evil." Bishop Fulton J. Sheen warned us of its dangers in the 1930s, and the warnings seemed vindicated as Eastern Europe, China and later Cuba "fell" to Communism. The early 1950s brought graphic accounts of missionaries tortured and imprisoned in China, reports of repression of religion in Poland and Hungary, chilling photographs of Cardinal Mindszenty broken by Communist interrogation. U.S. citizens prayed for persecuted Christians behind the Iron Curtain, and worried about Communist infiltration into our own

1

State Department and about a Communist takeover of the world.

A dramatic reversal of this adversary position has occurred nonetheless among Christians in many parts of the world. A growing number of Christians have called for openness to Marxism and have even espoused it. A Catholic bishop, Dom Helder Camara of Olinda-Recife, Brazil, has called for a synthesis of Marxism and Christianity like the synthesis St. Thomas Aquinas achieved between Aristotle and Christianity in the Middle Ages. Other bishops from Third World countries have condemned capitalism and proclaimed socialism as a truer expression of Christianity. In Latin America, liberation theologians have made use of Marxist analysis and accepted a Marxist perspective on the necessity of class struggle. In Italy, large numbers of Catholics advocate a Communist government for their country and have joined the Communist Party. In Chile, the Marxist socialist system developing under Salvador Allende in the early 1970s was proclaimed by Christians as a harbinger of a just society. A Christians for Socialism movement which began in Chile now has affiliates throughout the world, including groups in several U.S. cities. In England, "New Left" Catholics have gone so far as to argue that Christians *should be* Marxists, that the only truly Christian response in the current world situation is to join in the struggle for revolutionary socialism.

The purpose of this book is to re-examine Marxism, especially in light of this new Christian attitude toward it, but also by weighing the traditional arguments against it. The book deals primarily with Marxist theory, but it studies that theory as it developed historically and as it became embodied in Communist countries and movements. A study of Christian social thought in its development regarding both Marxism and socialism is included. The focal issue throughout is whether Marxism and Christianity are compatible. No attempt is made to synthesize Marxism and Christianity. Theoretical discussions about what Christians might learn from Marxist philosophy or what Marxists could learn from Christians are minimized. The concern of the book is a very practical one. The Church finds many of its own members calling for the use of Marxist analysis and at times collaborating with Marxists to achieve socialism. How should the Church respond? How should Christians view Marxism? The very length of the book results from an effort to take into consideration, to the extent possible, all the factors needed for such an assessment.

The book is addressed mainly to Christians in the United States. It tries to present the best of recent studies on Marx and Marxism, to indicate controversies and differing interpretations on positions within Marxism, and hence to go beyond simplistic, stereotyped views of Marxism. Some readers may already be versed in Marxism or aspects of theology and Church social teachings covered in the book. But the book was written with a view to the widest possible use, as a possible textbook for students and for readers with relatively little knowledge of Marxism. The topic seemed too important, on the other hand, to treat in a popularized fashion; so it was written with Marxist scholars in mind as well.

Three important terms which occur throughout the book need to be distinguished briefly at the outset—Communism, Socialism, and Marxism. Their meanings often overlap and some authors define them differently, but the following distinctions will indicate how they will be used in this book. "Communism," with a capital "C," will be used to refer to actual political-economic systems in countries which claim to have embodied Marxist ideas. "Communist," as an adjective, quite obviously also applies to all Communist Parties and Party members whether in power or not, and it may sometimes be used to designate official Party doctrines. All modern Communists are Marxists, and they constitute the great majority of Marxists in the world. But there are also many Marxists sharply critical of existing Communist regimes and many who would dissociate themselves from official Party ideology. Hence Communism and Marxism are not interchangeable terms.

"Socialism" will be used in a wider sense to refer to any actual or proposed economic system which advocates "public ownership of property." Some socialists may draw upon a Marxist critique in their opposition to capitalism. But many socialists are not Marxists; some socialist movements have been in sharp conflict with Communist Parties. There are socialist countries, such as Tanzania, which are not Communist or Marxist. "Public ownership of property" can mean different things. Some textbooks define socialism as "state ownership," and socialism is often thought of as a highly centralized, bureaucratic system. But many socialists explicitly reject this narrow meaning and advocate democratic, decentralized models of group and community ownership. Some proposals for socialism call for a "mixed economy" to include private and socialized enterprises. "Socialism" will be used in this book in a broad sense to include various forms of public ownership.[1]

"Marxism" will be used to refer to the theory or body of ideas originated by Marx and developed by others. Marx's theory stressed practical, revolutionary activity; reference to Marxism as a "theory" in no way denies this. But the point to be emphasized is that his theory, his method, and his ideas have been appropriated by many who would not call themselves Communist. The question whether Marxism and Christianity are compatible would be settled at the outset if Marxism and Communism were identified. Communism— granting the possibility of Eurocommunist exceptions—proclaims an atheistic, materialist worldview as an essential component of Marxism. Christians may learn to live with this, as they have in Poland, but Pope John Paul II can hardly be criticized for speaking of two diametrically opposed worldviews. It may be that atheism proves essential to any form of Marxism; this is one issue to be investigated. But only by distinguishing between Marxism and Communism can the question even be asked. What many Christians want to affirm is Marxist analysis of and opposition to capitalism. They feel that Marxist analysis and *socialist* goals are quite consistent with Christianity, if Communist ideology is not. Hence what constitutes Marxism and what ideas are essential to Marxism are critical issues discussed throughout the book.

In a book *On Synthesizing Marxism and Christianity,* Dale Vree proposes using the term Marxism to mean "whatever most Marxists, most of the time, have believed," and by Christianity "whatever most Christians, most of the time, have believed."[2] Arguments over what constitutes "true" Marxism, he feels, would be decided by this normative definition of Marxism. As orthodoxy and heresy are determined in Christianity by Church authorities, so should orthodox Marxism be determined by the Communist Party, which represents what most Marxists have traditionally held. His normative definition does draw attention to one important point: the *dominant* Marxist tradition is represented by Communism, and when Christians weigh a decision about collaborating with Marxist groups or movements this fact has to be taken into account. But Vree's definition fails both because it rules out in advance the claims of many who call themselves Marxists and because it forecloses on the possibility of change within the dominant Marxist tradition. If Christianity is defined as "whatever most Christians, most of the time, have believed," then Protestants could never have claimed to be "Christian" in the sixteenth century since "most Christians" until that time believed in Catholicism. Thus, in contrast to Vree's position, the openness of Marxism to different interpretations and possible embodiments is a basic premise in this book.

A quite important practical issue underlies these distinctions of terms. What most Christians who advocate Marxism really want to achieve is a new social order which embodies socialist values of cooperative work, shared control of power, and a more just distribution of goods. The immediate identification of socialism with Communism, and of Marxist analysis with Communist ideology, creates a strong bias against such a possibility.

The book is divided into three main parts, each composed of three chapters. Part I offers an historical perspective. Chapter 1 deals with Marx's own writings. It situates his writings in the socio-political and intellectual context of his times and traces the development of his thought from his early years to his death. Two significant points emerge from the study of Marx's early years. His atheism preceded his commitment to socialism and hence was not linked at the outset to socialist goals. His advocacy of socialist revolution preceded his study of capitalism and hence was not at first even linked to the overthrow of capitalism. Chapter 2 on the history of Marxism traces the development of "Classical Marxism," the dominant Marxist tradition, from Engels' dialectical materialism and the German Social Democrats, through Lenin and Stalin, and into post-World War II developments with special reference to Eurocommunism. This history is essential for understanding how a total Marxist worldview took shape and became an official, and often very dogmatic, ideology. The second part of the chapter deals with "Critical Marxism," with important figures in Western European Marxism who have challenged many of the classical views in the dominant tradition. A grasp of the main thrust of this current within Marxism is quite important to the issue of what is essential to Marxism, but an understanding of each specific figure is not. Gramsci and Althusser have significantly influenced recent Christian socialist thinking; Marcuse and Habermas are relevant to Marxist thought in the United States. Chapter 3 studies the history of the Church's attitudes toward Marxism and socialism. It looks at the "mind-set" of the Church in the nineteenth century and conditions which made it resistant not only to revolutionary socialism but to social change in general. It then traces developments in Church social teachings from Pope Leo XIII to the present. The chapter focuses especially on papal social encyclicals but includes also the important writings of Protestant theologians on Marxism/socialism, Catholic social thinkers, and Christian-Marxist encounters in recent years.

Part II studies the impact of Marxism on Christian social thinking and action. The appeal of Marxism stems chiefly from the forcefulness of its critique of capitalism. Chapter 4 thus presents "The Case Against Capitalism." It focuses particularly on neo-Marxist and other radical criticisms of U.S. capitalism, but the section on imperialism should help to explain why Latin American and other Third World Christians blame the United States and Western Europe for the underdevelopment and dependency of their countries. Chapter 5 attempts to explain and evaluate liberation theology in Latin America. Opponents of liberation theology have accused it of simply using theology to justify Marxist revolutionary views. This accusation will be addressed in an effort to determine the nature and the extent of the role Marxism plays in liberation theology. The chapter also includes discussions of two issues which relate to Marxism itself: to what extent "praxis" provides a criterion for truth, and whether Marxism is a science. Chapter 6 on "Chile Under Allende and Christians For Socialism" provides an important case study in respect to Marxist-Christian relations. In sharp contrast to experiences in other countries where Communism gained power, Church-state relations in Chile were relatively cordial. The official Church did not oppose Allende's election; Allende, for his part, showed respect for religious liberties. Tensions did arise, however, within the Church between the bishops who maintained a stance of neutrality and Christian groups who pushed for an active commitment to socialism.

Part III addresses the major difficulties raised as Christian objections to Marxism. Chapter 7 takes up the question: "Are atheism and materialism essential to Marxism?" The chapter explores the various sources of Marxist atheism in an effort to resolve the question—the humanistic atheism of the young Marx, the ideological critique of religion by Marx and Engels, the scientific atheism and materialism of Engels, the militant atheism of Lenin, and neo-Marxist re-evaluations of religion. Chapter 8 focuses on the political-moral problems evoked by classical Marxist views: abolition of private property; the use of revolutionary violence; the invoking of class struggle; dictatorship of the proletariat as a threat to democratic freedoms. Chapter 9 offers some concluding personal reflections about Marxism and Christianity especially in relation to the problem of the feasibility and desirability of socialism in the United States.

An historical-genetical method is used frequently throughout the book, and this accounts in large measure for its length. A critical factor in determining the compatibility of Marxism and Christianity is whether the "way things are" is the way they need be. The historical conditions which gave rise to certain Christian and Marxist positions no longer exist. But positions tend to become fixed or "reified," to use a Marxist term, with new justifications given to legitimize them. Church views on the right to property and Marxist views on the necessity for a unified, atheistic worldview may be understandable in the light of history but may serve poorly for the present. A dialectical effort at understanding by looking at both sides of an issue also characterizes the method used. But this is inevitably a selective process and my own views have undoubtedly influenced the stressing of certain points and the neglect of others.

The book is intended not as a definitive statement, but as a lengthy "working paper," as a basis from which to begin. First and second drafts of chapters were submitted to various readers with special expertise or experience in areas covered. Criticisms and suggestions have been incorporated into the text. The book remains nevertheless only a beginning, a first step. Many chapters, such as Chapter 3 on the Church, provide a historical survey of views that call for more sharply focused analysis. Chapter 4, "The Case Against Capitalism," because it deals with highly complex economic issues, must especially be considered only as a working paper. The chapter surveys what seemed to me the most forceful arguments of the Left against capitalism. But the chapter does not provide an original or professional economic analysis, nor does it even attempt to assess all the anti-capitalist arguments given. If the book succeeds, nevertheless, in gathering together the materials most needed for a reappraisal of Marxism-Christianity and in defining the major issues, its most important goal will have been achieved.

Two aspects of the book as a whole render it particularly vulnerable to criticism—its comprehensiveness and its dependency on books rather than direct experience. The book aims at providing an overview of a topic that is vast and complex in its scope. Marxism raises critically important questions about human society and proposes solutions for achieving a new social order. Any adequate Christian response must take up the issues it poses as fully as possible, considering all their possible ramifications. A Christian concerned about justice and wanting to work for a more humane society needs to have as clear a perspective as possible in order to judge and act intelligently. Hence a book of this scope seemed needed.

But the effort to be comprehensive creates some obvious problems. A study such as this involves numerous disciplines—philosophy, theology, economics, sociology, political science, history. Each chapter, each subsection, could demand years of research to be fully adequate. The risks of missing an important factor or source and the risks of being inaccurate multiply as the scope of the book increases. Some may object, on the other hand, that it is not comprehensive enough, that more should have been included on Cuba, on China, on Church-state relations in Communist countries, on positive features of capitalism, etc. The great complexity of issues in contemporary society can of itself create a sense of powerlessness and paralysis. The book recognizes the complexity of the Marxism-Christianity issue, but tries to face this as a challenge.

The book is vulnerable to criticism on a second score: it is based on books and not grounded in experience. Some Marxists and radical Christians may feel that I have stripped Marxism of its revolutionary force, and that evaluations are based on ivory-tower research and do not grow out of "praxis" and a commitment to socialism. A study based on such a commitment would bring a very different perspective, one perhaps far more critical of the Church and less critical of Marxism. Opponents of Marxism may feel that evaluations are too "soft" on Marxism and far too obliging to Marx himself. If I had lived under Communism my thinking would be quite different; if I worked in the business world my experience of economic problems would be quite different. Again, different lived experiences might have led to a far different book.

An effort has been made throughout the writing of the book to be fair, to strive for objectivity, to invite criticism, and to be self-critical. But especially in a book such as this, which "appraises" certain positions and doctrines, one's experiences, class origins, values, and temperament all influence judgments reached and what one selects to emphasize or overlook. The influence of Saul Alinsky's views on tactics ("taking people where they are and building on their concerns"), liberal rather than radical political involvements, and most especially a cautious temperament which leads me to consider and reconsider issues and decisions, these and other personal factors have undoubtedly affected the conclusions reached in the book. The book looks for what is positive in Marxist positions, agrees with much of the Marxist critique, disagrees with the Communist worldview and most Marxist-Leninist tactics, is cautious about easy solutions, and hence ends up more reformist than revolutionary, at least in respect to the United States. For those already committed for or against Marxism the book may only serve as a target for criticism. But the book is addressed primarily to Christians who want to understand Marxism, to use it to the extent that it helps in building a more just society, or to reject it to the extent that it does not. The hope of contributing to the construction of a more just and more humane society motivated the writing of the book.

I am indebted to many people who agreed to read first drafts of chapters and to offer criticisms and suggestions. Peter Steinfels made suggestions on the manuscript as a whole. Loyd Easton, Joe Holland, and Ken Gregorio, S.J., offered comments on several chapters. Many others gave invaluable help on particular chapters or materials: John Bokina, Fr. Charles Curran, Anton Donoso, Raya Dunayevskaya, Msgr. John Tracy Ellis, George Hampsch, Kathy Schultz, IHM, and Nancy Sylvester, IHM. For comments and suggestions on various chapters I am also indebted to several Jesuit friends: Gerald Cavanagh, Mike Czerny, Joe Daoust, Al Hennelly, Philip Land, Gap LoBiondo, Joe Mulligan, Jack O'Callaghan, Paul Schervish, Tom Schubeck, and Brian Smith. Some of these intitial readers may remain quite critical of conclusions reached in the book, but I gained much from their suggestions. Susan Daoust did a masterful job in typing the manuscript. Jesuits Mike Evans and Ken Gregorio helped greatly by checking references. Paul Dungan, S.J., read over several chapters for grammatical errors. Many beautiful friends and students have contributed more than they know by their encouragement. Finally, I am indebted to the Woodstock Theological Center and to the Jesuit Council on Theological Reflection for their financial assistance.

Notes

1. R. N. Berki, *Socialism* (New York: St. Martin's Press, 1975), snows how broad the term "socialism" can be. See especially Chapter 1, "What is Socialism?"

2. Dale Vree, *On Synthesizing Marxism and Christianity* (New York: John Wiley & Sons, 1976), p. xii.

PART I
HISTORICAL PERSPECTIVE

Chapter 1

Marx: the Evolution of His Ideas

Marxism takes its name from its controversial but certainly brilliant originator, Karl Marx (1818–1883). The ideas of this revolutionary German writer have profoundly influenced the course of world history. But they have also been the source of much dispute, even among his followers. The debate over what constitutes true Marxism and what is essential to Marxism significantly affects the issue of whether Marxism and Christianity are compatible, though no clear test exists to resolve the debate.

What did Marx "really hold"? Communist parties lay claim to a "correct" interpretation of Marx's ideas and Communist nations present themselves as embodiments of his doctrines. Party leaders often define what is essential to Marxism. But other contending socialist groups and independent Marxist thinkers argue that his thought has often been misrepresented and that Communist socialism in practice is not a true expression of Marx's views. Marx's writings, much like the gospels, lend themselves to very different and even conflicting interpretations. In the long run, moreover, what dominant and contending Marxist groups hold today may have a far more practical bearing on Christians than what Marx himself wrote. Yet some initial presentation of Marx's thought would seem essential to understanding Marxism, if only to locate the points of agreement and of controversy.

A second issue with regard to the study of Marx concerns the historical context of his thought. Marx espoused a dialectical method which stressed that consciousness and ideology change as historical conditions change. How much of Marx's own thought remains essential and applicable today and how much was simply a "product of his times"? Marx professed himself an atheist years before he began his critique of capitalism. Was his atheism, then, merely a reflection of the intellectual climate of his times, or does it remain nevertheless integrally linked to the achievement of a Marxist socialism? Marx lived in an epoch of recurring economic crises and of revolutionary ideologies generated by the French Revolution. How much were his views on the overthrow of capitalism affected by these historical factors? Hegel was the dominant influence in Marx's intellectual formation. How much of what Marx borrowed from Hegel or reacted against in Hegel remains still significant? While this initial chapter does not attempt to resolve all these questions, it does take note of differing interpretations of Marx and of historical conditions which may have influenced him.

Marx's Times and Background

The Dual Revolution

In writing on *The Age of Revolution* (Europe from 1789 to 1848), E. J. Hobsbawm speaks of a "dual revolution" which shaped the course of European history in the nineteenth century.[1] The industrial revolution brought the triumph of capitalist industry and bourgeois society; the French Revolution generated, in its wake, the political ideologies which would dominate Western Europe for decades to follow. Both parts of this dual revolution influenced significantly the development of Marx's thought. From 1844 on, the problem of capitalist society would be a focus of analysis. But he came to the problem of capitalist society first by addressing the issue of the state and political emancipation, and the French Revolution would continue to influence his reflections on the goals and strategies of social change.

The social effects of the industrial revolution, according to Hobsbawm, became evident only with the 1830s.[2] But the economic "take-off," especially in England, began in the last decades of the eighteenth century. At first industry and factory work meant primarily cotton mills, and cotton was closely tied to colonialism and slavery. Raw cotton imports into Britain rose from 11 million pounds in 1785 to 588 million pounds in 1850. The manufacture of cotton cloth jumped from 40 million yards to 2,025 million yards during the same period. The social effects of the cotton industry, with slavery abroad and exploitation at home, soon became evident. A harsh labor discipline in England, with laws in its support, forced workers to labor steadily all through the week in order to make a minimum income. Women, girls, and young boys under the age of eighteen constituted three-fourths of the workers in English cotton mills in 1834–1847, providing the cheapest and most tractable labor force available.[3] The coal industry, the building of railways, and the industrialization of other textiles, augmented the conquest of industrial capitalism. Crowded slums, fourteen-hour working days, the heat and dust of factories, and periodic economic crises which threw masses of workers out of jobs, created an almost universal urban discontent.

The French Revolution provided a vocabulary and political ideas for response to this discontent. Social radicals drew upon the language of "equality, fraternity, and liberty" to proclaim the need for a new social order. Political radicals sought to reawaken its spirit in backward countries which resisted even the most modest steps toward constitutional government. Conservatives pointed to the Jacobin "reign of terror" and saw the French Revolution and subsequent efforts to evoke its name as threats to the fundamental order of European society. The Churches, remembering the Revolution's attempts to enthrone "the goddess of reason," feared its resurgence in other parts of Europe. Moderate liberals, such as Hegel, sought to preserve some of the freedoms proclaimed by the French Revolution without destroying other traditional values and institutions. Marx, using Hegel at first as a counterpoint, would argue that the political freedoms promised by the French Revolution did not go far enough to effect a truly human liberation.

Hegel and the Dialectic

The dual revolution touched England and France most directly. Germany lagged behind both economically and politically. Only in Hegel's philosophy, as Marx would later observe, did Germany stand as an equal to other modern nations.[4] But it was in Germany and through Hegel that Marx first developed his own social and political thought. Hence some grasp of Hegel is essential for understanding Marx.

In the introduction of his *Philosophy of Right* (1821), Hegel wrote: "What is rational is actual and what is actual is rational."[5] This one cryptic statement provides an opening for understanding his political philosophy. By "actual" (*wirklich*) Hegel meant something that has been actualized, not just a passive given;[6] and by "rational" he meant not only intelligible but of positive value. "What is actual is rational." In the century of enlightenment preceding Hegel, a new confidence in the power of human reason and in the progress of the human spirit had emerged. Philosophers still warned of the "limits' of human understanding, but Newtonian physics had proved that the natural world is governed by "laws" which the human mind could discern and formulate. Technological advancements proved the practical control human beings could exercise over the world. Hegel ambitioned even more. He believed that human history, the state, religion, and all that pertained to civilization could be proven rational (i.e., of positive value for human progress). He argued this on the grounds that all of these (history, the state) "embodied" human reason, for they were creations of past generations.

"What is rational is actual." Yet not all we find is "rational." There have been apparently senseless wars, tyrannical governments, religious superstitions and persecutions, corrupt laws, customs and institutions that appear to block rather than further human development. True, Hegel admitted, not everything that exists (*Dasein*) is rational. The role of philosophy is to discover the rational core, the substantial elements of truth within what exists. Only that which is "true" at any given time should be affirmed and kept. The word "apparent" becomes critical also. History can "appear" to make little sense; the state can "appear" to be quite arbitrary and forced upon us. The process of discovering the rational is *dialectic*, on the part of both the knower and the thing known. The knower must constantly question the "appearances" of things, not allowing any single definition or single instance to determine meaning. But the "thing itself" can only be known in the process of development. Thus, says Hegel, we do not know the most essential factor about an acorn until we recognize, through experience in time, its potential to be an oak tree. Similarly we can only come to an understanding of "human nature" through the whole of human history. So, too, in understanding the state, a Persian living under a despotic rule centuries ago would never grasp the true "Idea" of the state as the embodiment of reason.

Hegel's own attitudes on history exemplified the dialectic at work. As a student he viewed the world of ancient Greece as "a paradise of human nature," as the harmonious embodiment of all that is great, beautiful, noble and free.[7] But then, influenced by his reading of Gibbon's *The Rise and Fall of the Roman Empire,* he came to blame Christianity for the disrupture and decline of the ancient world. A reading of Immanuel Kant on the moral values of Christianity, however, gave him a new perspective. He saw the sense of "individuality" and personal dignity which Christianity had introduced into the world as a positive consequence of Christianity's negation of the Greek world. Medieval Catholicism impeded the realization of a new synthesis. But with the Protestant Reformation and the coming of the modern "constitutional" state, a new synthesis was beginning to emerge which would combine the best of Greek "harmony" and Christian "individuality."

Similarly, Hegel's earliest political works (1796–1806) were highly critical of the state and civil society in Germany. Germany had no unified national life; before 1800 it was a conglomeration of nearly three hundred princedoms. Civil society (the socioeconomic world) was composed of competing individuals and clashing interest groups with no mediating power to regulate their conflicts. But through what Hegel would later describe as "the cunning of reason" (i.e., the goals of world history realized unwittingly by world leaders acting for their own interests) Napoleon unified much of Germany. Then Baron Karl von Stein, the Prussian king's prime minister, began in 1807 a series of political reforms which appeared destined to give Germany a modern, constitutional state. Hegel believed, moreover, that in his *Phenomenology of Mind* (1807) he had devised a philosophical system which would enable people to become truly conscious of all that "Spirit"[8] had achieved and was achieving in the world. Thus he could look back and see how the true idea of the state had developed dialectically through the major "stages" of history. The modern constitutional state, he felt, would embody human strivings for a state which harmoniously balanced and united individual freedom and social cooperation.

"What is rational is actual and what is actual is rational" then took on a very specific sense in reference to the French Revolution and what Germany should learn from it. French Jacobin radicals had failed to recognize that "the actual is rational." They failed to respect French history and customs and the rationality embodied in French institutions. Instead they made a goddess of "pure reason." They destroyed previous structures, even abolishing the traditional calendar, and tried to build a constitution from pure idealistic principles. So Hegel attempted to devise for Germany a constitution which would retain the traditions of an hereditary monarch and of a privileged role for land-owners, while including representation from the new industrial sectors of society.

Marx would reject Hegel's defense of the constitutional state and his criticisms would lead him to the conviction that only social revolution could bring true freedom. But he took much from Hegel: the concepts of "praxis" and "alienation," a sense of "stages" in history and of the cunning of reason, and most especially the idea of dialectics. Marx would use the dialectical method to challenge and negate what "appears" to be the case (e.g., that the owner-wage earner relationship is the natural way things are); he would apply it to the interaction of human beings shaping the environment and being in turn shaped by it; he would employ it to analyze class struggles. Engels and later Marxists would extend the dialectic, in a way that has become quite controversial, by claiming that all of nature operates according to dialectical laws.

The Young Hegelians and Germany

Hegel died in 1831, but his philosophy still dominated German intellectual thought in the decade which followed. It soon became apparent, however, that Hegelian philosphy was susceptible to two quite divergent interpretations: (1) his mature system could be defended as valid and as needing only accommodation to changing conditions; or (2) a stress could be placed on the dynamism of the dialectic, which would mean negating many of the conclusions Hegel had reached. Had not Hegel himself said that spirit "is never at rest, but carried along the stream of progress ever onward"[9] and that every philosophic system is historically conditioned and limited? The actual split came in a controversy over David Strauss' *Life of Jesus* which appeared in 1835. Strauss contended that religious dogmas are myths expressing the desires of a community, so that Hegel's defense of religion as a symbolic presentation of philosophic truth could not be justified. Strauss's book led to the formation of a group known as the Young or Left Hegelians in opposition to the orthodox Right Hegelians who continued to defend Hegel's system. The Young Hegelians felt they must push beyond Hegel's system if they were to be faithful to his method.[10]

Though Marx broke with the Young Hegelians as he moved toward socialism, many of their ideas anticipated views held by Marx. August von Cieszkowski criticized Hegel for dealing only with the past and with thought alone. Philosophy must concern itself with the future and with practical action. It must analyze conflicts and tendencies in the present in order to discern the direction the future will take. But it must also now stress will and action over mere reflection and thought. Arnold Ruge led the Young Hegelian movement toward political issues and anticipated many of Marx's criticisms of Hegel's political philosophy. Bruno Bauer stressed ruthless criticism of all that is irrational. His main target was Christianity which he believed had become a serious obstacle to human progress.

Ludwig Feuerbach influenced the young Marx most directly through his method of criticizing Hegel, his humanism, and his views on religion. Feuerbach argued that Hegel made "Idea" or "absolute Spirit," which are only abstractions, into active subjects and turned concrete, real beings into predicates. But nature and human beings are not products of some "Idea"; they are the basic components of reality. Feuerbach thus stressed the need for a humanistic philosophy which would focus on the human species and its relation to nature, and one which would take into account human feelings and bodily senses, not just thought alone. Feuerbach sought also to demythologize religion. God, he argued, was simply a "projection." Primitive people projected their fears of nature by personifying the sun and the sea. Modern people project their own human qualities into an imaginary being. For what is "God" except a projection of knowledge, power, and love—human attributes imagined in their perfection? God's infinity is simply an expression of the infinite capacity of the whole human species. Likewise, Christian dogmas simply mask truths about the human species. The Incarnation tells us that each person has a spark of divine energy; the Trinity represents human community.

The political situation in Germany needs also to be considered as background for Marx's first writings.[11] Hegel had envisioned a constitutional monarchy for Germany. But decades had passed without even the first steps being taken in that direction. To demand a democratic republic, or even to call for a constitution, was a radical stance to take in Germany in the 1840s. For a brief moment in 1840, Prussia appeared on the verge of breaking with its autocratic past and moving toward a more representative form of government. In June 1840, the old monarch died and his son, Friedrich Wilhelm IV, ascended to the throne. He granted amnesty to political prisoners, his speeches conveyed great sympathy for the poor, he conceded new freedom to the press, and he promised to convene provincial assemblies. But the hopes aroused by these liberal moves soon came to naught. It soon became apparent that the king envisioned a traditional Christian state which would preserve Germany's heritage against the forces of unbelief, materialism, and revolution. He thought of himself as a loving father; to demand constitutional limits on his power was to betray an unbecoming lack of trust on the part of his "children." Since he represented God on earth, he should have the same absolute authority. Given this historical situation it is not difficult to see how someone of Marx's radical temperament would embrace atheism and eventually revolution.

Marx: The Early Years (1818-44)

Karl Marx was born in the ancient city of Trier in 1818, the third of eight children. Ancestors on both sides of the family had been rabbis. His father was a successful lawyer who converted to Protestantism to avoid anti-Jewish laws, and Karl was baptized as a six-year old. There is little indication of religious influence or practice in Marx's biographies.[12] His father's interest in the Enlightenment (Kant, Leibniz, Voltaire) seemed to have carried greater weight. Though we know little of his earliest years, they appear to have been rather normal and relatively happy.

His Student Years

Marx completed his secondary studies in Trier in 1835. His final essay exams were preserved and they give some indication of his values and concerns as a youth. In one of the essays, "The Union of the Faithful in Christ According to John 15, 1-4," Marx does speak positively of the need for Christ to help people overcome their egoism and moral weakness. He says even that in union with Christ we should turn loving eyes to God and "sink joyfully on our knees before Him."[13] Whether the essay reflected Marx's real sentiments, even at this point of his life, or whether he simply wrote to fulfill an assignment, is uncertain. In another essay, "Reflections of a Youth on Choosing an Occupation," Marx wrote rather impersonally throughout of "the Deity." More significant in this second essay were the criteria he chose for guiding vocational decisions: dignity and the welfare of humanity. "Only that position can impart dignity in which we do not appear as servile tools but rather create independently within our own circle."[14] Detestation of servility remained characteristic of Marx throughout his life.

After his graduation from Trier, Marx spent a rather wasted year at the University of Bonn before transferring to the University of Berlin in 1836. He became secretly engaged to Jenny von Westphalen, four years his senior, before he left for Berlin. From a long letter to his father, written at the end of his first year in Berlin, we have some idea of how prodigious Marx's intellectual activity could be.[15] He took jurisprudence formally, but law awakened his interest in philosophy. He became fascinated with Hegel and studied him "from beginning to end." He translated works of Aristotle, Tacitus, and Ovid, studied English and Italian, read extensively in art, history, and literature, wrote two pieces of drama, and composed three volumes of poetry. He also joined with many of the Young Hegelians in the "Doctors' Club."

His interest in philosophy led Marx to undertake a doctoral thesis on Greek philosophy after Aristotle. He saw a parallel between the situation in Greece after Aristotle's death and the situation in Germany since Hegel's death. In both instances he saw philosophy moving away from pure theory and system building and turning into practical energy. "Just as Prometheus, having stolen fire from heaven, begins to build houses and settle on the earth, so philosophy, having extended itself to the world, turns against the apparent world."[16] The Prometheus image appeared also in the foreword to his thesis, giving expression to his already strong atheism. Philosophy proclaims, with Prometheus, that it hates all the gods and that it is "better to be the servant of this rock" (to which Prometheus in the legend was bound) than to be a servant of Zeus.[17]

His First Political Writings

By the time Marx completed his doctoral work in 1841 he had determined to join Bruno Bauer at the University of Bonn and work with him on a journal of atheism. But Bauer's dismissal from the university, on the grounds that his atheism was inconsistent with his position as professor of theology, caused Marx to give up hopes for an academic career and to turn to journalism instead. Even before his first publications Marx had already impressed many with his genius. Moses Hess, a German socialist and already prominent author, wrote to a friend about Marx: ". . . prepare to meet the greatest—perhaps the only genuine—philosopher now alive, who will soon . . . attract the eyes of all Germany. . . . Imagine Rousseau, Voltaire, Holbach, Lessing, Heine and Hegel fused in one person—I say fused, not juxtaposed—and you have Dr. Marx."[18]

Marx lent his talents to a newly formed paper in Cologne, the *Rheinische Zeitung,* which by October 1842 he would edit as well. The topics of articles he wrote ranged over many areas: censorship, provincial diets and representation by social "estates," divorce laws, peasants accused of stealing firewood, poor vinedressers in the Moselle Valley. But he brought to each of these questions a unifying concept, the idea of a "rational state," which served him as a norm for criticism of actual political conditions. The concept of a rational state came from Hegel, but Marx's criticisms of the actual state in Prussia contained criticisms of many of the specific institutions Hegel sought to preserve in his constitution.

Marx attacked the "Christian State" as a contradiction in terms. It appeals to authority, not reason; it cannot base judicial laws on the Sermon on the Mount without hopeless contradictions.[19] Marx also attacked censorship in which "political intelligence" becomes the exclusive property of one bureaucratic organ of the state. If these censors are so capable, Marx asked sarcastically, why don't these encyclopedic minds come out as writers and solve all our problems?[20] Marx likewise criticized several instances in which private or class interests were permitted to destroy the "organic unity" which the state should have.[21]

What Marx meant by a "rational state" is important for understanding the development of his thought towards socialism and it suggests what Marx later envisioned as a classless society. "State" suggests a political government. But by "rational state" Marx intended one that unified life in society, not a separate governmental sphere apart. He speaks of the rational state, almost in "Mystical Body" language, as an organic body whose members must function in harmonious union and which is animated by an inner rational soul. The free press, "the spirit of the people," provides the guiding spirit or soul. Special or class interests destroy union. Mistreatment of peasants affects the whole body of which they are an integral part. His subsequent critique of Hegel's constitution, and of the "political state" in general, flows from the conviction that they fail to effect the kind or organic union which they claim to achieve.[22]

Early in 1843 the Prussian government suppressed the *Rheinische Zeitung* and Marx turned his attention to a critique of Hegel's philosophy of the state. This critique would be pivotal in convincing Marx that the "political state" could never achieve the integration of personal freedom and social benefits Hegel believed would result. His commentary included a critique of Hegel's method (which makes reality the product of a mystical "Idea" or Spirit) and the most conservative elements of Hegel's constitution (the hereditary monarch, representation by "estates" as opposed to popular suffrage). But Marx also considered Hegel's theory as an articulation of the basic principles of the modern state. Hegel intended to prove that the modern constitutional state would overcome the divisions and conflicts which characterize civil society. For Hegel, the sovereign provided unity, the executive branch provided a "universal" disinterested service, and the legislative branch provided representation of all sectors of society. In Marx's judgment all three failed to create union and in fact only reinforced the separation of civil society from the political state. The monarchy gave sovereign power to one individual; the bureaucracy assigned general interests to one self-interested group; the legislature, instead of incorporating the people into the state, created an organized opposition to the state, with each group seeking its own special interests.

The political state thus stood *above* civil society, an illusory "heaven" which promised union but which left the "earth" of real life unchanged. The state is bound to fail because civil society has no unity; it is characterized by competing, individualistic interests. The state is not a power over property interests but a power in support of them. If civil society were to be represented politically as it actually is, it would take the form of a disorganized mass of conflicting elements.[23] This insight would lead Marx next to the need for social revolution, for a restructuring of civil society without which true freedom and social unity could not be achieved.

The Need for Social Emancipation

Marx took this next decisive step in two articles written in the fall and winter of 1843 for a new journal, the *German-French Annals,* which he and

Ruge established in Paris. In the first article, "On the Jewish Question," Marx attacked the liberal hopes of those who expect human emancipation to be achieved through political freedom. His former colleague Bruno Bauer told Jews that if they wanted to be free they should give up any claim based on their religion and demand that the state give up its alliance with Christianity. Once religion became a private affair it would disappear. Marx challenged this line of thought. Separating religion from the state does not free the individual from religion, as proved by the United States where religion flourishes despite the state's political emancipation from religion. Thus "a state can be a free state without men becoming free men."[24] Marx, of course, assumes that the presence of religion in society proves that human beings have not yet achieved human freedom—"the existence of religion implies a defect."[25]

What occurs in political emancipation is the transfer of the spirit of religion, namely individualism, from the state to the sphere of civil society. As the spirit of civil society, the sphere of the *bellum omnium contra omnes*, religion "has become what it was originally, an expression of the separation of man from his community, from himself, and from other men."[26] Marx sees the so-called "rights of man" as confirmations of this same egoism. The right to property is a right to enjoy and dispose of goods without regard for other men and independently of society. The right to security serves only to preserve private interests and property. None of these rights goes beyond the egoistic person, "the man withdrawn into himself, his private interest and his private choice, and separated from the community as a member of civil society."[27]

Once again, then, the separation of civil society from the state is confirmed, as is the double life which the individual is forced to live.

> In the political community he regards himself as a communal being; but in civil society he is active as a private individual, treats other men as means, reduces himself to a means, and becomes the plaything of alien powers. The political state is as spiritual in relation to civil society as heaven is in relation to earth.[28]
>
> Actual man is recognized only in the form of an egoistic individual; authentic man, only in the form of abstract citizen.[29]

Put more concretely: the state creates the illusion of harmony and equality among its citizens, but in their real everyday life in civil society, some are rich and powerful, and others poor and powerless. The overcoming of this dualism, Marx now recognized, would require revolutionizing the basic elements of civil society and submitting them to criticism. Only when the actual, individual man has "organized his own powers as *social* powers so that social force is no longer separated from him as political power, only then is human emancipation complete."[30]

In his second article for the *Annals*, "Toward the Critique of Hegel's Philosophy of Law: Introduction," Marx carries the question of social emancipation a step further. In Paris, for the first time, Marx came into contact with various worker groups and was impressed with their revolutionary spirit and ardor. In France a plethora of socialist and communist groups already existed. The followers of August Blanqui stressed the need for an elite group of professional revolutionaries. Proudhon advocated anarchy or at least a completely free self-organization of workers. The followers of Saint-Simon called for state socialism. Fourier and Cabet advocated voluntary "communes" as models for the rest of society, and inspired the formation of such communes in the United States. But the French had to be convinced that atheism was essential to any complete human emancipation. So Marx begins his article with his most famous statement about religion:

> For Germany the criticism of religion has been essentially completed, and criticism of religion is the premise of all criticism. . . . The basis of irreligious criticism is: Man makes religion, religion does not make man. And indeed religion is the self-consciousness and self-regard of man who has either not yet found or has already lost himself. But man is not an abstract being squatting outside the world. Man is the world of men, the state, society. This state and this society produce religion, which is an inverted consciousness of the world because they are an inverted world. . . . Religious suffering is the expression of real suffering and at the same time the protest against real suffering. Religion is the sigh of the oppressed creature, the heart of a heartless world, as it is the spirit of spiritless conditions. It is the opium of the people.[31]

But Marx now recognized that religion was not the root cause of suffering and alienation. It was rather the symptom of a more basic problem. People turn to religion because they are oppressed and unhappy. The critique of religion thus led to a critique of the political world. Germany was backward politically and economically. Only in philosophy, as reflected in Hegel's political theory, did it stand on equal grounds with more advanced European nations. German liberals placed their hopes in a *political* revolution, with the achievements of the French Revolution brought to Germany. But Marx clearly saw no hope for freedom through politics. He looked for a revolution which would raise Germany not only to the level of modern nations but beyond them to a true human liberation.

For such a revolution to occur, Marx observed, two elements must be present: a revolutionary theory and a material force capable of carrying out the theory. Marx saw the revolutionary theory arising out of the criticism of religion, for it establishes humanity as supreme and ends with a "categorical imperative" to overthrow all conditions which debase and enslave people.[32]

But what of the material force needed? A *political* revolution requires a rebellious oppressed class and a dominant oppressor class. Thus in the French Revolution the rebellious bourgeoisie overthrew the monarchy and aristocracy. But with a weak, complacent bourgeois class and no clearly dominant ruling class, Germany lacked the conditions needed for a political revolution.[33] Germany's only real possibility for emancipation lay in a more radical, social revolution led by a class whose radical chains, universal suffering, and complete loss of humanity put it outside of society and traditional political struggle—the proletariat. The vital need of the proletariat for a radically new, truly human society, coincided with the goal of society as a whole.

Thus the original grounds for Marx's advocacy of a social proletarian revolution did not arise out of a confrontation with capitalism or from a scientific analysis of successive economic stages of development, but dealt with the overthrow of backward conditions in Germany. The proletariat constituted only 4 percent of the population.[34] But their numbers would swell in decades to follow, and Marx believed that he had correctly traced the true source of divisions in society to economic causes. Civil society had to be restructured if social harmony and true freedom were to be achieved.

The 1844 Manuscripts

In 1844 Marx turned his attention to economics. He had been impressed with an article for the *Annals* by Frederick Engels entitled "A Sketch for a Critique of Political Economy." Engels, too, spoke of social revolution but grounded his analysis on industrial conditions in England. Engels from the outset used a much more deterministic language, and spoke of the "laws" of private property, of price determination, of crises generated by capitalistic competition leading inevitably to social revolution.

Marx recognized the need to follow Engels' lead in investigating the assumptions of political economy. If German conditions presaged a social revolution, Marx's previous work fell short of explaining this on economic grounds. So he plunged again into studies to discover the root cause of human misery in the social and economic structure of civil society. He worked out the results of his study in a series of manuscripts, written in the spring and summer of 1844, which have become the most discussed and most important of all his early works.

In a commentary on Adam Smith's *The Wealth of Nations*, Marx challenged the thesis that the whole nation benefits, through an "invisible hand," when individuals pursue their own profit goals. Wealth is indeed produced, said Marx, but for whom? Technical progress and the factory system enabled the modern worker to produce a hundred times more than his forebears could. Yet the workers themselves were utterly impoverished. For Marx the reason was clear. The workers are no better than serfs. Their power to work is owned and controlled by a small group of capitalists who thus make enormous profits.

In the best known of his manuscripts Marx analyzed the "Alienated Labor" which results from the capitalist system. Hegel had shown that individuals realize their value and identity as persons by "objectifying' themselves, by expressing their potential in work and other activities. In working and producing objects I should be able to enjoy both the satisfaction of seeing my own personality "objectified" and the satisfaction of creating an object useful to the needs of other human beings. But under capitalism the whole process becomes alienating and hostile. First, workers are alienated from the *product* of their labor. Capitalism takes from workers the product and profit they produce. Their life energy is poured into their work, yet they have little to show for it. "The more the worker exerts himself, the more powerful becomes the alien objective world which he fashions against himself; the poorer he and his inner world become the less there is that belongs to him."[35] Second, workers are alienated from the *activity* of their labor. Their work is forced labor; they must work simply to survive. They have no choice as to how they will work. Far from experiencing their creativity, workers feel only miserable at work. Their work is not their own; it belongs to another. Third, workers are alienated from *nature*. The whole of nature ought to appear as an extension of the human body. They ought to be able to see not only their own personal work but the richness of the human species reflected in the world. Instead, the world stands opposed to them, dehumanized and hostile. Finally, workers are alienated from *others*. "A direct consequence of man's alienation from the product of his work, from his life activity, and from his species—existence is the alienation of man from man."[36] Workers are forced into competition with other workers. They ought to be able to see, as Feuerbach stressed, the richness of human nature reflected in others. Instead they see others only as they see themseves, as debased and struggling simply to survive.

In another essay, on "Private Property and Communism," Marx indicates what would result from a socialist restructuring of society once the means of production were owned communally. Communism = naturalism = humanism. Once human beings begin working in a new way (cooperatively) and sharing in a new way (collectively) their whole relationship to nature and the world will change. And as nature and society take on a more human form, each person becomes more fully human. "Society is the completed. essential unity of man with nature . . . the fulfilled naturalism of man and humanism of nature."[37]

The promise of a "new man" under communism has its origins in this essay. We have come to think of greed, ambition, selfishness, as ' natural traits." Marx sees them as consequences of an alienated economic system which builds on these traits and reinforces them. "Having" or possessing is the only relationship to objects a capitalist understands. With communism we will enjoy the whole of nature and human creations simply because we are part of them. The whole life of the senses will take on a new development. A hungry person can think only of food. Our senses need to be humanized. The ear will learn to appreciate music, the eye to appreciate art—all of which capitalism has denied the workers by exhausting their energy in dehumanized labor. The truly rich person is not one with material possessions. "The rich man is simultaneously one who needs a totality of human manifestations of life and in whom his own realization exists as inner necessity, as need."[38]

Finally, Marx reasserts atheism. Human beings must be able to stand on their own feet. Life must be their own creation. Atheism is needed only so long as alienations in society require us to assert our independence. Once socialism is fully established and human nature transformed, atheism will no longer be needed. "Positive self-consciousness" will suffice. (A third significant essay which deals with a critique of the Hegelian dialectic will be taken up in considering Marx's notion of "praxis".)

These manuscripts have been the source of both renewal and controversy within Marxism. They remained unpublished in Marx's lifetime and were edited only in the 1930s. They served as a focal point of interest for European existentialism after World War II. Neo-Marxists in Eastern Europe drew heavily upon them with a view to creating a "human face" for socialism and to counter Stalinism and state bureaucracy. Christian-Marxist dialogues found a meeting ground in this humanism. Many began interpreting later works of Marx in the light of these manuscripts. Raya Dunayevskaya, in *Marxism and Freedom* (1958), was one of the first Marxist scholars on the American scene to draw attention to the manuscripts and to defend their humanism against Soviet critics. But other Marxists have reacted strongly, arguing that these early writings were only idealistic, philosophic essays not to be compared in value to Marx's later "scientific" writings. Thus the French Marxist Louis Althusser claims that an "epistemological break" divides these early writings from the "true" and scientific later Marx.

In the fall of 1844 Marx began his lifetime collaboration with Frederick Engels in a book they co-authored called *The Holy Family,* directed against Bruno Bauer and the Young Hegelians. The major criticism of the Young Hegelians' belief that "ideas make history" (namely their *own* ideas!) will be taken up again at greater length in *The German Ideology.* But Marx's views on "the role of ideas" should be noted. "Ideas alone can achieve nothing." But ideas which capture the real needs of the people—namely, the communist idea of a new world system—can lead to real results. Bruno Bauer had charged that the French Revolution ultimately failed because its "idea" became diluted among the masses. Marx responds: it failed because its *political* idea did not correspond to the real needs of the masses; hence it was *only* "an idea" and not a real force for them.[39] Marx identifies his views as "materialist," stressing the influence of environment on society. But he used the term "materialist" ambiguously, creating a problem which will be taken up in Chapter 7.

Marx's "Materialist" View of History (1845–59)

In his polemic with the Young Hegelians Marx also began to dissociate his views from those of Feuerbach, whose ideas had influenced his own humanism and method of criticizing Hegel. The first indication of an expressly critical attitude toward Feuerbach took the form of eleven brief but important "theses," written in the spring of 1845 but published by Engels only after Marx's death.[40] These theses enunciated a concept of "praxis" which has played a central role in all Marxist thought since.

The Notion of "Praxis"

Marx agreed with materialists that society and human nature are shaped by environment. But he felt that they failed to stress the need for action to change the environment. The core of Marx's argument is contained in the very first thesis. Thesis 1: The chief defect of all previous materialism, including Feuerbach's, is that it adopts a purely theoretical attitude toward the world, ignoring the crucial importance of human activity ("praxis"). Other theses confirm this stress on praxis. Thesis 3: Materialists recognize that conditions influence human behavior and attitudes. They forget that *changing* circumstances involves revolutionary practice. Thesis 4: Feuerbach considered alienation resolved when he showed that religion is just a projection of the human world. He failed to recognize that religion is a product of an alienated society which must be revolutionized in practice before religious alienation will disappear. Thesis 6: Feuerbach likewise conceived of man's "essence" as something abstract and unchanging. But the essence of man "is the ensemble of social relationships." As conditions change, human nature changes. Thesis 11: Marx concluded with the celebrated thesis engraved upon his tombstone—"The philosophers have only interpreted the world in various ways; the point is, to change it."

If the "theses" correct Feuerbach's materialism, Marx had already distinguished his notion of "praxis" from Hegel's idealistic use of it when he wrote his *1844 Manuscripts*. In an essay critiquing Hegel's dialectic,[41] Marx credited Hegel for recognizing the primacy of activity in human history. But, Marx contended, Hegel viewed this activity only in terms of thought-process. For Hegel, "Spirit" creates history. Human institutions are consciously created by men and women in history, but they do not recognize the overall course of history. Consequently human history, state power, wealth, all "appear" to be alienated. The alienation is overcome once Spirit, working through human philosophic "consciousness," recognizes the rationality of what has been achieved.[42] For Marx, a human being is more than "consciousness"; it is a natural being. The "praxis" that creates the world and its institutions is work. Moreover, the systems people have created (the state, capitalism) do not merely appear alienated; they *are* alienated. Consequently only a "revolutionary praxis" which abolishes them can overcome their alienation.

Though "praxis" can mean the original productive activity which gave embodiment to human products and institutions, Marxists now use it more often to mean "revolutionary praxis" which transforms the world. Garaudy defines praxis as "social activity, as activity for the transformation of the world" and makes it broad enough to include technology, scientific research, as well as revolutionary struggle.[43] Perhaps the simplest definition of praxis is "action based on thinking," i.e., action based on an understanding of socio-economic structures and their development.[44] The most important idea to be stressed is that praxis is dialectical—theory and action constantly interrelated. Neither theory nor action is prior; both are constantly modified in the light of the other and in response to changing conditions.

Finally in Hegel's behalf it should be noted that he recognized the role of action and change. If he stressed "consciousness'" in overcoming alienation, it was because he believed what history had achieved (e.g., the modern state) was *good*. Marxists once in power, once they believe the socialist society they have constructed is basically good, tend also to be Hegelians, defending the rationality of the new system rather than calling for new revolutionary activity to abolish it.

The German Ideology

Engels joined Marx in Brussels in the spring of 1845 to work on a new book which would refute the Young Hegelians' idealist view of history and criticize utopian socialism. This joint work, *The German Ideology*, was never published in Marx's or Engels' lifetime, but it has become an important source. Some view the book as the beginning of Marx's "scientific" work and a break with his earlier more philosophic writings, but a strong case can also be made for "continuity."[45] In either case, this book did set down for the first time the basic "materialist" theory of history.

The idealists—Ludwig Feuerbach, Bruno Bauer, Max Stirner—all assume, according to Marx, that ideas rule the world and determine history. The study of history becomes a mere question of determining which ideas have been dominant at different moments of history. Idealism "descends from heaven to earth" and starts from "what men say, imagine, and conceive" to be the real causes of history. "The exponents of this conception of history have only been able to see in history political action and religious or other theoretical struggles. In each historical epoch they have had to share the illusion of that epoch."[46] To put Marx's point more concretely, the idealist would explain the French Revolution as the result of Rousseau's ideas, and Napoleon's conquests as the consequence of his conscious intentions. Change in history, *praxis*, thus becomes a matter of changing people's thinking. Overcome the illusions of consciousness, the idealists believe, and reality itself will be changed. It is against this view, which exalts the role of ideas, that Marx and Engels stress the economic ("material") forces in history and the subordinate role of ideas.

1. The Basic Premises of the Materialist View: a. The Primacy of Production in History. The real premises for understanding history are not ideas. "They are the real individuals, their actions, and their material conditions of life, those which they found existing as well as those which they produce through their actions."[47] All history must set out from these material bases, from real individuals and their activity and the way in which these bases are modified in history. Human beings distinguish themselves from animals when they begin to *produce* their means of subsistence. What human beings are thus depends on the material conditions which determine their production. A few pages later Marx describes man's "first historical acts": (1) the production of means to satisfy basic human needs for food and shelter; (2) the fulfillment of these needs which triggers new needs (for better food, better instruments of work, etc.); (3) the production of the human race itself through propagation of the species; (4) this social factor enters into production; production involves definite relationships between people.[48]

b. The Subordinate Role of Consciousness. Marx could not rest content with a positive presentation of the real premises of history. He was dealing with adversaries who exalted the power of ideas. It was therefore necessary to counter their deification of consciousness with a materialistic explanation which showed that ideas also depend on practical activity for their origin and development. "The production of ideas, of conceptions, of consciousness is directly interwoven with the material activity and the material relationships of men; it is the language of actual life."[49] Thus morality, religion, philosophy, and political theory are the results of material human behavior. So instead of studying ideas and then looking for the material consequences of these ideas, Marx reverses the process. "Rather one sets out from real, active men and their actual life-process and demonstrates the development of ideological reflexes and echoes of that process." Ideas are thus merely "sublimations of man's material life-process." In short, *"Consciousness does not determine life, but life determines consciousness."*[50] Once Marx explains how division of labor leads to class struggle, he will also show how the "ruling ideas" of a given epoch simply reflect the ideas of those in power. Thus, when aristocracy was dominant in medieval society, concepts of honor and loyalty were stressed. With the rule of the bourgeoisie, concepts of freedom and equality prevail.[51]

c. Division of Labor and Private Property. Division of labor is a key concept in Marx's later philosophy. Marx traces the origins of division of labor to the family "where wife and children are the slaves of the man."[52] The man thus also possesses "property" in a primitive form, i.e., the power of disposing of the labor-power of his wife and children. Marx later developed more sophisticated distinctions about the forms which division of labor takes. Natural social divisions of labor have always existed. Hunting, fishing, cooking, tool-making, child-bearing could be distinguished in primitive societies; agriculture, specialized crafts, and trade developed in later societies. These could and did result in class distinctions when one class controlled the work of others, for example, feudal lords requiring serfs to work for them. Marx's main target, however, was artificial *planned* division of labor in which capitalist owners hire workers to carry out detailed, monotonous work, divorcing it from intelligence.[53]

By private property Marx always intends ownership of the "means of production." Ownership of my own clothes or home, or even of the plot of land upon which I work, creates no problems. But if I possess the only land available or monopolize the machines and raw materials needed for industrial production, others are excluded from ownership and must relate to me as tenant farmers or wage-laborers. In discussing "alienated labor" we have seen how Marx describes the dehumanizing effects of division of labor and private ownership on the workers. Here it should be seen how these same factors lead to class divisions and class struggle.

d. Classes and Class Struggle. Classes for Marx are defined by their role in the process of production. To determine class distinctions, one can ask: who owns? who controls? who profits? In the capitalist society of Marx's day, the capitalists or bourgeois class owned the means of production, controlled the division of labor, and by virtue of ownership profited by the work of others. Proletarians or workers owned only their power to work, gave over control of their work to the owners who hired them, and received only the wages needed to keep them in subsistence. The peasants and the petty-bourgeosie, on the other hand, might own their own land, trade, or profession, enabling them to control their own work, but received only the product of their own labor (unless they employed others). These divisions lead to "class struggle" because of conflicting interests (e.g., owners want to keep wages at a minimum to increase profits; workers press for better wages, better working conditions, etc. which would reduce profits).

Marx says that these conflicts between classes provide the real clue to struggle within the state and in history as a whole. "It follows from this that all struggles within the state, the struggle between democracy, aristocracy and monarchy, the struggle for franchise, etc., etc., are nothing but the illusory forms in which the real struggles of different classes are carried out among one another...."[54] Civil society, the social relations with the economic structure, are the "true focus of all history."

The state represents an "illusory communal life" but has a real function of regulating conflicts and maintaining order on behalf of the ruling class. Thus every class which strives to gain control "must first win political power" and to win support it must claim to represent the interests of all.[55]

2. The Materialist Method of Historical Analysis. The idealist view looks only to ideas in history. The materialist view first studies the tools, resources, work, and property relations which constitute the mode of production in a given society. It then shows the social structure (class antagonisms) which such productive forces engender, and finally the political and ideological forms (the state, law, philosophy, ethics, etc.) which reflect class interests.

> This conception of history depends on our ability to set forth the real process of production, starting out from the material production of life itself, and to comprehend the form of interaction connected with this and created by this mode of production, that is, by civil society in its various stages, as the basis of all history. We have to show civil society in action as State and also explain all the different theoretical products and forms of consciousness, religion, philosophy, ethics, etc., and trace their genesis from that basis.[56]

In *The German Ideology* Marx and Engels present two detailed accounts which illustrate their method of analysis. The first account deals with the evolution of tribal, ancient-communal, and feudal societies.[57] They show in each case the kinds of productive forces which dominated, and the corresponding forms which division of labor and property took. A second and more lengthy analysis deals with the evolution of division of labor and property from the middle ages on into modern times.[58] The "stages of history" are thus specified on economic grounds—primitive, ancient, feudal, capitalist, with socialism as the next progression.

   3. *The Materialist View of Revolutionary Praxis.* The materialist view of history leads to very practical conclusions. Historical change does not occur by proposing new "ideas." Economic conditions must be present for change to happen. Thus Marx insists:

> Communism is for us not a state of affairs still to be established, not an *ideal* to which reality [will] have to adjust. We call communism the *real* movement which abolishes the present state of affairs. The conditions of this movement result from premises now in existence.[59]

The conditions which Marx sees as present are two-fold: (1) productivity has reached a point of development where the human needs of all can be met, though the system of productive forces lies outside of human control; (2) the majority of individuals are not served by these productive forces and in fact lack even the basic requisites for survival. "Things have come to the point where individuals must appropriate the existing totality of productive forces not merely to achieve self-activity but to secure their very existence."[60]

   What Marx then foresees is a revolution which will overthrow the present system. It will involve a complete transformation of man and society. Past revolutions only rearranged division of labor and brought one segment of the population, one class, into power. The communist revolution will end division of labor, as such, and will abolish not merely the bourgeois class, but all classes. The communist revolution will be a complete appropriation of all productive forces. It will be accomplished by the proletarians because they alone can achieve a complete and unrestricted self-activity. The very act of revolution, moreover, will further develop their universal character and energy.[61]

Communism, then, as Marx sees it, puts an end to division of labor and private property. It transforms work into free activity and changes social relations from class relationships to relations between individuals. Finally, the revolution puts an end to illusory substitutes for communal life, such as the state, and creates a real community in which individuals obtain their freedom in and through their association with each other. Marx stresses throughout the "individual," not the sacrifice of the individual to a collectivity—as critics of Marx often charge.

The greatest and most lasting achievement of Marx's view of history has been his demonstration of the influence of economic conditions in history. But the grounds for many of the later criticisms of Marx can also be traced to this initial formulation of his materialist view. We will return later to the issue of "economic determinism," but some initial questions might be asked in respect to *The German Ideology* itself. All deal with the *extent* to which production can be said to be the determining factor in history. Most of the questions deal with the relationship between consciousness and work. Marx argues that what distinguishes human beings from animals is not that humans think but that they produce.[62] One can show "empirically" (Marx's term) that people do work. But one cannot return to primitive history and empirically establish the origins of consciousness. Could it not be argued that productive activity was only possible *because* primitive humans "grasped" intellectually the possibility of using tools? This holds true even if one "surmises" that the first use of a tool happened by chance; further use required "conscious" understanding. Does not productive activity assume consciousness from the outset? Can production, then, be proven "more primary"?

Marx also moves from saying that productive activity is "*a* definite way" human beings express their lives to the conclusion that "what they are, therefore, *coincides* with what they produce" and how they produce.[63] *A* factor becomes *the* factor. "Consciousness does not determine life, but life determines consciousness." As an insight into the *influence* of economic structures on ideology Marx's point is quite valid. Again, one of his greatest contributions has been to show that "morality, religion, metaphysics, and all the rest of ideology" are not independent of life conditions and do often reflect economic self-interest. But taken literally it cannot be said "that life determines consciousness", for human life, human work, always involve consciousness.

Similarly, one can point to the influence of economic factors in history. But can one assert, as Marx does, that lack of sugar and coffee caused the

Germans to rise against Napoleon, that "lack of sugar and coffee thus became *the real basis* of the glorious Wars of Liberation of 1313"[64]? And what does it mean, in reference to a *future* event, to say that it is "empirically established" that a communist revolution will end alienation and accomplish 'the liberation of each single individual"[65]? These questions do not negate the validity of Marx's insights but they do point up how easily his theory can become "reductionistic."

Historical Materialism Further Developed

With the publication of *The Poverty of Philosophy* (1847), directed against Pierre Proudhon, Marx's "historical materialism" became more publicly known. In the same year Marx published an article in which his great disdain for religion again manifested itself. In response to an article which claimed that communists would be put to silence if responsible powers would only develop "the social principles of Christianity," Marx retorted:

> The social principles of Christianity have now had eighteen hundred years to develop, and need no further development by Prussian consistorial councilors. The social principles of Christianity justified the slavery of Antiquity, glorified the serfdom of the Middle Ages, and equally know, when necessary, how to defend the oppression of the proletariat, although they make a pitiful face over it. The social principles of Christianity preach the necessity of a ruling and an oppressed class. . . . The social principles of Christianity preach cowardice, self-contempt, abasement, submission, humility. . . The social principles of Christianity are cringing, but the proletariat is revolutionary. So much for the social principles of Christianity.[66]

In 1848, just prior to the outbreak of revolution in Europe, Marx and Engels published *The Communist Manifesto* at the request of the Communist League. It gave popular and forceful expression to the materialist theory of history, the history of class struggle. It described the rise of the bourgeoisie out of feudalism, the technological achievements of capitalism, and the conditions which would now lead to its collapse, i.e., productive forces too powerful for a small group of capitalists to control, crises, over-production, mass unemployment, lack of wide buying power. Above all, capitalism had created the seeds of its own destruction in the proletariat, whose development as a class Marx shows. The *Manifesto* also points up an element which must be present, in addition to a definite role in production, before one can speak strictly of the proletariat as a "class." It must be "conscious of" being a class, union struggles against capitalism and political struggles against the state had given the workers this sense of unity as a class.

A revolution broke forth in Paris in late February 1848 and triggered revolutionary attempts through most of Europe. Marx returned to Paris from

Brussels to help organize the communist movement there but he discouraged, as reckless and futile, an attempt by German emigrants to form an army with the purpose of marching on Germany. In April he returned to Cologne to edit the *Neue Rheinische Zeitung*. He downplayed the demands of the proletariat and urged alliances which would first win a democratic, political revolution, after which the proletariat could push towards socialism. His writings in this period analyzed European revolutionary struggles, and these writings show that in practical application Marx was quite nuanced and sophisticated in using "the materialist analysis of history." His *Class Struggles in France* traced various stages of struggle in that country in 1848–49, from the original victories of the more radical bourgeosie with strong worker support, through the crushing of a worker revolt, to peasant support for Louis Bonaparte and the clash for power in the assembly between contending bourgeois forces in 1849. By 1850 Marx concluded that the moment of revolution had temporarily passed and must await another period of financial crisis. His *18th Brumaire of Louis Bonaparte* (1852) traced the new Napoleon's rise to power. Throughout the 1850s Marx also contributed numerous articles to the *New York Daily Tribune*.

The Issue of "Determinism"

Through the mid and late 1850s Marx, now in London, again focused on economic analyses. His manuscripts of this period, the *Grundrisse*, which will be taken up later, suggest that what Marx hoped to write on economics and society was far more ambitious than his volumes of *Capital*. His *A Contribution to the Critique of Political Economy* (1859) contained only a small part of his project. But the "Preface" to this work contains a brief statement of "the materialist conception of history" which has become a rather classic summary of his theory of history.

> In the social production which men carry on they enter into definite relations that are indispensable and independent of their will; these relations of production correspond to a definite state of development of their material powers of production. The sum total of these relations of production constitutes the economic structure of society—the real foundation, on which rise legal and political superstructures and to which correspond definite forms of social consciousness. The mode of production in material life determines the general character of the social, political, and spiritual processes of life. It is not the consciousness of men that determines their existence, but, on the contrary, their social existence determines their consciousness.[67]

The language of economic structure versus political and ideological superstructure, stated in quite deterministic language, reinforced the impression of Marxism as an "economic determinism" based on a series of "upwardly moving" causes. Productive forces at the bottom level—natural resources and geographical factors, human labor and skills, and the level of technology, which some Marxists singled out as *the* main causal factor—caused certain relations of production to appear, forms of division of labor and property ownership. Together these cause class divisions, and on top the whole superstructure of political states, laws, religion, morality, and philosophy "simply" reflect the economic order and class consciousness.[68]

But economic determinism and the complete subordination of ideology runs into some obvious contradictions. Marx himself spent his life trying to change people's *ideas* by his writing, and Lenin and others realized that the decisive struggle for revolution might indeed lie at the level of changing consciousness. In a now frequently cited letter to Joseph Bloch in 1890, Engels wrote:

> According to the materialist conception of history, the *ultimately* determining element in history is the production and reproduction of real life. More than this neither Marx nor I have ever asserted. Hence if somebody twists this into saying that the economic element is the *only* determining one, he transforms that proposition into a meaningless, abstract, senseless phrase. The economic situation is the basis, but the various elements of the superstructure . . . (constitutions, political theories, religious views, etc.) . . . also exercise their influence upon the course of the historical struggles and in many cases preponderate in determining their *form*.[69]

Roger Garaudy articulates a position now increasingly accepted, in its general form, by neo-Marxists. The contradictions of capitalism are such that they cannot be resolved without socialism. Therefore one can speak of an "external necessity" or inevitability about the effects of capitalism. But if we are not "conscious" of the necessity for socialism (an "internal necessity") the contradictions, crises, and wars generated by capitalism could continue unresolved.[70] Bertell Ollman argues in great detail that "economic determinism is a misinterpretation of Marx based on a misunderstanding of his idea of causes, which are always interacting, not "serial."[71] Even Soviet Marxists appear to have abandoned determinism.

Yet it remains important in Marxism to recognize the "contradictions" that conflicts within the economic order generate. Marx continues in his 1859 statement:

> At a certain stage of their development the material forces of production in society come into conflict with the existing relations of production, or—what is but a legal expression for the same thing—with the property relations within which they had been at work before. From

forms of development of the forces of production these relations turn into their fetters. Then comes the period of social revolution.[72]

What Marx intends is this: productive forces outgrow earlier forms of relations of production. With the introduction of manufacture—"serial" production by many workers rather than one craftsman creating an entire product—and of machinery, the medieval guilds had become fetters blocking the growth of production. Under capitalism *private* ownership (i.e., relations of production) is in conflict with productive forces which are now almost entirely social (i.e., all our commodities are mass produced, not hand made). The contradiction occurs because capitalism is geared only for profit and lacks social planning. The needs of the masses are not met. In Marx's time the lack of social planning, or any coordinated economic planning, resulted in regular cycles of financial crises, overproduction, the closing of factories, and massive unemployment.

In this summary statement Marx also reasserted the idea of successive *stages* in history (Asiatic, ancient, feudal, capitalist) and he contended: "No social order ever disappears before all the productive forces for which there is room in it have been developed."[73] This point would become a major problem for Marxists in Russia and China where capitalism had not yet fully developed. How could they promote a socialist revolution until capitalism and political democracy had become fully established and in decline?[74]

Marx's Critique of Capitalist Economy (1857–67)

In 1867 Marx published Volume I of *Capital,* his most famous work. Engels published two later volumes by Marx after his death. These volumes, together with his manuscripts, the *Grundrisse,* provide the main source of his economic thought. Since my own Chapter 4, "The Case Against Capitalism," presents a detailed neo-Marxist economic analysis, we might at this point simply note the most salient points of Marx's economic theory.

The Grundrisse

If the *1844 Manuscripts* drew the attention of Marxist scholars earlier, a more recently published set of Marx's manuscripts, the *Grundrisse* (Outlines or Foundations of the Critique of Political Economy), have become a focus of special interest over the past decade.[75] The *Grundrisse* tend to support those who argue for "continuity" in Marx's thought. They show the continued influence of Hegel; they take up again Marx's humanistic concern for the social individual and the theme of alienated labor. The growth of productive forces, Marx observes, has made possible the "universal development of individuals"[76] and conditions which could allow them to actualize their potential as full human beings. But under capitalism the universal nature of this production "creates an alienation of the individual from himself and others."[77] The creative power of the worker "establishes itself against him as an alien force, the power of capital."[78]

Of special contemporary interest, the manuscripts show that Marx recognized that the growth of technology and even of automation could be of enormous benefit. Productive activity meant for Marx not simply hours spent on a job, but also the creative and disciplined use of leisure time. "Really free labor, the composing of music, for example, is at the same time damned serious and demands the greatest effort."[79] By reducing the necessary labor of society to a minimum "all members of society can develop their education in the arts, sciences, etc., thanks to the free time and means available to all."[80]

Marx's Economics

Truly free labor and the universal development of individuals were Marx's vision of what "could be" under socialism. His criticisms were aimed at what capitalism instead had created. In page after page of *Capital*, and most vividly in his chapter on "The Working Day," Marx chronicles the price paid in human suffering for industrial growth: workers suffering from pulmonary diseases caused by the dust and heat of factories, small children working fifteen hour days, a young girl dying of exhaustion after twenty-six consecutive hours of work.[81]

But Marx intends far more than a description of the sufferings caused by capitalism and the industrial revolution. Using a dialectical method—going from "appearances" to a deeper grasp of reality—Marx challenges the basic assumptions of the prevailing economic theory. First, political economy assumed the owner-wage earner relationship, that some people should own and others work for them, to be the "natural" way things are. Marx sees the system of private ownership as a "historical" development and therefore subject to change. Second, political economy assumed that economics deals with "things," e.g., commodities, wages, prices. Marx insists that economics does not deal simply with things but with *social relations*. Every commodity produced and sold, every wage paid, involve very definite relationships between human beings. In failing to recognize these social relations, capitalism and capitalist theory consequently ignore the real effects of the system on human society. This insight, according to the American Marxist economist Paul Sweezy, distinguishes Marx from all other economists and is the key to his method of analysis.[82] Third, Marx challenges the explanation of profit in capitalist theory, and this leads him to his theory of capitalist "exploitation" of the worker.

1. Exploitation in Commodity Production. Grounds for the charge of exploitation were not difficult to find in nineteenth-century Europe. Some capitalist owners had accumulated vast fortunes while millions worked ten to fourteen hour days for bare subsistence wages. But many critics remained at a level of moral condemnation of the greed of owners. Marx sought to demonstrate "scientifically" that exploitation is *intrinsic* to the capitalist system, that profit can be explained *only* by the surplus-value created by workers. Serfs in the Middle Ages worked three days for themselves and three days for their landowners without compensation. So, in a more disguised and subtle way, do factory workers receive wages that represent only part of the value they have contributed to production with the rest going to owners in profits.[83]

Marx defined capitalism as commodity production, with surplus value as the central aim of the system. Men and women have always produced goods for their own use or to exchange them for others. But capitalism is characterized by "production of commodities for profit." Thus Marx begins *Capital,* I, with a study of commodities and what determines their value. Marx argues that while all commodities must have a "use-value" (i.e., the power to satisfy some human need or desire), this alone is not sufficient to explain the basis for exchange. "Exchange-value" (i.e., how much of everything else any one thing can command in a market) is determined by the quantity of labor necessary to produce it. The quantity of labor is measured by the length of "socially necessary" time needed to produce the commodity.[84]

How then does "surplus value" fit into the explanation of commodities? Surplus value originates with the private ownership of the means of production, when production ceases to be simply exchange for use and becomes production for profit. Surplus value is the uncompensated labor the wage worker gives to the capitalist without receiving any value in exchange. What workers receive in wages is determined not by the value of their work or the time they put in (labor-time), but by the amount they need to sustain life (labor-power). The difference between the two, the value created by work and the amount the worker needs in order to subsist, is surplus value.[85] Marx states his position quite graphically: "Suppose the working day consists of 6 hours of necessary labor and 6 hours of surplus labor. Then the free laborer gives the capitalist every week 6 x 6 or 36 hours of surplus labor. It is the same as if he worked 3 days in the week for himself, and 3 days in the week *gratis* for the capitalist."[86]

Non-Marxist critics reject Marx's explanation. They contend that the value of a commodity cannot be measured by the labor put into it, and that, in fact, there is no purely "objective" measure of the value of commodities. Some further discussion of this issue will be taken up in Chapter 4.

2. The Collapse of Capitalism. Marx did not intend simply a moral judgment on exploitation. He argued that the internal contradictions of capitalism create crises which will eventually lead to its collapse. Marx considered overproduction, combined with lack of buying power, as the ultimate cause of all economic crises. Capitalism is driven by a law of constant expansion. Its natural dynamism pushes it to seek ever greater profits by producing more and by producing more cheaply (by intensifying labor and by replacing human labor by machines). Competition also drives capitalists to save on labor costs, reduce wages, and push smaller capitalists out of business. But this very expansion contains the seeds of capitalism's destruction. For less wages to pay and fewer small capitalists to compete with also mean less buying power. Consequently, factories must be closed when goods lay unsold, and mass unemployment results. Crises rack the whole system and the jobless masses must necessarily revolt eventually, if only to subsist.

Marx's views on the inevitable collapse of capitalism have left him quite vulnerable to critics who respond that he has been refuted by history. Workers have not revolted, at least not in the highly developed capitalist countries where revolution was predicted. Workers' wages have not remained at a subsistence level; union negotiations have taken the place of revolution; long-range corporate planning has diminished problems of unforeseen overproduction. Neo-Marxists, as will be seen in subsequent chapters, have offered various explanations for the continuance of capitalism: investment of surplus and the creation of new markets through foreign imperialism; heavy investment in military weapons; the stimulation of false needs through massive advertising; the intrusion of the state to subsidize private business and placate the masses. But Marx himself, though he may have been too sanguine in anticipating socialism, did not expect the revolution to occur "automatically." He recognized that workers must be organized and become conscious of their revolutionary goals. Hence he wrote also on revolutionary strategy and the ways socialism might come about.

Marx's Revolutionary Strategy and Program

Marxist tactics have come to be identified in the popular mind with Marxist-Leninist tactics. Marx never hedged on the necessity of doing away with capitalism. But his tactics varied, and his followers often disagreed on what tactics were best. His immediate followers, in the Social-Democratic Party, would opt for a more "reformist" strategy to achieve socialism. Lenin would insist on revolution. Both claimed to be following Marx.

If his immediate tactics on working toward socialism varied, Marx's views on establishing socialism *after* the workers won power remained quite general and undefined. On the political organization of the new society, Marx spoke at times of the need for a "dictatorship of the proletariat" as a transitional step, and the disappearance of the state as an ultimate result. But practical details were never spelled out. Understandably reluctant to project a complete plan for the future, he indicated only briefly two economic phases of communism, one as it emerged from capitalism, and the other one after division of labor had been eliminated. In practice, then, revolutionary leaders since Marx have been left with the task of working out strategies for revolution and for constructing socialism after the revolution has succeeded. Thus what we have come to know about the role of the Communist Party, tactics for achieving socialism, and the political organization of Communist countries in practice often reflect Lenin's views or even Stalin's views more than those of Marx. But we should note what Marx himself had to say about strategy, revolution, and the state.

The Communist Party

In the *Manifesto* Marx stated: "The Communists do not form a separate party opposed to other working-class parties." They have no separate interests, said Marx, and no sectarian principles by which they intend to shape the proletarian movement. They differ only from other working class parties in pointing out the common interests of the proletariat in all countries independent of nationality, and in representing the interests of the movement as a whole. Their main contribution is that Communists have a clearer "theoretical understanding" of "the line of march, the conditions, and the ultimate general results of the proletarian movement."[87]

Only for a period of about five years could one speak of a "Communist Party" in Marx's lifetime. The Communist League formed in 1847 with at most 300 members. It was dissolved and then reorganized in 1850 with London as a center. There it lasted only two more years. From 1846 to 1873 Marx worked with the first International Association of Working Men, but it was an association which represented a wide spectrum of leftist views (followers of Proudhon, Lassalle, Bakunin, etc.). Otherwise Marx worked with no specific party. The political work he did do shows that he favored a democratic organization run by the workers themselves, but not dependent on any other political party. He wanted it, though, to have a clear theoretical understanding of its goals.[88]

It was Lenin, in *What is to be Done?* in 1903, who insisted on the need for disciplined "professional revolutionaries," drawn chiefly from the bourgeois intelligentsia. Only the masses could ultimately make the revolution, but without trained leadership they would "spontaneously" develop a trade-union consciousness, not the revolutionary consciousness needed to achieve socialism. Some have hailed Lenin for giving Communism the driving force and leadership it needed. Others, including Marxists of his day—Karl Kautsky, Rosa Luxemburg, the Mensheviks—accused him of substituting an elitist party for the proletariat.

Revolution

The *Manifesto* and the years 1848–50 mark the most revolutionary period of Marx's writings. He spoke in the *Manifesto* in immediate terms of "the conquest of political power by the proletariat,"[89] and said that the first step in the revolution would be to raise the proletariat to the position of ruling class.[90] But by the end of 1850, convinced that economic factors determine the possibility of revolution, he told workers that they might have to go through twenty or even fifty years of struggle before they would be ready to take power.[91] In his address to the International in 1864, he seemed to stress the gains that could be and had been achieved by structural reforms in England—the ten-hour working day, the growth of co-operative factories.[92] In 1872 and again in 1879 he spoke of the possibility of peaceful revolution in America and England where the working class could become a majority in Congress or Parliament. In such a case, however, the displaced opposition might resort to violence. He also strongly criticized the use of terror by the Jacobins in the French Revolution. A revolution was immature and weak which had to impose by sheer force what was not yet inherent in society.[93] Yet it would be wrong to conclude that Marx "abandoned" the idea of revolution.[94] He felt force was justified in overthrowing oppressive systems and would probably be needed since those in power do not relinquish power without struggle.

Marx's tactics varied considerably also. Where the "democratic" revolution had yet to be achieved, as in Germany, he urged alliances with the more radical sectors of the bourgeoisie. But in his "Address to the Communist League" in 1850 he warned, as a lesson learned from the revolutions of 1848–49, that the workers must retain their independence from bourgeois democrats. The revolutionary workers' party "marches together with them against the faction which it aims at overthrowing, it opposes them in every-thing whereby they seek to consolidate their position in their own inter-ests."[95] The workers should make the "revolution permanent" by pushing the democratic revolution to its most radical conclusions and ultimately to conquest of power by the proletariat. The question of alliances with the bourgeoisie would be an issue at many points in the history of Communism (e.g., in 1905 and 1917 in Russia and for Mao Tse-tung in China). Mao perhaps went the furthest in proposing the inclusion of the "national bourgeoisie" in the new revolutionary government.

Dictatorship of the Proletariat

Marx first used this term in 1850, and perhaps no other expression in Marxism has evoked more reaction. Explaining Marx's thought in *State and Revolution*, Lenin insisted that the dictatorship is needed to crush the resis-tance of the exploiters and to lead the enormous masses of the population in the work of organizing a socialist economy. "Only he is a Marxist who extends the recognition of the class struggle to the recognition of the dictatorship of the proletariat. . . . This is the touchstone on which the real understanding and recognition of Marxism should be tested. . . ."[96] Karl Kautsky, Rosa Luxemburg, and other Marxists of Lenin's day, while not denying Marx's use of the term, insisted that he intended a workers' democracy, and they feared that it could be used to justify a dictatorship *over* the proletariat. In Lenin's defense many argue that he always maintained vital contact with the workers and never intended to erect a Party elite in their place. But what of Marx?

Because the issue of whether Marxist socialism can be truly democratic or not is closely related to the meaning of dictatorship of the proletariat, the main discussion of it will be taken up in Chapter 8. Significant studies by Richard Hunt and Hal Draper will be explored more fully then. Some of the principal conclusions of their study, however, might be briefly noted. In some forty-odd volumes of Marx's and Engels' work this expression was used in only eleven places. In an effort in 1850 to achieve some common front with Blanquists, Marx and Engels used the term "dictatorship" but added "of the proletariat" precisely to show that it would be exercised by a whole revolutionary class, not an elite. In only *one* locus is the expression used to signify "crushing the resistance of the bourgeoisie" (and that is the passage which Lenin emphasized). Later use of the expression was intended to counteract Bakunin and the anarchists who wanted an immediate and complete abolition of the state. In a response to Bakunin who asked if the rule of the proletariat meant all forty million Germans would be members of the government, Marx answered: "Certainly, because the thing starts with the self-government of the township."[97] Finally, in an introduction to Marx's *The Civil War in France,* Engels pointed to the Paris Commune, which was extensively democratic in its measures, as an example of the dictatorship of the proletariat.[98]

The Future Communist Society

The power of the state remains an all too evident feature in Communist countries and, as noted before, Marx said very little about the political organization of a socialist society. In his *Critique of the Gotha Programme* (1875), in response to the question "what transformation will the state undergo in communist society?" Marx said only that "this question can only be answered scientifically" (presumably meaning it can be decided only when the time comes). He repeated that the dictatorship of the proletariat would be operative in "a political transition period."[99]

His statement in the *Manifesto* about "conquest of the state" became modified, however, in his *Eighteenth Brumaire* when Marx observed that the state machine would have to be "smashed."[100] This "smashing of the state machine," according to Engels, was described by Marx in reference to the Paris Commune of 1871.[101] Thus what "smashing the state machine" meant was replacing the professional army and police with a people's army and police. Bureaucracy was replaced by popular rule—universal suffrage, administrators receiving only workers' wages, short terms and the possibility of recall for all office holders, elected magistrates and judges.[102] Ultimately the state would "disappear" or "wither away" (Engels' term) since force would no longer be needed in a classless, cooperative society. Again, what purely "administrative" functions would remain was not specified.

What about the state in reference to the economy? In the *Manifesto* Marx and Engels indicated various measures aimed at *centralizing* banks, transport, and industry. Yet this cannot be taken as an indication that *state* socialism or ownership was intended as the lasting structure of the economy. For this would contradict Marx's views on the state and his descriptions of the economy as the "free association of individuals." In the *Critique of the Gotha Programme* Marx indicates the divisions of the "total social product" which would have to be taken into account before individuals received their "personal" share. But what administrative bodies would take over these functions is not indicated. Funds would have to be set aside for various purposes: to replace worn out machines and to invest for expansion, to provide for accidents and disasters, to meet social needs such as schools and health services, and to care for those unable to work.[103] With a view to the elimination of money, Marx speaks of workers then receiving "certificates" enabling them to draw from "the social stock of means of consumption." In the first phase of socialism people would be paid "according to their work." In the highest phase of communist society, once goods were abundant and class distinctions were overcome, the slogan would be: "From each according to his ability, to each according to his needs."[104] Marx offers only these brief schematic ideas of how communist society would function.

Marx's Final Years

These notes on the Gotha Programme would constitute Marx's last major work. Illness prevented him from ever fulfilling the work he had planned. He had been tortured by boils in the years he prepared for the publication of *Capital*. Headaches, insomnia, bronchitis, and tumors plagued him in his final years. He sought respite, from time to time, at the health "spas" on the continent. He tried to work on the third volume of *Capital*; he devoted time to studies in the natural sciences; he developed a special interest in Russia and its potential for revolution. But his strength was gone. The death of his wife, Jenny, in 1881, proved shattering to his morale, and the death of his first-born daughter, Jenny, crushed his spirits still more. Marx died on March 14, 1883, and was buried three days later in Highgate cemetery on the outskirts of London, where the final decades of his life had been spent.

His lifetime colleague, Frederick Engels, and other German followers, would undertake the effort to systematize his ideas. The revolutionary transition to socialism he had predicted appeared only a remote possibility at the time of his death. Toward the end Marx believed that England might move toward socialism by "peaceful" means. Marx had attracted followers and admirers, but no "Communist Party" existed to carry out his ideas. The German Social-Democrats would prove to be the most organized Marxist political force up to the end of the nineteenth-century. But in Marx's lifetime they were hindered by Bismarck's "anti-socialist" laws and they were an amalgam of Lassalle's followers as well as Marx's. A Marxist movement had developed in France, but Marx himself had expressed grave disappointment with the way his sons-in-law had represented his thought there.

Russia would, in fact, hold the key to the future of Marxism, but this was not yet evident. Revolutionary thought had taken hold of Russia in the 1870s, but it had been spurred by a "populist" movement which stressed peasant revolution and peasant socialism rather than a proletariat revolt against capitalism. The possibilities of revolution in Russia stirred Marx's interest and he did not rule out the possibility of Russia by-passing the capitalist stage of development. In a reply to Vera Zasulich he affirmed that his research had convinced him that the rural commune "is the mainspring of Russia's social regeneration."[105] But his last statement of the issue, in a preface to an 1882 translation of the *Communist Manifesto,* left ambivalent the issue of how Russia would fit into his own theory of historical development. Marx observed: "If the Russian Revolution becomes a signal for a proletarian revolution in the West, so that both complement each other, the present Russian common ownership of land may serve as the starting point for a communist development."[106]

If Marx left a controversial and disputed legacy of ideas, so also did he evoke quite different evaluations of his character and personality. Those who had met him and judged him unfavorably invariably spoke of his abrasive and domineering way of speaking; those who respected him and loved him spoke of his honesty, his humor, his love for his family. Thus, on the one hand, we read:

> Marx himself was the type of man who is made up of energy, will and unshakable conviction. . . . He always spoke in imperative words that would brook no contradiction and were made all the sharper by the almost painful impression of the tone which ran through everything he said. This tone expressed the firm conviction of his mission to dominate men's minds and prescribe them their laws. Before me stood the embodiment of a democratic dictator such as one might imagine in a day dream.
>
> To no opinion which differed from his own did he accord the honour of even condescending consideration. Everyone who contradicted him he treated with abject contempt; every argument that he did not like he treated either with biting scorn at the unfathomable ignorance that had prompted it, or with opprobrious aspersions on the motives of him who advanced it. . . .[107]

But a friend and his daughter wrote quite otherwise:

> No one could be kinder and fairer than Marx in giving others their due. He was too great to be envious, jealous or vain. . . . Of all the great, little or average men that I have known, Marx is one of the few who was

free from vanity. . . . No man could be more truthful than Marx—he was truthfulness incarnate.

Marx was the cheeriest, gayest soul that ever breathed, . . . a man brimming over with humour and good-humour, whose hearty laugh was infectious and irresistible, . . . the kindliest, gentlest, most sympathetic of companions. . . . In his home life, as in his intercourse with friends, and even with mere acquaintances, I think one might say that Karl Marx's main characteristics were his unbounded good-humour and his unlimited sympathy. His kindness and patience were really sublime.[108]

Whatever judgment one makes of his ideas or of Marx as a person, Engels judged rightly when he said at Marx's graveside: "His name will live through the centuries and so also will his work."[109]

Notes

1. E. J. Hobsbawm, *The Age of Revolution: Europe 1789–1848* (London: Wiedenfeld and Nicolson, 1962) , p. xv.

2. Ibid., p. 27.

3. Ibid., p. 50.

4. *Writings of the Young Marx on Philosophy and Society,* ed. and trans. Loyd D. Easton and Kurt H. Guddat (Garden City, N.Y.: Doubleday Anchor, 1967), p. 255. References hereafter given as: Easton, *Writings*

5. *Hegel's Philosophy of Right,* trans. with notes by T. M. Knox (London: Oxford at the Clarendon Press, 1962), p. 10. Confer also the commentary by Eugene Fleischmann, *La Philosophie politique de Hegel* (Paris: Plon, 1964), and the comprehensive study of Hegel's political writings in Shlomo Avineri, *Hegel's Theory of the Modern State* (Cambridge University Press, 1972).

6. Avineri, *Hegel's Theory,* p. 126.

7. Friedrich Hegel, *On Christianity: Early Theological Writings,* trans. T. M. Knox (New York: Harper Torchbooks, 1961). Introduction by Richard Kroner, pp. 1-20.

8. Hegel often personified "Spirit" (*Geist*) in his writings. as if it were a force akin to divine providence working through nature and history. Marx, and many Hegel scholars up to the present, have taken the personification literally, as a force striving to achieve its goals. Some recent Hegel scholars, however, believe that Hegel's main intention was to argue simply that the world is intelligible; it has rationality and hence spirit. See, for example, J. N. Findlay, *Hegel: A Re-Examination* (New York: Macmillan, 1958), Chapter 2.

9. G.W.F. Hegel, *The Phenomenology of Mind,* trans. J. B. Baille (London: George Allen & Unwin, 1964), p.75.

10. For more on the Young Hegelians see David McLellan, *The Young Hegelians and Karl Marx* (London: Macmillan, 1969); William J. Brazill, *The Young Hegelians* (New Haven: Yale University, 1970); and Karl Lowith, *From Hegel to Nietzsche* (London: Constable, 1965).

11. On the history of Germany in this period see: *Treitschke's History of Germany in the 19th Century,* Volume VI, translated by Eden and Cedar Paul (London: Jarrold & Sons, 1919), and Jacques Droz, *Le libéralisme rhénan, 1815–1848* (Paris: Fernand Sorlot, 1940).

12. David McLellan, *Karl Marx, His Life and Thought* (London: Macmillan, 1973) is perhaps the best biography of Marx. Boris Nicolaievski and O. Maenchen-Helfen, *Karl Marx, Man and Fighter* (London, 1933, 3rd edition, 1973) and Franz Mehring, *Karl Marx, The Story of His Life* (London: George Allen & Unwin, 1936; 3rd impression 1951), long served as standard biographies of Marx.

13. Karl Marx and Frederick Engels, *Collected Works, Volume I, Marx: 1835–1843*

(New York: International Publishers, 1975), pp. 637–8. Referred to hereafter as *Collected Works, I*.

14. Easton, *Writings*, p. 38.

15. Ibid., pp. 40 ff.

16. Ibid., p.52.

17. *Collected Works, I*, pp. 30–31.

18. McLellan, *Karl Marx*, p. 47.

19. Easton, *Writings*, pp. 126ff.

20. Ibid., p. 86.

21. My own article, "Karl Marx First Political Writings: The *Rheinische Zeitung*, 1842–1843," in *Demythologizing Marxism*, ed. F. J. Adelmann, S.J. (Chestnut Hill, Mass.: Boston College, 1969), pp. 19–63, studies these early writings in detail.

22. Ibid., pp. 60–63.

23. See Karl Marx, *Critique of Hegel's 'Philosophy of Right,'* ed. Joseph O'Malley (Cambridge University Press, 1970), p. 77. See also pp. 93, 115.

24. Easton, *Writings*, p. 223. Marx often gave underlined emphasis to many words in a single sentence. I have generally omitted these in quoting him.

25. Ibid., p. 222.

26. Ibid., p. 227.

27. Ibid., p. 237.

28. Ibid., p. 225.

29. Ibid., p. 240.

30. Ibid., p. 241.

31. Ibid., pp. 249–50.

32. Ibid., p. 257.

33. Ibid., p. 261.

34. As late as 1850, Prussia had only 700,000 factory workers, roughly 4 percent of the population, with an additional 9 percent in various artisan establishments See T. S. Hamerow, *Restoration, Revolution, Reaction* (Princeton University Press, 1958), pp. 17, 36. Hamerow cites statistics from official records in Berlin.

35. Easton, *Writings*, pp. 289–90.

36. Ibid., p. 295.

37. Ibid., p. 306.

38. Ibid., p. 312.

39. Karl Marx and F. Engels, *The Holy Family or a Critique of Critical Critique* (Moscow: Foreign Languages Publishing House, 1956), pp. 160–57.

40. Easton, *Writings*, pp. 400–02.

41. Ibid., "Critique of Hegelian Dialectic and Philosophy in General," pp. 314–37.

42. The explanation of this comparison between Marx and Hegel owes much to Nathan Rotenstreich, *Basic Problems of Marx's Philosophy* (Indianapolis: Bobbs-Merrill, 1965), pp. 39 ff.

43. Roger Garaudy, *Karl Marx: The Evolution of his Thought* (New York: International Publishers, 1967), p. 67.

44. The definition given for "praxis" by Bernard Delfgaauw, *The Young Marx* (Westminster, Md.: Newman, 1967), p. 36.

45. Nearly every writer who deals with Marx's development has taken some stand on whether there is a break or continuity between the thought of the young and the later Marx. Louis Althusser, *Pour Marx* (Paris: Maspero, 1965), pp. 23–32, and others

have argued for a decisive break. Bertell Ollman, *Alienation* (Cambridge University Press, 1971), and many others uphold continuity. In *The German Ideology,* Marx himself did ridicule his own earlier philosophical language, and in 1859 he looked back on this work as an effort to "settle accounts" with his earlier philosophical consciousness. But he quite clearly had a strong *political* reason for changing his language in 1845. Max Stirner, one of the main targets of *The German Ideology,* had identified Marx as a follower of Feuerbach whom Stirner criticized for making "Man" or "species-being" into a new and abstract god. Stirner likewise accused Communism of exalting "Society" as a replacement for God. Thus Marx's efforts to dissociate himself from Feuerbach, and from utopian socialism, and to prove that Communism is "not an ideal" but "the real movement which abolishes the present state of affairs" (Easton, *Writings,* p. 426) seem strongly influenced by Stirner's critique. Overlooked also by critics of "continuity" is Marx's own explanation, in Part III of *The German Ideology,* that his materialistic outlook had been already indicated in earlier works, but that his "philosophical phraseology" had given critics an excuse for misunderstanding *"the real trend of thought."* Marx, *The German Ideology* (London: Lawrence & Wishart, 1965), p. 254.

46. Easton, *Writings,* p. 433.

47. Ibid., pp. 408–9.

48. Ibid., pp. 415–21.

49. Ibid., p. 414.

50. Ibid., p. 415. Emphasis added.

51. Ibid., p. 439.

52. Ibid., p. 424.

53. On forms of division of labor see: Karl Marx, *Capital,* Volume I (New York: International Publishers, 1967), Chapter XIV, and a discussion of Marx's views in Vernon Venable, *Human Nature: The Marxian View* (Cleveland: Meridian Books, 1966, first published 1945), Chapter 9.

54. Easton, *Writings,* p. 425.

55. Ibid.

56. Ibid., p. 431.

57. Ibid., pp. 410ff.

58. Ibid., pp. 442ff.

59. Ibid., p. 426.

60. Ibid., p. 467.

61. Ibid., p. 468.

62. Ibid., p. 409.

63. Ibid. Emphasis added.

64. Ibid., p. 429. Emphasis added.

65. Ibid.

66. Lewis S. Feuer, ed., *Marx & Engels, Basic Writings on Politics and Philosophy* (Garden City, N.Y.: Anchor Doubleday, 1959), pp. 268–69.

67. Ibid., p. 43.

68. See Marx and Engels on the ideas and morality of the ruling class in Easton, *Writings,* pp. 438–39.

69. Engels to Joseph Bloch, 1890, in Robert C. Tucker, ed., *The Marx-Engels Reader* (New York: W. W. Norton, 1978, 2nd ed.), p. 760.

70. Garaudy, *Karl Marx,* p. 101.

71. Ollman, *Alienation*, parts I and IV.

72. Feuer, *Marx & Engels,* pp. 43–44.

73. Ibid., p. 44.

74. In response to the issue of how a socialist revolution could occur prior to capitalism's full development, some Marxists have argued that backward countries were part of an already developed *world* system of capitalism. These countries were the "weakest links" in world capitalism. Trotsky used this point to argue that socialist revolution also had to become international and that Stalin's "socialism in one country" could not succeed. Others affirm simply that Marx only intended the stages to describe the path of Western Europe, and not to give a universal law for all countries.

75. The *Grundrisse* was published in Moscow in 1939–41, and became known in the West only after a 1953 German edition appeared. E J. Hobsbawm's edition of *Precapitalist Economic Formations* in 1964 brought part of the *Grundrisse* into English translation; English translations by David McLellan and by M. Nicolaus appeared in 1973; Tucker's second edition of *The Marx-Engels Reader* now contains long excerpts from the *Grundrisse.*

76. Karl Marx, *The Grundrisse,* ed. David McLellan (New York: Harper Torchbooks, 1971), p. 121.

77. Ibid., p. 71.

78. Ibid., p. 81; see also pp. 96ff., 120ff.

79. Ibid., p. 124.

80. Ibid., p. 142; see also p. 148.

81. *Capital, I,* pp. 243–56.

82. Paul Sweezy, *The Theory of Capitalist Development* (New York: Oxford University Press, 1942), pp. 1–5, and Chapter 2, *passim.*

83. For a study of Marx's concept of exploitation see Ernest Mandel, *An Introduction to Marxist Economic Theory* (New York: Pathfinder Press, 1970), pp. 7–9.

84. *Capital, I,* pp. 35–41, 89–93.

85. Ibid., pp. 186–98.

86. Ibid., p. 236.

87. Tucker, *Marx-Engels Reader,* pp. 483–84.

88. See David McLellan, *The Thought of Karl Marx. An Introduction* (London: Macmillan, 1971), pp. 167–71. See also Richard N. Hunt, *The Political Ideas of Marx and Engels, Volume 1: Marxism and Totalitarian Democracy, 1818–1850* (University of Pittsburgh Press, 1974), Chapters 5 and 8.

89. Tucker, *Marx-Engels Reader,* p. 484.

90. Ibid., p. 490.

91. See McLellan, *The Thought of Karl Marx,* p. 200.

92. Tucker, *Marx-Engels Reader,* pp. 517–18.

93. McLellan, *The Thought of Karl Marx,* p. 202. See also "The Possibility of Non-violent Revolution" by Marx. in Tucker, *Marx-Engels Reader,* pp. 522–24.

94. In a letter to F. Bolte and a circular letter to A. Bebel and others Marx again sounds more revolutionary and criticizes "bourgeois reformist" tendencies in the Social-Democratic movement. See Tucker, *The Marx-Engels Reader,* p. 520 and pp. 549–555, respectively.

95. Tucker, *Marx-Engels Reader,* p. 504.

96. James E. Connor, ed., *Lenin on Politics and Revolution, Selected Writings* (New York: Pegasus, 1968), p. 203.

97. Tucker, *Marx-Engels Reader,* p. 545.
98. Ibid., p. 629.
99. Ibid., p. 538.
100. Ibid., p. 607.
101. Ibid., pp. 627–28.
102. Ibid., pp. 632–33.
103. Ibid., pp. 528–29.
104. Ibid., pp. 530–31.
105. Ibid., p. 675.
106. See McLellan, *Karl Marx,* p. 442.
107. Quotes taken from McLellan's biography, *Karl Marx,* pp. 452–59.
108. Ibid.
109. Mehring, *Karl Marx,* p. 532.

Chapter 2

Marxism: Its Development since Marx

Marx never wrote a systematic account of all his teachings. As he took up new issues, as conditions changed, Marx's interests shifted and new insights emerged. He wrote no "treatises" on atheism or philosophical materialism. Even such central concepts as "class" and "class struggle" never received a detailed, systematic development. The idea of a "dictatorship of the proletariat" occurred in some letters and writings, but its limits and its precise purposes were never spelled out. In short, as Richard De George observes, "The Marxism which Marx left as a legacy was amorphous. He left no systematic body of doctrine and no unified presentation of his thought." His followers found themselves with a vast array of material from which to pick and choose. The problem of interpreting his thought has consequently led to countless conflicts and controversies. Before his death Marx himself objected to the way his ideas were being used. Commenting on the French "Marxists" of the late 1870s, Marx said: "All I know is that I am not a Marxist."[2]

The openness of Marx's thought to different interpretations raises a number of difficult questions. "What is Marxism?" "What constitutes a Marxist?" "Who decides what Marxism is?" The answers to these will significantly affect the issue of whether Marxism and Christianity are compatible. Two different ways of answering what Marxism is serve as the basis of this chapter.

The Dominant Marxist Tradition,[3] would insist that Marxism, by its very nature as a system of "praxis" within history, should be identified with the actualized dominant form it has taken in history.[4] Three sources of "authority" most influenced the development of this dominant tradition: Engels, Lenin, and the Communist Party. Frederick Engels systematized Marx's views on history and put them into a larger framework of a dialectical materialism which explained the laws of nature and thought as well as of history. His writings carried great authority because of his lifetime collaboration with Marx. Lenin fortified Engels' views by insisting that Marxism is an integral worldview with philosophical materialism as its basis, and he added his own emphases on the role of the vanguard Party, the necessity of revolution, and the dictatorship of the proletariat. As the successful leader of the Bolshevik Revolution in Russia, his views won wide acceptance as authoritative. The Communist Party, especially in countries where it acceded to power, laid claim to being the authentic interpreter and guardian of this tradition, though its authority has been sharply contested by Trotskyist groups and others who adhere to the Marx-Engels-Lenin tradition. The first half of the chapter deals with the history of this classical, and dominant form of Marxism. One can argue that Christians can accommodate to this form of Marxism, as they have to some extent in Eastern Europe, and affirm what is positive in a socialist economy. But it is a Marxism which, at least in its most doctrinaire articulations, is hardly compatible in theory with Christianity.

There is, however, a second view of Marxism, a *Critical Marxism*. It adopts a position quite similar to that taken by the Young Hegelians in respect to Hegel. True Marxism is an open, constantly changing system of ideas. The dialectic of "praxis" requires moving beyond the historically conditioned nineteenth-century expression of Marxism and certainly is in opposition to the closed, dogmatic form which Marxism assumed under Stalin. This view tends to treat Marxism primarily as a method of analysis and not as a complete system of all knowledge. It contends that classical, dominant Marxism has often misrepresented or distorted the "true" Marx.

Not all these generalizations would apply equally to all the Marxists discussed in the second half of the chapter. Certain similarities in thought permit them to be loosely grouped together (e.g., all undertake a "rethinking" of Marx and Marxism), but they often differ considerably in their concerns and in their conclusions. Almost all critical Marxists would reject Marxism as a theory of "economic determinism." Some would claim that Engels' expansion of dialectics to explain nature runs counter to Marx's use of dialectics. Some do not consider philosophical materialism as essential to Marxism. Others would argue that Marx's later doctrines should be read and interpreted in the light of his early humanistic writings. Still others would argue that many of Marx's views, for example his atheism, were historically conditioned and no longer are necessary components of Marxism.

For the most part, Critical Marxism represents the stance of neo-Marxist "intellectuals" rather than any determinate social movement. It is represented by dissident individuals and groups within Communist Parties (e.g., "the Yugoslavian school"), by independent Marxist thinkers (e.g., "the Frankfurt school," Ernst Bloch, Roger Garaudy), and it claims Marxist intellectuals of the past (e.g., the early Georg Lukács, Antonio Gramsci) as its forerunners. But it also represents a growing number of adherents, including a sizeable number of "democratic" socialists in the United States, Europe, and Latin America, together with Christian socialists who claim that certain aspects of Marxism, separable from official Communist ideology, are quite compatible with Christianity.

Some would dispute critical Marxists' claim to represent Marxism, but their claim is of great importance in determining the compatibility of Marxism and Christianity. They agree, on the other hand, with dominant Marxists in calling for a Marxist method of analysis, a critique of capitalism, a denunciation of exploitation, and socialism as a goal.[5]

The Dominant Marxist Tradition

Frederick Engels and Dialectical Materialism

Engels' collaboration with Marx began early in both their careers and lasted until Marx's death. If Marx arrived initially at communism through critiques of political theory and the state, Engels came to communism through a more direct confrontation with capitalism. Born November 28, 1820, in Barmen, Westphalia, Engels grew up in a Protestant capitalist family. As a youth he saw and was repelled by factory conditions in Germany. After studies at the University of Berlin where he also came in contact with the young Hegelians, Engels went to England where his father's spinning firm had a factory in Manchester. Engels himself would later hold a managerial position in the firm. He wrote a critique of capitalist economy for the *German-Franco Annals* (1844) which Marx co-edited. This essay spurred Marx's own interest in economics and led to Marx's and Engels' collaboration first on *The Holy Family* (1844), then on *The German Ideology* (1845) and *The Communist Manifesto* (1848). Engels assisted Marx in writing articles for the *New York Daily Tribune,* provided considerable financial aid to Marx, and edited the final volumes of *Capital.* But Engels also made a very distinctive, if today controversial, contribution to Marxism. He systematized and popularized Marx's ideas, and it was his philosophical writings, rather than those of Marx, which became the source of the distinctive worldview known as "dialectical materialism."[6]

One of Engels' greatest concerns was to show that Marxism was "scientific socialism." He became convinced, moreover, that the same dialectical and materialistic principles which govern history also govern nature. He felt that recent scientific discoveries—the discovery of the cell, the transformation of energy, and the theory of evolution—proved that all of reality could be and should be explained by a materialistic, dialectic view. His most important work, *Anti-Dühring,* thus presented Marxism as a systematic, scientific view of both history and nature. The summary which follows is drawn chiefly from this work and from his *Ludwig Feuerbach.*[7] Discussion of the issue of dialectical materialism will be taken up again in Chapter 7.

1. Materialism. When Marx spoke of the "materialist" view of history he stressed the role of material, economic factors as opposed to the "idealist" stress on ideas and conscious goals. Engels gives the word "materialist" a far more sweeping sense. "Matter" is the sole, or at least the primary, factor at every level of reality: in nature, in history, in the explanation of human life and thought. "God," "Spirit," "Soul," "Consciousness," and "Ideas" are all either nonexistent or products of matter.

Materialism asserts first of all the primacy of matter in explaining change both in nature and history. Hegel's idealism made Spirit or the Absolute Idea the primary creative force in the world. Hegel recognized dialectical development and change in the world but he attributed the change to Spirit. Thus, says Engels, nature and history for Hegel are nothing more than a divine "Idea" or plan working its way through the world.[8] Materialism, in contrast, shows that the source of dialectical development is in reality iself. The material forces of nature and the material, economic forces within history explain change without requiring some hidden, underlying "Spirit" at work.

Materialism, as a consequence, has a different theory of knowledge from idealism. If Hegel made the dialectic a product of Spirit, for materialism the dialectic is simply "the conscious reflex of the dialectical motion of the real world."[9] Ideas are images of real things, whereas Hegel treated real things as mere expressions or embodiments of an "Idea." Hegel's dialectic is thus put back on its feet. The real movement is of nature and history; thought, even dialectical thinking, is only a reflex of this movement. "Dialectical philosophy itself is nothing more than the mere reflection of this process in the thinking brain."[10] The material sensible world is the only reality; our consciousness and thinking are the products of a material, bodily organ, the brain. "Matter is not a product of mind, but mind itself is merely the highest product of matter."[11] Engels thus subscribed to a "copy-theory" of knowledge, to a materialistic realism in which thought mirrors reality precisely because it is itself a product of nature, of matter.

Materialism also resolves the issue of the existence of the world and of the human race. No God or Spirit prior to nature is required to explain matter. The existence of matter needs no explanation because it is itself eternal, uncreated and indestructible. Movement and development in the world can be fully explained by the motion which belongs to matter by its very nature. "Motion is the mode of existence of matter. Never anywhere has there been matter without motion, nor can there be. . . . Matter without motion is just as unthinkable as motion without matter. Motion is therefore as uncreatable and indestructible as matter itself."[12] Science has shown that matter alone can explain the origin of the world and of the human race. Kant's theory of the origin of the universe out of nebulae masses or gasses rendered obsolete the religious doctrine of creation. Darwin's theory demonstrated that human beings are the product of the evolution of nature.[13]

2. Dialectics. If Engels stressed the material basis of all reality against idealism, he found it necessary to insist on the dialectical nature of reality and to differentiate Marxism from classical materialism. Reality, he argued, should be viewed as a complex of "processes." Engels rejected a teleology based on Spirit, but in its place he attempted to show a new teleology inherent in matter itself. Matter has undergone an evolution, an upward movement of progression toward higher forms in both nature and history. Nature has its own final cause such that it necessarily develops from simple aggregate forms to more complex, thinking beings. The failure of the old materialism, and of Feuerbach's materialism, was that they did not see the world as process.

Engels believed that the dialectical process of nature had been proven or confirmed by three great scientific discoveries of his day. The cell was discovered to be the basic structural unit of all living organisms and shown to develop dialectically through a process of multiplying itself. The law of the conservation and transformation of energy showed that nature was a continuous process of one form of universal motion changing into another. Darwin's theory of evolution proved not only the evolution of species but also their transformations through series of dialectical "leaps."

Engels proposed three great dialectical laws, already noted by Hegel, as governing the whole of reality. (1) "The Union and Struggle of Opposites." Contradictions pervade the whole of reality. Curves and straight lines can no longer be sharply distinguished in modern mathematics; neat distinctions cannot be drawn between vertebrae and invertebrae; even death and life appear to merge at times. Tension of conflicting forces characterizes every sphere of reality: attraction and repulsion in magnetic fields; positive and negative charges in the atom; oppressing and oppressed classes in society. Change occurs when one element breaks through the balance and begins to dominate the other.[14] (2) "The Transition from Quantity to Quality." Changes occur quantitatively up to a certain point at which point a "leap" to a new quality takes place. Merely quantitative changes in temperature can produce qualitative changes of water into steam and ice into water. A quantitative difference in the molecular structure of the same atomic elements gives vastly different chemical compounds: N_2O (nitrogen monoxide) is laughing gas; N_2O_5 (nitrogen pentoxide) is nitric analyde. Similarly in society, gradual changes in modes of production eventually cause a complete revolution in the economic structure of society, and gradually increasing numbers of proletarians reach a stage where a whole breakthrough in class relations in necessitated.[15] (3) "The Negation of the Negation." Dühring charged that this Hegelian law was simply an invention based on the religious ideas of fall and redemption. Engels sought to show it operative in nature. The grain of barley must be negated and die in order to bring forth new life. In mathematics, $-A \times -A = A^2$. A negation is itself negated to produce a positive synthesis. In philosophy, the old materialism was negated by idealism which has now been overcome by a new dialectical materialism. In history, an oppressed class, the bourgeoisie in feudal society, gains power and then is itself overthrown by the proletariat.[16]

Dialectical Materialism thus gives a comprehensive and "scientific" explanation of all reality. "Dialectics is nothing more than the science of the general laws of motion and development of Nature, human society, and thought."[17] It is "not a question of building the laws of dialectics into Nature, but of discovering them in it and evolving them from it."[18] Philosophy is thus restricted to the science of thought and its laws, to formal logic and dialectics, and "everything else is merged in the positive science of Nature and history."[19] In short, dialectical materialism puts an end to philosophy and replaces it with a scientific view which embraces nature, history, and thought.

Engels consequently presented Marx's analysis of history and society as a scientific discovery of laws. History is to be explained "by the discovery of the general laws of motion which assert themselves as the ruling ones in the history of human society."[20] Marx's "great law of the motion of history," which demonstrates that all historical struggles are the expressions of class struggle conditioned by definite modes of production, has the same significance for history as the law of the transformation of energy has for natural science.[21]

Engels' systematization of Marxism and the generalized laws of dialectical materialism became, in the final decade of the nineteenth century, the touchstone of "orthodoxy" for most Marxists. Though Engels himself later complained that Marxism was being presented *too* deterministically, his own systematization led to a much greater stress on "historical necessity" and a tendency to present Marxism as a doctrine describing a causally determined process.[22] His extension of dialectics to explain laws of nature and his view of dialectics as simply a "reflection" of external laws in nature and history have been challenged by many critical Marxists, as will be seen later. His systematization of a total "materialist worldview," a view still considered essential by most in the dominant Marxist tradition, remains one of the chief obstacles to Christian advocacy of Marxism.

Reform and Revisionism: Social-Democracy and Bernstein

After Marx's death his largest and strongest group of followers, the German Social-Democrats, adopted a strategy which stressed politics rather than revolution. While not abandoning revolution in principle they worked in practice to build up a strong political party. Their strength peaked in 1912 when they won 34.8 percent of the vote. If Lenin would later cite the writings of the "revolutionary Marx," the Social-Democrats could appeal to the Marx who argued that proletarian insurrections were often the sign of political immaturity, who opposed terrorism and secret societies, who praised reform laws, and who made compromises to include worker groups with differing ideologies in the First International.[23]

The relaxation of Bismarck's anti-socialist laws allowed the German Social-Democrats to engage openly in politics. The Erfurt Program of 1891, and the Workers Program enunciated by Karl Kautsky the next year, spelled out their position. They clearly envisioned a radical restructuring of the economic system into socialism. They were not reformist in the sense of believing that an adaptation of capitalism to workers' demands would suffice. But the Erfurt Program contained no suggestion of violent revolution and stressed a strategy of immediate political rights and the development of political power within the system. Commenting on the Program in his h story of socialism, G.D.H. Cole concludes:

> Let us say that the Erfurt Programme, in emphasizing the need for political action by the working class, left the long run method of action undefined, but clearly contemplated in the short run the exclusive use of parliamentary methods, and that there was no hint of any sort of proletarian dictatorship as contemplated at any stage.[24]

The German Social-Democrats sought Engels' advice and won his enthusiastic support.[25]

The strategy of legal political action, however, led directly to the first serious breach in Marxist theory. Eduard Bernstein claimed that the unity of theory and practice essential to Marxism was being violated by his own Social-Democrat Party. It was reformist in practice but still revolutionary in principle. Bernstein argued that the Party should drop its facade of insurgency and appear in fact as it was—a democratic, socialistic party of reform.[26]

Many of his criticisms, which first appeared in articles on "Problems of Socialism" and then in his work *Evolutionary Socialism* (1899), were aimed at Marx's own thought. Bernstein felt that while Marx was often a superb social scientist in gathering and analyzing data, he introduced a metaphysical "scaffolding" through his use of materialism and Hegel's dialectic. This was especially evident in Marx's position on the "inevitability" of socialism. It derived not from empirical facts but from the determinism implied in materialism and from Hegel's dialectical stages. Use of the dialectical "struggle of opposites" led Marx to overstress the creative strength of violence and the power of single, decisive, revolutionary acts.[27]

Social-Democracy, Bernstein argued, cannot judge reality from an a priori position. Science must be open to whatever social reality presents. Marx's views on the increasing misery of the working class and the decline of the middle class into the ranks of the proletariat had not proved accurate. But why tie the achievement of socialism to a dialectical scheme which says that conditions must deteriorate for it to come about? Why not look instead to a process of social progress and development?[28] Bernstein also rejected the materialist theory of knowledge and the monistic identification of ethics and reality. Ethical interests, what ought to be, necessarily involve a utopian element and cannot be determined by science.[29]

Bernstein insisted on democracy as the very substance of socialism and on the gradual buildup of democratic structures for workers and peasants alike.

In short, Bernstein argued that the Social-Democrats should replace an inevitable, revolutionary view of socialism, based on a materialistic dialectic, with a linear, evolutionary view of the progressive realization of socialism.

Criticisms similar to those made by Bernstein would be taken up later by critical Marxists, but Bernstein was branded a "revisionist" by his own party and that label remains a term of opprobrium in the dominant Marxist tradition. The German Social-Democrats rejected Bernstein's theories on Marxism but they continued reformist tactics in practice. After World War I the Social-Democratic tradition experienced a strong upsurge. The German Social-Democrats became a leading political party in the 1920s. Leon Blum helped form and lead a Socialist Party in France. Social-Democrats in Sweden would eventually gain political power, though without creating a socialist economy. Socialist and Social-Democrat parties in Europe continue the same tradition into the present. But even prior to World War I the Social-Democratic strategy was challenged by the revolutionary Marxism of Rosa Luxemburg in Poland and Germany, and by Lenin in Russia. After the Bolshevik Revolution in 1917, revolutionary Marxism-Leninism replaced social democracy as the dominant Marxist tradition.

Lenin and the Bolshevik Revolution

The ferment of revolution had grown strong in Russia before Marxism arrived on the scene there. Nineteenth-century Russia lagged far behind the rest of Europe both politically and industrially. The Czar still ruled with absolute authority; serfdom was not ended until 1861; Russia remained basically a peasant-aristocratic society as it had been for centuries. But the Russian "intelligentsia" reflected a growing unrest. It was the great golden age of Russian literature and nearly every writer pondered the "destiny of Russia" and "awakening the soul of Russia." Emancipation of the serfs and the moderate reforms of the 1860s tended only to accentuate the backwardness of Russia and to radicalize those who sought change. A populist movement arose with a goal of replacing the old order with a new peasant-based socialism. When propaganda and organizing efforts failed, some turned to terrorism, and Czar Alexander II was assassinated in 1881. Revolutionary literature flourished underground—Nechayev's *Revolutionary Catechism,* Chernyshevsky's *What Is to Be Done?,* and the writings of Tkachev. These writers placed great emphasis on the need for ruthless, professional revolutionary leaders. Lenin's opponents would later accuse him of following this tradition.

Marxism came to Russia in the 1880s, chiefly through Georg Plekhanov, who had been a Populist but who was converted to Marxism during a stay in Geneva in the early 1880s. The Marxists argued that the Populists placed too great a stress on the "subjective" side of revolution, on sheer will and revolutionary leaders, and that revolution must instead be based on objective conditions and carried out by the masses, led by the proletariat. Lenin would strive to show the need for both the subjective and the objective.

Lenin, whose real name was Vladimir Ilyich Ulyanov, was born in Simbirsk in April 1870. His father was a liberal, middle-class supervisor of education. Lenin's brother Alexander was executed in 1887 for involvement in a plot to assassinate the Czar. Lenin himself was expelled later that year from Kazan University for taking part in student demonstrations. His first contact with Marxism came through reading Plekhanov and Marx's *Capital*. In the early half of the 1890s Lenin studied for and passed law exams, joined a Marxist circle in St. Petersburg, and then traveled to western Europe to meet Plekhanov and other Russian Marxists in exile. On his return to Russia he was arrested for possessing contraband literature, spent a year in prison waiting for trial, and then was exiled to Siberia in 1897. While in Siberia he wrote a study on *The Development of Capitalism in Russia*. In 1898, the year the Russian Social-Democratic Party was founded, Lenin married Nadezhda Krupskaya. He left Russia in 1900 to join the staff of the Marxist paper *Iskra* and most of his subsequent years until 1917 would be spent in different locations in Europe.

1. The Party, and Theory from Without. In 1902 Lenin wrote his now famous *What Is To Be Done?*, taking the title from Chernyshevsky's novel. His attack was directed against a group of Russian Marxists, the "Economists," who argued that the Party, which was still predominately made up of intellectuals, should take workers "where they are." The Economists contended that the Party should help workers achieve their own immediate demands for better working conditions, higher wages, and the right to organize. The Party should allow workers to lead themselves; workers would become revolutionary when objective conditions created the right situation.

Lenin opposed such a strategy. Revolutions do not just happen spontaneously. A revolutionary movement requires a clear, unified theory, and such a theory will not just develop automatically. The theory of socialism was developed by intellectuals (Marx, Engels) from the bourgeois class; it must be brought to the workers "from without." The working class, left completely on its own, tends to develop only a trade-union consciousness and to see only short-range goals. Revolutionary theory, moreover, must compete with bourgeois ideology, which has far greater resources at its disposal. Needed then are "professional revolutionaries," a small disciplined, secret, and well-organized "vanguard" with skills in agitation, propaganda, organizing, and theorizing. Needed are revolutionaries who can raise the consciousness of workers and enable them to see the necessity of revolution.[30]

Lenin's views on strict criteria for membership in the Party met with resistance from many of the leading Marxists within his own party. The issue created a split within the Party between the Bolsheviks ("Majority") and the Mensheviks ("Minority"), a split which lasted into the Russian Revolution. Though Lenin modified his views after 1905 to include broader membership, the notion of a "professional vanguard Party" would continue to be one of the central features of Leninism. Defenders of Lenin point to its success and argue that the masses still remained the essential driving force of the revolution. Critics of Lenin, including Marxists of his time, have contended that Party leadership of the workers before the revolution leads to Party rule *over* the workers and all others after the revolution.

Lenin also reinforced philosophic positions which had already become part of the dominant Marxist tradition. In *What Is to Be Done?*, he attacked those who denied the possibility of putting socialism on a scientific basis and of demonstrating its necessity and inevitability from the point of view of the materialist conception of history. He insisted on the unity of every aspect of dialectical materialism, a philosophy which he said was cast from a single piece of steel so that not even one basic premise could be eliminated from it without departing from objective truth.[31] He insisted also that atheism was essential to party membership and that religion should be combatted (see Chapter 7). He reaffirmed the copy-theory of knowledge and the objective reality of dialectical laws in his *Materialism and Empirio-Criticism* of 1908.

Though the last-mentioned work was appropriated by the Communist Party of the U.S.S.R., some would sharply dispute it as representative of Lenin's thought. Raya Dunayevskaya contends that Lenin rediscovered the subjective side of Hegel's dialectic and separated himself from the "vulgar materialism" of his own earlier work. His *Philosophic Notebook* (1914) stated that "cognition not only reflects the objective world, but creates it." This insight, Dunayevskaya argues, changed Lenin's whole outlook.[32]

2. The Necessity of Revolution and of the Dictatorship of the Proletariat. According to the Marxist view of dialectical stages in history, Russia appeared to lack the objective conditions required for a socialist revolution. Though it had begun, in the late nineteenth-century, to experience rapid industrialization, it was not yet a fully developed capitalist economy and it had not yet undergone a "bourgeois revolution." But Trotsky several years before had argued that unique conditions in Russia made it *more* apt for a socialist revolution. A bourgeois capitalist revolution would require a strong bourgeois class. The bourgeois class in Russia, however, was weak because towns and cities had not become productive centers over long periods of years as had happened in the West, and because much of the capital investment in Russia was in foreign hands. The workers, on the other hand, were more revolutionary than their counterparts in the West. They had no long tradition of trade-unionism and political compromises; they were concentrated in large factories in two major cities; they could draw upon a fully developed revolutionary theory in Marxism.[33]

The first Russian Revolution of February 1917 erupted without planning, however, and without socialist orientation. The long war had demoralized the nation; government leadership had deteriorated; inflation and food shortages stirred anger and great unrest. International Woman's Day brought crowds of demonstrators to the streets and they were joined the next day by masses of strikers. Soldiers, called in to restore order, refused to fire upon the people. A provisional government was created which demanded the resignation of Czar Nicholas II, who had gone to the front to lead the army. The Soviet workers reorganized and became so strong that a virtual "dual government" existed.

Initially the new government won support, even from Marxists in Russia. But Lenin, in Switzerland when the revolution occurred, wrote immediately to express his opposition. The provisional government, Lenin charged, was a bourgeois government, an ally of the imperialists, and it could never provide what the people demanded—peace, bread, and freedom. From the time he returned to Russia in April he sought to push for a socialist revolution, but the Bolsheviks had to first win control in the workers' Soviet.

A "July Uprising," for which the Bolsheviks were blamed, caused Lenin to escape to Finland to avoid arrest. There he wrote his famous *State and Revolution* to justify the overthrow of the Kerensky government. Drawing upon the most revolutionary writings of Marx and Engels, he sought to prove that socialism could only be attained through revolution and the establishment of a "dictatorship of the proletariat." Gradualism was impossible; socialism could not be reached through democratic political processes within the existing state. "It is clear," wrote Lenin, "that the liberation of the oppressed class is impossible . . . without a violent revolution."[34] The dictatorship of the proletariat, needed to put down counterrevolution and to construct a new socialism, was also seen as an essential of Marxism. "*Only he is a Marxist* who extends the recognition of the class struggle to the recognition of the dictatorship of the proletariat."[35] These positions on the state and revolution would become in time "essential" doctrines of Marxism-Leninism.

The Bolshevik revolution of late October 1917 met little resistance and involved relatively little bloodshed. The election of delegates to a Constituent Assembly, planned by the Kerensky government, was carried out in November. But the Assembly itself was dissolved in January on the grounds that its members did not really represent the true desires of the people for a new social order. A peace treaty was signed with Germany in March 1918, but a civil war led by Czarist loyalists soon enveloped the country. Faced with a civil war, with the anarchy created by two revolutions and by the devastation left in the wake of World War I, Lenin was forced to take measures which ran counter to the ideals of socialism—a "dictatorship" or boss-rule within factories until workers could be prepared for self-management; a strong army and police; a large bureaucracy to administer the distribution of scarce goods; and compromises with capitalism to retain bourgeois managers and spur production.

Mutual enmity existed between the Bolsheviks and the Russian Orthodox Church. The Church energetically opposed the Bolsheviks, excommunicated Party members, and attacked government policies. The Bolshevik government separated Church and state, prohibited religious instruction to the young, banned religious literature, expropriated Church lands, and executed or imprisoned thousands of priests.[36] "Left-wing" Communists and right-wing opponents pressured Lenin from both sides. Strokes debilitated him for the last two years before his death in January 1924. His early death left unanswered what direction Communism might have taken in Russia once it emerged from the problems of "Civil War Communism" and of economic recovery from World War I.

The legacy of Lenin's thought and actions raises almost as many questions as Marx's. Given the success of the Bolshevik revolution, Lenin's words came to be treated as "the official interpretation" of Marx. Thus, his insistence on strict "unity of doctrine" based on an atheistic dialectical materialism, his stress on the need of a "vanguard Party" to raise the consciousness of workers, his conviction that socialism can be achieved only through violent revolution and sustained only through dictatorship of the proletariat, all these tended to become "correct" positions in opposition to "revisionist," "opportunist" and "bourgeois reformist" theories and tactics proposed by other Marxists. For Lenin had succeeded in "praxis" while his Marxist critics—Karl Kautsky, Rosa Luxemburg, the Mensheviks, and others—had failed.

Non-Marxist critics of Lenin blame him for the Stalinism which followed. The creation of an elitist Party which designates the correct line to be followed during the revolutionary struggle naturally leads, they maintain, to a Party which rules "in the name of the workers" after the revolution. Dictatorship of the proletariat becomes dictatorship of the Party *over* the proletariat.

One might also, however, assess Lenin in terms of his historical context, considering his positions as "relative" to that context rather than as universally and eternally established doctrines. But even this perspective does not resolve the issue, for some Marxist-Leninists will argue that the necessity of revolution and dictatorship of the proletariat remain true for all present situations, given the powerful hold of capitalism; and Lenin's critics will still argue that Leninism leads inevitably to Stalinism.

Stalin and Dogmatic Marxism

Almost all Marxists today, including most Communist Parties, want to dissociate themselves from Stalinism. The de-Stalinization of the Khrushchev era in the U.S.S.R. serves as perhaps the major historical expression of this dissociation, though critics of Communism are cynical about the extent of the change. Lenin had serious misgivings about Stalin. In a "last testament" written a year before his death, Lenin first warned that Stalin might misuse his power as General Secretary of the Party. Two weeks later he added that Stalin, because of his rudeness, should be removed from office. But Lenin's testament did not become public, and Stalin remained on. His undisputed power, however, took several years to achieve. First Trotsky, then Zinoviev and Kamenev, and finally Bukharin and Rykov, had to be eliminated from power positions.

The story of Stalin's ruthlessness has been told elsewhere. His forced "collectivization" of peasants at the end of the 1920s included the liquidation of the "kulak" or rich-peasant class. His purges in 1935–38 sent millions to Siberian labor camps and brought the execution of renowned Bolshevik leaders. By 1938 only 15 of the 140 members of the top Soviet Council remained free; 65 percent of all the top army officers had been imprisoned, killed, or removed from office.[37]

If for most people the history of Stalinism is simply the story of ruthless dictatorship Trotsky sought to explain Stalin's power, and the bureaucratic Party rule he commanded, as a result of "objective conditions." The danger of anarchy after the revolution, followed by civil war, created the need for an army, police, and discipline in factories. A strong state was required to control distribution of scarce goods. But even after "war communism" ended, conditions made rules by the workers themselves unrealistic. They had no experience in management or government; the wars had greatly diminished their numbers and left them weary.[38] More importantly, Marxist socialism always envisioned an *international* revolution, and not one backward country like Russia struggling on its own, as Stalin sought to defend.[39] Marx envisioned socialism as replacing a fully developed capitalism with a wealth of productive forces. Where socialism is required to "build up" an economy, the problems of capitalism, the "struggle for goods," reassert themselves.[40] Consequently a strong state, a large bureaucracy, and the power of individual dictatorial power arose contrary to Marxist theory.

The need to engender strict unity of purpose in order to build up a new socialist economy may also help to explain the development of a strict official ideology.[41] Whatever the explanation, once Stalin solidified his power any deviance from "correct" doctrine was not permitted. Through the international Comintern, moreover, the Soviet Communist Party sought to impose this same correct unity of doctrine on all Communist Parties in the world. The Party, and under his rule Stalin himself, became the official guardian and interpreter of Marxism. Party members were expelled, disciplined, or at very least charged with revisionism for not adhering to what Communist officials claimed was essential and correct. Marxism was presented as *the* correct picture of all reality and all adversary positions were reduced to bourgeois idealism or some other "false" stance. This official Marxism tended also to place great stress on objective laws, historical necessity, and inevitability. It also quite clearly viewed the whole Marxist worldview as one logically integrated system, so that to challenge any of its basic principles would be destructive of its unity.

Stalin's own *Dialectical and Historical Materialism* (1938) exemplified these characteristics. If in historical fact Marx's historical materialism developed first and Engels' dialectical materialism only later, Stalin presented the former as an "extension" of the latter. Historical analysis thus became an application or confirmation of general, and presumably always valid, principles governing all reality.

> Dialectical materialism is the world outlook of the Marxist-Leninist party. It is called dialectical materialism because its approach to the phenomena of nature, its method of studying and apprehending them, is *dialectical,* while its interpretation of the phenomena of nature, its conception of these phenomena, its theory, is *materialistic.*
> Historical materialism is the extension of the principles of dialectical materialism to the study of social life, an application of the principles of dialectical materialism to the phenomena of the life of society, to the study of society and its history.[42]

Stalin first explains the general features of the dialectical method with emphasis on the dialectics of nature. Not surprisingly the sources he cites are from Engels or Lenin, not Marx. His own use of dialectics in respect to social change illustrates Bernstein's criticism that conclusions are based on a priori dialectical principles rather than empirical analysis. Stalin contends that changes in society follow the law of "transition from quantity to quality." Thus while changes in modes of production are gradual, the liberation of the working class cannot be effected by slow changes and by reforms but only by a qualitative change of the capitalist system, by revolution. "Hence in order not to err in policy, one must be a revolutionary, not a reformist."[43] The law of "the struggle of opposites" similarly shows why class struggle is inevitable under capitalism. Stalin omits, on the other hand, the law of "the negation of the negation," perhaps to avoid the problem of explaining what "negations" arise in socialism and need to be overcome. Writing in another work on linguistics Stalin asserts that while leaps and revolutions apply to the contradictions of capitalist society they do not apply to classless Soviet society.[44]

Stalin's explanation of the principal features of philosophical materialism follows the main lines already noted in Engels. The world by its very nature is material; change results because matter is always in motion; hence God is not needed to explain the world. The world exists independently of our knowing; thought is a product of matter which has reached its highest development in the brain. The world is knowable; nature and its laws are fully knowable and this knowledge has "the validity of objective truth."[45]

Again these features serve as a priori principles to which empirical data must conform. Laws of society "follow from" the general truth of materialism.

> If the connection between the phenomena of nature and their interdependence are laws of the development of nature, it follows, too, that the connection and interdependence of the phenomena of social life are laws of the development of society, and not something accidental.[46]

It follows, says Stalin, that the science of the history of society can become as precise a science as, for example, biology.

Stalin does introduce a "subjective" element into history in reference to ideas. In respect to their *origin,* ideas are to be explained as reflections of material reality. But they have a "certain independence" and reciprocal influence on the economic, if one considers their *role* or significance.[47] Stalin's explanation of historical materialism, however, is then presented in very deterministic language. Productive forces are *the determining element* in the development of production. "Whatever are the productive forces such must be the relations of production."[48]

"Dogmatic" Marxism did not, unfortunately, come to an end with Stalin's death and the de-Stalinization of the Khrushchev era. Two "popular" presentations of Marxism-Leninism serve as examples of its continuation— *Fundamentals of Marxism-Leninism,* a voluminous "manual" by several authors, and V. Afanasyev's *Marxist Philosophy,* both published in the early 1960s.[49] The very absence of references to Stalin in both books only emphasizes how much "correct authority" determines Party-approved doctrines. The nearly nine-hundred page *Fundamentals,* in describing not only the theory but also the achievements of Soviet Communism, makes no reference to Stalin's contributions and includes only three brief quotations by him out of 331 citations, this despite the fact that he had led the nation for nearly thirty years and was quoted during those years as *the* authoritative interpreter of Marxism-Leninism. *Marxist Philosophy* mentions Stalin only twice in 380 pages, in both cases to refute his erroneous views.

The language of both volumes presents Marxism-Leninism as providing *the correct* and "scientific" truth about philosophy, science, history and knowledge. "Contemporary materialism is a progressive, scientific world outlook. Materialism gives a correct picture of the world, presenting it as it really is; it is a true ally of science." Consequently, "Materialism is an implacable foe of religion: in a world where there is nothing else but matter in motion there is no room for a god."[50] Idealism serves the reactionary forces in society. "Idealism and religion have always been tools for the spiritual enslavement of the working people by the exploiters, a means of justifying and reinforcing their rule." On the other hand, "Because socialist society has no exploiters there are no people interested in idealism. . . . Under socialism a scientific, materialist outlook prevails."[51]

The history of philosophy becomes, from this world outlook, the triumph of "progressive materialist science" against reaction, ignorance, and idealism. All the great names in the history of philosophy are then categorized according to their "correct" or "false" stances on materialism and dialectics. Aristotle was a materialist but vacillated in the direction of idealism by bringing in the notion of a "prime mover"; Hobbes was a materialist but a "metaphysical" one; Hume was an idealist; Kant was a materialist in recognizing the influence of reality on sensations, but an idealist in speaking of concepts as "constructs" of the mind.[52]

The "opponents of philosophical materialism" include almost every contemporary philosophical movement: bourgeois positivists, existentialists, logical positivists, neo-Thomists, pragmatists.[53] The leading scientists of history, on the other hand, were "spontaneous materialists," though some, like Einstein, slipped into idealism when they tried to philosophize about their work.[54] Dialectics, because it sees the world as it really is, "is the *only* scientific method."[55]

The reasons for referring to this kind of Marxism as dogmatic should be evident to most readers. For those convinced, on the other hand, that it does represent "the correct picture of reality," any criticisms will be dismissed as bourgeois, reactionary thinking. But one might object to the presentation of this section on dogmatic Marxism on several scores.

First, the sources cited are "popularized" versions of Marxism-Leninism, written some time ago. They hardly represent the best in Soviet philosophy or Communist Party Marxism any more than pre-Vatican catechisms or scholastic textbooks represent Catholic theology or Thomistic philosophy. But more recent textbooks continue to insist on "militant materialism" and to claim that Marxist philosophy gives a "strictly scientific explanation" of the world.[56] Opponents of Communism fear that such convictions lead inevitably to the imposition of text-book Marxism-Leninism as an educational system on all citizens under a Communist Party rule.

Second, one might certainly object: "What right does a Catholic priest have to criticize dogmatism among Marxists? The Catholic Church has for centuries imposed dogmatic beliefs on its members." Indeed this can be said. The "scholastic" textbooks long used in Catholic seminaries, with their "correct" theses and "false adversaries," conveyed the same attitude towards truth as the Soviet textbooks cited above. But this very objection is based on a reaction *against* dogmatism, a reaction most likely shared by most readers.

Third, one might object that this section places far too much emphasis on "official ideology." What counts are the economic and social changes brought about. Many Communist countries pay only lip service to this ideology in any case. But again the fear of a "monolithic" ideology is the one frequently expressed by many Christians and by many other non-Marxists. Hence the problem raised at the beginning of the chapter remains: "What is Marxism? How open to change is it?" Certainly the question of whether one can speak of a "Christian Marxism" depends on the possibility of distinguishing Marxism from the dogmatic Marxism noted in this section.

Communism since World War II/Eurocommunism

Until World War II the U.S.S.R. remained the only "model" of a communist nation. A Stalinist interpretation of Marxism prevailed not only in the Soviet Union, but through the leadership of the Third International it tended to dictate the ideology and policies of Communist Parties elsewhere in the world. After World War II, Communist Parties acceded to state power in

Eastern Europe, China, and later, Cuba. But this expansion also led to divergence. Unity of doctrine, in respect to historical and dialectical materialism, remained constant for the most part. The leading Communist Parties and nations continued to adhere to the "total world outlook" first expounded by Engels and defended by Lenin. Atheism and philosophical materialism remained essential parts of official ideology. Even the dissident Trotskyist groups adhered to these. But sharp differences, focused mainly on "praxis," put into question the authority of the Soviet Communist Party and the way it had carried out communism.

Trotskyists had challenged Stalin's policies for decades. They charged that Stalin's defense of "socialism in one country" ran counter to the true Marxist *and* Leninist view that revolution must become *international*. Socialism cannot develop correctly in a single, underdeveloped nation. Trotsky judged the Soviet Union a "degenerate workers' state" governed by a Party bureaucracy; some Trotskyists rejected it as simply "state capitalism." Trotsky's ideas, and offshoots from Trotskyism, served as the basis for several Marxist parties (e.g., Socialist Workers' Party, International Socialists) contending with Communist Parties in many nations.

Shortly after World War II, Tito proclaimed independence from the Soviet Union, and Yugoslavia developed its own distinctive form of socialism which emphasized workers' self-management of industries and "market" competition. Suppression of the Hungarian uprising in 1956 and the overthrow of the liberal Dubcek regime in Czechoslovakia in 1968 prevented such independence from spreading elsewhere in Eastern Europe.

But the conquest of Mao Tse-tung's Communist Party in China in 1949 led to the greatest "rift" in Communism and to a significantly different approach to Marxist socialism. First, the conquest of power was quite different. Mao's chief force was peasant armies, fighting guerrilla warfare and gradually encircling the cities. The classical Marxist theory made the urban proletariat the leading force. Second, Mao proclaimed a "People's Democratic Dictatorship" in place of the "dictatorship of the proletariat," and it included peasants, workers, petty-bourgeoisie, *and* the "national bourgeoisie," i.e., members of the capitalist class not allied with imperialists and willing to work for socialism. Third, Mao gradually developed a commune system with a stress, especially after the Cultural Revolution, on de-centralized economic units. The Cultural Revolution (1966–69) also brought certain "stresses" which the Chinese felt were not operative in Soviet Communism—initiative from the "masses" vs. Party rule or rule by technological experts; working for others vs. individualistic, material incentives; "permanent revolution" vs. a sliding back into bourgeois attitudes. To the chagrin of many who extolled Mao's efforts, the "modernizations" and opening of China to world trade, introduced in the late 1970s, appear to be a move back to a bureaucratic, technocratic economy. China's antagonism toward the Soviet Union, however, remained unabated.[57]

Latin America has become in recent decades a focal point of discussion regarding Marxism, particularly in respect to its relationship to Christianity. The Cuban revolution led by Fidel Castro pre-dated the period of "new thinking" about this relationship and hence tended to reflect the situation of Marxism and Christianity in Eastern Europe—mutual hostility at the outset and somewhat improved relations in recent years. The election of Salvador Allende in Chile in 1970, on the other hand, appeared for a time to mark a significant "turning point" in the relationship of Marxism and Christianity. Many Christians had become increasingly critical of capitalism and open to socialism; Allende had been elected democratically and made no attack on the Church or religion; the hierarchical Church did not oppose his election and many Christian groups worked actively to support him (see Chapter 6).

Eurocommunism also became, in the mid-1970s, a phenomenon of great interest for evaluating changes within official Party thinking and for studying possible shifts in Christian-Marxist relations. The term "Eurocommunism" refers especially to the stance adopted by the Communist Parties of Italy, France, and Spain, though other Parties, including the Japanese Communist Party, have moved in a similar direction.

Two main features have been distinctive of Eurocommunism: (1) a declaration of independence from Moscow, and (2) a commitment to a democratic path to socialism.[58] For many decades Communist Parties had been dependent on guidelines from the Soviet Union, or at least they were reluctant to express openly any disagreement. The prestige of the Bolshevik Revolution and loyalty to the unity of "proletarian internationalism" helped the Communist Party of the Soviet Union to maintain its hegemony over other Parties. Dissidents either left the Party or joined Trotskyist movements. The suppression of the Hungarian uprising in 1956, the revelation of Stalin's purges and ruthless excesses, and continued restrictions on political freedoms in the U.S.S.R. led to great losses in Party membership. But it was the Soviet Union's effort to win international Party support for its "normalization" of affairs in Czechoslovakia in 1968 that triggered a rift between it and other Communist Parties. Italian Party leader Enrico Berlinguer and many others refused to accept the Soviet Union's justification for intervention in Czechoslovakia, and several Communist Parties refused to sign a document upholding the Soviet Union's action.[59] The Soviet Union also came under attack for its treatment of Russian Jews, of writers, and of political prisoners. Santiago Carrillo, secretary-general of the Spanish Communist Party, became the most outspoken critic of the Soviet Union. He claimed that the U.S.S.R. was not truly socialist and that it had been deformed and had degenerated to a degree once only associated with imperialism. Somewhat less stridently the Communist Parties of Italy and France also declared their independence and revised positions once deemed essential to Marxism-Leninism.

The Eurocommunist Parties have declared themselves committed to democracy. They have decided to seek power not through violent overthrow but by open, peaceful, parliamentary means. The Italian and French Communist Parties spelled out their positions at a meeting in Rome in November 1975. They affirmed that both the path to socialism and the building up of socialism must be achieved within the framework of democracy. They affirmed the right of existence and activity of opposition political parties, the freedom and autonomy of labor unions, and the guarantee of religious freedom and all the freedoms gained through bourgeois-democratic efforts of the past.[60] Above all they affirmed respect for the verdict of universal suffrage. If voted out of office, they would step down. They insisted, moreover, that this commitment to parliamentary democracy was not merely a strategy but was based on the conviction that true socialism requires democracy. They assigned also an important role to small and medium-sized farms and industrial enterprises in the building up of socialism.

The French Communist Party, which had been generally considered the most intransigent of the Eurocommunist Parties, after considerable debate voted to drop the expression "dictatorship of the proletariat," which had long been an essential of Marxism-Leninism. French Party chief Georges Marchais sought also to convince Christians that they could and should in good conscience collaborate to achieve a socialist democracy. While he had maintained that "between Marxism and Christianity no theoretical conciliation is possible nor any ideological convergence," he did not believe that philosophical differences should hinder the achievement of common objectives.[61] He insisted that religious freedom would be safeguarded in a socialist society, that socialism excluded categorically all recourse to totalitarianism, and that Communists had no intention of imposing their philosophy on others.[62]

The Italian Communist Party, through the influence of Antonio Gramsci and Palmiro Togliatti, had embarked much earlier along the lines Eurocommunism has taken in recent years. The Party Congress of 1961 stated that religious faith was not incompatible with socialism and could be a stimulus for social change. The Party's constitution states that all citizens can join the Communist Party "independent of race, religious faith or philosophical convictions" as long as they accept the political program of the Party and work for its realization. In the light of this rule, Berlinguer has stated that it is therefore "inexact" to say that the Party explicitly professes a materialistic, atheistic philosophy. The Party recognizes as a decisive patrimony the teachings of Marx, Engels, and Lenin, but even these do not represent an ideological creed or immutable texts.[63] Marxism-Leninism was declared an "optional creed" by the Party in April 1979.

The stance of Eurocommunist Parties has, not surprisingly, been the subject of much controversy. Opponents of Communism see it simply as a strategy to win support and do not trust the Parties' claims to observe democratic rules and to preserve democratic freedoms. They see a lack of democracy within the Parties as an indication of what would occur if Communists come to power. Other critics trust individual leaders such as Berlinguer, whose wife is a practicing Catholic, but fear that more Stalinist elements would gain control if political power were obtained.[64] Many Marxist-Leninists, on the other hand, feel that Eurocommunism is leading Communist Parties back to a merely reformist Social-Democracy. Even if they win power, these critics maintain, the Eurocommunists will simply become "managers" of a capitalist society without ever achieving socialism.

The future of Eurocommunism is unsettled. In the mid-1970s Marxists perceived a new structural crisis in capitalism. For two decades after World War II capitalism in Europe had experienced growth and expansion. The 1970s, however, brought new crises of unemployment and discontent leading to a marked increase in electoral support for Communist Parties. But after appearing on the verge of a united socialist victory in France in 1978, the Communist and Socialist parties split and the Communists returned to their role as an opposition party. The "historic compromise" which the Italian Communist Party adopted did not lead to new political gains. Their decision to work in coalition with Christian Democrats and to support sometimes unpopular austerity measures made them vulnerable to attacks from the left. They lost electoral support in the late 1970s and did not gain the official cabinet posts they sought to obtain.

Eurocommunism has, however, significantly influenced Christian-Marxist relations. Considerable distrust remains and the issue of Communism became significant in the elections of both Pope John Paul I and John Paul II. Positions could harden, but the interaction of Christians and Marxists in the 1970s could also lead to significant change. On the Christian side, groups such as the "Christians for Socialism" have collaborated with Marxists; priests and Catholic laity have publicly declared in favor of socialism. On the Marxist side, this support and the need for support have influenced Marxist thinking on religion. The fact that Eurocommunist Party leaders and intellectuals have put into question what had been considered essential to Marxism-Leninism is a step toward a more open Marxism. The "Critical Marxism," to be discussed next, which often developed independently of, or even in opposition to, official Party Marxism in the past, could conceivably become more significant in years to come.

Critical Marxism

The legacy which Marx left, as we noted earlier, was quite open-ended. His writings have lent themselves to quite different interpretations and developments. After Hegel's death, the Young Hegelians had argued that the very dynamism of his dialectical principle demanded a rejection of all "closed systems," including Hegel's own systematic conclusions. This same aversion to closed systems characterizes Critical Marxism. But the equivalent of a Young Hegelian movement did not occur after Marx's death. For one thing,

Marx himself did not leave a "system." The task of constructing a coherent system, as opposed to challenging an old one, became a central concern for Marx's followers. Engels initiated this project in the final years of Marx's life; Kautsky, Plekhanov, and other Marxists in the last decades of the nineteenth-century carried it through to its completion.[65] Historic conditions called for the *need* of a coherent system, a "scientific socialism," to distinguish Marxism first from other worker revolutionary movements. The reasons Lenin gave for *maintaining* an integral, coherent system once it had been constructed, and the reasons Communist nations and parties have given since, have both been noted in the previous section. Thus, the first challenge to the "system" from within Marxism by Eduard Bernstein at the turn of the century, ran counter to the need for unity which Marxists were experiencing. Like early Christianity, which needed to combat gnostic "heresies" in order to safeguard a relatively new Church, the new Marxist parties sought to ward off "revisionists" as destructive of a needed Party unity.

The advocacy of Critical Marxism is itself the product of a felt need corresponding to new conditions. In the United States and Western Europe, it often represents a commitment to a *democratic* socialism, a desire to dissociate Marxist socialism from existing Communist nations and their ideology while maintaining "Marxist analysis." In Eastern Europe it has often expressed dissatisfaction with "statism," Party-rule, and dogmatism, in an effort to create a "truer" Marxist socialism. For Christians in Latin America it is important for distinguishing between Marxist analysis and Marxist atheism-materialism.

If the designation "Dominant Marxist Tradition" includes divergences, the term "Critical Marxism" is even more of an umbrella. Along the lines suggested by Wittgenstein one should perhaps speak of "family resemblances" rather than any set of characteristics which define it. It is not a Marxist movement as such. Much as Bernstein was rejected as a "revisionist," so almost every school or individual noted in this section has been accused of "abandoning Marxism." But such was also often true of many Christian theologians whose views in time won acceptance.

The expression "Western Marxism" has been used by recent authors to designate the Marxists discussed in this section, since most of the leading figures have been Western Europeans.[66] But the designation "Critical Marxism" underscores a common epistemological note, the criticism of at least some aspects of the dominant Marxist tradition with a greater awareness of the subjective factors that influence society and Marxism itself.

Critical Marxism: An Overview

The economic structure of society, Marx wrote in 1859, is the real foundation "on which rises a legal and political superstructure and to which correspond definite forms of social consciousness. . . . It is not the consciousness of men that determines their being but, on the contrary, their social being that determines their consciousness."[67]

The influence of this statement has been great. The Soviet text *Marxist Philosophy* argues that the principal postulate of historical materialism is "social being determines social consciousness."[68] This postulate seemingly provides the basis for considering Marxism as "scientific" and able to determine the "objective laws" of social and historical change. Empirically observable "material conditions" (the base) are seen as primary, first causes; the realm of consciousness and politics (the superstructure) are determined by material factors (as diagrammed). But it is this relationship between economic base and superstructure that has been a primary focus of reevaluation by critical Marxists.

Superstructure
Ideology
State/Law
[Classes]
Relations of Production
Productive Forces
Base

If the text cited above has long served as a principal postulate of the dominant Marxist tradition, a different text from Marx suggests a very different emphasis in Critical Marxism. In his *The Eighteenth Brumaire of Louis Bonaparte* (1852) Marx wrote:

> Men make their own history, but they do not make it just as they please; they do not make it under circumstances chosen by themselves, but under circumstances directly found, given and transmitted from the past.[69]

The second part of the quotation retains the importance and influence of objective conditions, but the first phrase stresses the centrality of the active, "subjective" factor. Another simple diagram might bring out the implications of this difference.

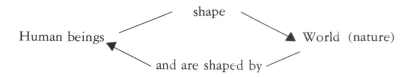

Dominant Marxism stressed the "underside," the influence of material conditions in the world upon human thought and activity. Moreover, it established the dialectic as an objective movement in the world, independent of human interaction. Critical Marxism argues that the dialectic which Marx stressed was the interaction of human beings with the world, as in the second diagram. Consequently the relationship between base and superstructure, in the first diagram, should not be viewed as a "linear causality," from material conditions up, but as dialectical also, with a constant interplay between the base and the superstructure.

The issues of Critical Marxism nearly all deal with the "subjective" factors in social history—a re-examination of the relationship between the superstructure and the base, and *how* consciousness is formed; the dialectical relationship between active human beings and the world, and generally a rejection of dialectical materialism applied to nature; the role of subjectivity in the formation of theory, and a rejection of the copy-theory of knowledge; a concern for the interiority and individuality of each person versus an over-emphasis on society; and in some cases a re-evaluation of religion, as possibly more than a "reflection" of material, social conditions.

One could also characterize Critical Marxism by its use of sources. Critical Marxists insist on a return to Marx himself, often making use of texts unknown to earlier Marxists, e.g., the *1844 Manuscripts, The German Ideology*, the *Grundrisse*. Many place great stress on re-examining the relationship between Marx and Hegel, including studies of the early, more radical, Hegel. Their investigations have frequently been enriched by the use of other sources, Freud most especially, but Max Weber, Husserl, and others also.

Some of the critical Marxists have been staunchly revolutionary and pro-Leninist, attributing to Lenin the recognition of the importance of subjective factors. Others are highly critical of Lenin, especially of the role he assigned to the Party. As "western" Marxists in advanced capitalist countries, many critical Marxists have focused on a "critique of everyday life," attacking the culture produced by capitalism as a bureaucratic, technological culture which deprives individuals of freedom and autonomy. The major criticism leveled against Critical Marxism is its remoteness from actual proletarian struggles and socialist action.[70]

In selecting examples of Critical Marxism, many names have been omitted—Karl Korsch, Henri Lefebvre, Jean-Paul Sartre and others—that some might consider of great importance. Moreover, the summaries which follow only highlight certain aspects of the authors that are treated. The figures selected were chosen because their influence, or the issues they treat, seemed especially relevant for Christians and for Americans interested in Marxist analysis. Gramsci and Althusser should be noted especially for their influence on Christian proponents of Marxism.

The Forerunners: Lukács and Gramsci

The Hungarian philosopher George Lukács (1885–1971) ranks, without question, as one of the greatest Marxist thinkers of this century. In contrast to some other critical Marxists, Lukács strongly defended Lenin for having seized upon the heart of Marx's theory—the task of revolution.[71] Lukács' other writings often brought him into conflict with the Communist Party and his career reflected the tensions of a person striving to be both critical and orthodox. He felt compelled to exercise self-criticism when the Communist International condemned some of his positions. He renounced his most famous work, *History and Class Consciousness* (1923), during his exile in the

Soviet Union; in a 1967 preface to his book he renewed the self-criticism of his earlier views. He was nevertheless condemned by the Hungarian Communist Party when it came to power after World War II and was forced out of public life. He returned to public life during the period of de-Stalinization, but the young Marxist intellectuals he formed were still barred from university teaching.[72]

In the opening chapter of his most famous work, *History and Class Consciousness* (1923), Lukács asked a pivotal question: "What is Orthodox Marxism?" Lukács challenged the dominant Marxist tradition, which he felt had reduced Marxism to a set of fixed, determined, objective theses. Orthodox Marxism, Lukács insisted, does not mean uncritical acceptance of Marx's investigations. It is not a "belief" in this or that thesis, nor the exegesis of a sacred book. On the contrary, "orthodoxy refers exclusively to method."[73] The key to Marxism is its revolutionary dialectic. Drawing upon Marx's notion of "praxis" in the *Theses on Feuerbach,* Lukács stressed the active role of the subject in such a dialectic. Consciousness must become a decisive step in the historical process and this consciousness requires a class, the proletariat, which becomes both the subject and object of knowledge. The proletariat must be able to recognize itself as "object." It must understand both the historical process which led to its present conditions of alienation and at the same time recognize its capability to change the situation. As "subject" of this change the proletariat must be active both in the appropriation of theory and in acting upon it.

This emphasis on consciousness, on praxis, and on the proletarian class as the subject of the dialectic led Lukács to a critique of dialectics as developed by Engels and uncritically taken over by other Marxists. Engels said that the dialectic should be considered as interaction and not of rigid causality.

> But he does not even mention the most vital interaction, namely the *dialectical relation between subject and object in the historical process,* let alone give it the prominence it deserves.[74]

The very purpose and central problem of the dialectical method is how to *change* reality; it is not a passive understanding of how reality dialectically changes itself.

"Totality" is, for Lukács, an essential category for understanding the dialectic correctly. The dominant Marxist tradition viewed causality in a linear, deterministic fashion (see diagram 1). Productive forces cause relations of production to take definite forms; resulting class divisions determine politics and ideology. Lukács contended that Marx never intended such a reductionism and that he looked always to "concrete totality," to the dynamic, dialectical relationship of all parts to the whole. Society should not be studied, therefore, as if one factor caused the others, but as a system of organically and mutually interacting elements.[75]

Lukács used these insights into the proletariat as the subject/object of history and into society as a totality to study the problem of "class consciousness." Marx had never explained adequately *how* class consciousness develops nor what might block it from developing. Class consciousness often involves a class-conditioned *unconsciousness* of one's condition, according to Lukács. This was an insight which led later critical Marxists to complement Marxism with Freud. A "false consciousness" often masks the real material interests of a class; a moral appeal to "rights," for example, safeguards property relations. Where class consciousness does become explicit, the bourgeoisie has the advantage of wealth and media control to promote its ideology. The proletariat, on the other hand, has the advantage of being able to see society "from the center, as a whole." Marxism permits the proletariat to go beyond symptoms and to grasp the unity of the total socio-economic system. But such class consciousness does not simply arise out of material conditions; it must be freely and actively developed. The fate of the revolution, and with it the fate of humanity, depends on the ideological maturity of the proletariat, on the strength of its class consciousness.[76]

Lukács' chapter on "reification" attempts to show how the capitalist mode of production affects consciousness. The workers' subjective, creative activity becomes submerged and lost in "objects." Objects produced and workers themselves come to be viewed simply as commodities. All sense of human relations is lost and economists recognize only 'things' in relation, viz., wages, prices, commodities.[77] This reification leads bourgeois economists and ideologists to see only isolated facts and problems. The proletariat can develop a consciousness of the whole, but the pervasiveness of this reification impedes such consciousness from developing.

Lukács' stress on Marxism as a method, on the need for re-examining Marxist tenets, on the relative independence of the superstructure and its interaction with the economic, would be significant for later critical Marxists. Of importance for the Marxism-Christianity issue, his views put into question a strict materialist view of consciousness and, by implication at least, the reductionistic explanation of religion as a mere reflection of economic conditions.

Antonio Gramsci (1891–1937) was a contemporary of Lukács. But in another sense he is a contemporary of our day. His *Prison Notebooks* came to light only after World War II and only during the past decade has he become widely known outside Italy. His writings have become a focus of special interest for Christian Marxists and Socialists. His friend and compatriot Palmiro Togliatti called Gramsci "the first Italian Marxist." He became an active anti-war socialist in Turin during World War I. He broke with reformist socialists in 1921 and helped in founding the Italian Communist Party. He struggled against the rising power of fascism until 1926 when he was arrested and later sentenced to twenty years in prison. His prosecutor shouted: "For twenty years we must stop that brain from working."[78] In poor health from the outset, Gramsci lived on sheer will alone under deplorable jail conditions. His teeth rotted, he developed tuberculosis, Potts' disease and various stomach disorders, yet somehow he managed to fill notebooks with nearly 3,000 pages of writings before he died.

Just as Lukács stressed subjective factors in Marxist theory and analysis, so Gramsci insisted that Marxism is a doctrine of action. Revolutionary praxis rather than any set theses determines its content. Historical process is complex and not reducible to any formula. Marxism is not a science of objective laws and inevitable outcomes. Scientific analysis can only determine "possibilities"; the fulfillment of these possibilities is a question of will, of subjectivity. Marxism must complement historical analysis with political analysis, and politics is an "art" rather than a science.[79] Gramsci's discussions of "hegemony" and his critique of "scientism" gave fuller expression to this general thrust.

The concept of "hegemony" served as a unifying thought for Gramsci. Socialism will not be achieved simply by gaining state power. As John Cammett in his study of Gramsci observes: "The fundamental assumption behind Gramsci's view of hegemony is that the working class, *before* it seizes State power, must establish its claims to be a ruling class in the political, cultural, and 'ethical' fields."[80] Hegemony means a predominance achieved by consent rather than force. Economic conditions do not simply determine the political and the ideological superstructure of society. The ideological terrain shapes the outcome of revolutionary struggle. Thus hegemony requires the permeation throughout society—in trade unions, schools, churches, and family—of an entire system of values, attitudes, beliefs and morality.[81]

Winning hegemony involves both a negative and a positive task. The prevailing hegemony, its political rule and its ideological control, must be challenged and criticized. A new hegemony throughout civil society must be built up. If a new society is to be built upon worker participation and self-development, workers must be prepared to take on their role. Encouraged by worker takeover of enterprises in Turin in 1919, Gramsci believed that "factory councils," as self-governing worker organizations, could serve to develop and prepare workers. Gramsci helped establish study groups, "Clubs of Moral Life," among workers to encourage their self-development. Their preparation also had to include developing leadership and overcoming their biases against southern peasants in order to build a common front.[82] A whole new way of thinking, being, and relating to others must be adopted before the revolution. Socialist attitudes do not simply take form at the moment of revolution, nor do they simply "result" from objective conditions after the revolution. Attitudes and views must be consciously created and freely willed. The Party must find ways to respond to the everyday concerns, fears, and hopes of the people if they want them to move in a new direction.

Gramsci recognized the importance of Catholicism in Italy and did not simply dismiss religion with disdain. At the same time he viewed it as a negative model of hegemony. The Church maintained its spiritual hegemony at the price of the creative growth of the people it was meant to serve. It maintained an iron discipline over its intellectuals and exercised a protective, pacifying control over the simple people.[83]

While never directly critical of Lenin's own efforts, Gramsci criticized the classical Marxist preoccupation with force and coercion as the basis of ruling class domination, and he was critical of elitist Party models and of bringing consciousness from without.[84]

Along with the concept of hegemony, Gramsci also developed a sharp critique of "scientism" and determinism in Marxism. In a 1917 essay on "Revolution vs. *Das Kapital"* Gramsci argued that the Bolshevik revolution could not be explained as the result of historical inevitability, since Russia did not fit the capitalist stage of history. The revolution was the result of organized action. In his prison notebooks Gramsci developed much more fully his objections to any purely "scientific" interpretation of Marxism. Many Marxists, he believed, remained bound to cultural currents of the nineteenth century, for example to positivism and scientism, and they thought they were being orthodox in identifying Marxism with traditional materialism. They combatted religious ideology but in doing so made a prejudice and superstition of Marxism itself.[85] In an effort to make Marxism scientific they reduced the world to mechanical formulas. One cannot scientifically "foresee" the future of society. One foresees only to the extent to which one contributes a voluntary effort to create the foreseen result. "Therefore, to hold that one particular conception of the world and of life has in itself a superior capacity for foresight is a mistake of the crudest fatuity and superficiality."[86] The openness of Gramsci's Marxism to new ideas, and his great concern that socialist attitudes and political power develop internally and organically, have made him attractive to socialists striving to attain a more democratic and popularly-based socialism.

Contending Schools of Critical Marxism

Once one goes beyond the early Lukács and Gramsci the selection of figures representative of Critical Marxism becomes somewhat arbitrary. The goal of this section, moreover, is a limited one: to give "some idea" of different strains within Critical Marxism and of how they diverge from the dominant Marxist tradition. Noting three somewhat different orientations may fulfill this purpose.

1. *The "Frankfurt School": Marcuse and Habermas.* In the advanced capitalist countries of the Western world two related issues have surfaced for Marxists: why revolutionary consciousness has not developed, and the impact of science and technology on society. While these issues by no means define the work of the Frankfurt School they help to give some focus to this

section.[87] Herbert Marcuse belonged to the first generation of Frankfurt social theorists; Jürgen Habermas came later. Marcuse retained a more revolutionary stance than Habermas. Both became prominent in the 1960s as "philosophers of the New Left" in the United States and Germany respectively.

Marcuse addressed an issue which has pre-occupied Marxists of this century in Western capitalist countries. Objective conditions have long been present for the replacement of capitalism by socialism. Why hasn't a corresponding revolutionary consciousness developed? How might it develop? Marcuse became one of the first Marxists, in the 1930s, to draw attention to the previously unpublished works of the young Marx and to "rediscover" also the critical thought of the early Hegel. In *Reason and Revolution* Marcuse showed the similarity between the early critiques of society and the state by Hegel and the critiques by Marx. The driving force in both was the power of "critical thinking," of dialectical reason. But the power of critical thinking has become repressed in modern society, much as sexual instincts have become repressed, a comparison Marcuse developed in *Eros and Civilization*. Marcuse's best known work, *One Dimensional Man* (1964), analyzed how critical thinking, and hence revolutionary consciousness, have been subtly absorbed and eliminated in modern advanced societies.

Modern society so dominates the individual, Marcuse contended, that it leaves no room for qualitative change and for radically new and different institutions. Society is "one-dimensional" because it contains social change by absorbing potentially antagonistic forces and ideas into its own web. "A comfortable, smooth, reasonable, democratic unfreedom prevails in advanced industrial civilization, a token of technological progress."[88] If freedom of thought and freedom of conscience once meant essentially critical ideas designed to replace obsolete cultures with more rational ones, ideas have lost this power. We need freedom *from* economy, freedom from politics, and freedom from the "false needs" created by our present consumer society. But the individual has become so identified with society as to lose all sense of true needs and of the autonomy needed to be free.

The political universe has become a closed world.[89] The laboring class has been absorbed. The classic Marxist view presumed that the proletariat would be a liberating force *within* society. But the working class no longer appears as a contradiction to society. Labor unions are now a part of the system. Capitalists are bureaucrats and no longer seen as class enemies; domination is transformed into administration. Soviet society, in Marcuse's estimation, was no better because it is an educational dictatorship into which workers have been similarly absorbed.

The artistic world is likewise a closed world. The challenging "two-dimensional" power of art and literature has been liquidated. Everything becomes a commodity to be sold; great literature is in paperback, great music on records. Even nature is commercialized into vacation resorts. The impression of a "different order of things," of lost paradises and unforgettable hopes, has been eliminated. Psychologists explain away the Hamlets and Fausts of this world as neurotics. Sublimation is now a repressive "desublimation." Even war is now a very rational thing planned by "think tank" corporations.

The universe of discourse is a closed world. Words like "freedom" and "equality" now have limited, functionalized meanings. All sense of what "ought to be" and what "could be" is lost. Thus the word "democratic" is reduced to methods and rules for a fair election and any other meaning is called unrealistic.[90] Technological thinking is an acceptance of the status quo. We are told that business must go on and that alternatives to the present system are utopian.

Marcuse sought to find a "new historical subject" which would embody critical, oppositional thought to the domination of the present system. In *One Dimensional Man* he argued that groups "outside" of society—minority groups, the unemployed, the marginal—might have to be that force. He was accused of abandoning Marxism for a pessimistic, nihilistic position, since the marginal elements of society seemed hardly capable of becoming a revolutionary force. But in his later *An Essay on Liberation* (1969) he contended that national liberation movements in the Third World, the new strategy of the labor movement in Europe, the underprivileged in affluent societies, and intellectuals spurred by student activists, combined to give hope of revolutionary change.[91]

Jürgen Habermas attempted to further this analysis on the absorption of all critical consciousness in a society dominated by technological and scientific thought. If Marcuse contrasted critical reason to one-dimensional thought, Habermas contrasted "practical reason," in the sense of overall life-value decisions, to "purposive-rational" thinking which is limited to specific, partial, pragmatic objectives.

Contemporary society is dominated by purposive-rational thought. Science and technology as used presently are not concerned with "why" certain research is undertaken or what the long-range consequences may be for human society. They ask simply "does it work?" "Is it an efficient method?"[92] This very restriction of questions to pragmatic concerns assures protection for the status quo so that science and technology become an ideology in support of capitalism. Decision-making comes to rest in the hands of those who have technological expertise or can manipulate its uses. Ordinary citizens are left powerless in the face of an ever-expanding growth of highly specialized, technical knowledge. For Habermas, then, the critical question is how knowledge, used at present for technical manipulation and control, can be shared with "communicating individuals" whose lives and future are affected by it.[93]

The recognition of technology and science as "ideology" requires, according to Habermas, significant changes in Marxist analysis. First, the role of ideology must be reconsidered. In former times certain myths were used, such as the divine right of kings, to legitimize political power. In present society "rational" planning of economic growth and of welfare services appears to be for the benefit of all. Hence the capitalists need no explicit ideology to legitimize their power in society; they do not even appear to be a ruling class. Second, the traditional Marxist analysis of the relationship between economic base and superstructure must be revised.[94] State and society no longer stand in the same relationship they once had. Science and technology have become the leading productive forces; the state intervenes consistently in their use. Thus the economic base is itself now a function of government activity, taken up into the superstructure. An economic critique of society becomes inadequate. Third, the concept of class struggle cannot be employed as it once was. The new capitalist rationality strives to win the loyalty of the working class by satisfying its demands as much as possible. Class conflict remains hidden, though still latent. Discontent manifests itself not as exploiters versus exploited but as the demands of those neglected by rational planning—the unemployed, the aged, women, and minority groups—who direct their protest against the *state* primarily. Moreover, the underprivileged are often not classes at all in the Marxist sense, as determined by their role in production. Capitalism often does not depend on their labor power and hence they cannot gain power by withdrawing their cooperation as workers had the potential to do.[95]

These changes, however, do not mean that capitalism has safely escaped from its problems. The increased intervention and role of the state in the service of capitalism creates special "legitimation" problems for the state. (This is an issue taken up again in Chapter 4 of this book.) The state attempts to maintain the allegiance of all its citizens. In prosperous times it uses tax rebates, urban subsidies, medical care, etc. to achieve these. But as crises, inflation, and unemployment appear, the state itself reveals the strain. Demands are made on it at every level—to help failing industries, to take over ecological costs, to aid agriculture, to help the unemployed, and at the same time to reduce taxes. But these very demands call for increasing tax burdens and eliminating government expenditures. Caught in this bind, the state's structural class bias begins to show itself. The legitimation crisis has thus become the central focus of neo-Marxist critique for Habermas.[96]

These reflections may seem to have little direct bearing on the Marxism-Christianity issue. But their very challenge to oversimplified, materialist-reductionist uses of Marxism creates an openness for a more pluralistic adaptation of Marx.

2. "Humanistic" Marxism: East European Marxists. The discovery of the writings of the young Marx, particularly his *1844 Manuscripts,* created in the decades after World War II a great interest in Marxist humanism. Existentialism, with its concern for individual freedom, challenged dominant Marxism's neglect of the individual but found common ground in the writings of the young Marx. The common theme of humanism served as a base for Christian-Marxist dialogues in the 1960s (see next chapter). Many Marxists agreed that the dominant Marxist tradition had neglected the individual in its stress on societal change.[97]

In Eastern Europe the appeal to the humanism of the young Marx became a critical political issue because it often served as a way of expressing dissent against bureaucratic statism within Communist countries. In Poland, Adam Schaff attempted to address the issue while remaining loyal to existing Communism. Leszek Kolakowski's dissent, on the other hand, led him out of the country and ultimately to a rejection even of the label "Marxist."[98] In Czechoslovakia, the appeal to Marx's humanism was part of the effort to create "socialism with a human face" prior to 1968. In Yugoslavia, where Tito's break with Stalin had permitted greater freedom to criticize Stalin, a "Yugoslavian School" of Neo-Marxism developed. Its eventual suppression, on the other hand, indicates the continuing problems faced by critical Marxists within Communist countries.[99]

Gajo Petrovic's *Marx in the Mid-Twentieth Century* (1961) represented an early effort of the Yugoslavian School to liberate Marxism from Stalinism and to return to Marx's original thought, especially his early writings. "Stalin simplified, distorted, and made rigid philosophical views contained in the works of Engels and Lenin, and almost completely ignored Marx's own philosophical inheritance."[100] What Stalin excluded was Marx's humanism. The individual person is the center of authentic Marxist philosophical thought, according to Petrovic. Marx was not concerned with defining "matter" or reducing mind to matter, but with human liberation. The human being for Marx is defined by praxis, by free creativity, and not as some object determined by the productive process.[101] Marx's humanism is incompatible with dialectical materialism; the human person cannot be reduced to matter; spirit and matter represent two sides of the person.[102]

Yugoslavian Marxist Mihailo Marković, in *From Affluence to Praxis* (1974), calls also for a return to the "real Marx." He attacks the "fallacy of objectification," a fallacy initiated by Engels which projects a limited view of the world into the external world and declares it eternally true. While theory must be based on reality it necessarily involves subjective human features. It is *we*, Marković insists, who select, interpret, clarify and build up our systems.[103] Marković challenges a monistic Marxist interpretation which makes the individual a "product" rather than a free, imaginative creator of history, and which reduces values and ethical norms to reflections of society. Certain values about the capabilities of human nature are "normative" in working toward goals and developing praxis.[104] The dialectic, similarly, is a creative theory of action. But dogmatic Marxism turned it into a universal, ontological theory of reality with the paradoxical consequence that a theory which proclaims constant change became a closed system with eternal, unchangeable laws.[105] This false view of the dialectic led also to a false concept of

Marxism as "scientific." Marx's theory contains a highly articulated a priori element, a vision about what "ought to be" which cannot be reduced to an empiricist description. Marković then employs his own normative criteria, drawn from Marx's humanism, to confront problems which Marx did not foresee regarding Communism—statism, bureaucracy, and Party rule which impede the realization of a truly democratic socialism.[106]

3. *In Defense of "Scientific" Marxism: Althusser.* The French Marxist, Louis Althusser, certainly ranks as one of the most influential contemporary Marxists.[107] Yet some would contest his inclusion as a "critical" Marxist. He has been accused of "Stalinism" for many of his political stances. He opposes both the humanistic Marxism just considered and the historicism of many critical Marxists noted earlier. But, while defending both dialectical and historical materialism, Althusser does criticize the reductionist interpretation of them which developed in the dominant Marxist tradition. He is important, in any case, to the issue of Marxism and Christianity because his views have been very influential on many Christian proponents of Marxism. They stress particularly his emphasis on Marxism as a scientific method distinct from Marxism as an ideology.

Althusser sees Marxist philosophy as a theory of science and of the history of science, and it is needed to safeguard Marxist scientific method. In opposition to those who find continuity between the writings of the young, humanistic Marx and the later Marx, Althusser argues that an "epistemological break" separates the two.[108] Philosophic categories such as "alienation" and "species-being," drawn by the young Marx from Feuerbachian humanism, are replaced by scientific categories in the later Marx. Some of the old concepts continue to appear in the later Marx but the problematic has changed. No longer did Marx contrast what should be, based on the fulfillment of the social nature of "man," with what is. Traditional epistemology viewed knowledge as comparing ideas with reality. The young Marx, and Engels with his copy theory of knowledge, remained locked in this problematic. The later Marx worked from a new problematic recognizing theory as a product not of reality but of consciously formulated concepts drawn from the past.[109]

In the light of this new problematic, and the persistence of old categories, Althusser calls for a "symptomatic reading" of Marx's *Capital,* an attention to what is *not* said. This insight Althusser took from Freudian psychoanalysis which views as important what a patient does not say. Misreading Marx's "inversion" of Hegel, many Marxists fell into the same reductionism which characterized Hegel. Hegel reduced all to manifestations of Spirit; Marxists substituted matter or economic forces as *the* cause or driving force of all social change. Marx himself, in contrast, recognized the complexity of reality; no one element determines the rest.[110] Marx analyzed specific modes of production, not economy in general. He recognized that ideological, political, scientific, and economic production, while interrelated, cannot be reduced to any one common determining factor. Althusser therefore rejects the idea of linear causality—productive forces causing classes which in turn cause political and ideological structures—though he also rejects Lukács' idea of "totality" in which all elements simply exercise mutual causality.

What then is the scientific method of Marx according to Althusser? First, he argues that there are different forms of praxis, of the transformation of materials into products, which make scientific, political, and economic production very different. Scientific-practice is thought-power used to produce new concepts through a critique of previous ones. Science, then, is not a "reflection" of economic or other conditions. Second, Marx's dialectical method is not an analysis of how the economic determines the superstructure. Rather it is a study of how different structures affect each other—productive forces and relations of production, the economic and the political, etc. It is an investigation of "structural causality," of the relationship between parts of a social formation and the whole. It rejects both a linear causality which would make one cause the prime mover of all else and Lukács' circular causality which views no element as any more important than another. Structural causality allows for one factor being "determinant in the last instance" but retains the recognition of mutual interaction.[111]

Third, the concept of "overdetermination" becomes a key concept for Althusser. Each element of the whole—the economic, the ideological, the political—has its own history and trajectory. The economic is *determinant* in the last instance, thus preserving the primacy of the economic stressed by Marx, but the economic is not always the *dominant* element in a social formation. Religion was often the dominant factor in the Middle Ages; politics and ideology were recognized by Lenin as dominant in Russia; science and technology may indeed be dominant in advanced industrial countries today. Marx recognized a multiplicity of contradictions, not just the ones most cited between productive forces and relations of production or between the economic base and the superstructure. Consequently Marxist method does not mean reducing one level to another but studying the interactions and contradictions that develop between them.[112]

A major obstacle to Christian acceptance of Marxism has been its adherence to an atheistic ideology and its reduction of religion to a reflection of societal sickness. Althusser's criticism of reductionist uses of Marxism and his separation of scientific method from ideology would make his Marxism more acceptable to Christians. On another score, however, his interpretation of Marxism makes it more difficult to reconcile with Christianity. While the critical Marxists noted earlier place great stress on the subjective, on humans *making* history freely and creatively to a significant extent, Althusser has been criticized for eliminating the role of free, human creativity by his stress on the scientific study of structures alone as determinants of society. He holds to a rigorous, monistic materialism which treats free will as an ideological illusion and which sees Christianity as an ideology using this illusion of free will to justify itself.[113]

Atheism Revisited: A Concluding Note

A basic principle underlying Critical Marxism, the critical reassessment of Marxism itself to discover what is essential and what are only historically-conditioned formulations of Marxism, makes it more open to possible reconciliation or synthesis with Christianity. But the explicit question, "Is Marxism necessarily atheistic and antagonistic toward religion?" remains an obviously important concern. Given the length of this chapter already it seems advisable to take this up in the context of Chapter 7 on atheism. A reconsideration of atheism has not been a major thrust of Marxists, even of critical Marxists, though many practical efforts have been made by Marxists in Italy and Latin America to develop a new stance toward Christianity. Some important theoretical reappraisals, however, have been undertaken. The German Marxist Ernst Bloch stands out in particular for his pioneering work in re-evaluating the Marxist critique of religion. In his effort to show the importance of the "principle of hope" in history, Bloch credited Judaism-Christianity with bringing the concept of messianic hope into the world. Other critical Marxists have followed suit. The French Marxist Roger Garaudy, though his expulsion from the Party diminished his role as a spokesperson for Marxism, has gone so far as to call for a rejection of atheism and to speak of "Christian Marxism" as a needed alternative vision. But before returning to these Marxist reappraisals of religion we need to turn now to the history of Christian attitudes toward Marxism.

Notes

1. Richard T. DeGeorge, *The New Marxism* (New York: Pegasus, 1968), p. 20.

2. Engels, in a letter to Conrad Schmidt in 1890, cited Marx's comment about French Marxists. See Feuer, *Marx & Engels,* p. 396.

3. The phrase "the dominant Marxist tradition" is not very elegant, but other general terms that might be used are also unsatisfying. "Orthodox" Marxism is sometimes used but it tends to suggest that critical Marxists are thereby unorthodox. "Official Party Marxism" covers the stance taken toward Marxism in Communist nations but would not cover Trotskyist and other Marxist-Leninist groups who contest Communist Party ideology. "Classical" Marxism might be used, if extended to include Lenin and Stalin.

4. George H. Hampsch, *The Theory of Communism. An Introduction* (New York: Philosophical Library, 1965) defends the Marxism-Leninism which became dominant in the U.S.S.R. as "the only interpretation of Marx viable at present" and as "the only exposition of Marxism in which the theory and the actual practice can be said to be unified" (p. vii).

5. See also DeGeorge, *The New Marxism,* on points of agreement among Marxists (p. 27).

6. The expression "dialectical materialism" was not used by Engels but it gained acceptance through the writings of the Russian Marxist Georg Flekharov.

7. Frederick Engels, *Anti-Dühring, Herr Eugen Dühring's Revolution in Science,* translated by Emile Burns (New York: International Publishers, New World Paperbacks, 1966), was intended as a refutation of Eugene Dühring, a reformist socialist who had written a book on the new physics and chemistry. Engels began work on a refutation in 1876, published it first as articles for *Vorwärts* in 1877, then as a book in 1878. Some have called his work the "bible" of Communism. The chapters devoted to historical materialism were later published separately as *Socialism: Utopian and Scientific.* Engels prepared for a new and complete account of the dialectical movement in nature. But his work was interrupted by the more pressing task of editing and publishing the second volume of Marx's *Capital.* He never completed his own work, but his notes were published in 1926 and entitled the *Dialectics of Nature* (Moscow: Progress Publishers, 1966, 4th printing). Engels further developed his own ideas on philosophical materialism in a work on *Ludwig Feuerbach and the Outcome of Classical German Philosophy* (New York: International Publishers, 1967 printing).

8. Engels, *Anti-Dühring,* p. 30; *Ludwig Feuerbach,* p. 43 and also p. 21.

9. Engels, *Ludwig Feuerbach,* p. 44.

10. Ibid., p. 12.

11. Ibid., p. 25.

12. Engels, *Anti-Dühring,* p. 68.

13. Engels, *Dialectics of Nature,* pp. 33–36.

14. Engels, *Anti-Dühring,* pp. 131–33.

15. Ibid., pp. 138–41

16. Ibid., pp. 147–52.

17. Ibid., p. 155.

18. Ibid., p. 17.

19. Ibid., p. 31. See also *Ludwig Feuerbach,* pp. 47, 59.

20. Engels, *Ludwig Feuerbach,* p. 48.

21. From Engels' preface to Marx's *The Eighteenth Brumaire of Louis Bonaparte,* edited by C.P. Dutt (New York: International Publishers, New World Paperbacks, 1967, 3rd printing), p. 14.

22. See Engels' "Letters on Historical Materialism," in Feuer, *Marx & Engels,* pp. 395–412. Engels insists that Marx and he never claimed that the economic element was the *only* determining one, that the political and ideological can influence the economic, that the former is not simply the "effect" of the latter. On the tendency of Marxists to present Marxist doctrines as simple cause and effect, see George Lichtheim, *Marxism, An Historical And Critical Study* (New York: Praeger, 1963, 3rd printing), pp. 234ff.

23. See Leslie Derfler, *Socialism Since Marx* (New York: St. Martin's Press, 1973), Chapter 1, and also our own discussion of Marx's revolutionary strategy in the first chapter.

24. G.D.H. Cole, *Socialist Thought, Volume II: Marxism and Anarchism, 1850–1890* (London: Macmillan, 1954), p. 431.

25. In a preface, written in 1895, for a new edition of Marx's *Class Struggles in France,* Engels looked back on the revolutionary tactics of 1848–1850 and observed that such tactics now seemed obsolete in Germany and that a successful utilization of universal suffrage introduced an entirely new method of struggle. He felt that the workers were thriving far better on legal methods than on illegal methods and overthrow. But sections of his full text were suppressed when it was first published, sections which still spoke of the "right to revolution" and on the possible need for revolution in other countries. *The Marx-Engels Reader,* Tucker rev. ed., contains the full text of Engels' preface, pp. 556–73.

26. Eduard Bernstein, *Evolutionary Socialism* (New York: Schocken Books, 1978 edition), p. 197. Bernstein had been editor of a German-Social Democrat paper and played an important role in the adoption of the Erfurt Program. His criticisms of Marx were spurred in part by contact with English Fabian socialists.

27. Peter Gay, *The Dilemma of Democratic Socialism, Eduard Bernstein's Challenge to Marx* (New York: Collier, 1962), pp. 145–149, and Bernstein, *Evolutionary Socialism,* pp. 210ff. on the dialectic, and Chapter 1 on materialism.

28. Bernstein, *Evolutionary Socialism,* pp. 212–13, and p. 93.

29. Gay, *Bernstein,* pp. 150–61.

30. James E. Connor, ed., *Lenin on Politics and Revolution, Selected Writings* (New York: Pegasus, 1968), p. 35 on unified theory, pp. 44–45 on theory from without, pp. 67–76 on professional revolutionaries. For a complete text confer V. I. Lenin, *Selected Works in Three Volumes, Vol. I* (New York: International Publishers, 1967), pp. 117, 127–33, 182ff. For background see Bertram D. Wolfe, *Three Who Made a Revolution* (New York: Delta, 1964, 2nd printing), pp. 160 ff.

31. See Lenin's *Collected Works,* Vol. 21, p. 54, cited in the Soviet textbook, *The*

Fundamentals of Marxist-Leninist Philosophy (Moscow: Progress Publishers, 1974), p. 35. Writing on three souces of Marxism Lenin asserts: 'The Marxian doctrine is omnipotent because it is true. It is complete and harmonious, and provides men with an integral world conception which is irreconcilable with any form of superstition, reaction, or defence of bourgeois oppression." V. I. Lenin, *Selected Works*, Vol. XI, (London: Lawrence & Wishart, 1943), p. 3.

32. Raya Dunayevskaya, *Philosophy and Revolution, From Hegel to Sartre, and From Marx to Mao* (New York: Delta, 1973), Chapter 3; the quote, p. 101. The Soviet textbook cited above views the philosphic notebooks, on the other hand, as a "continuation and further elaboration of the basic propositions put forward in his *Materialism and Empirio-Criticism*," p. 65.

33. Leon Trotsky, *The Permanent Revolution* and *Results and Prospects* (New York: Pathfinder Press, 1970). The summary we have given is from *Results and Prospects* written in 1906. Chapter 1 of Trotsky's *The Russian Revolution*, abridged ed. (Garden City, N.Y.: Doubleday Anchor, 1959) also contains a summary of Trotsky's views on the "uneven and combined development" of Russia prior to 1917.

34. *Lenin on Politics*, pp. 186, 195.

35. Ibid., p. 203. Emphasis is mine.

36. Georg von Rauch, *A History of Soviet Russia*, rev. ed. (New York: Praeger, 1960) pp. 141–43.

37. Ibid., pp. 238–53. See also Leonard Schapiro, *The Communist Party of the Soviet Union*, rev. ed. (New York: Vintage, 1971) pp. 403 ff.

38. Leon Trotsky, *The New Course* (Ann Arbor: The University of Michigan Press, Ann Arbor Paperbacks, 1965), Chapter IV.

39. Trotsky, *The Permanent Revolution*, pp. 105, 115, 129–135.

40. Trotsky, *The Revolution Betrayed*, 5th ed. (New York: Pathfinder Press, 1972) p. 56.

41. DeGeorge, *The New Marxism*, p. 17, cites three major functions which a strictly regulated "official ideology" provides: (1) a coherent world view to replace religion and previous philosophical views, and to provide its people with a single and new set of values; (2) justification and moral sanction for the policies of the new regime; (3) a guide for the development of society as a whole. See also Gustav Wetter, S. J., *Dialectical Materialism, A Historical and Systematic Survey of Philosophy in the Soviet Union* (New York: Praeger, 1963), pp. 268 ff.

42. Joseph Stalin, *Dialectical and Historical Materialism* (New York: International Publishers, 1970 edition), p. 5.

43. Ibid., p. 14.

44. Wetter, *Dialectical Materialism*, p. 224.

45. Stalin, *Dialectical and Historical Materialism*, pp. 15–17.

46. Ibid., p. 19.

47. Ibid., p. 22.

48. Ibid., p. 32. For a fuller study of Stalinist philosophy and current reactions to it, see Anton Donoso, "Stalinism in Marxist Philosophy," *Studies in Soviet Thought*, No. 19, 1979, pp. 113–41.

48. *Fundamentals of Marxism-Leninism, Manual* (Moscow: Foreign Languages Publishers House, 1961); V. Afanasyev, *Marxist Philosophy, A Popular Outline* (Moscow: Foreign Languages Publishing House, n.d.). The more recent (1974) and shorter *Fundamentals* textbook cited earlier (note 31) continues to defend the integrity and

irrefutable logic of Marxist-Leninist philosophy. But it does affirm a greater distinction between philosophy and science and it recognizes that the dichotomy between materialism and idealism has been oversimplified in the past. It continues, however, to defend the latter distinction claiming that in the light of class struggle one must opt between the two (pp. 39–44).

50. Afanasyev, *Marxist Philosophy*, p. 11.

51. Ibid., pp. 12–13.

52. Ibid., p. 22ff.

53. *Fundamentals of Marxism-Leninism*, 1961 Manual, pp. 45–64, 136.

54. Ibid., p. 26.

55. Afanasyev, *Marxist Philosophy*, p. 14.

56. *Fundamentals of Marxist-Leninist Philosophy*, 1974 text, pp. 10, 16.

57. In the first years of Chinese Communism, the Soviet Union was supportive. But several factors led to a rift in the late 1950s and early 1960s: China's criticism of an "unbalanced" de-Stalinization; the U.S.S.R.'s criticism of China's "great leap forward" in 1958; the U.S.S.R.'s hesitancy or refusal to back the People's Republic of China in its border disputes with India and its claim to Taiwan; Soviet refusal to help the Chinese develop atomic weapons; the U.S.S.R.'s adoption of "peaceful coexistence" with the West.

58. Fernando Claudin, *Eurocommunism and Socialism*, translated by John Wakeham (London: NLB, Schocken Books, 1978), p. 8. Claudin was a leader in the Spanish Communist Party, expelled from the Party in 1964 by Santiago Carrillo for ideas which have now become basic tenets of Eurocommunism.

59. Ibid., p. 42–45.

60. Ibid., pp. 65–66.

61. Georges C. Marchais, *Communistes et Chrétiens* (Paris: Editions Sociales, 1976), pp. 121–22. The quote from an interview in 1970.

62. Ibid., pp. 34, 38. From an address to Christians in June 1976.

63. Enrico Berlinguer in a statement on Communists and Catholics in the Communist daily newspaper *L'Unita* for October 13. 1977. See Gerry O'Connell, "Communists and Catholics in Italy," in *America*, April 1, 1978, pp. 266–68.

64. For a negative assessment of Eurocommunism see James V. Schall, S.J., "Italian Communists and 'Revisionism,' " in *America*, April 10, 1976, pp. 312–15.

65. See Lichtheim, *Marxism*, p. 235.

66. Perry Anderson, *Considerations on Western Marxism* (New York: NLB, 1976); *Western Marxism, A Critical Reader*, edited by New Left Review (London: Verso, 1978); Neil McInnes, *The Western Marxists* (London: Alcove, 1972); *The Unknown Dimension, European Marxism Since Lenin*, ed. Dick Howard and Karl E. Klare (New York: Basic Books, 1972); Dick Howard, *The Marxian Legacy* (New York: Urizen Books, 1977).

67. From Marx's 1859 Critique in *Marx-Engels Reader*, Tucker 2nd ed., p. 4.

68. Afanasyev, *Marxist Philosophy*, p. 185.

69. Tucker, *Marx-Engels Reader*, p. 595.

70. Anderson, in *Considerations on Western Marxism*, criticizes the isolation of critical Marxists from socialist praxis, and feels that the hidden hallmark of Western Marxism is that it has been the product of defeat (pp. 34, 42, 52–55, 92–93). Howard's *The Marxian Legacy* is an effort to analyze the failure of the New Left in the

United States, and by stressing freedom, autonomy, and self-management, to move to a socialist theory which can be more effective. See especially his Chapter 2.

71. Georg Lukács, *Lenin, A Study on the Unity of His Thought,* translated by Nicholas Jacobs (Cambridge, Mass.: MIT Press, 1971). Lukács defends Lenin s concept of a vanguard Party (Chapter 3) and his revolutionary use of the state to achieve socialism (Chapters 5, 6). In an essay on ' The Marxism of the Early Lukács," Gareth Stedman Jones views Lukács' work on Lenin as a reversal of his more famous *History and Class Consciousness,* published the year before (Jones, in *Western Marxism,* pp. 50ff.).

72. See Andrew Arato, "Georg Lukács: The Search for a Revolutionary Subject," Chapter 3 in *The Unknown Dimension,* and also Michael Löwy, "Lukács and Stalinism," in *Western Marxism.*

73. *Georg Lukács, History and Class Consciousness,* trans. Rodney Livingstone (Cambridge, Mass.: MIT Press, 1971), p. 1.

74. Ibid., p. 3. In criticizing the empiricists' emphasis on "facts," Lukács argues that "facts only become facts within the framework of a system—which will vary with the knowledge desired" (p. 5).

75. Ibid., p. 13.

76. Ibid., p. 70, and the whole chapter on class consciousness. Gareth Jones, in *Western Marxism,* is sharply critical of Lukács analysis which he claims puts so much emphasis on consciousness that it makes ideology the ultimate key to political power (pp. 45–46).

77. Lukács, *History and Class Consciousness,* pp. 84–36.

78. From an introduction by Louis Marks to Antonio Gramsci, *The Modern Prince and Other Writings* (London: Lawrence and Wishart, 1957), p. 55. A more extensive set of Gramsci's prison writings can be found in *Selections from the Prison Notebooks of Antonio Gramsci,* ed. Quintin Hoare and Geoffrey Nowell-Smith (London: Lawrence & Wishart, 1971).

79. This main thrust of Gramsci's thought is spelled out by Leonardi Paggi, "Gramsci's General Theory of Marxism," in *Telos* 33, Fall 1977, pp. 27–70. I am indebted to Paul Zancanaro and Gerry O'Connell for suggestions in this section.

80. John M. Cammett, *Antonio Gramsci and the Origins of Italian Communism* (Stanford, Calif: Stanford University Press, 1967), p. 205.

81. Carl Boggs, *Gramsci's Marxism* (London: Pluto Press, 1976), p. 39, and the whole of his second chapter on ideological hegemony.

82. Gramsci, *The Modern Prince,* p. 30.

83. Ibid., p. 65.

84. Boggs, *Gramsci's Marxism,* pp. 38, 74–75, 83, 102–4.

85. Gramsci, *The Modern Prince,* pp. 82, 87.

86. Ibid., p. 162.

87. Andrew Arato and Eike Gebhardt, eds., *The Essential Frankfurt School Reader* (NY: Urizen Books, 1978), offers a wide selection of texts from the writings of the first members of the Frankfurt School. Martin Jay, *The Dialectical Imagination* (Boston: Little, Brown & Co., 1973) provides an overall study of the School. The journal *Telos* reflects the continuing Frankfurt tradition. Books already noted on Western Marxism also include studies of the School.

88. Herbert Marcuse, *One Dimensional Man* (Boston: Beacon Press, 1964), p. 1.

89. Ibid., Chapter 2.

90. Ibid., p. 115. Chapters 4–7 deal with "clcsed discourse" in different forms.

91. For an overview of Marcuse's political ideas, see George Kateb, "The Political Thought of Herbert Marcuse," in *Commentary,* 49:48–63, January 1970.

92. Jürgen Habermas, *Toward a Rational Society, Student Protest, Science, and Politics,* trans. Jeremy J. Shapiro (Boston: Beacon Press, 1970), pp. 6ff.

93. Ibid., p. 79.

94. Ibid., p. 100.

95. Ibid., pp. 107ff.

96. Jürgen Habermas, *Legitimation Crisis,* trans. Thomas McCarthy (Boston: Beacon Press, 1975). This summary drawn from Howard, *The Marxian Legacy,* pp. 120–27. See also his sections on Habermas' reformulation of Marxist theory, pp. 127ff.

97. See Czech Marxist Karel Kosik, "Marxism and Philosophy," in *Socialist Humanism,* ed. Erich Fromm (Garden City, N.Y.: Anchor Doubleday, 1966), p. 165. The book contains essays by Adam Schaff, Ivan Svitak, Raya Dunayevskaya, and many other Marxists writing on the question of humanism.

98. See Adam Schaff, *Marxism and the Human Individual,* ed. R. S. Cohen (New York: McGraw-Hill, 1970); Leszek Kolakowski, *Toward a Marxist Humanism,* trans. Jane Zielonko Peel (New York: Grove Press, 1968). Kolakowski offers two striking examples of Stalinist "dogmatism" in the Party's complete reversal of positions on language theory and on revolution, which it had shortly before contended were essential to Marxism-Leninism, p. 174.

99. Mihailo Marković and R. S. Cohen, *Yugoslavia, The Rise and Fall of Socialist Humanism: History of the Praxis Group* (Nottingham: Spokesman Books, 1975).

100. Gajo Petrovic, *Marx in the Mid-Twentieth Century* (Garden City, N.Y.: Anchor Doubleday, 1967), pp. 10–11.

101. Ibid., pp. 22–23.

102. Ibid., p. 59.

103. Mihailo Marković, *From Affluence to Praxis, Philosophy and Social Criticism* (Ann Arbor, Mich.: Ann Arbor Paperbooks, The University of Michigan Press, 1974).

104. Ibid., pp. 14, 36–37.

105. Ibid., pp. 21–22.

106. Ibid., pp. 182–83 and throughout the final chapters of the book.

107. Louis Althusser's best known works are *For Marx* (London: NLB, 1977, written 1965); with Etienne Balibar, *Reading Capital* (London: NLB, 1970); *Lenin and Philosophy and Other Essays* (London: NLB, 1971). The following studies have proved helpful in summarizing Althusser's thought: Norman Geras, "Althusser's Marxism: An Assessment," in *Western Marxism;* Robin Blackburn and Gareth Stedman Jones, "Louis Althusser and the Struggle for Marxism," in *The Unknown Dimension,* Chapter 15; Miriam Glucksmann, *Structuralist Analysis in Contemporary Social Thought* (London: Routledge & Kegan Paul, 1974).

108. Althusser, *For Marx,* pp. 32–37.

109. Ibid., pp. 175–76; Glucksmann, *Structuralist Analysis,* p. 99; Geras, in *Western Marxism,* p. 238.

110. Althusser, *For Marx,* pp. 101–4; *Reading Capital,* pp. 46–47.

111. Althusser, *For Marx,* p. 111; *Reading Capital,* pp. 180–93; Geras in *Western Marxism,* pp. 250–52, 256–58.

112. See Blackburn and Jones, in *The Unknown Dimension*, pp. 370–71.

113. See Perry Anderson, *Considerations on Western Marxism*, pp. 54–65, 34–85. Anderson states that Althusser borrows his monistic determinism from Spinoza. See also Althusser, *Reading Capital*, pp. 187–89 and *Lenin and Philosophy* pp. 151–52, 160–65.

Chapter 3

The Church: From Anathemas to Christian Marxists

The historical fact of Christian opposition to Marxism requires little confirmation. The reasons for the opposition, however, do need to be studied if the debate over the compatibility of Marxism and Christianity is to be resolved. The Church was slow to respond at all to social issues in the nineteenth century. When it did respond, the Catholic Church showed itself unhappy with capitalism but almost totally opposed to socialism. Marxism did not really become a focal issue until the present century. The history of the Church's social doctrines thus raises numerous questions. Why did the Church wait so long to address the problems raised by the industrial revolution, and why was socialism rejected from the outset? Do the arguments against socialism differ from those against Marxism and Communism? Have official Catholic views on socialism changed? Have any changes, or signs of change, occurred to suggest a more positive attitude on the part of the Church toward Marxism? Why have Protestant theologians and Church groups often been more supportive of socialism and more open, at times, to Marxism?

This chapter on the Church attempts to address these questions, to look at the original reasons for Church opposition to socialism/Marxism,[1] and to investigate what changes may have occurred over the years. Catholic social thought receives much fuller treatment than Protestant thought. The author's own greater familiarity with Catholic social thought, the more clearly discernible lines of development in papal encyclicals, and the importance for Catholics of "squaring" their views with official teachings if they wish to gain Church support account for this greater stress on Catholic social doctrines.

The Church Against the World: Nineteenth-Century Europe

Resistance to social change characterized the official stance of the Catholic Church and most Protestant Churches through most of the nineteenth-century. Pope Pius IX's "Syllabus of Errors" (1864), with its condemnation not only of socialism but of "progress and modern civilization," manifested this resistance in its most intractable form. Movements of Social Catholicism and Social Protestantism made efforts to involve the churches in social problems, but generally with very limited success. Historical conditions, however, offer some explanation as to why the churches reacted as they did.

The Scars of the French Revolution

Liberals invoked the French Revolution in their quest to win political rights. Revolutionary socialists sought to go beyond its political freedoms to a complete transformation of society. The Catholic Church could only remember its terrorism and the destruction it brought. This memory influenced all the Church's responses. Any doctrines which spoke of "revolution" evoked emotions of fear and repugnance. The very words "liberty," "equality," and "democracy," because of their association with the French Revolution, often carried threatening connotations. It may be helpful to recall why.

When the Estates-General met at Versailles in 1789, the Assembly opened with a solemn Mass. Most delegates seemed quite ready to work with the Church. Most clergy delegates recognized the need for reform, including reforms within the Church.[2] The conflict began when Talleyrand, concerned about the deteriorating financial situation of the state, proposed that the goods of the clergy be placed in the hands of the nation. In 1790 a transfer of all Church property was voted and the Church lost every source of revenue.

The Civil Constitution of the Clergy, legislated in the same year, required priests to take an oath of loyalty to the French Constitution and called for bishops to be popularly elected. Hostility toward the Church escalated in 1791-92. Clerical dress was prohibited; religious congregations were suppressed. Any priest judged by several witnesses to be a "non-juror" would be deported. An estimated 30,000 priests were deported or fled. Those caught remaining faced ten years in prison. In August 1792, the monarchy was overthrown. Hundreds of priests were arrested; many were simply lynched. The September Massacres of 1792 saw the execution of over one thousand "enemies of the revolution" including some 250 priests and bishops. Many victims were hacked to death as they left the courtroom which sentenced them.

Anti-religious measures continued through 1794. Abbeys were razed to the ground; statues and monuments were destroyed or defaced. Saints' names were prohibited. Substitute religions flourished—the cult of great men (e.g., Rousseau, Voltaire), the cult of Nature, the enthronement of the goddess of Reason in Notre Dame Cathedral.

When the French Revolution ended, and after an uneasy concordat with Napoleon, the Church looked once again to the monarchy for protection. "The Church had been driven . . . as a fellow sufferer at the hands of the

[French] Revolution, into a closer union with the monarchy and the aristocracy."[3] Eighty percent of the new bishops in France came from the nobility. Most of the parish priests came from peasant stock. It was not a combination that would lend itself to an understanding of the problems of future urban factory workers.

Pius IX and the Papal States

If scars from the French Revolution would influence the Church's first responses to revolutionary socialism, protection of the Papal States also significantly affected its judgments. "Throne and altar" were united in the office of the Pope. The popes were not only monarchical in their sympathies but temporal monarchs themselves. The Papal States in central Italy were governed entirely by ecclesiastical authorities under the Pope, with no lay voice or even grievance procedures available. The popes believed that they needed temporal power to safeguard their spiritual authority and independence. Any Catholic who spoke out even for separation of Church and State was seen as a threat to the papacy itself. Thus Gregory XVI in his *Mirari Vos* (1832) condemned the view, advanced by the French Abbé Félicité de Lamennais, that political liberty of the state could aid the Church's mission.[4] Pius IX, in his *Qui Pluribus* (1846), condemned the Young Italy movement and the secret societies formed to promote the unification of all Italy.

When revolutions swept through Europe in 1848, the Pope's prime minister, Count Pellegrino Rossi, was assassinated. Saint-Simonian socialists were blamed for his death. Pope Pius IX fled in fear. On his return in 1850, he named the conservative Cardinal Giacomo Antonelli as his secretary of state.[5] All radical groups, democratic as well as socialist, were seen as threats to the Papal States and the authority of the Church.

Pius IX's famous "Syllabus of Errors" was appended to an encyclical *Quanta Cura*, promulgated on December 8, 1864. The Syllabus condemned political liberalism, rationalism, Gallicanism, and numerous other "isms." It concluded by saying: "If anyone thinks that the Roman Pontiff can and should reconcile himself and come to terms with progress, with liberalism, and with modern civilization, let him be anathema."[6]

Of the eighty errors condemned by the Syllabus only one paragraph condemned socialism and communism. But from Pius IX's many encyclicals one can form a summary view of the subversive tendencies the pontiff attributed to socialism and communism. They have as their aim "to destroy the worship of God," "to wage a fierce war against the Catholic *religion*." They attack the power of all higher *authority* (Church, family, government); their doctrine is destructive of the natural law, of the *natural order* of things. They provoke revolution "in order to pillage, ruin and invade first the *property* of the Church and then that of all other individuals."[7]

The Socialists Pius IX most probably had in mind, says Arturo Gaete, were Bakuninists, for they were especially active in Italy, promoting terrorism and insurrection. [8] Socialism and communism, at this point, embraced a plethora of different and even conflicting doctrines. Marxism had not yet developed enough strength and unity as a movement to be singled out.

From what has been noted thus far, several reasons can be given for the Catholic Church's opposition to socialism from the outset. First, the Catholic Church itself was seen as a major target of socialist and communist movements. Religion, Church authority, and Church property were threatened with destruction. Second, these movements were "revolutionary" and hence evoked memories of all the terrors of the French Revolution. Third, these movements were viewed as the culmination of ideas which had already proved destructive of the Catholic Christendom and "natural order of things" which God intended for the world. The Reformation had challenged Church authority, the Enlightenment introduced pernicious secularized values, the French Revolution subordinated the Church to the state, and laissez-faire capitalism had destroyed the harmony of guild structures. Socialism seemed bent on carrying these disruptive ideas and tendencies to their radical conclusion, the destruction of all that is sacred, holy, and "natural."

Social Catholicism and Protestantism in Europe

Throughout the nineteenth century in Europe individual Christians and small Christian groups did attempt to awaken the official Church to the plight of the working class.[9] In France, the Abbé Félicité de Lamennais condemned the capitalist wage contract as a form of enslavement long before Marx came on the scene. Philippe Buchez, a socialist converted to Christianity, likewise spoke out vigorously in the 1830s about the misery of workers' lives. Frederic Ozanam founded the St. Vincent de Paul Society in 1833 and he inspired a generation of lay apostles to work with the poor.

These efforts, however, did little to affect official Church policy. The Church was preoccupied with maintaining its own threatened authority and reacted adversely to the democratic ideas of Catholic social reformers. The hierarchy, drawn chiefly from the aristocratic class, had little grasp of workers' problems and the peasant-based lower clergy lost contact with the urban proletariat.[10]

The 1848 revolution turned the French Church more decidedly to the right, leading to further alienation of the working class. When Social Catholicism did experience a rebirth in France and Belgium in the latter part of the nineteenth century, its promoters were often monarchists (e.g., Albert de Mun, René de la Tour du Pin) or reformers (e.g., Frédéric Le Play, Edouard Ducpétiaux) who favored a "paternalistic" model of business. The reformers, influenced by the medieval tradition, promoted business corporations small enough that the employer could act as a "father" to his employees. They assumed the natural division between rich and poor, but believed the rich had a serious Christian obligation to the poor. To their credit, Albert de Mun and others did work hard and successfully to obtain governmental legislation providing higher wages and shorter hours for workers.

The Protestant response to the industrial revolution did not differ significantly from the Catholic one. The Protestant Church in Germany identified with the Prussian state, and the Lutheran "two kingdoms" doctrine tended to assign a mission of personal salvation to the Church and to leave social and political issues to the state. Individual Protestant efforts were made to raise social consciousness, but official Church policy remained quite conservative.

Among the individual Protestant efforts, the work of Johann Heinrich Wichern stood out. He initiated an Inner Mission in the 1840s to help workers and their families.[11] His writings depicted in graphic detail the deplorable housing and working conditions to which the proletariat was subject. Wichern urged the cooperation of employers and workers, the reform of morals, and the safeguarding of family life as ways of dealing with the new industrial revolution.

Wilhelm Weitling became a prominent revolutionary figure in the 1840s. He proclaimed a revolutionary socialism based on Christian principles. He portrayed Jesus as a champion of the working class. A worker himself, Weitling attracted many workers to his cause. But he gained little Church support, and an angry confrontation with Marx weakened his position with other revolutionary groups.

After the turbulence of 1848–49, the German Protestant Church allied itself even more strongly to the Prussian state. Formal ecclesiastical statements on social responsibility continued to be infrequent and vague.[12] Some Protestant spokespersons did attack capitalism. Hermann Wagener denounced capitalism as anti-Christian and used Marxist language in condemning the reduction of workers to mere commodities.[13] But like their Catholic counterparts in France and Belgium, most German Protestant efforts tended to be paternalistic. Carl Stumm symbolized the paternalistic approach to worker problems. He was an authoritarian owner, but his workers were the highest paid in the Saar, and he provided them with a hospital, a restaurant, a library, and support for their children's schools.[14]

Even in England, the most advanced industrial country of Europe, churches were quite slow to respond to problems created by the industrial revolution. But a significant Christian socialist movement did emerge in the mid-nineteenth century.[15] John F. D. Maurice and Charles Kingsley became its leading figures. They were drawn especially to French socialist ideas, and in particular to the idea of national workshops advocated by Louis Blanc. Kingsley dramatized the plight of the workers and the need for socialism through novels and stories. Maurice developed a theological support for socialism based on the "mystical body of Christ" in which all members are called upon to work in harmony as one organism. Their work led to the creation of a federation of workers' associations. Their efforts were short-lived (1848–54), but as clergymen they succeeded at least in developing within the Church the idea of Christian socialism as an alternative to capitalism.

Among Catholics, Bishop Wilhelm Emmanuel von Ketteler (1811–77) was the first significant "official" Church figure to speak out progressively on social issues.[16] He came to prominence in 1848 when he won election to the Frankfurt Parliament and spoke out for democratic freedoms and for workers' rights. In a series of six sermons on "The Great Social Questions of our Time," (1848), he condemned laissez-faire capitalism and argued that the right to property was not an absolute right. His major written work, *The Labor Question and Christianity,* was published in 1864, the same year as Pius IX's Syllabus of Errors. Bishop Ketteler proposed a solution to the labor problem which would greatly influence Catholic social thought in years to follow, the idea of producers' cooperatives.[17] He believed that these cooperatives, in which workers would hold a share of ownership, offered an alternative both to liberal capitalism which wanted free competition without state intervention, and to socialism which was viewed as total state or collective control. Ketteler also addressed more immediate social issues. He told worker audiences that their demands for higher wages, shorter hours, and protective labor legislation were just and Christian. He urged clerics to be knowledgeable about labor issues, to study economics, and to gain direct experience of working conditions in different parts of the country. His work would impress Pope Leo XIII who would finally lead the Church into an era of greater social concern.

The Church Confronts the World: 1890–1930

For the Catholic Church the papacy of Leo XIII marked a decisive turning point in its stance toward the world. When Leo became pope in February 1878, few could have anticipated the impact he would have on Catholic social thought. Though his reputation as an intellectual presaged a more modern outlook, Leo was already sixty-eight years old and the Church was still besieged with a multitude of problems other than social justice. The French Church wanted a return to the monarchy and clashed with the French Republic over education, religious orders, and marriage. The German Church was still locked in battle with Bismarck and his *Kulturkampf* and divided internally by the defection of Döllinger and the Old Catholics. In Italy, the recent loss of the Papal States was a festering wound, and Pope Leo would make efforts throughout his papacy to win them back.

Leo's first encyclicals, in 1878, did little more than to attack the same evils which his predecessor had combatted. The encyclical *Inscrutabili* condemned revolutionaries who oppose every form of authority, enemies of Church education, and those who would confiscate Church wealth. *Quod Apostolici*

Muneris condemned socialism for its hatred of all authority, its rejection of God and religion, its attacks on the sacredness of marriage, and its goal of abolishing private property.[18] The Pontiff offered little to workers by way of an alternative. Workers should accept their status in life as intended by divine providence. Worker societies were encouraged but they were to be under the tutelage of the Church to help workers to be "content with their lot." Pope Leo also concurred in the prohibition of Catholic participation in the Knights of Labor in Canada.

Strong voices for change, however, began to be heard. Attention was drawn to the lifework of Bishop von Ketteler and to the efforts of Catholic theorists in the Freiburg Union. Cardinal James Gibbons of Baltimore, while in Rome in 1887, intervened personally on behalf of Catholic participation in the Knights of Labor. Cardinal Henry Edward Manning of Westminster intervened in 1889 in behalf of the London dock workers and demands for labor legislation. Pope Leo made his move when he commissioned Cardinal Francesco Zigliara to draw up the first draft of an encyclical "On the Condition of Workers." While the encyclical *Rerum Novarum* (May 1891) continued to reflect the traditional mind-set of the Church in many respects, it also dramatically changed the Church's stance toward the world.

Leo XIII's Rerum Novarum[19]

The encyclical confronted two major problems created by the capitalist industrial revolution—the plight of the working class and class conflicts. But to understand the encyclical's efforts to deal with these it is important to draw out into relief the mind-set that governed its analysis.

1. Its Method of Analysis. The method of the early social encyclicals has been described as deductive, as the application of set moral principles to particular situations. Critics have challenged this method as "a-historical." In fact, however, a very definite historical analysis underpins Leo's appeal to set moral principles and the natural law. A comparison with Marxist historical analysis may prove helpful to illustrate this.

The Marxist analysis (1) begins with the situation, viz., wealth concentrated in the hands of the few, the mass of workers impoverished, the two classes in conflict; (2) it then traces the principal cause of the situation to private ownership of the means of production and control of division of labor; (3) it consequently calls for the overthrow of the private property system with means of production to be owned communally.

Implied in *Rerum Novarum* is a quite different perspective, rooted in an historical judgment about Christian society in the past. Leo XIII (1) begins with the same situation as the Marxists; he cites "the enormous fortunes of individuals and the poverty of the masses" which have created "conflict" and "moral deterioration" (RN, n. 1). He then (2) traces the principal causes to the loss of religion and of medieval guilds. "The ancient workmen's Guilds were destroyed in the last century, and no other organization took their place. Public institutions and the laws have repudiated the ancient religion" (RN, n. 2). Consequently (3) Leo calls for a return to the moral principles of the gospel and of natural law, and the establishment of new associations to safeguard the worker.

While these historical judgments remain implicit for the most part, they are made explicit later in the encyclical. Recalling the medieval past Leo writes: "Of these things there cannot be the shadow of doubt; for instance, that civil society was renovated in every part by the teachings of Christianity . . . the human race was lifted up to better things . . . to so excellent a life that nothing more perfect had been known before or will come to pass in the ages that are yet to be" (RN, n. 22). "History attests what excellent results were effected by the Artificers' Guilds of a former day' (RN, n. 36). One may certainly question this glorification of medieval society, but these historical judgments are the key to understanding the encyclical as a whole. They explain why Pope Leo insisted on the need to "restore" society, "to recall it to the principles from which it sprang" so that "to go back to it is recovery" (RN, n. 22). This historical analysis, one might add, rests on definite assumptions about human nature and society very different from the premises of the Marxist analysis.[20]

2. Its Critique of Socialism. The correct "principles" of natural law and religion which governed medieval society are then applied to socialism. Pope Leo actually uses much sharper language in criticizing capitalism than he does in speaking of socialism. He denounces "the callousness of employers," "the greed of unrestrained competition," and the dealings of "avaricious and grasping men." But capitalism escapes condemnation in principle because it is based on private property. Socialists, on the other hand, base their doctrines on false principles. First, they want to take away the right to property (RN, nn. 3–12, 30). Second, they propose solutions which are "clearly futile"; they believe that all inequalities can be overcome and the hardships of work eliminated (RN, nn. 3, 14). Third, they assume that hostilities between classes are natural and inevitable (RN, n. 15). Fourth, they want to bring the state into a sphere not its own, making rights come from the state, letting civil government penetrate into the family, and risking the complete absorption of the individual and the family by the state (RN, nn. 3, 6, 11, 28).

The encyclical says surprisingly little about socialists promoting violence and revolution, and the anti-religious philosophy of socialism is addressed only indirectly when the encyclical rejects solutions which exclude the need for religion and do not recognize the importance of the after-life (RN, n. 18). *Rerum Novarum* does, however, condemn nearly all the major points which have remained Catholic criticisms of Marxism/socialism up to the present: abolishing private property, proposing unrealistic solutions, encouraging class antagonisms, advocating state or collective control over individuals and the family, and adopting a materialist philosophy of life.

3. On Private Property. The most pronounced argument against socialism in the encyclical is based on the right to property. "For every man has by nature the right to possess property as his own" (RN, n. 5). The encyclical offers several reasons "from natural law" for this right. First, human beings, as distinct from animals, need the stable and permanent possession of goods. As rational beings they see the necessity of providing for the future (RN, nn. 5–6). Second, natural law teaches that the goods produced by labor should belong to the one who performed the labor. Hence the worker has a right to "what his own labor has produced" (RN, nn. 7–8). Third, the right to property is needed so that the father of a family may provide for his wife and children, to be able to transfer by inheritance what he has gained. This responsibility lies with the family, and the state should intervene only if the family is in great need (RN, nn. 9–11).

In Chapter 8 some reflections will be made about the force of these arguments today. A few brief observations, however, might be made at this point. First, Leo clearly sees the defense of this right as a defense of the *worker's* right to own, though later he does apply it to the capitalist as well (RN, n. 30). Second, Leo paradoxically uses the same argument put forward by Marx that workers *should* be entitled to the fruits of their labor. The difference is that Leo views this as possible under capitalism, though all his images suggest the work of a farmer rather than a factory worker.[21] Marx, in contrast, argues that the factory workers have already been robbed of the fruits of their labor and that the system denies them the power of ownership. Third, only under the "right use of money" do the limits of the right to property become clear, with the principle that the goods of the earth should be considered "common to all" (RN, nn. 19, 7). Recent Church pronouncements, as will be seen, have reversed this priority and have placed the common purpose of created things over individual rights to property.

4. Pope Leo's Solutions. Aware that capitalism had created severe problems, but convinced that socialism violates the natural law, Leo offered the Church's solutions to these problems. Assuming as natural the division of owners and workers, the Pope spells out their mutual obligations. The workers should carry out agreements made, never injure capital, never employ violence or engage in riots or disorders. The rich and employers must recognize that workers are not slaves and therefore must not be treated as "chattels to make money by." The employer's principal obligation is to give a just wage (RN, nn. 16, 17).

The second half of the encyclical enunciates several other proposals. Given the premise that loss of religion and decline of morality were major factors in the deterioration of society, the role of the Church, as teacher and inspirer of charity, is seen as crucial (RN, nn. 22–23, 13). The State must also play a critical role. It must recognize justice for all, stepping in when the general interest of any particular class suffers. It must secure the safeguarding of private property; it must remedy the causes, such as overly long hours and

hard work, that lead workers to strike (RN, nn. 26–31). Of signal importance, the encyclical argues that "wages fixed by free consent" may *not*
constitute a just wage because the worker often has no option but to take a
job. The Pope encourages mutual associations of employers and workers, but
he also affirms the right of workers to their own unions (RN, n. 36).

To the contemporary reader these may seem very cautious steps. The
assumption of a "natural order" of classes,[22] and the reliance on appeals to
morality and the authority of the Church reflect a traditional and conservative
mind-set. But judging the 1890s by late twentieth-century criteria can give a
very unbalanced perspective on the encyclical. Many of Leo's proposals were
considered bold and daring in their day. They directly challenged liberal
capitalism's contention that there should be no interference with the laws of
the free market. The very approval of labor unions, independent of the
patronage of employers or the tutelage of the Church, placed Leo among the
avant-garde thinkers in the Church. The affirmation of state intervention to
protect workers also marked a significant step forward. The insistence on a
"just wage" made justice, and not simply charity, a focus of Church concern.
Above all the encyclical brought to serious attention the condition of the
working class and the weight of the Church's influence in its defense.

Social Catholicism in the United States

In the closing years of the nineteenth century and the first decades of the
twentieth-century, social issues and socialism itself became the focus of
considerable debate within Protestant churches and the Catholic Church in
the United States. Within the Protestant Church the "social gospel" movement became quite prominent and a Christian Socialist fellowship developed. Such movements gained little momentum within the Catholic Church,
but the writings of Father John A. Ryan provided progressive U.S. Catholics
with an articulate voice on issues related to labor and socialism.

The Catholic Church in the United States related to the working class far
more naturally than did the Church in Europe. Most of the U.S. clergy and
most of the bishops came from working class families. But perhaps due to the
minority status of the Church in the U.S., Catholic clergy and laity alike
tended to avoid involvement in social reform movements other than labor
organization. Until late in the nineteenth-century, most of the U.S. Catholic
response to problems created by industrial capitalism took the form of
welfare to the poor.[23] Centers and settlement houses were established to
help immigrants find jobs, to educate them for trades, to provide for them in
case of unemployment, sickness, or accident. Temperance became a major
crusade, since drinking was seen as a major cause for the breakup of families
and of unemployment. Reliance on voluntary charity remained strong in the
decades to follow.

In the late 1880s, Church leaders did turn their attention to the industrial conflict and trade unions. Bishop John Lancaster Spalding of Peoria and Bishop John Ireland of St. Paul endorsed Catholic participation in unions. Cardinal Gibbons, as already noted, went personally to Rome in 1887 to argue for the Knights of Labor and Catholic participation in unions.

Catholic Church response to socialism was generally negative. Henry George's quasi-socialist ideas did win some strong Catholic backing, and George found an ardent disciple in Father Edward McGlynn of New York. A small Catholic Socialist Society developed after the formation of the Socialist Party in 1901. But Catholics in general opposed socialism. Pope Leo XIII's rejection of socialism in *Rerum Novarum* evoked a greater response among U.S. Catholics than did his proposals for social reform.[24] Many socialists were openly anti-Catholic and anti-religion in general. Catholic critics of socialism noted that only after heated debate and by the narrow margin of one vote did the Socialist Party in the U.S. pass a resolution declaring that "socialism is not concerned with matters of belief."[25] Catholic participation in labor unions was often encouraged precisely on the grounds of combatting socialism.[26]

Monsignor John A. Ryan, esteemed by many as the foremost Catholic social thinker in U.S. history, articulated a very carefully nuanced evaluation of socialism. In a 1909 essay, "May a Catholic be a Socialist?"[27], Ryan distinguished three aspects of socialism: socialism as a social movement (hostile to religion), as a social philosophy (materialistic, deterministic), and as an economic system. Many Catholics, Ryan observed, dissociate themselves from socialist ideology but advocate an "essential, economic socialism" which would compensate owners for nationalized property, would permit smaller private enterprises, and would retain private possession for one's own home and personal goods. Ryan judged that, if the system could be shown to work:

> We cannot say that it falls under the condemnation of either the moral laws or the Church. For the moral law merely requires that the rights and the opportunities of private ownership be sufficiently extensive to safeguard individual and social welfare. In theory, at least, the proposed scheme seems to meet this end.[28]

What Pope Leo XIII intended to condemn, said Ryan, was an extreme position where all is possessed by the state. Essential socialism does not do this. Thus, Ryan concluded, again subject to the hypothesis that the system could be practicable, a Catholic may believe in Essential Economic Socialism.[29]

Ryan himself agreed with socialists on many issues: public ownership of public utilities, mines, and forests; the break-up or control of monopolies; taxes focused on land and inheritance.[30] But he believed that the materialist philosophy and complete state ownership advocated by the Socialist Party precluded membership by Catholics.

61086

Ryan's sustained debates with the socialist Morris Hillquit, in 1913–14, offered a level of informed, respectful exchange, quite possibly unmatched in value since.[31] They touched on nearly every key issue. Who speaks for socialism? Is socialism anti-religious, and without a morality? Is Marxism scientific? Would socialism bring state domination? What combinations of state ownership and private enterprise could be feasible?

In his *The Church and Socialism* (1919) Ryan urged, as a Catholic alternative to socialism, the cooperatives suggested by Pope Leo XIII, which would distribute ownership rather than absorbing it completely into the state.[32] But Ryan also sharply attacked the capitalist system: "A social order in which the majority of the wage-earners do not own the tools with which they work, nor any important amount of other productive property, is abnormal and cannot endure permanently."[33]

Father Ryan became the chief author of the "Bishops' Program for Social Reconstruction" in 1919. Many of its proposals have since been adopted,[34] but at the time they provoked outrage among leaders in big business. The president of the National Association of Manufacturers denounced the program as "partisan, pro-labor union socialistic propaganda."[35] The Bishops' Program might have marked the beginning of a very progressive era in U.S. Catholic social thought. But the national mood of the 1920s was conservative and strongly anti-socialist. Valuable Catholic reflection on the issues raised by socialism would remain fallow for years to come.

Protestant Social Thought in the United States

Protestant concern about problems created by capitalism developed late in the nineteenth-century. Through much of that century Protestantism in the United States remained for the most part conservative and concerned about personal salvation.[36] Henry Ward Beecher typified most of the clergy in his enthusiastic defense of the free enterprise system.[37] Socialism met with strong opposition as being either too utopian or too willing to give power to a centralized state.[38] The radical rhetoric of John Most in the 1870s and the 1886 Haymarket riot in Chicago, for which socialists were blamed, served to further discredit socialism.

The industrial crises of the last decades of the nineteenth-century, however, together with a great alienation of workers from the Church,[39] stirred many voices in the Church to speak out. Clergy like Washington Gladden began to challenge the principles of capitalism, its ruthless competition and its exploitation of workers. Between 1860 and 1890 national wealth had increased at an incredible rate, from $16 billion to $78.5 billion. But one-half of it was owned by 40,000 families, representing only one-third of one percent of the population. Workers' wages, in the meantime, had often sharply declined.[40]

The writings of Josiah Strong and Richard T. Ely, and the social-gospel novels of Charles Sheldon, evoked concern for the "social message" of the gospel. Edward Bellamy's utopian novel, *Looking Backward 2000–1887,* presented a fictitious account of a national cooperative in which all persons were economic equals. George Herron, as an outspoken proponent of socialism, represented the radical wing of the new social Christianity.[41] In the late 1890s Christian socialists made an unsuccessful attempt to establish a communist colony in Georgia. Its newspaper, *The Social Gospel,* gave a lasting name to the new theological movement,[42] though most within the movement stopped short of advocating socialism.

Walter Rauschenbusch became the leading figure in the social gospel movement. His own early ministry among the poor in New York and the writings of Henry George prompted his interest. His major works, beginning with *Christianity and the Social Crisis* (1907), then *The Social Principles of Jesus* (1916), and *A Theology for the Social Gospel* (1917) gave theological articulation to the movement. Rauschenbusch argued that capitalism embodied principles hostile to the spirit of the Gospel (e.g., competition, monopoly, profit-motive). He recalled the great concern of the Old Testament prophets for the poor and Jesus' denunciation of riches, and he argued that the message of the Kingdom *was* the social gospel.

Rauschenbusch sought to balance an increased socialization of property and maintenance of private property at some levels. He felt that great natural resources essential to society should be publicly owned, for example, mines, forests, and water resources. Those industries which are monopolistic by their very nature, such as the railways, telephone and telegraphs, gas and electric power, should also be socialized.[43] He also urged strong laws to create a more equitable distribution of wealth. Other Protestants stood more unqualifiedly in favor of socialism. A Christian Socialist Fellowship grew out of the publication of *The Christian Socialist,* begun in 1903.

Social-gospel pastors would seek to implement the social message of Christianity in the 1920s.[44] Christian socialism would await the 1930s, however, to receive new impetus. But even at its strongest point Christian socialism was just that, a "Christian" socialism, critical of capitalism but opposed to Marxist movements and uneasy with the anti-clericalism that often pervaded other socialist groups.[45]

The Church in Search of Alternatives: 1930–60

The world had already experienced the crashing impact of the great depression when Pope Pius XI promulgated an encyclical, *Quadragesimo Anno* (May 15, 1931), to recall and develop the social doctrines set down forty years before by Leo XIII. The new encyclical, consistent with the deep sense of tradition that characterized all Catholic teachings, repeated and clarified much that *Rerum Novarum* had taught, but it also proposed more clearly its own alternative to liberal capitalism.[46]

Pope Pius XI's Quadragesimo Anno

1. Continuity and Change. Pius XI retained the basic method of analysis and most of the premises operative in Leo XIII's encyclical. After recalling the basic social teachings of Leo XIII and noting the responses to his encyclical (QA, nn. 1–40), Pius XI enunciated the "principles" which govern the Church's moral doctrines. The natural law provides general principles for determining social doctrines; the Church has the right and the duty to pronounce on the moral implications of economics; the right to private property remains as a fundamental principle governing the evaluation of economic systems (QA, nn. 41–44). The ideal of reconstructing the social order along lines which once prevailed in medieval Christendom again emerges.[47] In light of this ideal the goal of restoring harmony between social classes is again stressed. Both liberal capitalism and collectivist socialism are rejected (QA, nn. 105ff.). The importance of renewing morals and the spirit of the Gospel receives renewed emphasis.

But notable shifts, at least in emphasis, can also be discerned in Pius' encyclical. Leo XIII had insisted upon the right to private property; Pius XI clarifies the "two-fold" aspect of ownership which takes into account both the rights of the individual and the common good of the whole human race (QA, n. 45).[48] Leo XIII began with a rejection of socialism; Pius XI gives equal weight to the rejection of liberal capitalism. The main thrust of the encyclical, in fact, is the need to find a "middle course" between the individualism of a laissez-faire capitalism and the collectivism of socialism (QA, nn. 46, 88).

If defenders of capitalism believed that great progress in justice for workers had been made since the nineteenth-century, Pius XI condemned its abuses in even stronger language than his predecessor had used. While noting that "the system itself is not to be condemned" and that it is "not vicious of its very nature" (QA, n. 101), Pius nevertheless castigates its abuses. Capitalism had become more abusive of its power than when Leo XIII confronted it. It now represented not only great wealth, "but immense power and despotic economic domination is concentrated in the hands of a few" (QA, n. 105). "Free competition is dead; economic dictatorship has taken its place." The whole economic life "has become hard, cruel and relentless in a ghastly manner." Capitalism has made the state a slave to special interests; it spreads its power to an "international imperialism" (QA, n. 109).

Pius XI continued to argue for a "just wage" and more equitable distribution of goods. But he recognized a condition that Leo XIII had not really acknowledged, that immense numbers of wage earners were in fact propertyless and that many rural laborers had no hope of ever owning land (QA, nn. 59–60). While the new encyclical still stressed harmony between classes, it abandoned the notion that class divisions are part of a "natural order" intended by God.

2. Toward a Corporative Society. The most distinctive contribution of *Quadragesimo Anno* was its advocacy of a corporative state or society as a middle way between individualistic capitalism and collectivist socialism. Leo XIII had discussed the idea of associations involving both owners and workers, but the practical effect of his encyclical had been the defense of independent labor unions and specific worker demands. Pius XI wished to emphasize a new, long-range vision and plan for reconstructing the social order.

The basic plan was to reconstruct the whole economic system gradually through the creation of corporations based on vocational or professional groupings (QA, nn. 81–97). Workers would have a share in the ownership of these corporations (QA, nn. 64–65) and a voice in their management. Owners would have to belong to these corporations and would no longer have complete control over investment, work, and distribution of wages and profits. Workers would gain job security by belonging to a corporation and would escape the status of being mere wage-earners. Policy decisions would be governed by the common good and would build upon values of mutual help and willingness to sacrifice for others. The profit motive would no longer serve as a governing principle in decisions about automation, plant location, and production goals.[49]

These corporations would not be state-owned. The state would serve to encourage and protect them but would not take over the operation of the economy. Pius insisted on the "principle of subsidiarity":

> . . . as it is wrong to withdraw from the individual and commit to the community at large what private enterprise and industry can accomplish so, too, it is an injustice . . . for a larger and higher organization to arrogate to itself functions which can be performed efficiently by smaller and lower bodies (QA, n. 79).

The encyclical thus insisted upon a decentralized economy to the extent to which it could be realized.

This plan for a corporative society derived its inspiration from the ideal of guilds in medieval society and from the vision of an "organic" society in which all members would contribute. This conception of a corporative society came principally from Catholic social theorists in Germany where guilds had continued to function well into the nineteenth century.[50] These theorists blamed individualism, which liberal capitalism extolled, as the root cause of society's dissolution. Pius XI's criticisms of economic liberalism echoed this sentiment. Still, the pontiff did not accept socialism as an alternative because he viewed it as imbued with a materialist philosophy and as a *complete* takeover of society by the state or a total collectivity.

3. Socialism. "No one can be at the same time a sincere Catholic and a true Socialist" (QA, n. 120). This one sentence, if taken literally and as an unchanging doctrine, would rule out not only Marxism but even socialism as a political option for Catholics. Hence, it is important to weigh what Pius meant by a "true" socialist. Pius noted the often hostile division which had emerged, especially in the 1920s, between Communism and Socialism. Communism the Pope saw as clearly evil (QA, n. 112). Socialism was now much less radical in its views, according to Pius. It condemned recourse to violence; it even mitigated and moderated to some extent class warfare and the abolition of private property. Its programs, in fact, often strikingly approached the just demands of Christian social reforms. "If these changes continue," Pius observed, "it may well come about that gradually the tenets of mitigated Socialism will no longer be different from the program of those who seek to reform human society according to Christian principles" (QA, n. 114).

If such convergence seemed to be occurring, why did Pope Pius conclude that a Catholic cannot be a true socialist? He did so because he equated "true" socialism with doctrines inimical to Catholic truth. True socialists saw only the material side of production; they felt people must submit themselves wholly to society; all other human values, including freedom, were subordinated and even sacrificed for the sake of efficient production; loss of human dignity was considered less important than abundance of material goods (QA, n. 119). It is in light of *these* tenets that Pius concluded a Catholic cannot be a true socialist. His attack, in short, was directed against a definite ideological form of socialism and not against all socialist parties or all who called themselves socialists.[51]

Pius XI's Divini Redemptoris

Six years after *Quadragesimo Anno,* Pius XI promulgated a condemnation of "Atheistic Communism" in the encyclical *Divini Redemptoris* (March 19, 1937). The reasons for an encyclical on Communism were evident. Stalin had just purged, imprisoned, or executed millions in Russia. The Civil War in Spain and revolution in Mexico had threatened Communist domination of those traditionally Catholic countries. The Comintern in 1935 had made the Church a target for opposition.[52] Yet the danger of the "appeal" of Communism remained strong because of conditions created by the depression. Maurice Thorez, leader of the Communist Party in France, had offered an "outstretched hand" to Christians to work together for social change in one united front. Pius XI felt strongly the need to condemn Communism and to warn of its deceptive propaganda.

The condemnation focused on "the principles of Atheistic Communism as they are manifested chiefly in Bolshevism" (DR, n. 7).[53] Several ideological or philosophical principles of Communism came under attack (1) false promises—Communism proposes a false messianic idea and deceptive promises about what a new society will be; (2) materialism—it holds that only matter exists, a view which rules out all belief in God, the soul, and hope in an after-life; (3) violence and hatred—class struggle and consequent violent hate and destruction become a crusade for progress; (4) denial of rights—there is no recognition of any individual rights in respect to the collectivity; (5) rejection of authority—it rejects all hierarchy and divinely constituted authority, including the authority of parents; (6) the natural right to property is abolished; (7) marriage and the family are completely undermined; (8) dominance of the collectivity makes production of goods its only goal and gives unlimited discretion over individuals; (9) morality is reduced to being simply a product of the economic order; (10) the state is given unlimited power, though Communists claim it will "wither away" (DR, nn. 8–14).

If the pontiff focused primarily on the "principles" of Communism, he also condemned it in practice—its persecution of religion, the brutal slaughter of clergy and laity in Mexico and Spain, the terrorism of Soviet Communism (DR, nn. 19–23). Much of the encyclical is then devoted to a reaffirmation of Catholic social teachings enunciated in earlier encyclicals. But Pius's unqualified condemnation of Bolshevik Communism would characterize Catholic anti-Communism for many years to come. "Communism is intrinsically wrong, and no one who would save Christian civilization may collaborate with it in any undertaking whatsoever" (DR, n. 58). Whether distinctions can be made between the Stalinist Communism of that period and Marxist thought and movements today becomes an obvious issue.

Aided by the stimulus and encouragement of Pius XI's encyclicals, Catholic Action groups swelled in numbers. Christian-Democratic parties were formed to promote a middle course between capitalism and Communism. Catholic philosopher Jacques Maritain proposed the ideal of a "new Christendom." He did not promote any specific form of political organization and he was too realistic to suggest a new Catholic hegemony over society. But he did believe that efforts to build a new society must be inspired by moral principles with a special stress on the dignity of every individual. He felt capitalism was decadent, but he rejected Marxism as a pseudo-religion with no underlying morality, or at least none which could guide decisions before the eschaton of a classless society could be reached.[54]

Pius XII made a significant contribution to the Church's teaching on property by insisting that "the primordial right to the use of material goods" can outweigh property rights and that the Church's defense of private property was not a defense of capitalist property relations.[55] Corporatism faded as a Catholic ideal because fascist regimes had corrupted the idea by making corporations artificial instruments of the state. The post-war years brought Communist dominance in Eastern Europe and the threat of Communist domination in Italy and France. It marked the strongest period of anti-Communism in Catholic Church history. Under Pius XII, a decree of the Holy Office, in July 1949, forbade Catholics to join the Communist Party or to encourage it in any way. Moreover it forbade the faithful to publish, distribute, or even read books and papers which upheld Communist doctrines.[56]

Protestant Thought

No one Protestant body or set of writings defines Protestant social thought in the way in which papal social encyclicals have formed Catholic social teachings. One could study the assemblies of the World Council of Churches,[57] but these more often represent "great debates" of contending theological movements in a given period than a continuous and set body of doctrines. But the very freedom to explore all possible alternatives led many of the most prominent Protestant theologians to consider socialism more seriously and to evaluate the truth claims of Marxism more closely.[58] A strong sense that the Church itself stands "judged" by God for its failures in respect to social justice also made Protestant thought self-critical in a way that was little evident in papal encyclicals. Two Protestant theologians, Paul Tillich and Reinhold Niebuhr, might be singled out for their efforts to deal with the issues of Marxism and socialism.

1. **Paul Tillich.** From the end of World War I to his exile from Germany in 1933, Tillich developed a theology of "religious socialism." He became a member of the Independent Social Democratic Party and some of his colleagues referred to him as a "Red Socialist."[59] Religious socialism, according to Tillich, accepted the basis of Marx's analysis of capitalist society.[60] It recognized the structure of contemporary society as determined by the capitalist economy. It argued, with Marx, that this economy creates an opposition between owners and workers and that class struggle results from this. It agreed with Marx's assessment that the proletariat was the main force of resistance to capitalism. Consequently, religious socialism allied itself with the proletarian movement as expressed in socialist parties.

Even in these strongly pro-socialist years Tillich drew certain reservations. He refused the views that only by advocating socialism can one truly fulfill the Christian commitment to love or that the very promotion of socialism is religious.[61] Above all Tillich recognized that religious socialism must always stand in criticism of political socialism when its efforts become misdirected. Religious socialism should support the struggle for socialism only in so far as it intends to break the power of political and social domination.[62] In particular, Tillich recognized the tendency of Communism to become a religious movement by absolutizing its truths and its authority.

This tendency of Marxism to become a religion and to absolutize its insights was the focus of Tillich's criticisms decades later in 1960. "The Marxist elite identifies itself with *the* truth, and thereby gains the good conscience to persecute and, if possible, destroy every opponent."[63] Whereas Christianity sees the "fall" of human nature as universal and holds that all human groups are under judgment, the Marxist view claims that alienation belongs only to a special period of history and it exempts the proletariat from judgment. When its messianic claims to achieve a classless society are not achieved, Marxism substitutes methods of terror to secure its rule. While these later judgments did not negate Tillich's earlier vision of religious socialism they constituted an obviously harsh critique of Communist efforts to achieve socialism.

2. Reinhold Niebuhr. Niebuhr stands out as the most influential American Protestant writer on Marxism. Like Tillich, Niebuhr moved from views supportive of Marxism, in the later 1920s and 1930s, to sharply critical positions in his late career. Thirteen years (1915–28) of church ministry at Bethel Evangelical Church in Detroit led him to champion the "social gospel" and to criticize the empire of Henry Ford's auto industry. For a time in the 1930s large numbers of U.S. Protestant pastors adopted pro-socialist positions.[64] Niebuhr went further and spoke of himself as a "Christian Marxist."[65] He defended Marxist analysis and Marxism's claim to represent the attitudes of the working class. He felt that socialism, more or less Marxist, was the political creed of the industrial worker of Western civilization. If this had not yet proved the case in the United States, Niebuhr predicted that "the full maturity of American capitalism will inevitably be followed by the emergence of the American Marxian proletarian."[66] He felt that Marxism correctly expressed the workers' feelings, through its moral cynicism, its egalitarian idealism, its rebellious heroism, and its sense of class loyalty.

Even in this period, however, Niebuhr worried about the "religious" character of Marxism, its apocalyptic vision of classless society and the messianic role attributed to the proletariat. Advocacy of Marxism could thus lead to a deification of the proletarian class and to ruthless vindictiveness, as was happening under Stalin.[67] He remained sharply critical, on the other hand, of efforts to dismiss Marxism as too radical. Comfortable classes dream of automatic progress in society. "They do not suffer enough from social injustice to recognize its peril to the life of society."[68]

By the late 1930s Niebuhr had become far more critical of Marxism. Stalin's purges, the Hitler-Stalin pact, the subservience of the American Communist Party to the Soviet Union, together with the recovery of the U.S. economy after the depression, all contributed to his changed outlook. Whatever value he still recognized in Marxist social analysis, he judged Communism to be evil. The sources of Communist evil he traced to its monopolization of power, its utopianism, its uncritical acceptance of the Party and of the proletariat as forces of good, and its dogmatic pretensions to scientific truth.[69]

In his great work *The Nature and Destiny of Man,* Niebuhr included several pointed criticisms of Marxist theory.[70] His criticisms all related in some way to the Marxist failure to recognize radical sinfulness as a part of the human condition. First, according to Niebuhr, Marxism has an erroneous view of human nature. Its uneasy combination of voluntarism and determinism fails to account for the will to power as intrinsic to human nature, and hence it projects unrealistic expectations of social harmony once extrinsic economic conditions are changed.[71] Second, it reflects the sin of intellectual pride. It detects ideological taints in its opponents but not in its own thought. "The Marxist detection of ideological taint in the thought of all bourgeois culture is significantly unembarrassed by any scruples about the conditioned character of its own viewpoints."[72] Its inability to criticize or even recognize its own a priori tenets accounts for the uncompromising polemics of Marxists against each other. Third, Marxism promises an unrealistic solution to the problems of society because it reduces evil to external factors, to alienating economic structures, without recognizing any intrinsic, sinful egoism in human nature.[73] Fourth, Marxism absolutizes the claims of the proletarian class. Its truth is untainted; its goodness unsullied. Such pretensions to sanctity lead too easily to fanaticism and to the absence of any spirit of tolerance or forgiveness.[74] Fifth, by making true justice only realizable in a future classless society, Marxism fails to provide any norms through which justice might be "approximated."[75]

This stress on "approximations" became the characteristic of Niebuhr's "political realism." Niebuhr retained, through all of this, an appreciation for the values of Marxist analysis, its critique of the injustices of capitalism, its valid critique of ideological elements in Christianity, its suspicion of moral idealism, and its drive for justice. But he believed that justice could best be achieved through democratic politics, proximate solutions, and a pluralism of social strategies for change.

Shifting Attitudes: The Church in the 1960s

The Church, and the Catholic Church in particular, underwent a succession of dramatic changes in the 1960s. Pope John XXIII and the Second Vatican Council adopted new attitudes which profoundly affected the Catholic Church and its relationship to the world. The changes began with seemingly contained goals. Pope John wanted the Church to exert positive leadership in addressing world problems. The Council wished to examine the Church's understanding of itself and its relation to the world in order to make it a more effective means of transmitting the gospel message to a modern world. But once new questions were asked, and new responses encouraged, far greater changes occurred than were ever anticipated. The Church would experience, especially in the second half of the 1960s, many of the tensions which traditional societies undergo when they strive to modernize. Thus the "shifting attitudes" discussed in this section met with great resistance from some sectors of the Church and impatience for more radical changes from other sectors.

Pope John XXIII and Vatican II

Three important documents, in the early 1960s, gave new articulation to the Church's social teachings. Pope John's *Mater et Magistra* (May 15, 1961) commemorated the seventieth anniversary of *Rerum Novarum;* Pope John's *Pacem in Terris* (April 11, 1963) addressed the whole world on issues of peace and justice; Vatican II's *Gaudium et Spes* (December 1965) attempted to define, for the first time in any conciliar document, the relationship of the Church to the world.[76] A more detailed study would call for separate treatment of each of these, but for our purposes it may suffice to note the new trends that emerged from these documents in contrast to earlier social teachings.

1. New Attitudes toward the World. The early 1960s marked a period of great hopes. The emergence of African nations from colonialism, alliances to aid developing nations, the civil rights movement in the United States, the promise of a new space age, and de-Stalinization in the U.S.S.R., all seemed to hold open the promise of a brighter future. This new spirit of hope seemed both engendered and embodied by such leaders as John F. Kennedy, Martin Luther King, Jr., and Pope John.

Pope John's *Mater et Magistra* captured much of this new spirit. It was far more positive in tone, more optimistic, more pastoral and more future-oriented than any previous papal encyclical.[77] It spent little time on condemnations or correcting false ideologies and sought to promote practical, creative responses to the world's problems. It reflected far less concern about the Church's own authority and showed far greater openness to different approaches. *Pacem in Terris* strove even more explicitly to find a common base and common principles about human dignity, to which all people of good will might respond.

Vatican II's *Gaudium et Spes* went a step further. If the social encyclicals of Leo XIII and Pius XI seemed to place the Church "above" the world, offering its wisdom somewhat paternalistically, Vatican II sought to place the Church "in" the world. It identified the joys, hopes, griefs, and aspirations of humanity, especially of the poor, as its own. It saw itself intimately linked with humanity and its history (GS, n. 1). It recognized that the Church does not always have at hand the solutions to particular problems (GS, n. 33).

After centuries of teaching that stressed the relative insignificance of this life compared to eternal life, the Vatican Council put great emphasis on the importance of transforming *this* world, and it made much greater use of Scripture and biblical theology. It spoke of Christ's mission as breaking the power of evil "so that this world might be fashioned anew according to God's design and reach its fulfillment" (GS, n. 2). It affirmed the importance of human activity in transforming the world. It insisted that human achievements, far from opposing God's power, are a sign of God's greatness (GS, n. 34). Its new eschatology stressed no longer heaven alone but "a new earth where justice will abide." Though it rejected any reduction of the Kingdom of God to earthly progress, the Council affirmed that progress is of "vital concern" to the Kingdom (GS, n. 39). These and similar passages would give great impetus, in years to follow, to Catholics convinced that achieving a just new social order should be the primary concern of the Church. The Council did, however, insist that the proper mission of the Church is religious and not political (GS, n. 42) and that Christians who take political stands should not claim to do so in the name of the Church (GS, n. 76). But as Pope John Paul II would discover in Mexico in 1979, the press can distort these distinctions and leave an impression, contrary to the whole thrust of *Gaudium et Spes,* that the Church should simply stay out of politics.

2. *New Methodology and a New Sense of History.* The encyclicals of Leo XIII and Pius XI began with basic natural law principles, such as the right to property, and drew solutions from these somewhat deductively. The principles were assumed to be meta-historical; a "natural order" intended by God was often presumed. Where history was invoked it served to recall the past ideals of a corporative, medieval, Christian society.

The new social teachings broke significantly away from this mind-set. Concern for "the dignity of the human person" provided a more personalist ontological ground or principle for evaluating socio-economic issues and solutions. But the new documents proceeded much more inductively, relying on data from the social sciences. *Mater et Magistra* analyzed "trends" and characteristics of modern society; *Pacem in Terris* repeatedly began with "signs of the times." Concrete proposals for change consequently became less sweeping and more flexible. The grand plan for a "corporative society" was quietly buried, though the importance of co-determination and active participation of workers in decision-making continued to be stressed.[78] Pope John asserted that no one formula or no one form could be universally applied (MM, nn. 84, 91). Both Pope John's encyclicals and the Vatican Council reflected a shift away from the more somber, natural law approach of German theologians to the more optimistic, world-affirming, and inductive views of the French.

Of signal importance, a whole new historical consciousness emerged from these documents. Catholics had long accepted the Church's doctrines and practices as "unchanging." But historical studies, for example those on the Mass, revealed how much change had occurred over the centuries. The Church thus became more aware of the impact of culture on its teachings and practices and of its power to change religion to meet the needs of modern times.[79] *Gaudium et Spes* acknowledged the growing consciousness of men and women "that they themselves are the artisans and authors of culture" (GS, n. 55). This new historical awareness would lead some Christians to accept the validity of the Marxist insight that owner-worker relations and economic systems in general are not natural "givens" but changeable products of human history.

3. *New Views on Property.* The Church's defense of private property, one might justly argue, was always intended as a defense of the individual. Thus, Jean-Yves Calvez supports Pope John's reaffirmation of the right to property

in *Mater et Magistra* (MM, nn. 19, 30, 109) as a means of countering the ever-increasing power of society, capitalist as well as socialist, over the individual.[80] But if Pope John reaffirmed the right to property, he also made much more explicit the subordination of this right to the good of individuals. He cites Pius XII's declaration that the right of every person to use material goods "is prior to all other rights in economic life, and hence prior even to the right of private ownership" (MM, n. 43). Moreover, he began his own proposals, in Part II of *Mater et Magistra,* not with private property but with "private initiative" (MM, n. 51).[81] The need for finding a correct "balance" between private initiative and state or social planning is a recurring theme in the encyclical.[82]

Both *Pacem in Terris* and *Gaudium et Spes* establish the dignity of the human person, and the social relationships needed to respect and develop individuals, as the fundamental principles of social morality.[83] *Pacem in Terris* makes only passing reference to the right to private property as a "suitable" means for safeguarding the dignity of the person (PT, n. 21). *Gaudium et Spes* makes no mention at all of the "right" to property, saying only that ownership and private control over goods "contribute to the expression of personality" and lead to other benefits. The Council goes on to say, moreover, that the common good may require the expropriation of property if it is being misused (GS, n. 71). The universal purpose of created goods, rather than private property, becomes the primary normative principle. In using created goods "a man should regard his lawful possessions not merely as his own but also as common property in the sense that they should accrue to the benefit not only of himself but others" (GS, n. 69).

4. Shifting Attitudes on Socialism/Marxism. One might argue that any shift in attitude toward Marxism or socialism in these documents of the early 1960s reflected a difference in tone rather than in substance. Pope John, in *Mater et Magistra,* still saw Communist and Christian views as "radically opposed," and he still rejected socialism for its philosophical outlook which considers only temporal welfare and production of goods (MM, n. 34). He also seemed clearly to intend Communism in his criticism of countries which deny private initiative (MM, n. 109) and which deny religious freedom and other freedoms (MM, nn. 216–17). But the encyclical contained so little by way of condemnation, compared to earlier social teachings, that many commentators referred to the "virtually complete silence" of the Pope on the issues of Communism and socialism.[84]

The Pope's use of the term "socialization" (MM, nn. 59–68) provoked considerable controversy when *Mater et Magistra* appeared. Some interpreted it as an affirmation of socialism. But the Pope seemed rather to intend by the term a recognition that people's lives had become increasingly interdependent with the multiplicity of social relationships created by modern technology and industrialization. State interventions into all aspects of societal life, the growth of voluntary associations, and the development of international organizations, all reflected the fact of increasing socialization.[85]

In *Pacem in Terris* Pope John avoided any direct discussion of Communism or socialism. But he did set down an important distinction which would take on great importance after Pope Paul VI used it again, in application to socialism, in his *Octogesima Adveniens* of 1971. Without explicit reference to socialism, Pope John distinguished between "historical movements" containing positive and deserving aspirations within them and the "false philosophical teachings" from which these movements arose (PT, n. 159).

Although many bishops wanted the Council to include a renewed condemnation of Communism, it avoided doing so.[86] In treating of systematic atheism, however, the Council did seem clearly to have Communism in mind when it repudiated atheists who view religion as opposed to socio-economic liberation and who consequently "vigorously fight against religion" once they gain political power (GS, n. 20). But the Council also opened the way to dialogue in place of condemnation. "While rejecting atheism, root and branch, the Church sincerely professes that all men, believers and unbelievers alike, ought to work for the rightful betterment of this world in which all alike live" (GS, n. 21). Efforts at "sincere and prudent dialogue," which the Council encouraged, had already begun to develop.

Christian-Marxist Dialogues

Serious studies of Marxism by Fathers Jean-Yves Calvez, Gustav Wetter, Pierre Bigo, Henri Chambre, and others, and the work of centers such as *Action Populaire* and *Frères du Monde* paved the way for dialogue in the 1960s.[87] The new Pope, Paul VI, spoke of the Church's need to dialogue with the world in his *Ecclesiam Suam* in 1964. By their actions as well, both Pope John and Pope Paul symbolized a new openness to dialogue. In 1962 Pope John had held a personal audience with Aleksei Adzhubei, Khrushchev's son-in-law. In April 1966, Pope Paul had a forty-five minute private audience with Soviet Foreign Minister Andrei Gromyko, and he met with President Nicolai Podgorny in January 1967.

In Czechoslovakia, Protestant theologians carried on lengthy and serious exchanges with Marxist theoreticians, contributing to the great effort of the Dubcek regime to create "socialism with a human face." Similar dialogues were undertaken in Yugoslavia and Hungary.

But the dialogues which would receive the greatest attention were initiated by the Paulus Society (*Paulus-Gesellschaft*), a German-speaking group formed originally to carry on a dialogue between theologians and natural scientists. The German Marxist philosopher Ernst Bloch was invited to a meeting in Munich in early 1964, along with the German theologian Karl Rahner, to discuss false concepts of materialism in both Marxist and Christian thought. Polish Marxist Adam Schaff attended a meeting in August 1964 and presented his efforts to develop a philosophy of the individual person, a problem generally neglected in Marxism. Theologian Johannes B. Metz served as a reactor and offered his own ideas on an "anthropocentric" Christianity.[88]

These meetings set the stage for the major conference held in Salzburg, April 29–May 2, 1965. Invitations were sent to the Academies of Science of the Soviet Union and other Eastern European countries. The Soviet Academy did not respond, and some Communist countries rejected requests of their philosophers to participate. But an impressive list of scholars did attend. The Christian representation was predominately Catholic at this first conference (Karl Rahner, Johannes B. Metz, Marcel Reding, Gustav Wetter, Jean-Yves Calvez, Dominique Dubarle, and others). Among the Marxist scholars were Ernst Bloch of Germany, Roger Garaudy and Gilbert Mury from France, Lombardo-Radice and Cesare Luporini from Italy, and several Yugoslavian scholars.[89]

Nearly 300 attended the next conference held at Herrenchiemsee in Bavaria in 1966.[90] Several Protestant theologians, including Josef Hromadka of Prague, attended. Rahner and Metz again participated along with Giulio Girardi of Italy. The Italian Communists were strongly represented, but only Roger Garaudy came from France, and both Bloch and Schaff were absent. Metz argued that the Church needed to develop an eschatological understanding of the faith, one which recognized Jesus as a revolutionary who acted and suffered in conflict with the existing social order. Garaudy challenged as a misconception the view that Marx intended the individual to be "sacrificed" to a collectivity. He argued also that one could find in Marx and Engels a more positive view of religion as a "protest" against human suffering.

A third major conference was held for the first time within a Communist country, at Marianske Lazne (Marienbad) in Czechoslovakia. The *Herder Correspondence* characterized this meeting as a "set of polished monologues" rather than a dialogue since the participants developed very different themes.[91] But the conference did include talks by the Czech Marxist Milan Machovec, by the theologian Jürgen Moltmann, and again by Metz who stressed his thesis that the Church should be an institution for the collective criticism of society.

The invasion of Soviet troops into Czechoslovakia in August 1968 ended for a time the dialogues within that country. It also brought a temporary end to the international dialogues sponsored by the Paulus Society, though efforts to revive them were made in Florence in the fall of 1975 and again in Salzburg in September 1977. What lasting effects these dialogues may have had cannot easily be judged; one journalist who attended them now views their results with great skepticism.[92]

There have been some efforts at Christian-Marxist dialogue in the United States. Gus Hall, longtime leader of the Communist Party in the United States, responded in the early 1960s to Pope John's *Pacem in Terris*. Herbert Aptheker, perhaps the best known philosopher with the U.S.

Communist Party, has engaged in several dialogues with the Christian groups. Roger Garaudy visited the United States and spoke with Christians on college campuses. Vitezslav Gardavsky and other Czech Marxists, who were in the United States at the very moment of the Soviet invasion of their country, participated in a dialogue at the Aquinas Institute of Theology in Dubuque, Iowa, in the fall of 1968. Several books on Christian-Marxist dialogue have appeared in the United States.[93] An "international encounter" of Marxists and Christians took place at Rosemont College (Rosemont, Pennsylvania) in January 1977, with Soviet, East German, and Hungarian Marxists in attendance. Over 150 participants attended a second conference in May 1978 at Rosemont with U.S. Marxists, representing very different positions, as co-speakers with Christians. A third conference was planned for February 1980 in Dayton, Ohio.

The Church and the Third World

The 1960s brought into more prominent light the problems of the "developing nations." With relative prosperity and governmental welfare programs in most countries of Europe and North America, the urgency of owner-worker issues diminished for a time. The emergence of new African nations, the aid and alliances promised to Latin America, the Cuban revolution, Chinese Communism and the war in Vietnam, brought a shift of attention. Part of the original concern grew out of the cold-war era. "Third World" at first usually designated the "non-aligned nations," with aid often closely linked with efforts to win over these nations to the Communist or to the "free-world" camps. With China, Cuba, and then Vietnam as examples of "liberation," Marxist analysis focused upon foreign imperialism. Failures to achieve "development" created unrest and revolutionary movements in Third World countries.

Protestants made these issues the focal point of their discussions at the World Conference on Church and Society in Geneva in 1966. They focused, in particular, on Christian attitudes toward revolution. Inquiries were made into the nature of the different revolutionary movements active in many parts of the world. Questions were raised as to what stance toward revolution would be most consistent with the faith. Should one be maximalist or a reformist, violent or non-violent, utopian or realist? The tension between commitment and solidarity became a concern. Christian commitment would seem to demand being partisan to the poor and the oppressed; but such commitment also risks the loss of objectivity.[94]

1. *Populorum Progressio.* Pope Paul VI's major social encyclical, "On the Development of Peoples"[95] (March 26, 1967), dealt extensively with the issue of developing nations. Some critics and supporters alike felt the encyclical marked a complete change from previous social encyclicals. The *Wall Street Journal* called it "warmed over Marxism." Certainly Pope Paul was

sharply critical of affluent nations. Some of the arguments he used regarding rich and poor nations reflected positions taken in earlier encyclicals on owners and workers. Some critics challenged precisely the parity of such an analogy.

Pope Paul blamed the policies of rich nations for being at least partially responsible for the conditions of hunger and misery in which developing nations find themselves. Colonialism, the pontiff noted, while it had provided some beneficial results, had often left colonized countries with one-crop economies dependent on fluctuating world prices (PP, n. 7). Within these countries a small group often dominates while the remainder of the population is left poor and powerless (PP, n. 9). Modernization and industrialization compound the problem by breaking down traditional values and supports. But Pope Paul was far from conceding Communist revolution as a solution. Without mentioning Communism by name, the pontiff warned:

> In this confusion the temptation becomes stronger to risk being swept away towards types of messianism which give promises but create illusions. The resulting dangers are patent: violent popular reactions, agitation towards insurrection, and a drifting towards totalitarian ideologies (PP, n. 11).[96]

Pope Paul set down as an alternative a "Christian vision of development" which looks to the whole of humanity from a "duty of solidarity" (PP, nn. 43–44, *passim*) and which promotes the good of the whole person (PP, nn. 16–18, 42–44).

Populorum Progressio continued the shift away from making the right to property a dominant principle, and insisted that rights to property and free commerce are subordinate to the rights of individuals to find in the world what is necessary for their growth and development (PP, n. 22). This subordination of ownership to universal use is backed up with the strong words of St. Ambrose to the rich, that they have arrogated to themselves what has been given in common for the use of all. The pontiff drew two very concrete conclusions from this position, that if certain landed estates are being unused or poorly used "the common good sometimes demands their expropriation," and that it is wrong for citizens with abundant incomes from the resources of their own country to transfer this income abroad for their own benefit (PP, n. 24).

With capitalism quite clearly intended, Pope Paul expressed dismay that "a system had been constructed which considers profit as the key motive for economic progress, competition as the supreme law of economics, and private ownership of the means of production as an absolute right that has no limits and carries no corresponding social obligations" (PP, n. 26). Unchecked liberalism leads to economic dictatorship which Pius XI denounced as producing "the international imperialism of money."

While neither Communism nor socialism fell under any explicit condemnation, the pontiff warned against the danger of "complete collectivisation" which would deny the exercise of human rights (PP, n. 33), and he insisted that a Christian cannot accept social action based on a materialistic and atheistic philosophy (PP, n. 39).

With the gap between rich and poor nations a major concern, the main body of the encyclical then dealt with the duty of foreign aid and the duty in justice of rectifying inequitable trade relations (PP, nn. 43ff.).

2. *The Church in Latin America.* Perhaps far more important than the evolution of papal social teachings were the changes occurring within the Church itself. In Latin America, in particular, a dramatic transformation seemed under way.[97] Through most of its history the Catholic Church there had played a very conservative role, allying itself with the landed aristocracy. But new voices were being heard within the Church, and they could call upon documents such as *Populorum Progressio* to support their claims that social justice and solidarity with the poor should be the most important mission of the Church. Bishop Helder Camara of Olinda-Recife, Brazil, and Bishop Sergio Mendez Arceo of Cuernavaca, Mexico, became leaders in championing reforms and defending the rights of the poor.

The Medellín Conference of Latin American Bishops, which took place August 24–September 6, 1968, in Colombia, gave witness to the new spirit developing within the Catholic Church. It challenged the unjust politico-economic structures which dominated much of Latin America, and it spoke of the need for authentic "liberation," thus encouraging the emerging theology of liberation (see Chapter 5). Pope Paul VI made a historic visit to Latin America in the same year, and in his talks spoke of the urgent need for reforms and changes in social structures.[98] A center for social research (ILADES) was established in Chile, and the progressive Chilean hierarchy gave active support to the reforms envisioned by Eduardo Frei and his Christian-Democratic Party. But liberal reformist movements often create demands for more radical change. So, within the Latin American Church did the reformism of the 1960s lead to more radical demands in the 1970s.

The Church in the 1970s: The Issue of Christian Marxism

Christian-Marxist dialogues of the 1960s often assumed two "opposed" ideologies coming together to discuss points of unity and difference with a view to a more peaceful coexistence. In the 1970s the issue of Marxism and Christianity took on a very different form in many parts of the world. Many Christians, deeply disturbed by the enormity of poverty and powerlessness in most of the world and frustrated by efforts or promises of reform, began increasingly to question the whole socio-economic system of capitalism. They found in Marxism a tool for critical analysis of capitalism and a socialist vision of a new society. They began also to rediscover in the Bible the centrality of prophetic denunciations of injustice, and to experience God as a liberator of the poor and oppressed. Marxist socialism, far from appearing inimical to the faith, seemed to them much more consistent with the Christian message than corporate capitalism. Some Christians argued for the usefulness of Marxist analysis; others moved to direct collaboration with Marxist groups.

Latin America drew attention to this new direction. Groups of priests reflecting a wide range of more radical perspectives were formed in the late 1960s: the Priests Movement for the Third World in Argentina, Golconda groups in Colombia, and ONIS in Peru. Camilo Torres became a symbol of revolutionary Christianity when he was killed after joining a guerrilla force in Colombia.[99]

With the election of Salvador Allende in Spetember 1970, Chile became the first major testing ground of direct collaboration with Marxists (see Chapter 6). The official, hierarchical Church remained neutral, but individual Christians, including many priests and religious, worked actively in support of the new Marxist-socialist regime. Such support, at least on any large scale, had failed to materialize a decade before in Cuba where the Church served more often as a rallying force for anti-Communist sentiment. Only with the Chilean experiment did significantly large groups of Christians begin actively to advocate Marxism. A movement of Christians for Socialism developed out of Chile and spread to other parts of Latin America, to Europe, and into the United States.

Paul VI's Octogesima Adveniens *(80th Year Letter)*[100]

With strong negative reactions to Pope Paul's encyclical on birth control *(Humanae Vitae,* 1968), and with authority in general under attack everywhere, responsiveness to Church documents began to suffer a serious decline. Pope Paul's *Octogesima Adveniens* (May 14, 1971), on the 80th anniversary of *Rerum Novarum,* passed almost unnoticed in many parts of the world. It was promulgated as an "apostolic letter" rather than as a full-fledged encyclical, but it had great significance for the Church in countries which were wrestling with the problem of Marxism-socialism. It drew some very important distinctions about both Marxism and socialism.

First, the pontiff insisted that a Christian cannot adhere to ideological systems which go against the faith. "He cannot adhere to the Marxist ideology, to its atheistic materialism, to its dialectic of violence and to the way it absorbs individual freedom in the collectivity, at the same time denying all transcendence to man and his personal and collective history" (OA, n. 26). But neither, the pontiff continues, can a Christian adhere to the liberal ideology which exalts individual freedom without limits.

Second, Pope Paul applied to socialism the distinction which Pope John had made between "historical movements" with economic and political ends, and the "false philosophical teachings" which have accompanied these movements.

> Distinctions must be made to guide concrete choices between the various levels of expression of socialism: a generous aspiration and a seeking for a more just society, historical movements with a political organization and aim, and an ideology which claims to give a complete and self-sufficient picture of man (OA, n. 31).

The pontiff went on, however, to caution that these three aspects of socialism are often not separable in practice.

Third, Pope Paul offered, for the first time in the history of papal social teachings, several distinctions regarding Marxism. He avoided affirming these distinctions as his own by noting that "some Christians" feel that the unitary, atheistic ideology of Marxism has been splintered, leading to various meanings of Marxism:

> For some, Marxism remains essentially the active practice of class struggle . . . to be pursued and even stirred up in permanent fashion. For others, it is first and foremost the collective exercise of political and economic power under the direction of a single party. . . . At a third level, Marxism, whether in power or not, is viewed as a socialist ideology based on historical materialism and the denial of everything transcendent. At other times, finally, it presents itself in a more attenuated form, one also more attractive to the modern mind: as a scientific activity, as a rigorous method of examining social and political reality, and as the rational link, tested by history, between theoretical knowledge and the practice of revolutionary transformation (OA, n. 33).

But having noted these distinctions Pope Paul warned that these different aspects of Marxism have generally been linked together, and that Marxist interpretation and practice of class struggle have led to violent, totalitarian societies (OA, n. 34). Those attracted to Marxism make much of the Pope's official recognition of these distinctions in Marxism; opponents of Marxism stress the dangers noted by the pontiff in conclusion.

Papal social encyclicals had from the outset condemned 'abuses' of capitalism, but never the system itself. Pope Paul judged both "bureaucratic socialism" and "technocratic capitalism" as *systems* which have failed to solve the problem of humans living in justice and equality. He called for creative "utopian" thinking which will go beyond present systems and ideologies (OA, n. 37). The letter, it might be noted finally, brought some recognition to the problem of discrimination against women (OA, n. 13).

The synod of Catholic bishops meeting in Rome in November, 1971, also promulgated a document on "Justice in the World" which took up themes of importance to Christian socialists. The Synod recognized the violence and oppression created by "unjust systems and structures" and spoke of God "as the liberator of the oppressed and the defender of the poor."[101]

Christian Socialists/Marxists in Europe

If the Marxism issue has had great impact on the Church in Latin America, it has stirred controversy in many quarters of Europe as well. The "Catholic Left" in England began speaking out in favor of socialism and Marxist analysis in 1963 when a group of undergraduates at Cambridge University, with the help of some priests, launched a periodical called *Slant*. The "Slant Manifesto," published in 1966, spelled out their fundamental argument why Christians should be socialists. To be a Christian, the *Slant* authors insisted, is to be committed to creating community in the world. But if Christians are really aware of what creating community demands, they will be led logically to condemn vital aspects of capitalism.[102] For capitalism is thoroughly destructive of community; it is a system which creates class antagonisms and encourages egoistic competition and possessiveness.[103] Socialism alone provides the grounds for community, not a dogmatic Stalinist socialism, but a true, democratic, participatory socialism.[104]

In an article for *New Blackfriars* (June 1975), Denys Turner carried the Catholic Left position a step further, arguing that not only can a Christian be a Marxist but a Christian *should* be one. Philosophical materialism is not essential to Marxism; what is essential to both Marxism and Christianity is "praxis." The only real issue, for Turner, is whether one is for or against capitalism. Since community is not possible under capitalism, the only rational response of a Christian is revolutionary socialism.[105]

Eurocommunism has spurred the Communist parties of southern Europe to seek actively the support of Christians. Many Christians, including groups like the Christians for Socialism (see Chapter 6), have adopted Marxist perspectives and worked actively with Marxist groups. Some do not hesitate to call themselves Christian Marxists or even to join the Communist Party. Most view Marxism primarily as a scientific tool for analyzing capitalism and as an efficacious strategy for achieving socialism. They do not believe that materialism and atheism are essential to true Marxism. But many realize that a Christian political commitment to Marxism raises serious questions which need to be addressed.

Phillipe Warnier attempts to face these questions squarely in his *Marx pour un chrétien*.[106] He headed a group in France, the *Vie Nouvelle*, which found itself relying more and more on Marxist concepts and Marxist analysis, but whose members wanted to remain fully loyal to the Church. "A Christian in faith, a Marxist in practice"—can the two be reconciled? In successive chapters of the book Warnier attempts to answer the difficulties most often posed by Christians in respect to Marxism. Isn't it simply Communism, dogmatic in theory and domineering in practice? Doesn't Marxism lead inevitably to Party dictatorship, to the "Gulag Archipelago"? Isn't Marxism necessarily atheistic and materialistic? Doesn't it suppress the individual and eliminate all real morality?

In answering these objections, Warnier adopts a stance toward Marxism which is characteristic of many reflective Christian socialists. He is critical of those who idolatrize Marxism. He is critical of Marx's own failure to develop any true theory of power, and of Marxist-Leninist practical failures to deal with political power, failures which led to Party dictatorship rather than workers' democracies.[107] Warnier clearly espouses a "critical" Marxism and rejects dogmatic formulations of Marxism.[108] But he speaks for a growing number of Christians when he witnesses, in his conclusion, to a "double fidelity," to his Church and to the socialist movement, with Marxism as a dynamic factor informing his existence.[109]

Recent Episcopal Declarations and Some Conclusions

The growing influence of Marxist ideas among Christian students, workers, and other groups became a source of great concern for many Catholic bishops. When several Italian Catholics ran for election on a Communist ticket in May 1976, Cardinal Antonio Poma, Archbishop of Bologna, made it publicly known that Communism and Christianity are still irreconcilable, and that no Catholic may adhere to, favor, or support a Marxist movement. Other bishops in Italy and France issued pastoral letters on Marxism.[110]

In June 1977, the permanent council of the French episcopacy decided that a more unified response was needed and promulgated an official declaration on the relations of Christians to Marxism.[111] While some critics viewed the declaration as an effort to influence national elections in 1978, the document seemed more directly intended as a response to an address given the year before by French Communist Party leader Georges Marchais. In his June 1976 address to French Christians, Marchais sought to allay the fears of Christians by assuring them that the Communist Party wanted a socialist *democracy* which would fully respect their religious convictions and practice. While Marchais acknowledged that Communist theory was based on scientific materialism, he insisted that Communists have no intention of imposing their philosophy on others.[112]

The French bishops, in response, left open the possibility of Christian dialogue and even collaboration with the Communist Party. But at the same time they declared Marxism incompatible with the Christian faith,[113] and they insisted that serious guidelines must be considered in making any political option. The declaration took note of the distinctions made by Paul VI about different senses of Marxism and of the different ways a Christian might relate to Marxism, from use of Marxist analysis to party membership. But the bishops found Marxism incompatible with Christianity both because it declares dialectical materialism as its foundation, and because of certain "tendencies" in Marxism. The bishops singled out the following tendencies: (1) Marxism seeks to acquire a "quasi-monopoly" over democratic relations, with the result often leading to a totalitarianism and the exclusion of all real pluralism; (2) its materialistic vision tends to reduce the human person to a reflection of the relations of production, and to make religion only a reflection of social conditions; (3) it tends both in theory and practice to atheism; (4) it claims a scientific monopoly for its social analysis.[114] What the declaration did *not* say is also significant; it raised no objection to "socialism" as such, though in 1977 the prospects of the Socialist Party gaining power were evident.

The declaration of the French bishops helps to pinpoint the core objection of the Church to Marxism for more than a century. It is an objection that runs through the early encyclicals, through the writings of Tillich and Niebuhr, through Pope Paul VI's writings and into the present. The objection centers on Marxist ideology. But it is not simply that Marxism as a worldview is based on atheism and materialism. Christians and atheists could learn and have learned in many parts of the world to live together. Nor is it a question of Marxist opposition to capitalism, which many Christians oppose, nor even of class struggle, if it is taken to mean a struggle against unjust structures and systems and not as a vindictive clash against persons. The core objection or fear is that Marxists will "impose" their views once in power, believing that they alone possess the "truth."

Later chapters of this book will argue, on the side of those who hold a "critical" Marxism, that Marxist analysis can be separated from traditional Marxist philosophical views, and that any true socialism must be a democratic socialism which respects a plurality of lifeviews. But prevailing Christian objections to Marxism are likely to perdure, especially since the free exercise of proclaiming the Christian message is at stake, until a more critical Marxism becomes prevalent. How much such a critical Marxism already has developed in Latin America, in Europe, and elsewhere remains a very practical question.

A statement (November 21, 1975) by the bishops of the Antilles reflects the evolution and change in the Church's attitude toward socialism as such. Especially in Latin America a growing consensus has developed in the Church about the "economic violence" engendered by present economic structures. Thus the Antilles' bishops, representing various Caribbean countries, noted the mounting dissatisfaction in their countries with the prevailing economic system. Their statement recalled past papal criticisms of capitalism and then presented what the bishops saw as "the current teaching of the Catholic Church on socialism":

> In the first place, the Church has never defended an absolute right to private property. The only absolute right it does defend is that of the universal purpose of created things and the consequent right of every

individual to possess what is necessary for himself. . . . It follows from this that any society in which a few control most of the wealth and the masses are left in want is a sinful society.

Secondly, the Catholic Church does not condemn indiscriminately all forms of socialism. In the past it denounced three particular aspects of socialism, namely: the denial of God and the spiritual, the insistence on the need for class warfare, and the suppression of all types of private property. In so far as these are to be found in some forms of socialism, a true Christian cannot accept them. But today there are other forms of socialism in the world and the very word "socialism" is used in many different ways. Past Church statements referring to socialism must therefore be understood in the light of these new developments. Thirdly . . . when looking at socialism, or Marxism, or capitalism for that matter, it is important to distinguish carefully between (a) basic aspirations, (b) ideologies or systems of thought, and (c) concrete historical movements.[115]

The bishops recognize the "basic aspirations" of socialism, for a more just society and for greater independence and equality, as not only not wrong but "profoundly Christian." They reject the "ideology" of Marxism for the reasons given by Paul VI. In respect to concrete "historical movements" and specific political parties, they say that Christian support will depend on how closely these are linked to atheistic-materialistic ideologies and what methods are employed by them to achieve their basic aspirations.

The Antilles bishops' statement helps to pinpoint the issue of socialism as such. Apart from ideological considerations, the primary objections to socialism over the years has been the danger of a "total collectivity absorbing the individual." The Catholic Church, first in stressing private property, then the principle of subsidiarity and free initiative, and finally in stressing the dignity and responsibility of the individual, has consistently insisted on the need for a balance between societal or state power and protection of the individual. Both a totally collectivist socialism and concentrated monopoly capitalism impair the possibility of individuals determining their own life decisions. Quite clearly the Church still stands opposed to the either-or option of capitalism, with power concentrated in the hands of a few, or a totally collective socialism, with power likewise concentrated in the hands of a ruling state or party. But the Church seems clearly more open to the possibility of a democratic, participatory socialism, especially as a "mixed economy" with a balance of small private enterprises and larger public ownership. Whether socio-political movements exist or will emerge to bring about changes in this direction remains an obvious question.

What direction Church teachings will take in the 1980s remains uncertain. Three different levels of leadership will affect the outcome. Pope John Paul II seems destined to exert greater leadership than his predecessor. He may possibly promulgate a social encyclical in 1981 on the ninetieth anniversary of *Rerum Novarum*. His experience of Marxism in Poland has been of an institutional Communism which does not consider its materialist worldview and Marxist analysis as separable. The pontiff, therefore, may take little note of varieties within Marxism. He has, on the other hand, already distinguished between various types of socialism in comments to the press. The most certain prediction is that Pope John Paul II will do as his predecessors have: he will draw upon past Church teachings, so that whatever new directions he spells out will be a "development," carrying with it an *imprimatur* from the past.

More important, however, in shaping future Church actions and teachings, could be the pronouncements of national or regional groups of bishops. This chapter concluded with declarations of bishops in France and the Antilles. The Church in Latin America has been greatly influenced by bishops' conferences at Medellín and more recently at Puebla. What bishops in local areas determine as guidelines may prove of greater consequence than more generalized social teachings from Rome.

Finally, popular movements within the Church, especially in developing countries of the world, could play a significant role. Church teachings once proceeded only from the top down. A new consciousness of the Church as "the people of God" may make the influence of popular movements far more important.

Notes

1. The general term "Church" is used in this chapter when it seems unnecessary to distinguish between Protestant and Catholic or when the context indicates that one or the other is clearly intended. The expression "socialism/Marxism" is sometimes used when Church teachings have not clearly distinguished the two.

2. H. Daniel-Rops, *The Church in an Age of Revolution*, trans. John Warrington (New York: E. P. Dutton, 1965), pp. 1–8, Chapter I. Other points in this section are drawn from this work or from Friedrich Heyer, *The Catholic Church from 1648 to 1870*, trans. D.W.D. Shaw (London: Adam & Charles Black, 1969), Chapter V. See also *Church and Society, Catholic Social and Political Thought and Movements, 1789-1950*, ed. Joseph N. Moody (New York: Arts, Inc., 1953), pp. 109–18.

3. Lillian P. Wallace, *Leo XIII and the Rise of Socialism* (Duke University Press, 1966), p. 14. See also Joseph Moody in *Church and Society,* p. 119.

4. Daniel-Rops, *The Church in an Age of Revolution,* p. 208.

5. Ibid., p. 253.

6. Ibid., p. 284. See also the documents in *Church and Society,* pp. 232–34.

7. The encyclicals of Pius IX are cited and discussed by Henri Chambre, S.J., *Christianity and Communism,* trans. R. F. Trevett (New York: Hawthorn, 1960), pp. 17–21. Emphasis on key words is my own.

8. Arturo Gaete, "Socialism and Communism: A Problem-Ridden Condemnation," in *Latin Americans Discuss Marxism-Socialism* (Washington, D.C.: LADOC, 1975), no. 13 in the LADOC "Keyhole" series.

9. Alec R. Vidler, *A Century of Social Catholicism, 1820–1920* (London: SPCK, 1964), provides an extensive study of Social Catholicism. See also Daniel-Rops, *The Church in an Age of Revolution,* Chapter VI; Wallace, *Leo XIII and the Rise of Socialism,* Chapter VIII; and Moody in *Church and Society,* pp. 121ff.

10. Speaking of the French Church Vidler concludes: "With rare exceptions its hierarchy was incapable of reading the signs of the times and was without any sense of the prophetic office of the Church." Vidler, *Social Catholicism,* pp. 77–78. See also Daniel-Rops, *The Church,* p. 337.

11. William O. Shanahan, *German Protestants Face the Social Question, Volume 1: The Conservative Phase, 1815-1871* (Notre Dame, Ind.: University of Notre Dame Press, 1954), pp. 70ff.

12. Ibid., pp. 4 and 379.

13. Ibid., p. 363.

14. Ibid., pp. 394ff.

15. See Charles E. Raven, *Christian Socialism, 1848–1854* (London: Macmillan, 1920). Raven speaks quite critically of all the Churches in England in the initial stage of the industrial revolution. The Church of England gave loyal support to privilege and the status quo; the Methodists preached a contempt for this life and were generally blind to social problems; the Oxford Movement was openly hostile to social

reformers (ibid., pp. 6–16). When Robert Owen, the English pioneer of socialism, embarked on his New Lanark experiment to create a new community for industrial workers, Church leaders attacked his views and provoked his strong antipathy toward religion (ibid., pp. 44–47). Raven also notes, however, that some clergy did speak out in favor of the 1832 Reform Bill and that Thomas Carlyle's writings won their sympathy for the Chartist movement (ibid., p. 53).

16. On Bishop von Ketteler and Social Catholicism in Germany, see Edgar Alexander in *Church and Society,* pp. 407ff. See also Vidler, *Social Catholicism.* Alexander notes that Bishop Ketteler did not hesitate to cite Frederick Engels in one of his writings, p. 415.

17. Vidler, *Social Catholicism,* p. 107.

18. For Leo XIII's early encyclicals see Joseph Husslein, S.J., *Social Wellsprings, Fourteen Epochal Documents by Pope Leo XIII* (Milwaukee: Bruce, 1940). Gaete, in "Socialism and Communism," argues that Leo's encyclical *Quod Apostolici Muneris* intended Bakunin's Alliance as its main target in condemning socialism.

19. The text of *Rerum Novarum* can be found in *Five Great Encyclicals* (New York: Paulist Press, 1955, first edition 1939). References in this chapter are given according to paragraph numbers of the text.

20. The premises underlying the pope's analysis and those of a Marxist analysis diverge in several ways. The pope accepts different classes in society as natural (RN, n. 15); Marxism sees them as created by private property. The pope assumes change must begin with the moral and religious attitudes of individuals (RN, nn. 13,16); Marxism contends that material conditions create attitudes and hence the conditions must change. The pope assumes that human nature can never be completely free of original sin (RN, nn. 14, 27); Marxism believes a "new person" will result from socialism.

21. The pontiff uses agricultural images consistently to defend private property: "God has given the earth" for the use of all. 'Those who do not possess the soil, contribute their labor." When a person works "he makes his own that portion of nature's field which he cultivates . . ." (RN, nn. 7–8).

22. A still later statement by Pius X to Italian Christian Democrats, in 1903, provides a striking example of this traditional mind-set in respect to class distinctions: "It is in conformity with the order established by God that there shall be in human society princes and subjects, capitalists and proletarians, rich and poor, the learned and the ignorant, nobles and plebeians." Cited in Vidler, *Social Catholicism,* p. 138.

23. Aaron I. Abell, *American Catholicism and Social Action: A Search for Social Justice, 1865–1950* (Garden City, N.Y.: Doubleday, 1960), chapter 2.

24. See David J. O'Brien, *American Catholics and Social Reform, The New Deal Years* (New York: Oxford University Press, 1968), p. 33, and Francis Downing, "American Catholicism and the Socio-Economic Evolution in U.S.A.," in *Church and Society,* p. 862.

25. Abell, *American Catholicism,* p. 171.

26. Downing, in *Church and Society,* pp. 853, 862, 869.

27. John A. Ryan, "May a Catholic be a Socialist?" in *The Catholic Fortnightly Review,* First February issue, 1909, Vol. XVI. n. 3., pp. 70–73.

28. Ibid., p. 72.

29. Ibid., p. 73.

30. Francis L. Broderick, *Right Reverend New Dealer John A. Ryan* (New York:

Macmillan, 1963), pp. 59–61.

31. The Ryan-Hillquit debates were published in Morris Hillquit and John A. Ryan, *Socialism: Promise or Menace?* (New York: Macmillan, 1914). For background on the debates see Broderick, *Right Reverend New Dealer,* pp. 87–89.

32. John A. Ryan, *The Church and Socialism and Other Essays* (Washington, D.C.: The Catholic University of America Press, 1919), p. 21.

33. Ibid., p. 22.

34. The bishops' Program called for minimum wage legislation, insurance against unemployment, sickness and old age, a minimum age limit for work, the legal enforcement of the right of labor to organize, public housing for the working class, government prevention of excessive profits and incomes, and the participation of labor in management. See *Church and Society,* pp. 874 and 889–92.

35. Broderick, *Right Reverend New Dealer,* p. 106.

36. Charles H. Hopkins, *The Rise of the Social Gospel in American Protestantism, 1865–1915* (New Haven: Yale University Press, 1940), Chapter 1.

37. Henry F. May, *Protestant Churches and Industrial America* (New York: Harper & Brothers, 1949), pp. 69ff.

38. Hopkins, *Social Gospel,* pp. 73–76.

39. Ibid., p. 84.

40. Ibid., pp. 79–81.

41. May, *Protestant Churches,* pp. 249ff.

42. Hopkins, *Social Gospel,* pp. 195–96.

43. On Rauschenbusch's economic proposals, see Frank Grace, *The Concept of Property in Modern Christian Thought* (Urbana, Ill.: University of Illinois Press, 1953), pp. 103ff.

44. See Donald B. Meyer, *The Protestant Search for Political Realism. 1919–1941* (Berkeley: University of California Press, 1960), Chap. I and II.

45. See ibid., p. 232, and May, *Protestant Churches,* pp. 257–61.

46. The text of *Quadragesimo Anno,* on "Reconstructing the Social Order " can be found in *Five Great Encyclicals.* See also the commentary by Oswald von Nell-Breuning, S.J., *Reorganization of Social Economy* (Milwaukee: Bruce, 1936).

47. In reference to medieval society Pius XI speaks of "the highly developed social life which once flourished" but which is now so damaged or ruined that only individuals and the state remain (QA, n. 78). "At one period there existed a social order which, though by no means perfect in every respect, corresponded nevertheless in a certain measure to right reason . . ." (QA, n. 97). His stress on restoring harmony can be seen in QA, nn. 81, 95, 147.

48. Charles P. Bruehl, *The Pope's Plan for Social Reconstruction, A Commentary on the Social Encyclicals of Pius XI* (New York: Devin-Adair, 1939) places great stress on the *limits* of private property in commenting on Pius' views. See Chapters 5–8.

49. Bruehl, *The Pope's Plan,* devotes eleven chapters (Chapters 19–29) to the ideas of "corporatism" touched on in Pius XI's encyclicals. See also Chapter XIX of Jean-Yves Calvez, S.J., and Jacques Perrin, S.J., *The Church and Social Justice, The Social Teachings of the Popes from Leo XIII to Pius XII, 1878–1958* (Chicago: Regnery, 1961).

50. On the history of "corporatist" ideas see Ralph H. Bowen, *German Theories of the Corporative State, With Special Reference to the Period 1870–1919* (New York: Whittlesey House, McGraw-Hill, 1947). See also Richard L. Camp, *The Papal Ideology*

of Social Reform (Leiden: E. J. Brill, 1969), pp. 66, 97.

On corporatist opposition to individualist capitalism see Bowen, *The Corporative State*, p. 98. See also Pius XI, QA, nn. 10, 14, 25–30.

51. Christopher Hollis, *Christianity and Economics* (New York: Hawthorn, 1961), pp. 66–73, discusses in detail what forms of socialism Pius intended to condemn and what forms he was not attacking.

52. On the background to *Divini Redemptoris,* see John P. Lerhinan C. Ss. R., *A Sociological Commentary on 'Divini Redemptoris'* (Washington, D. C.: The Catholic University of America Press, 1946), pp. xvi–xx.

53. The text of *Divini Redemptoris,* "On Atheistic Communism," can also be found in *Five Great Encyclicals.*

54. Dennis McCann, "Reinhold Niebuhr and Jacques Maritain on Marxism: A Comparison of Two Traditional Models of Practical Theology," in *The Journal of Religion,* Vol. 58, No. 2, April 1978, pp. 140–68. Maritain's own work on political theology was *Integral Humanism, Temporal and Spiritual Problems of a New Christendom* (Notre Dame, Ind.: University of Notre Dame Press, 1973 edition).

55. Calvez, *The Church and Social Justice,* pp. 194 ff.

56. Henri Chambre, *Christianity and Communism,* pp. 27–29.

57. See André Dumas, "The Social Thought of the World Council of Churches from 1925 to 1966," in *Church Alert* (Sodepax), No. 17, November–December 1977, pp. 7–12.

58. Charles C. West, *Communism and the Theologians, Study of an Encounter* (Philadelphia: Westminster Press, 1958) has long served as an important study of Niebuhr, Tillich, Barth, and other Protestant theologians on Marxism/socialism.

59. Paul Tillich, *Political Expectation* (New York: Harper & Row, 1971), from the Introduction by James Luther Adams, p. xvi.

60. Ibid., from an essay on "Religious Socialism," pp. 48ff.

61. Ibid., pp. 40–41.

62. Ibid., from an essay on "Basic Principles of Religious Socialism," p. 88.

63. Ibid., from an essay on "Christianity and Marxism," p. 92.

64. Meyer, *The Protestant Search for Political Realism,* pp. 174–75, notes that of 20,000 clergymen who responded to a questionnaire in 1934 only 5 percent favored capitalism as a system and 28 percent favored socialism. Among members of the progressive Fellowship for Reconciliation, in a poll on preferred presidential candidates, 75 percent indicated support for Norman Thomas of the Socialist Party.

65. Gordon Harland, *The Thought of Reinhold Niebuhr* (New York: Oxford University Press, 1960), p. 236.

66. Reinhold Niebuhr, *Moral Man and Immoral Society* (New York: Charles Scribner's Sons, 1960, original 1932), p. 144.

67. Ibid., p. 157.

68. Ibid., p. 165.

69. Harland, *The Thought of Reinhold Niebuhr,* pp. 175–79.

70. Reinhold Niebuhr, *The Nature and Destiny of Man, A Christian Interpretation,* Volumes I–II (London: Nisbet, 1941, 1943). The five points of criticism noted in this chapter are drawn from McCann, "Reinhold Niebuhr and Jacques Maritain."

71. Niebuhr, *The Nature and Destiny of Man,* Volume I, pp. 49–50.

72. Ibid., Vol. I, p. 209.

73. Ibid., Vol. II, p. 91.

74. Ibid., p. 251.

75. Ibid., pp. 262–64.

76. The texts for these three documents can be found in *The Gospel of Peace and Justice*, ed. Joseph Gremillion (Maryknoll, N.Y.: Orbis, 1976).

77. See Donald R. Campion, S.J., "The World-wide Response," in *The Challenge of Mater et Magistra*, ed. Joseph N. Moody and Justus George Lawler (New York: Herder & Herder, 1963), pp. 155–62.

78. On the idea of "co-determination" see Jean-Yves Calvez, S. J., *The Social Thought of John XXIII, Mater et Magistra*, trans. G.J.M. McKenzie, S.M. (Chicago: Regnery, 1964), Chapter III. On silence about "corporatism" see Campion, *The Challenge of Mater et Magistra*, pp. 174–76.

79. On the new historical consciousness of the Catholic Church see John W. O'Malley, S.J., "Reform, Historical Consciousness, and Vatican II's Aggiornamento," in *Theological Studies*, Vol. 32, No. 4, December 1971, pp. 573–601.

80. Calvez, *The Social Thought of John XXIII*, pp. 22 ff.

81. On private property in *Mater et Magistra* see also Gremillion's Introduction in *The Gospel of Peace and Justice*, pp. 27–35.

82. The need to find correct "balances" is expressed at various points in *Mater et Magistra*, especially in its discussion of private initiative and state intervention (MM, nn. 52–58, 66), and in its reaffirmation of the principle of subsidiarity (MM, nn. 53, 117). See also Calvez, *The Social Thought of John XXIII*, Chapters IV and V.

83. On the dignity of the person, see *Pacem in Terris*, n. 11, and *Gaudium et Spes*, n. 63.

84. See Paul Emile Bolté, S.S., *Mater et Magistra, Commentaire*, Volume I (Montreal: Université de Montreal, 1964), pp. 103–10. See also Campion, *The Challenge of Mater et Magistra*, p. 186.

85. On "socialization" see Calvez, *The Social Thought of John XXIII*, Chapter 1 and Bolté, *Mater et Magistra*, pp. 231ff.

86. On the council debate as to whether Communism should be condemned, see the note in *The Documents of Vatican II*, ed. Walter Abbott, S.J. (New York: America Press, 1966), p. 217.

87. Pierre Bigo, S.J., *Marxisme et humanisme, Introduction à l'oeuvre économique de Karl Marx* (Paris: Presses Universitaires de France, 1953); Jean-Yves Calvez, S.J., *La Pensée de Karl Marx* (Paris: Editions du Seuil, 1956); Henri Chambre, S.J., *From Karl Marx to Mao Tse-Tung*, trans. Robert J. Olsen (New York: Kenedy & Sons, 1963); Gustav Wetter, S.J., *Dialectical Materialism*, trans. Peter Heath (New York: Praeger, 1958).

88. The history of these first meetings of the Paulus Society and of the Salzburg conference is taken from "Dialogue Between Catholics and Communists" in *Herder Correspondence*, Vol. 2, Nos. 9–10, September–October 1965, pp. 325–30. Thomas J. Reese, S.J., *The Christian-Marxist Dialogue*, an unpublished master's thesis, St. Louis University, 1968, was also a helpful source.

89. The Salzburg conference focused on the theme of "Man and Religion." Several Marxists acknowledged the inadequacy of the Marxist critique of religion. Roger Garaudy's book *From Anathema to Dialogue* developed out of a paper he gave. Conference papers were published in *Marxistes et chrétiens, Entretiens de Salzbourg*, trans. Michel Louis (Paris: Mame, 1968).

90. See "Christians and Marxists at Herrenchiemsee," in the *Herder Correspondence*,

Vol. 3, No. 8., August 1966, pp. 243–47. The theme of this conference was "Christian Ideal of Humanity and Marxist Humanism."

91. "Juxtapositions at Marienbad," in the *Herder Correspondence,* Vol. 4, No. 9. September 1967, pp. 267–71. Quote, p. 268.

92. Peter Hebblethwaite reported on the 1960s dialogues for *The Month* (June 1966; June 1967) and for the *Tablet* (May 6, 1967). In his book, *The Christian-Marxist Dialogue* (New York: Paulist Press, 1977), he concludes that the record of these dialogues provides no evidence of convergence between the two sides (p. 37). The Marxists who participated, he claims, were revisionists and heretics who had no power. Institutional Marxists never shared their doubts and questioning (p. 30).

For a more positive evaluation of what these dialogues were achieving in Czechoslovakia prior to 1968 see Jan M. Lochman, "Marxism, Liberalism, and Religion: An East European Perspective," in *Marxism and Radical Religion, Essays Toward a Revolutionary Humanism,* ed. John C. Raines and Thomas Dean (Philadelphia: Temple University Press, 1970).

93. Books and periodicals on Marxist-Christian dialogue from the United States include: Gus Hall, *Catholics and Communists, Elements of a Dialogue* (New York: Political Affairs, June 1964); Herbert Aptheker, *The Urgency of Marxist-Christian Dialogue* (New York: Harper & Row, 1970) and *Marxism and Christianity* (New York: Humanities, 1966); Roger Garaudy and Quentin Lauer, *A Christian-Communist Dialogue* (Garden City, N.Y.: Doubleday, 1968); *The Christian-Marxist Dialogue,* ed. Paul Oestreicher (Toronto: Macmillan, 1969); *Openings for Marxist-Christian Dialogue,* ed. Thomas W. Ogletree (Nashville: Abingdon, 1968); *From Hope to Liberation: Towards a New Marxist-Christian Dialogue,* ed. Nicholas Piediscalzi and Robert B. Thobaben (Philadelphia: Fortress, 1974), several issues of the *Journal of Ecumenical Studies* (Spring and Summer 1967, Winter 1972, Summer 1978) and *New Catholic World,* (May-June 1977).

94. See André Dumas, in *Church Alert* (SODEPAX), No. 17, November–December 1977, p. 11.

95. The text of *Populorum Progressio* can be found in Gremillion, *The Gospel of Peace and Justice.*

96. Later in the encyclical, addressing the issue of violence and revolution, the pontiff declared that "a revolutionary uprising—save where there is manifest long-standing tyranny . . . produces new injustices" (PP, n. 31). This statement led to subsequent controversy since quite different conclusions could be drawn from it, depending on whether one stressed the "long-standing tyranny" or the "new injustices."

97. Two studies which reflect changes within the Church in Latin America are: Enrique Dussel, *History and the Theology of Liberation,* trans. John Drury (Maryknoll, N.Y.: Orbis, 1976), and Hugo Latorre Cabal, *The Revolution of the Latin American Church,* trans. Frances K. Hendricks and Beatrice Berler (Norman, Oklahoma: University of Oklahoma, 1978).

98. See Dussel, ibid., p. 114.

99. See Cabal, ibid., pp. 49ff.

100. The text of *Octogesima Adveniens* can be found in Gremillion, *The Gospel of Peace and Justice.*

101. "Justice in the World" found also in Gremillion, nn. 5, 30.

102. Adrian Cunningham et al., *Catholics and the Left: Slant Manifesto* (Springfield, Illinois: Templegate, 1966), pp. 7–9.

103. Ibid., p. 23.

104. Ibid., pp. 47–49. Chapter 11 of the Slant Manifesto argues for points of similarity between Marxism and Christianity: both are historical movements working for "liberation"; both are committed to changing the world; both are committed to the unity of all humanity.

105. Denys Turner, "Can a Christian be a Marxist?" in *New Blackfriars*, June 1975, Vol. 56, No. 661, pp. 244–53. A response to Turner's argument was made by Brian Wicker, "Marxists and Christians: Questions for Denys Turner," and in turn to Wicker by Terry Eagleton, "Marxists and Christians: Answers for Brian Wicker," in *New Blackfriars*, October 1975, Vol. 56, No. 665, pp. 467–70.

106. Phillipe Warnier, *Marx pour un chrétien* (Paris: Fayard-Mame, 1977).

107. Ibid., pp. 64–73.

108. In espousing a critical Marxism Warnier builds especially on Althusser's distinction between ideology and science. He argues that humanism, ethical choices, and freedom all form a necessary part of revolutionary praxis, which is *not* science. Praxis uses science, but it is not determined by it (pp. 127–34). Warnier argues also from this distinction that Marx's thought is necessarily dualistic and not monistic as is commonly held (p. 212).

109. Ibid., p. 222.

110. The declaration of Cardinal Poma can be found in *La Documentation Catholique*, June 6, 1976, No. 1699. The same periodicals contain episcopal statements by the bishops of Sees and of Strasbourg in France (April 4, 1976, No. 1695 and August 1–15, 1976, No. 1703).

111. The Permanent Council of French Bishops, "Le Marxisme, l'homme et la foi chrétienne," in *Cahiers de l'actualité religieuse et sociale*, September 15, 1977, No. 147. References to the text are given by paragraph numbers.

112. Georges G. Marchais, *Communistes et chrétiens* (Paris: Editions Sociales, 1976), p. 38.

113. French bishops, "Le Marxisme," n. 50.

114. Ibid., nn. 17–23. The Bishops also warn that Christian acceptance of Marxism risks reducing the faith and substituting a terrestrial mission for the kingdom of God (n. 54).

115. Bishops of the Antilles Episcopal Conference, 'Justice and Peace in a New Caribbean," in LADOC (Washington, D.C.: Latin America Documentation), Vol. VI, No. 33, July–August 1976.

PART II
THE IMPACT OF MARXISM
ON CHRISTIAN SOCIAL THOUGHT
AND ACTION

Chapter 4

The Case Against Capitalism

Why, after more than a century of opposition to Marxism, have many Christians turned toward Marxism, and toward the use of Marxist analysis especially. Three interrelated factors have contributed to this. First many Christians are deeply troubled by conditions in the world, by the vast gap between wealthy, affluent peoples and desperately poor ones, by vast expenditures on military weapons and luxury goods while basic human needs go unmet, by the growing power of giant corporations, and by a culture that undermines Christian values and true human needs. Second, many Christians have developed a new awareness of their faith, of its call to denounce injustice, to be on the side of the poor and the oppressed, and to transform the world. Third, many have come to the realization that ways of addressing these concerns in the past have failed. Charity toward the poor, appeals to the rich and the powerful, the promise of technology, reliance on political changes, all these have failed. Marxists have long argued that there are *structural* reasons for these failures, that inequality, oppression, powerlessness, and false values are natural consequences of the very logic of the capitalist system. Many Christians have become convinced that they should learn from Marxist analysis, if they want to create a more just and human society. This chapter thus investigates what Marxists and other critics have to say about the capitalist system.

The chapter will focus primarily on concrete socio-economic problems related to capitalism. Marxist critiques of capitalism are often highly technical and abstract. They include discussions of Marx's labor theory of value, his theory of crises leading to the collapse of capitalism, contending neo-Marxist theories of crises, Marxist theories of monopoly capitalism and imperialism, neo-Marxist theories of the capitalist state, and neo-Marxist analyses of class structures in advanced capitalist countries. Books are available which focus on Marxist economic theory as such.[1] But the present chapter deals rather with more concrete issues, issues which explain why Christians are drawn to Marxist analysis in the first place. Some of the theoretical issues emerge in the course of the chapter but others have been relegated to footnotes or to the conclusion of the chapter. This chapter does not claim, therefore, to offer a strict, consistently Marxist analysis. Some of the most convincing arguments against capitalism often come from non-Marxist sources. Some of the issues, for example on values, reflect Christian concerns rather than Marxist perspectives. But Marxist theories on imperialism, on ideology, on alienation, and on the state, do provide approaches to the major problem areas discussed in the chapter: poverty and inequality, materialistic values and priorities, and capitalist domination of the state.

If this approach proves less than satisfying to a Marxist, critics of Marxism will certainly challenge the one-sidedness of its views on capitalism. The chapter is one-sided and the radical views it presents should not be accepted uncritically. A far more critical and careful evaluation is called for, if truth and justice are the goals. But the case *for* capitalism hardly suffers from lack of defenders.[2] Most U.S. Americans have an awareness of specific problems besetting U.S. society but rarely read or hear of analyses which look at the system as a whole. *Time, Newsweek,* newspapers, television, textbooks in history and economics, all give constant reaffirmation that "for all its faults capitalism is still the best." Milton Friedman and Paul Samuelson have regular columns in popular periodicals; Marxist economists do not. The chapter does take note of contending views and it does challenge Marxist positions that seem without substance. While it focuses on the central issue raised by Marxism about capitalism as a system, it certainly recognizes the complexity of social reality and that no one factor ever explains all. Foreign imperialism is not the sole determining cause of Third World poverty; racism, sexism, and state power cannot be simply reduced to economic causes. Nor does a criticism of capitalism suffice to show socialism would be better; communism and socialism must both be evaluated on their own merits. But granting all this, it seems important to address forcefully the issue: does the capitalist system create fundamental obstacles to the realization of a more just and human society?

Opposition to capitalism, as will be seen in the next two chapters, is far stronger in Latin America than in the United States. The use of Marxist analysis is consequently far more influential there also. This chapter deals primarily with the United States, but the section on imperialism will help to explain Latin American attitudes as well.

Earlier we said that discussion of Marxist economic theory would be taken up in the context of specific issues or relegated to a concluding section of the chapter. An immediate exception to that needs to be made. Capitalism itself has changed dramatically since Marx first wrote. Giant corporations have gained ascendency over smaller competitive enterprises; technocratic bureaucracies with many levels of executive or managerial authority have replaced individual or family owner-managers; multinational corporations have extended the power of capitalism far beyond what Marx observed; the state, whose intervention in economic affairs laissez-faire capitalism strongly opposed, has become an integral part of the economic system. We need to begin, therefore, by discussing stages of capitalist development and corresponding developments in Marxist thought.

Developments in Capitalism and Marxist Analysis

Recognition of the dehumanizing effects of industrial capitalism in the nineteenth century required no special insight or analysis. Fourteen-hour working days, children working in mines, women in congested textile factories, workers crowded into slum dwellings sleeping several to a room, these were all too evident for anyone who had to live under such conditions or who took time to observe them. The novels of Charles Dickens, the pamphlets of utopian socialists, the sermons of clergy who allowed themselves to become involved, all decried the dark and dehumanizing side of capitalism. What made Marx different, and what caused social movements to develop in his name, was his effort to go beyond descriptions, impressions, and moral outcries to an analysis of capitalism as a system. He challenged the pretensions of a property system which assumed as natural and fair a division between capitalist owners and wage-earning laborers. He claimed that the system was not natural at all, and that the wealth it produced for owners could be explained only in terms of exploitation of workers. He also saw it as a system so riddled with inner contradictions that its collapse would be inevitable.

One central thesis of Marx's analysis has remained a constant in Marxism up to the present, whatever other developments or disagreements may have occurred. It holds that a fundamental cause of socio-economic problems can be traced to the capitalist mode of production in which ownership, control, and profit remain in private hands. Under capitalism maximization of profits is the driving force of the system. Profits, which accrue to the owners, are primary; other social priorities are secondary. Expansion and profit-maximization are not simply a consequence of the greed of individual capitalists; they flow from the very logic of the system itself. The system, Marxism argues, leads inevitably to contradictions and crises which necessarily generate inequality and unemployment, class divisions, and other problems noted earlier. Hence no real solution of these problems can come about until the capitalist system is replaced by social ownership and social planning.

As the century moved on, time seemed to be working against Marx's conviction that capitalism would be replaced by a new socialist society. Capitalists proved adept at making concessions when faced with the power of organized workers. Workers, even those within Marxist-inspired Social Democratic parties, began placing greater reliance on trade-union struggles and legal reforms. The Churches, more conscious of workers' conditions but still fearful of atheistic, revolutionary socialist movements, pleaded for reforms that would end conflict and would lead to a more just social order. Wages did increase; working hours were shortened; working conditions did improve. Political democracy and the legalization of unions seemed to provide an alternative to socialism. Capitalism seemed capable of surmounting its inherent problems and criticisms raised against it. But the very developments which gave new stability and strength to capitalism generated their own set of problems and new openings for Marxist criticism.

1. *Monopoly Capitalism and Imperialism.* In 1916 Lenin wrote *Imperialism: The Highest Stage of Capitalism.*[3] He sought to explain why capitalism had not collapsed, and why workers had grown less revolutionary and had abandoned "international solidarity" by supporting their governments in a capitalist World War. Lenin found the answer to these questions in the analysis of a new stage of development within capitalism. J. A. Hobson, Rudolf Hilferding, Karl Kautsky, Rosa Luxemburg, and others had made similar analyses, but the prominence which Lenin would gain through the Bolshevik victory in Russia lent special authority to his work.

Significant changes had occurred within the capitalist system. It had become increasingly "monopolistic" and increasingly "imperialistic." Lenin noted five characteristics of this new stage. (1) Concentration of production. Competition between many smaller companies was being transformed into the monopoly of a few. In the United States one percent of the enterprises accounted for half of the total production. Through different types of mergers and agreements—trusts, cartels, syndicates—industry had become concentrated. This change diminished dependency on a fluctuating market, it created greater price stability, and it eliminated much of the anarchy of earlier capitalism. (2) Concentration of finance. The same mergers were taking place in banking. Banks were no longer simply "modest middlemen" for the transfer of money. They were powerful monopolies in their own right, able to make or break industrial companies by their control of finance capital. (3) Export of capital. Overproduction had plagued capitalism earlier and had been partially relieved by the "export of goods" to foreign countries. Now capitalist countries were using foreign countries and colonies as the focus for investment of surplus capital, with the benefit of added profits through the use of cheaper labor and cheaper raw materials. (4) Division of territorial interests. As foreign markets grew and monopolies expanded, international agreements and cartels began to take shape. Agreements on "spheres of influence" permitted giant corporations to avoid price wars and loss of profit. (5) Division of the world into colonies. The most striking and obvious "imperialism" took the form of direct political conquest of colonies. In Africa alone, during the last quarter of the nineteenth-century, over 90 percent of the continent was taken over by various European powers. Colonies gave assured control over raw materials, provided the guarantee of new markets, and permitted surplus population to resettle. In short, an imperialistic, monopolistic capitalism had replaced the capitalism of free competition known to Marx.

These changes expanded the life-expectancy of capitalism. For the new capitalism included more planning, new markets for goods, new outlets for investment and expansion. Of great significance for Marxist revolutionary movements, this change shifted the focus of "exploitation." The greatest victims of exploitation were now poor *nations* of the world. This change also explained in part the loss of revolutionary consciousness among workers and their support of World War I. For a section of the working class, the "labor aristocracy," now profited from imperialism and could be bribed into accepting capitalism. Lenin viewed imperialistic expansion as "necessary" for capitalism and he also believed that wars between capitalist nations would inevitably result from competition for markets and colonies.

What Lenin considered monopolies in 1916 would be dwarfs in comparison to the giant corporations of today. While some corporate growth developed gradually over the century, the largest wave of mergers in U.S. history began in the 1960s. John Kenneth Galbraith drew popular attention to this phenomenon in his *The New Industrial State* (1967). The dominant feature of the new industrial system, he argued, was the influence and control exerted by 400-500 giant corporations.[4] Their growth continued through the 1970s. In 1970 the top four firms in motor vehicles accounted for 91 percent of all output, the top four in tires 72 percent, in cigarettes 84 percent, in detergents 70 percent.[5] The automobile industry dramatically illustrates the monopolization of industrial production. In 1909 there were 265 auto producers in the country, by 1921 only 88, by 1926 only 44, by 1955 only six.[6] There are still nearly 11 million business enterprises in the U.S., but 97 percent have business receipts under $1 million; wealth and profits are concentrated elsewhere. By 1973 the top 100 manufacturing corporations accounted for nearly 50 percent of all profits in manufacturing. The top 200 got 70 percent, the top 500 got 80 percent. These top 500 had assets of more than $500 billion, sales of more than $600 billion, and profits of almost $40 billion.[7] Banks show the same concentration of wealth and power, and the top five insurance companies account for nearly one-half of all life insurance in force.[8]

Industrial mergers have taken different forms. Some are horizontal, with one company buying out a company producing the same product; others have been vertical, with one company buying out its suppliers or customers. The most significant change has been in the growth of giant conglomerates controlling scores of disparate businesses. Now Gulf & Western includes in its conglomerate Paramount Pictures, Simon and Schuster publishers, Madison Square Garden sports, Dutch Master cigars, Schrafft candies, sugar companies in the Dominican Republic and Puerto Rico, Catalina swim wear, insurance companies and auto parts manufacturers—to name only some.

Studies of "interlocking directorates" show that representatives of the same banks and corporations provide boards of directors for each other.[9] Fewer than a thousand persons, Richard Barnet contends, are the principal decision makers in the 200 top industrial corporations and the 20 largest banks which control a huge proportion of the nation's wealth.[10] These few individuals plan what is best for the society.

The rise of multinational corporations (MNCs) has been even more dramatic. In 1970, 7 percent of American corporate profits derived from abroad; by 1974, 30 percent.[11] Profits from abroad run consistently higher than domestic profits, in some cases dramatically so. In 1972 United Brands reported a 72.1 percent return on net assets and Exxon 52.5 percent.[12] In the same year some $500 billion of the world's productivity was attributable to multinationals. Professor Howard Perlmutter of the Wharton School estimated that by 1985, 200 to 300 global corporations will control 80 percent of all productive assets of the non-Communist world.[13]

Big does not necessarily mean bad. But it does mean power. How the policies of some multinational corporations have affected many poor nations will be seen later in the chapter.

2. Monopoly Capitalism and the State. Increasing state intervention into the economy has become, along with multinationals, the most significant development in capitalism in recent decades. Conventional economists call it "Keynesian" economics. Conservatives have reacted against it since it interferes with the natural forces of a free market. For neo-Marxists it means that the state has become "the guarantor of capitalist profits" through its distribution of defense contracts and subsidies, its tax credits and reductions, its bearing the burden of welfare and social insurance which the economy itself should provide. The state no longer functions simply as a regulator of conflicts *above* civil society, as Marx described it, but as an integral part of the economic structure. Government spending now accounts for nearly one-third of the entire GNP.

Jürgen Habermas, James O'Connor, Michael Harrington, and others have analyzed this change. Concrete examples and implications of this analysis will be taken up later in discussing the "capitalist domination of the state." At this point it may suffice to indicate the main outlines of this analysis, drawing upon James O'Connor's *The Fiscal Crisis of the State.* The state, in modern capitalism, must fulfill two basic and often mutually contradictory functions—accumulation and legitimization. "This means that the state must try to maintain or create the conditions in which profitable capital accumulation is possible. However, the state must also try to maintain or create the conditions for social harmony."[14] The state, for the most part, does not enter into the race of commodity production for profit. Rather it creates conditions for *private* accumulation; it subsidizes private capitalist enterprises in their productive efforts. But it also bears the social costs, for example, of welfare, created by the private enterprise system. The fiscal crisis O'Connor speaks of is the "tendency of government expenditures to outrace revenues." Put in more concrete terms: everyone wants more government money. Corporations want more freeways, bankers want the government to underwrite more loans, welfare recipients want higher allowances and more housing. But no one wants to foot the bill and pay higher taxes.

State expenditures to aid accumulation take two forms: social investment and social consumption.[15] Social investment can take the form of building interstate freeways or airports, undertaking urban renewal, building dams or waterways, or perhaps funding research. This investment provides direct subsidies to capitalist enterprises. Auto companies, for example, do not have to bear the cost of roads essential for their product. Social consumption might take the form of providing job-training, workers' compensation, health insurance, etc. These, too, serve to subsidize private enterprises since the government carries the cost of programs which would otherwise have to be added to wages.

State expenditures to carry out the legitimization function of the state take the form of social expenses. Business enterprises have profits as their goal which means keeping costs at a minimum and operating as efficiently as possible. The state picks up most of the bill for all those left unemployed. The other major social expense is "warfare" or military spending. It is a 'social expense" because it produces no consumer goods but it also serves the legitimizing function of maintaining national defense. Together military spending and social welfare spending make up 75 percent of all government expenditures. Both serve the interests of private enterprise. Welfare mollifies the discontent created by unemployment; military spending provides an outlet for surplus productivity and a great source of profit. In the public eye, the state receives the blame when it fails to provide the expenditures demanded or when it increases tax burdens in an attempt to provide them. The real cause of the fiscal crisis, in O'Connor's analysis, is the economic system which the state attempts to subsidize.

The above analysis bears more directly on the issue of capitalist domination of the state; the following section draws more upon the preceding analysis of monopoly capitalism and imperialism.

Poverty and Inequality

The president of the World Bank, Robert S. McNamara, estimated a few years ago that nearly 800 million individuals survive on incomes estimated at 30 cents a day in U.S. purchasing power, and live in conditions of malnutrition, illiteracy, and squalor.[16] Hundreds of millions more can barely meet basic human needs. The overwhelming majority of these are in Third World countries, in Latin America, Africa, and Asia. In 1900 the gap between the per capita incomes of the more affluent nations and the poorer ones was two to one. Today the gap is nearly twenty to one.[17] Poverty and inequality are certainly also problems within the United States. But not surprisingly the greatest outcry against the prevailing world economy has come from voices within the Third World. Whether justly or not, they often blame their situation on their economic "dependence" upon the United States and other western European countries. In Latin America this accusation has grown particularly strong and the appeal to Marxist analysis more frequent. In the name of democracy and free enterprise, critics argue, U.S. and European business has gouged out the natural resources of underdeveloped countries, established corporations to exploit cheap labor and bring home immense profits, and influenced government foreign policy in favor of right-wing dictatorships willing to protect U.S. and European business interests. Some Marxists contend that without these markets in which to sell goods and reinvest profits, the capitalist system would face economic crisis. Even Franklin D. Roosevelt once acknowledged: "Foreign markets must be regained if America's producers are to rebuild a full and enduring domestic economy for our people. There is no other way if we would avoid painful economic dislocations, social readjustments, and unemployment."[18]

Critics of Marxism sharply contest these charges. Extreme forms of Marxist criticism, which would make imperialism *the* cause of poverty, and underdevelopment *the* explanation of capitalism's continued survival, do indeed invite refutation. Many factors contribute to underdevelopment—poor soil and poor climate, the lack of technology and capital to meet the needs of exploding populations, vast land holdings possessed by indigenous wealthy families, the failure to develop effective political leadership, and similar considerations. It would also be difficult to "prove" that the United States requires the exploitation of poor nations. Profits from these countries account for a very small percent of our total GNP, and the great bulk of U.S. capital exports goes to advanced, industrialized countries.[19] Nor do foreign investments and poverty go hand in hand; Canada has absorbed the lion's share of U.S. investment without suffering impoverishment.

But if charges can be exaggerated, the substance of the radical criticisms still needs to be examined. If Marxists and other critics sometimes create new myths about underdevelopment, the more prevalent capitalist myths about it should be challenged. For the impact of foreign influence on Third World conditions has been great.

The Third World: How It Got That Way

Since the term "Third World" was first introduced to express non-alignment and then underdevelopment, the terms "Fourth World" and "Fifth World" have been added to distinguish the poorest of these nations. But more controversial have been the expressions "underdeveloped" or "developing." Both can seem to imply that the First World is an ideal model or norm for development. "Underdevelopment" is a negative, pejorative term; "developing," on the other hand, suggests steady improvement and progress.

Paul Sweezy argues that even the term "underdeveloped" is not strong enough to convey the situation in most Third World countries. One should speak of "underdeveloping" countries, for their share of world output is declining. How did the Third World become so poor? Was it always poor? Sweezy challenges the explanation espoused most often by social scientists in

Western countries. The usual theory given is that all countries of the world were underdeveloped until 400-500 years ago when the countries of Western Europe "took off" into development, leaving the others behind. Sweezy responds that it is "absurd" to think of the Third World as similar to the world of Europe in A.D. 1500. "The truth is—and this is the key to understanding the whole of modern history—that the underdevelopment of the Third World is the product of the very same historical process which resulted in the development of the advanced capitalist world. The two, development here and underdevelopment there, are the opposite sides of the very same coin."[20]

From the very beginning, says Sweezy, capitalism advanced by subjugating, plundering, and exploiting foreign countries and territories. The result was a transfer of wealth from the periphery to the metropolis (Europe), destroying the old society in the periphery and concentrating the resources necessary for the "take-off" in the metropolis. Thus Spain and Portugal, then Holland, Britain, and France, extended capitalism across the earth. The social order which the "conquerors" found in Central and South America, in Asia and Africa, was forcibly transformed or destroyed. After the conquerors and looters did their damage, the investors, traders, and administrators came to turn the periphery into colonies and a lasting source of profit for the metropolis. They caused the periphery to specialize in producing raw materials needed in the center and to provide new markets for the manufactured goods of the metropolis. The underdevelopment of the periphery was thus perpetuated and deepened while the center advanced with the wealth it drew from the periphery.[21]

If this is described in rather broad strokes, others have spelled out this history in vivid and disturbing detail. Eduardo Galeano, in *Open Veins of Latin America,* writes angrily of "five centuries of pillage." For the Western world, Columbus, Cortes, and Magellan are remembered as heroes, as bold explorers or conquistadores. But what does history look like from the "underside," from the perspective of native Americans whose land this was and who had built up their own cultures and civilizations? The New World was rich in costly resources that Europe wanted—gold, silver, spices. Not only did the European conquerors plunder these resources, they forced native Indians to rob themselves by working mines and fields, and they only brought in Black slaves from Africa when the Indians could not bear the severity of the work. Christopher Columbus personally directed the pillage of Haiti. His soldiers decimated the Indians in battle; more than five hundred were shipped to Spain where they were sold as slaves in Seville and died miserably.[22] Muskets and cannons enabled the much smaller forces of Cortes and Pizarro to conquer large Incan armies.

The town of Potosi, in Bolivia, symbolizes the pillage of the whole continent. Because of its prolific silver mines it once stood as one of the wealthiest and most populated cities of the New World. Today it is an impoverished ruin. But its silver served to finance the "take-off" of industrialization and economic growth in Europe.[23] And far more than loss of wealth was involved. "Aztecs, Incas, and Mayas totaled between 70 and 90 million when the foreign conquerors appeared on the horizon; a century and a half later they had been reduced to 3.5 million."[24] Little wonder that angry Latin Americans, criticized for underdevelopment, charge that "equal opportunity" would allow them a century to plunder Europe and North America.

If plunder despoiled southern continents, foreign efforts to create "specialized" economies in them have been equally devastating. Today we associate certain products with certain countries—coffee in Brazil, tin in Bolivia, copper in Chile, sugar in Cuba. But the development of such economies came not from initiatives within those countries. Production of these raw materials was developed by European and U.S. companies to meet needs in the "developed world." The concentration on one or two products often upset a natural balance of production and created "one-crop" economies very dependent on the fluctuating prices in the world market for that one crop. Brazil's Northeast was once that country's richest area; now it is its poorest. Portugal granted lands to Brazil's first big landlords. Sugar production flourished for a time, but left a washed-out soil and eroded lands.[25] Barbados in the West Indies suffered the same fate. It once produced a variety of crops in small holdings: cotton and tobacco, oranges, cows and pigs. Canefields devoured all this; the soil was exhausted, unable to feed its population. The story was similar in Africa. Gambia once grew its own rice on land now used to grow peanuts. Northern Ghana grew yams and other foodstuffs on land now devoted to cocoa. Liberia was turned into a virtual rubber plantation. Seizures of land, taxation, the undercutting of domestic prices and forced migrations were all employed by colonizers to gain control of the land.[26]

The economies of most countries in the Third World thus now depend on one or two crops which foreign investors cultivated. Bananas accounted for 58 percent of Panama's export earnings and 48 percent of Honduras's in the early 1970s. Coffee brought in 53 percent of Colombia's foreign exchange and 61 percent of Uganda's. Moreover, their export earnings on foodstuffs have declined as the price of manufactured goods soared. In 1960 three tons of bananas could buy a tractor; in 1970, the same tractor cost the equivalent of eleven tons.[27]

The Third World: Who Profits from Its Production?

When ownership of property is the monopoly of a few, profit-maximization takes precedence over human needs. In nineteenth-century England, land once farmed for food crops by peasant farmers was "enclosed" and converted for sheep grazing to grow wool for the clothing market. Landowners profited from the conversion; thousands of peasants were forced into dire poverty. A parallel pattern has occurred many times over in Latin America and other areas of the Third World. Land that could be used by the poor to feed themselves becomes land given over to cash crops for export. Natural mineral resources that could be tapped to support the populace became instead sources of profit for foreign owners. Ownership and control rest predominately in two hands—wealthy domestic landowners and foreign corporations (plus some domestic capitalists and foreign corporations with vast land holdings). Together they decide in large measure what will be produced and who will profit from it.

In eighty-three poor countries of the world slightly more than 3 percent of all landowners control 80 percent of the farmland.[28] From 30 to 60 percent of all rural adult males in non-socialist countries are landless. Less than one percent of the farms in El Salvador comprise more than 250 acres, yet these few take up half of the total farm area of the country, including all of the prime land. The prime land of these large estates is devoted to exports: cotton, sugar, and coffee crops, and cattle ranches. In Barbados 77 percent of the arable land grows sugar cane alone. Much of the land goes unused. A study two decades ago in Colombia showed rich landowners controlling 70 percent of the country's agricultural land but actually cultivating only 6 percent.[29] In Guatemala the Del Monte corporation owns 57,000 acres but plants only 9,000.[30] In Brazil, one percent of the farms take up 43 percent of the farmland. Four out of five rural families earn less than $33 a month, though a family of three needs an estimated $65 a month just for food alone.[31] Brazil was hailed a few years back for its "miracle growth." The rich indeed did very well; the share of the top 5 percent grew from 29 percent to 38 percent; the living standards of the poorest 40 percent of the population declined.[32]

What can be said of foreign enterprises, of the fruit companies, sugar companies, mining corporations, manufacturers, and banks that invest in the Third World? Doesn't their presence insure needed capital, technology, and know-how to help poor countries to develop? Paul Sweezy noted that in the heyday of British imperialism (1870–1913) the flow of income to Britain exceeded the flow of capital from Britain by 70 percent. Foreign investments by U.S. corporations (1950–63) showed an almost identical percentage of profit: net flow of capital from the United States, $17.4 billion; flow of income to the United States, $29.4 billion.[33] In a study some years ago John Gerassi noted that in Venezuela during the decade of the 1950s barely 10 percent of oil profits—$600 million of $5 billion—remained within the country.[34] If a box of bananas retails at a price of $5.93 in the United States, producers in Honduras gross roughly 66 cents. Chain supermarkets in the United States gross $1.90 on the same box. Migrant coffee workers in Guatemala earn $1 a day; workers on tea plantations in Sri Lanka make $11 to $14 a month.[35]

"Let the market decide" and "consumer sovereignty" are bywords justifying the capitalist system. But the consumer who decides is the consumer who
has money, and profits are determined by this. The poor and hungry cannot
buy food enough to match the profits that can be made on exports. So Central
America sends its vegetables to the United States where 65 percent are
dumped or used as animal feed because their quality is not good enough or
markets are oversupplied. Mexico grows strawberries, cantaloupes, and as-
paragus for Del Monte and other U.S. corporations to sell in the United
States. Colombia grows flowers for export because one hectare of flowers
brings nine times the profit that wheat or corn could.[36]

Why don't governments in these countries make a change? Because their
officials often share in profit-making land or business enterprises, and when
countries do attempt revolutionary change, as Cuba and Chile did, the
United States uses punitive tactics. The United States cut its aid drastically to
Chile when Allende took power and pressured banks to cut off loans (see
Chapter 6). In response to radical critics of the multinationals, John Kenneth
Galbraith has attempted to defend their positive achievements and to distinguish these from their abuses. Multinationals differ considerably in the
responsibility they exercise in use of their power. The governments of
developing nations also differ in the control they exert, with some insisting
on measures which protect against socially damaging corporate policies and
others allowing great abuses to go unchecked. Galbraith feels that multinationals are necessary for transferring technology, management and capital to
countries which need these for development.[37]

Poverty and Inequality in the United States

The United States is the richest country in the world. Its very affluence
makes it a target for condemnation by poorer nations. The buying power of
its citizens enables multinationals to import the foodstuffs and goods needed
by the poor in exporting countries. Billions in the United States are spent on
cosmetics, entertainment, and junk food. But our very affluence raises a
disturbing question. How can the wealthiest and most powerful nation in the
world allow millions of its own people to remain unemployed, poorly
housed, and poorly fed? How can one judge capitalism successful, even in the
United States, when some 25 million of its people live below the poverty
threshold and nearly double that number would be in poverty except for
government aid?[38] A University of Michigan study in 1970 showed 5 percent
of family units had upwards of 40 percent of all personal wealth, and the
bottom *half* of wealth-holders accounted for only 3 percent of the net worth
of all Americans. It showed the top 20 percent of family units had three times
the net worth of the bottom 80 percent.[39] U.S. Census statistics for 1972
showed that wealthy families in the United States, with $60,000 or more in
gross assets, held $629 billion in corporate stocks. The wealthiest *one* percent

accounted for one-fourth the value of all gross personal assets, worth $1000 billion. They held 56 percent of all corporate stock, 60 percent of the bonds, nearly 90 percent of trusts.[40]

Countless studies have been made on inequality of income and wealth distribution in the United States.[41] The fact of inequality alone is unlikely to evoke the moral energy needed to effect radical change. The fact that millions of sports fans seem to feel that the million-dollar contracts offered their sports heroes are justified may be just one indication of this. Defenders of capitalism may point to the fact that while inflation has driven prices sky high, the median family income in the United States rose dramatically from $3,319 in 1950 to over $16,000 in 1977.[42] They may also point to the decline in poverty—thanks chiefly to government transfers—from 40 million (22 percent) below the poverty line in 1960 to 25 million (11.6 percent) in 1977. One *ought* to feel outraged, however, by the fact that there is poverty at all and that most U.S. families have little or no wealth to count on when 1 percent of the population has assets of over $1000 billion. The ratio between the income and wealth of the rich and the poor, moreover, has shown little change over the past thirty years. Black families, in the meantime, and despite civil rights legislation, have lost ground to whites. And to correct the impression that poverty continues steadily to decline, the number and percentage of poor *grew* between 1973 and 1977.

Prevailing ideology would suggest that the wealthy gain their money through earned incomes and that the government takes most of it away in taxes. Those "myths" call for a response.

Myths about Work, Wages, and Taxes. How are income and wealth gained in the United States? By hard work and enterprise, or is it due more often to ownership of property and control over the work of others? Certainly the "hard work" thesis has some notable exceptions. Over six thousand persons earned more than $25,000 a year in 1972 working a few days a week and less than fourteen weeks of the year. By contrast nearly three-quarters of a million men and women earned less than $1,000 a year working for thirty-five or more hours a week for fifty to fifty-two weeks of the year.[43]

Some have challenged the distinction between "owners" and "workers" as no longer applicable to the modern capitalist system since the executives who manage corporations are distinct from the stockholders who own. But even salary differences between executives and workers show where inequality begins. Leo Huberman provided a graphic, if now dated example:

In 1946, the union of shipyard workers in the Bethlehem Steel Company fought for and won an increase of 15 percent which raised the minimum shipyard rate to $1.04 an hour. That's $41.60 a week or $2,163.20 a year. In 1946, the executives in Bethlehem were given a 46 percent salary boost. Mr. J. M. Larkin, vice-president of Bethlehem, who insisted that the incentive rates for workers had to be cut, was given a bonus of $38,764 in addition to his salary of $138,416. That's $177,180 a year, $3,407.30 a week, $85.18 an hour.[44]

Top executives are not just salaried managers; they are also owners. Richard Barnet notes that chief executive officers in major corporations averaged about $380,000 in after-tax incomes in 1972. Fifty-three percent of that income came from stockholdings valued at over $5 million each. The top five executives in each company drew 42 percent of their incomes from stockholdings.[45]

"Let your money work for you," the advertisement reads. That is precisely the problem, say radical critics of the capitalist system. Great wealth, C. Wright Mills argued, has never resulted from work and salary alone. Great wealth derives from investment or ownership, not work. Mills illustrated this quite graphically in *The Power Elite*. If you had bought $9,900 worth of General Motors stock in 1913 and had gone into a coma for forty years, you would have awakened in 1953 worth $7 million.[46] A study of people who reported million-dollar incomes in 1961 showed that of their total income, less than $30 million came from salaries or partnership profits. Nearly $700 million was derived from dividends and capital gains.[47]

Graduated income taxes are supposedly designed to redistribute wealth. In fact they do not. The proportion of income held by the top 5 percent of the population drops less than two percent after taxes.[48] Middle income groups bear the heaviest burden of personal income taxes. But regressive payroll taxes, along with sales taxes, have also increased the burden of lower income groups. A 1974 study of the Brookings Institution stated:

Taxes on the poor are heavy, and the tax system as a whole does little to alter the very unequal distribution of before-tax income. . . .

The combined income and payroll tax of a four-person family with one earner is actually a smaller percentage of income if the family earns $25,000 than if it earns $10,000. While the affluent family pays a higher percentage in income tax, this is more than offset by the lower percentage of its income it pays in payroll taxes. . . .

Over the past few years the federal tax structure has become more regressive. Reliance on the payroll tax has increased from 16 percent of total revenue in fiscal 1960 to 30 percent in 1974, while the importance of the corporation income tax has declined from 23 percent of federal revenues in 1960 to 14 percent in 1974. . . .

In the last four years changes in the individual income and social security payroll taxes have dramatically increased the burden on those with very low wages and reduced the burden carried by lower-middle-income groups.[49]

At the other end of the spectrum special provisions have been written into the tax code to provide exemption or preferential rates on the incomes of the wealthy—depletion allowances on energy production, depreciation on housing, exemptions on capital gains, municipal and state bonds, to say nothing of "write-offs" for luncheons, trips, and other "business" expenses. The Brookings report found that: "On the average, even extremely rich people—those with incomes over $1 million—*pay less than a third* of their income to the government in personal income tax despite top bracket rates of 50% on earned and 70% on unearned income."[50] If income tax rates were applied to all income received in 1974 the Treasury would have been richer by an estimated $77 billion a year.

Philip Stern noted that no fewer than 394 families making more than $100,000 avoided paying even a nickel to the treasury in 1970. Tax loopholes granted to the wealthy of the country, he observed, really constitute our greatest "welfare program."[51]

The tax returns of two presidents only serve to confirm his conclusion. President Richard M. Nixon's net worth tripled between 1969 and 1973. Documents released by his tax accountants and lawyers revealed that he had paid no state income taxes in California or the District of Columbia during his presidency. President Carter was more gracious. He made a voluntary 'gift" of taxes in 1977 when he found that loopholes had almost fully exempted him. To the public these may have appeared to be the privilege of high office, but their very legality confirmed tax privileges available to all the wealthy. The liberal critic concludes that tax reform is urgently needed; the Marxist sees little possibility of substantial, effective change unless property relations are radically restructured.

Materialistic Values and Priorities

How does one judge an economic system? If one judges by quantitative norms alone, capitalism generally scores high. It has proved productive. If judged by more qualitative norms, its performance raises serious doubts. A treatise on social ethics would be needed to articulate what all these norms might be. But implicit in many of the Christian criticisms directed against capitalism and Communism alike are two normative principles: (1) does the system respect the dignity and freedom of all persons and promote their common good; (2) does the system engender attitudes of respect and concern for others. "Are persons treated as ends, not means, as persons and not as things, in the system?" "Are members of society led by the system to respect and care for each other?" The biblical grounds, especially for the second norm, can easily be seen in the parables of the Good Samaritan, the rich man and Lazarus, the Last Judgment scene in Matthew's gospel. These norms by themselves may be inadequate. A system must also be intelligent; goodwill does not assure a sufficient production of food and other goods needed by society.

Socialism in theory and even Communism in practice have scored best on the second norm, in inculcating concerns for society as a whole. Some supporters would add "and the system has proved intelligent and effective"; China and Cuba have devised ways to produce food enough and goods enough to meet basic human needs of their people as a whole. Judgments against Communism have generally focused on the first norm, that human freedom, rights, and dignity have been trampled on. But the purpose of this chapter is not to compare systems; and the possibilities of a more democratic socialism will be discussed later in the book. The focus at present is upon capitalism.

Capitalism, or at least free enterprise, certainly makes its claim to fulfill these norms. If the quantitative appeal to "goods produced" and to efficiency receive frequent stress, defenders of the system would also argue for its qualitative performance. It encourages initiative, creativity, and responsibility. It allows freedom for each individual to get ahead. By encouraging all to work for their own gain it produces enough for all. Millions of immigrants to the United States feel it has provided this opportunity for them.

If indeed every person began with his or her own land or business, and with equal educational opportunities, the case which Pope Leo XIII made for private property could be argued more favorably. But the vast majority of people in the world have no such opportunity. Even in the United States fewer than one out of ten working adults are self-employed. It is the *monopolization* of ownership under capitalism which is at issue.

The moral norms enunciated above were implicit in the discussion of poverty and inequality. The criticisms were not based on a norm of "absolute equality," that all income and all wealth should be distributed equally regardless of effort or work. The argument was rather that private control of ownership does not work for the common good of all, and profit-maximization takes precedence over concern for others. The present section explores other social consequences of the system, particularly its effects on human values and social priorities.

To begin with, value norms and priorities is a Christian perspective. Marxists tend to look at values only as part of ideology reflecting the prevailing economic system. But their approach provides a valuable heuristic method for analyzing prevalent values or loss of values. And while methodologically Marxism does not move from value norms to concrete situations, the whole enterprise of Marxism rests on certain value assumptions. Paul Sweezy contends that what distinguished Marx's method from conventional economics was precisely that it refused to treat economic factors (prices, commodities, wages) simply as "things." It sought instead to show the human, social relationships embodied in each of these factors.[52] Michael Harrington makes a similar point: the critical question for Marx is "what kind of *qualitative* social relationships" arise out of capitalist conditions as opposed to purely quantitative aspects of prices and costs.[53] The very endeavor to achieve socialism would have little meaning without the values Marx enunciated in his *1844 Manuscripts* and *Grundrisse*—development of the talents and potential of each individual, more humanized social relationships, etc. This section, then, involves both Christian value concerns and insights drawn from a Marxist method of analysis. Four main issues will be addressed: consumerism, military spending, alienated work, and alienated groups and classes.

Consumerism

Modes of production, Marx observed, condition social consciousness. As modes of production change so do society's values and ideologies. Loyalty, chivalry, honor, and trust were the esteemed values of the Middle Ages. The Puritan "work ethic," self-reliance, achievement, and frugality became important values as free enterprise grew to dominance. The growth of monopoly capitalism has produced its own distinctive form of consciousness—consumerism. If monopoly capitalism needs new markets, it develops them in large measure by stimulating new needs. The United States and other advanced industrial countries have changed significantly from production-oriented societies to consumer-oriented ones.[54] Some of the traditional work-ethic ideology remains in force. Most U.S. Americans do work hard, and poverty still has a "they-wouldn't-be-poor-if-they-worked" stigma attached to it. But the very goals of work are strongly influenced by the desire to obtain consumer goods and the status they bring.

Marx spoke of the fetishism of commodities, of capitalism's making "things" more important than persons. But his wrath was chiefly directed against turning workers into profit-making commodities. Today's capitalism turns *consumers* into "things." The average U.S. American watches 40,000 TV commercials a year. The strategy of affecting consumer behavior, moreover, is quite consciously manipulative. Textbooks use stimulus-response models of human behavior to predict and plan reactions to advertising.[55] Advertising is a scientifically planned process: how to stimulate the needs of children and adolescents, how to create subliminal messages to capture adults, etc. Advertising keeps consumers in a state of perpetual dissatisfaction with what they have. Automobiles could be made to last for years; but that would reduce production and profit. So new "styles" become the selling point. Advertising seeks to convince us of our "need" for ever-drier deodorants, automatic garbage-compactors, and even electric toothbrushes and combs. The barrage of ads telling women they should be "sexy," and conveying to men thereby that women are sex objects, far outweighs literature challenging sexism. Ads promoting sugar-coated cereal and candy override parents' advice, at least until ads promoting sugarless gum come to their aid. Food commercials nullify doctors' recommendations. Forty percent of U.S. Americans are overweight as beef consumption more than doubled since 1940 and sugar consumption has quadrupled over the past century. But profit-maximization requires expansion; expansion is assured by the creation of "false needs."[56] U.S. multinationals, in the meantime, promote the same needs abroad. So diet-deficient Mexican children drink Cokes, and transistor radios become status symbols.[57]

The 1970's generation became known as the "Me" generation, a "culture of narcissism."[58] The delayed gratification once characteristic of production-oriented societies has given way to the "gratification now" demands of a consumer-oriented society. The number of sexually active unmarried teenage girls jumped 30 percent between 1971 and 1976. The consumer society provides endless ways of *Looking Out for #1,* as one book encouraged people to do. There is something to stimulate and then satisfy every want: wines and gourmet foods, discos and saunas, magazines on self-care, jogging, and tennis, or *Playboy, Hustler,* and *High Society* to meet more prurient interests.

As consumerism grows, care about others seems to diminish. Daniel Bell speaks of the loss of "civitas" in this country, of spontaneous willingness to make sacrifices for some public good.[59] The United States after World War II gave over 2 percent of its GNP for foreign aid. Foreign aid has now dropped to less than three-tenths of one percent of the GNP, and it ranks as one of the lowest priorities of most citizens. Welfare programs took the brunt of the criticism in tax revolts of the 1970s. The pace, pressures, and frustrations of life in contemporary society certainly also explain the turning toward selfish needs and consumption. But the promotion of consumption for the sake of profits both diverts investment from more needed goods and makes popular support for needed social changes more difficult.

Military Spending

By the end of the 1970s military spending drew over $130 billion from the federal budget. Demands for a new MX missile system threatened to escalate even that considerably. Military spending accounts for nearly 60 percent of federal funds in the budget, though new budget procedures which include Social Security revenues-payments leave the impression that it counts for only 30–35 percent.[60] National security cannot simply be written off as a "false need," but the priority given to defense over other needs raises a serious issue. The military budget exceeds the GNP of whole continents.

The Leninist argument that capitalism needs war and military spending as an outlet for surplus capital would be difficult to substantiate. Germany and Japan have experienced great growth without it. The immense military spending of the Soviet Union, moreover, weakens the Leninist case attributing military spending simply to capitalist investment needs. A notable critic of military spending, Seymour Melman, argues conversely that our permanent war economy is highly detrimental *to* capitalism. It diminishes overall productivity; it lowers efficiency; it violates the basic cost-minimizing principle of market capitalism by maximizing costs and depending on maximum government subsidies.[61] Even using Melman's data, however, a Marxist argument can be made. Thus his main arguments against present levels of military spending are worth noting.

First, with its logic of subsidy-maximization and non-competitive contracts the Pentagon pays exorbitant amounts for military production. Compared to the cost per standardized unit of output in a competitive civilian industry, military production runs two, five, and even twenty times higher.[62] Cost overruns on weapons in 1971 amounted to $35 billion,[63] and billions have been spent on weapons never used or discarded. Second, federal budget increases for military spending and budget cuts for civilian purposes go hand in hand. As missiles are added, education for the handicapped and child nutrition are cut. Melman lists what civilian-military "trade-offs" in spending could mean; elimination of hunger throughout the United States in exchange for the C-5A aircraft program; 257 apartments in New York for 1 Navy Intruder plane; bringing all poor Americans over the poverty line for the estimated cost of the B-1 bomber program; meeting all of Newark's needs for urban renewal in exchange for 4 destroyer escorts; rebuilding blighted areas in all of our major cities for 1 nuclear aircraft carrier and escorts; etc.[64] Third, reduction of military spending would not mean less military security for the United States. Twice as much is spent on maintaining a worldwide military system and bases as on nuclear deterrence.[65] Moreover, no real defense against nuclear attack is feasible.[66] The comparing of who has the most missiles obscures the fact that by the most conservative estimate we already have the capacity to destroy Soviet population-industrial centers twenty-six or more times over.[67]

If Melman argues from a capitalist perspective, his own research would provide a Marxist case against capitalism. Defense contracts are immensely profitable. Melman notes 131 firms in 1972 whose after-refund profits exceeded 50 percent of net worth; twenty-two earned between 200 and 500 percent; and four exceeded 500 percent.[68] From a Marxist perspective, James O'Connor gives three reasons why military spending will continue to expand in years ahead. First, the expansion of capitalism into the Third World enlarges the possibilities of capital accumulation but also increases the possibility of class and national conflict. Overseas expansion meets more and more resistance and the defense of the U.S. "empire" becomes ever more costly. Second, private military producers have established what seems to be a permanent tap on the Federal budget. Industrial procurement amounts to about 50 percent of the Pentagon budget, with two-thirds going to the fifty largest defense contractors. Third, technological advance in monopoly sector civilian production is dependent on a large and growing military scientific and technological establishment.[69]

Alienated Work

Capitalist ideology places great stress on "efficiency." It judges and compares other systems by this criterion. Can they do the job efficiently? Efficiency also means cost-minimizing and hence profit-maximization. While the Marxist critique is popularly associated most often with issues of exploitation and social inequality, Marx himself emphasized *how* people work as an even greater concern. He believed that humans express their lives and actualize their human capabilities in their work. But to achieve this, work had to be *their* work, work freely chosen, work which developed their skills and their intelligence. Under capitalism, work was forced and dehumanizing. Workers, if they wanted to survive, had to accept the job offered them. They did the routinized work assigned them, at the pace designated. They were appendages to machines. From Marx's later *Grundrisse* (see Chapter 1) it is clear that Marx meant by work not simply the hours spent on a job, but also the creative and disciplined use of leisure time. Hence he favored the reduction of necessary labor to a minimum so that wokers could develop their skills and talents in leisure time. But the exhausted laborer of Marx's time had little hope for such personal development.

Many critics, Marxist and otherwise, believe that capitalism still sacrifices humanizing work to efficiency and profit-maximization. Kenneth Keniston describes the impact of alienated work in terms that echo Marx's analysis a century before. In most traditional societies, he observes, one's work was one's life. Work, play, and social life flowed into each other. Work meant simply tasks to be done, without any division of life into work and nonwork. For most Americans, in contrast, work has unpleasant connotations. The reason why lies in the characteristics of most jobs. With increasing specialization, each worker finds herself or himself assigned to a smaller and smaller portion of a task. The product is finished far down the line: out of sight and out of mind. There is little sense of satisfaction from work. Moreover, too few jobs challenge one's abilities, imagination, or spirit; most call simply for a capacity to follow exact routines in an orderly way. As a result, most Americans speak of "working for a living" and rarely "living for their work." We have long since stopped even expecting work to be meaningful.[70]

Harry Braverman's *Labor and Monopoly Capital* is an important Marxist study of "the degradation of work in the 20th century." He begins by noting rising discontent in the labor movement today about job dissatisfaction. Expressive of this discontent was the Lordstown, Ohio, strike in 1972 directed against the increased pace of work demanded in a General Motors plant.[71] What distinguishes *human* work from animal instincts, Braverman argues, is the power of conceptual thought. True human labor unites mental and material action. The degradation of labor in capitalist society results from their separation.

The "scientific management" which Frederick Taylor proposed in the late nineteenth century, and which greatly influenced the U.S. system of production, very deliberately divorced mental and material labor. Taylor wrote:

> The managers assume . . . the burden of gathering together all of the traditional knowledge which in the past has been possessed by the workmen and then of classifying, tabulating, and reducing this knowledge to rules, laws, and formulae. . . . All possible brain work should be removed from the shop and centered in the planning or laying-out department.
>
> The work of every workman is fully planned out by the management at least one day in advance, and each man receives in most cases complete written instructions, describing in detail what he is to accomplish, as well as the means used in doing the work.[72]

The introduction of assembly lines carried this concept of mechanized labor to its fullest expression. Henry Ford's decision in 1914 to raise workers' pay to $5.00 a day was hailed as an enlightened, progressive move to enable workers to become more affluent customers. This view overlooks the fact that Ford faced an angry revolt by workers against his new assembly lines. The turnover rate in 1913 had forced the Ford Motor Company to hire 963 workers in order to sustain the 100 needed.[73]

Far more than factory work has been affected by the separation of mental from manual work. The same principle enunciated by Taylor has been applied to clerical work. Some companies have so mechanized clerical work as to fix time standards for every minute task. The drive for speed and efficiency has reduced more and more work to simplified, routinized, and measured tasks.[74]

Tibor Scitovsky's reflections on our "joyless economy" suggest the carry-over of efficiency into every area of U.S. American life.[75] The desire to "save effort," to buy things, to recreate, to do things that require the least amount of energy, characterizes the "American way of life." Comfort triumphs over quality. Packaged foods, casual dress, careless buying, indiscriminate TV watching, leisure comfort rather than leisure development of skills, these indeed give evidence of a joyless economy.

But far more serious than these cultural effects of efficiency are its social consequences. U.S. capitalism prides itself on "building on the best." It looks for the brightest executives, the most skilled workers, the most efficient methods, the best plant locations. But in doing so it constantly widens the gap between the best and the less educated and less skilled, creating a permanent body of persons "on welfare" or at least unable to contribute to society's growth. John Gurley's insightful views on this will be taken up in chapter 8 in a discussion of the Maoist view of society.

Unemployment is, in large measure, a consequence of cost-minimizing efficiency for the sake of profits. If work has been dehumanized, unemployment proves far more degrading. To speak of "only" 6 percent unemployment—a figure once thought intolerable—does little to describe the powerlessness, frustration, and alienation of millions of unemployed people. Welfare may permit an income on which to live, but it can only be dehumanizing. In many critiques of capitalism the issue of unemployment would be a predominant concern; the chapter may be deficient in not giving it greater prominence.

Alienated Groups and Classes

Central to any Marxist analysis is the concept of "class struggle" and the divisions engendered by the capitalist system. The militancy of workers in the nineteenth century and the often violent suppression of their strikes and efforts to unionize did give clear evidence of class hostilities. In the United States today the issue of class struggle rarely is discussed except in Marxist journals and newspapers. Hence, unlike other issues discussed in this chapter it is not an obvious problem which would lead Christians to Marxist analysis. Neo-Marxist analysis focuses on such issues as how to define the working class and the capitalist class, on divisions within both classes, on the relation between class, race, sex, and other factors, on the state's role in dissipating or segmenting class conflicts, and on strategies to unite different alienated groups.[76]

Many non-Marxists feel that clearly defined social classes do not exist in the United States, if they ever did. Race, religion, ethnic origin, education, and other factors are more determinative of behavior and attitudes than class.[77] Most protest groups form on some basis other than class: Blacks, women, Chicanos, gays, anti-abortionists, anti-nuclear–energy protesters, etc. John Kenneth Galbraith contends that classical class struggle has dwindled because of four factors characteristic of corporate capitalism: power has passed from owners to managers, from capitalists to corporate bureaucrats who place high priority on maintaining smooth relations with workers; advanced technology has led to the replacement of blue-collar workers with white-collar workers who identify more with the firm; the general affluence of union workers has reduced conflict; Keynesian economics often shifts conflict to the government and its efforts to control wage hikes. But Galbraith does affirm that labor-management tensions have been passed on to other sectors of society.[78]

While disagreeing especially with Galbraith's first point, many Marxists would concur with his last contention. The conflicts and tensions have been passed on. Class struggles stay more often "latent" than openly apparent, with the state frequently becoming the target of discontent (see Chapter 2 on Habermas and the next section of this chapter on the state). Some social critics, on the other hand, find class consciousness still very evident among workers.[79] But most recognize capitalism's "success" in displacing class struggle by segmenting the labor force and creating divisions between workers. James O'Connor stresses the division between workers in the monopoly sector of the economy and the competitive sector. Workers in the monopoly sector, in large corporations, are generally unionized and make higher wages. Workers in the competitive sector—in smaller firms, groceries, restaurants, etc.—constitute the lower echelon of the working class. Wages in this sector tend to be low, unions are rare, employment is often seasonal or temporary, and Blacks and women are disproportionally represented.[80]

Race proves a divisive force within the working class. While workers may share the same class definition, white workers often see Blacks as a threat to their jobs, and Blacks accuse whites of "back-climbing" over them for advancement.[81] Sex differences add a further complexity to class analysis. The issue of women's oppression crosses class lines. But Marx and Engels did link woman's emancipation to liberation from capitalism, and some feminists have tried to combine the radical feminist perspective and the socialist perspective.[82]

Certainly the issue of economic inequality deeply affects the Blacks and women. The median family income for Blacks in 1977 was nearly $6,000 a year less than for whites; nearly three times as many Blacks as whites had median incomes under $3,000.[83] Women are very minimally represented in high-paying and high-prestige jobs. They work predominately in lower-paying, lower-status jobs: as secretaries, as primary school teachers, as waitresses, as nurses. Where they do work in predominately male professions their salaries tend to be significantly lower.[84]

Thus while racism and sexism have their own cultural causes, arguments can certainly be made to show their relation to capitalism. First, Blacks suffer most from high unemployment engendered by the capitalist system, and the pressure to keep women "domestic" seems certainly related to the insufficiency of job opportunities available. Second, for both groups discrimination becomes reinforced by the low-status jobs they most often occupy. Third, with the exception of women who have obtained wealth through inheritance or marriage, the dominant capitalist class quite clearly consists of white, and usually Anglo-Saxon, males.

Capitalist Domination of the State

U.S. Americans take pride in their democratic system: "Whatever its faults, it's the best in the world." Every citizen has a voice in the government. All can vote; all can aspire to political office. The two-party system offers alternatives in the choice of policies and candidates. The division of executive, legislature, and judiciary creates a balance of power. Opposition to

Marxist Communism most often expresses itself as a defense of democracy.

Marxists challenge this "pluralist" view of the state and its faith in U.S. democracy. Their quarrel is not with the principles and values of democracy as such, but with claims that they have been realized in the United States and in other capitalist nations. Marx had argued, in his early writings, that political freedoms created only an "illusion" of true human freedom. People's lives are determined far more by the conditions in which they live in civil society than by abstract political rights. Political power, moreover, reflects economic power. When John Locke, the seventeenth-century English philosopher, stated that the great and chief end of persons uniting to form a government was "the preservation of their property," he reflected all too clearly the goals of his social class. The democratic state in capitalist society claims to represent the common good of all its citizens, and indeed it must pass legislation needed to legitimize that claim. But it serves primarily to maintain the power and interests of the dominant capitalist class. Or as Marx expressed it in *The Communist Manifesto:* "The executive of the modern State is but a committee for managing the common affairs of the whole bourgeoisie."[85]

Marxists may be exaggerating and using heavy rhetoric when they speak of "capitalist domination of the state." But it is important to consider the arguments for the Marxist position. Their arguments are grouped under three questions in this section: Who Rules? Who Benefits? and Whose Interests Prevail? The responses draw upon three different, though complementary, types of analysis. The first two reflect a current controversy in neo-Marxism between an "instrumental" and a "structural" view of the state.[86] The third, and perhaps the most forceful critique, goes outside Marxism as such but focuses on the role of giant corporations in respect to the state.

Who Rules?

Most U.S. Americans would not be surprised to find the rich disproportionately represented in high office. But the degree to which this proves true offers one reason why Marxists view the state as an "instrument" of the ruling capitalist class. Thus an initial approach to a radical critique of U.S. political power would be to show the direct presence of wealthy persons in high office. One starting point requires no special research. Anyone can be president of the United States in theory. But millionaires and multi-millionaires, though they represent a miniscule fraction of the population, have contended in almost every presidential election of the last fifty years—Franklin D. Roosevelt, Adlai Stevenson, John F. Kennedy, Lyndon Johnson, with Richard Nixon and Jimmy Carter reaching the million mark while in office.

G. William Domhoff, in *Who Rules America?*, notes that five of eight secretaries of state and eight of thirteen secretaries of defense over the thirty-six year period he studied, were listed in the elite *Social Register.*[87]

Ambassadors have traditionally been persons of great wealth also. Indeed, many important ambassadorial posts were awarded to wealthy men or women because they contributed substantially to the successful candidate's treasury.

Congress has a broader composition, but the power of wealth is quite evident there also. Congressperson Torbert H. MacDonald, a Democrat of Massachusetts, noted that: "In the nation's seven largest states in 1970, 11 of the 15 major senatorial candidates were millionaires. The four who were not lost their bids for elections."[88] A Ralph Nader study in 1975 revealed that 20 senators were millionaires; well over half of those who responded to Nader's inquiry were worth $250,000 or more: only five were worth under $50,000. The "average" American that same year had a net worth of $4,000.[89] One would very likely look in vain for even one member of Congress representative of the average American. Legislators come from the ranks of business and the professions, law in particular. The main work force of the United States—factory workers, truckers, secretaries, etc.—goes virtually without any direct representation from its ranks.

Elected and appointed officials, however, tell only part of the story. The wealthy upper class exercise their influence through predominant membership on councils, committees and agencies which significantly influence U.S. foreign and domestic policy. In his *The Higher Circles,* Domhoff found that the ruling upper class, and the power elite which represents them,[90] dominated such groups as the Council on Foreign Relations, The Committee on Economic Development, The National Security Council, and the Federal Trade Commission. Still further research into the power structure of these groups was published in 1975 in *The Insurgent Sociologist.* One study showed that the Council of Foreign Relations in its planning during World War II, aimed at assuring a world market for U.S. business after the war while downplaying overt imperialism. Another study investigated the Industrial Advisory Council to the Department of Defense which met from 1962 to 1972 and included the presidents of AT&T, DuPont, Honeywell, Lockheed, IBM, Ford, and other large military contractors. It showed the Council's concern for maintaining defense spending and increased profit rates. A third study of the President's Cabinet from 1897 to 1973 concluded that 90 percent of all cabinet officials during that period belonged to either the social or business elite.[91] The conclusion of these studies is that the upper class constitutes a ruling class which operates through a power elite of its own members or persons who represent its institutions.

Who Benefits?

A neo-Marxist theory of the state proposed by James O'Connor and others does not depend on proof of direct links between the upper class and government bodies to show that the state serves to protect and promote capitalist interests. "The capitalist state is not an instrument but a structure,"

O'Connor contends.[92] The state, in fact, does far more than protect capitalism. It has descended from the superstructure and become an integral part of the economic system. Without its "subsidizing" of capitalism the system would collapse or face intolerable crises.

The main thesis of O'Connor's *The Fiscal Crisis of the State,* as already noted earlier, is that the state performs two contradictory functions. It maintains a climate for capital accumulation, and it performs legitimizing functions to give the appearance that the state tries to balance the interests of all classes and groups. State spending provides a basis for the private monopoly sector to grow. But it also creates a "contradiction." Only monopolistic interests really benefit, while the burden of social expenses, in the form of taxes and inflation, falls upon the great majority of citizens.

How the state subsidizes private industry can be shown in the automobile industry. Cars need roads, but private industry does not have to bear the cost of building them. The entire transportation budget from 1944 to 1961 was given to the construction of roads and highways; the railroads received nothing. The government assumes 90 percent of the cost of interstate free-ways and 50 percent of all other primary roads. 80 percent of the funds earmarked for the redevelopment of Appalachia went into roads.[93] The auto industry is thus richly subsidized.

This same subsidy of autos made possible the growth of suburbia at the expense of the inner-city. Highways enabled migration to the suburbs to occur; further government subsidy provided the use of water, fire service, hospitals, etc., at little or no expense to the suburbs. The benefits of the urban central city remain for suburbanites, but the city residents must bear all the costs of traffic control, police, and pollution.[94]

The state subsidizes private industry, and hence private profits, in a variety of ways: through loans as it did for Lockheed, through helping to finance building and developing land, through tax exemptions for building deprecia-tion and oil exploration, through funding research. By providing welfare it tempers the discontent created by unemployment. By assuming much of the cost of medical care it frees industry from paying higher salaries to cover these costs. It bears much of the expense for industrial pollution as well. The discontent of citizens demanding more benefits gets directed at the state, because it picks up expenses that private corporations escape.

Michael Harrington makes a similar case against "state management of the economy on behalf of the capitalists."

> Over the past three decades, the government helped to build ten million units for the better-off and 650,000 units of low-cost housing for the poor. In 1969, the *Wall Street Journal* reported that there were $2.5 billion in subsidies for the urban freeways, which facilitated the commuting of the privileged, and only $175 million for mass transit. All

of this made good commercial sense even though it helped to perpetuate the social disaster of the disintegration of the central cities, the consequent isolation of the racial and ethnic minorities, the subversion of the passenger-rail system, and so forth.[95]

Government policies regarding farming reveal the same priorities. Between 1960 and 1974, the number of farms in America decreased by 25 percent. The larger units, with more than $20,000 a year in sales, went up 80 percent. The "farmers" included ITT, Gulf & Western, Boeing Aircraft, and other giant corporations. But it was these giant agribusinesses which were the prime recipients of tens of billions in federal subsidy. From 1968 to 1973, just prior to the great inflation of food costs in the United States, Washington paid $15.5 billion to farmers for idling millions of acres which would have produced an estimated 23 million metric tons of grain.[96] In 1967 the poorest 20 percent of farmers received 1.1 percent of federal subsidies; the richest 5 percent, often corporations, received over 42 percent.[97]

Harrington directs his strongest criticism at government subsidy of oil companies, several of which rank among the fifteen largest multinationals in the world. He shows how the oil industry won multi-million-dollar subsidies and massive tax reductions by arguing that the defense and common good of the nation were at stake.[98] Government subsidy of defense industries we have already noted.

Whose Interests Prevail?

How do giant corporations affect democracy? Charles Lindblom, in *Politics and Markets,* presents a strong case against their presence in a democracy. He does not argue from a Marxist perspective as such. He clearly favors a "market" economy over the "authority" and "persuasive" models operative in the U.S.S.R. and China respectively, though his favorable comments on Yugoslavian "market socialism" make it evident that he distinguishes between private ownership of the means of production and a market economy. But it is his analysis of politics, not markets, that we wish to consider here..

Business executives, not government officials, make nearly all the public policy decisions that affect the economic life of the nation. Their decisions, in turn, affect almost every aspect of life—jobs, homes, consumer goods, leisure. These executives determine income distribution, allocation of resources, plant locations, the pattern of work, the technologies to be used, what goods should be produced, the quality of goods and services, and of course executive compensation and status.[99] These major decisions are turned over to business leaders and taken off the agenda of government. Thus citizens have no vote at all on policies that affect every sphere of their welfare.

But these major decisions only begin to describe the public role of business leaders. Their influence on government is quite different than that of any other group in society. Public functions in the market system rest in their hands. Jobs, prices, production, growth, the standard of living, and the economic security of everyone, therefore, rest in their hands also. Government officials cannot, consequently, be indifferent to how business performs its functions. Business leaders are not just representatives of one or more special interest groups; the whole welfare of society depends on what they do. They never get all they ask for or want, it is true. But whether they ask for subsidies for transportation and research, for aid in overseas promotion of business, for marines called in to protect investments in foreign countries, for laws to restrict stockholder liability, for tax reductions to stimulate investment, or for similar advantages, the state must respond.[100] Little wonder, one might add, that radical critics spoke of Jimmy Carter's "second election" in 1976. His need to win the confidence of business was more important than his election by popular vote. Populist campaign promises for tax reforms had to cede to the business demands.

Workers, Lindbloom argues, have no comparable clout. Business executives can choose or not choose to take risks depending on prospects for greater profits. Workers have no choice; they must work for a livelihood. Only through a general strike could they exercise any comparable power, but this the state would stop.[101] Contributions to political campaigns give some idea of relative influence. Union expenditures in the 1972 presidential election amounted to only $13 million of nearly $500 million spent.[102]

All citizen groups can compete in politics, but they depend on the use of their members' own incomes and energies. Business corporations can draw on extraordinary sources of corporate funds, organizations and personnel ready to use, and on special access to government. Business has myriads of avenues by which to do its own "consciousness forming or raising." Through lobbying, through entertainment, through advertising, through contributions to education, through litigations, business uses its profits to confirm its position and gain approval. Roughly $60 billion per year is spent on advertising and other sales promotion. A large part of this is institutional advertising with a political content like Exxon's "Energy for a strong America."[103] This matches all the funds spent on education or health in the country. Few radical or dissenting journals even exist to compete with dominant business views.

Democratic thought has not faced up to the private corporation's role in an ostensible democracy. The large, private corporation, Lindbloom concludes, does not fit into democratic theory and vision.[104] Yet even this does not tell the whole picture, for it speaks only of the United States, and not of the impact of U.S. business on "economic democracy" in other countries. The destinies of many poor nations of the world are greatly affected by the policies and decisions of multinational corporations, as the section on imperialism sought to show.

Marx's Critique Revisited: A Concluding Note

In the course of the chapter, in the text itself or in footnotes, an effort has been made to explain briefly some neo-Marxist theories about advanced monopoly capitalism, class structures, and the state. But little mention was made of two very central doctrines in Marx's own critique: his theory of surplus value explaining worker exploitation, and his theory of crises leading to the collapse of capitalism. This final section will attempt in a few pages to give at least a perspective on problems and divergent theories about these.

Marx argued that profits generated by capitalism resulted from exploitation of workers. As slave holders gained wealth through the work of slaves, and feudal lords from the work of serfs, so capitalist owners, in a more disguised and subtle way, take their profit from the work of wage-earners. Commodities sold bring a profit to the owner. But what accounts for this profit? A sale of commodities at a value greater than their worth does not. If every commodity sold for a price greater than its actual value, profits would cancel out. What was gained in selling would be lost in buying, at least at an aggregate level. Some quantitative measure must be had to determine the value of commodities. This measure of exchange-value, according to Marx, was determined by the quantity of labor necessary to produce it. This quantity of labor included the labor that went into making machines, into obtaining raw materials, into overhead, and into managerial work. Still profits remained over and above all these. Only one factor could account for this. The wages paid to workers were not determined by the actual value of their work but by the amount needed to sustain them and their families. The surplus value which creates profits derives from this exploitation.

Critics of Marxism have challenged this explanation, arguing that there is no "objective" measure of the value of commodities, that scarcity of goods, the risk and entrepreneurship of owners, technology, and what buyers are willing to pay, all influence the price of commodities. Some critics contend that Marx himself recognized the inadequacy of his labor theory of value and tried to revise it.[105] Neo-Marxists have responded to these criticisms in various ways. Ernest Mandel defends the labor theory of value.[106] Erik Olin Wright argues that, granting other ways of measuring value, the labor theory is the most useful for understanding class relations in production.[107] Michael Harrington contends that Marx's labor theory of value has been misread as a measure of prices, and that Marx's methodology in general has been misunderstood.[108] A group of British Marxists feels that the labor theory of value should be abandoned, and that a Marxist critique does not depend on it.[109]

A semantic difficulty also arises regarding the word "exploitation." Exploitation conveys a technical sense in Marxism which does not correspond fully to the moral connotations of the word. When workers draw bare subsistence wages and owners draw immense profits, the moral overtones of "unfairness" are also clear. But skilled workers drawing $20,000 a year are still exploited in a technical sense if their labor creates surplus value above what they receive in wages. That some surplus should be reinvested is not an issue; all socialist countries do this. The moral issue revolves around both personal profit and the power that comes from private control over investment.

It would seem that the burden of proof regarding exploitation should rest on the capitalist theorist rather than on the Marxist. In medieval society, the serfs' contribution of half their labor to the landowner obviously explains the owner's wealth. In capitalist society, especially where one finds great disparities between workers' wages and owners' profits, it is difficult *not* to believe that exploitation underlies the wage-contract system. Union struggles, moreover, have shown that owners under pressure have the resources with which to pay higher wages. If one imagines, along the lines suggested by John Rawls' theory of justice, people agreeing to a system before knowing their place in it, it is hard to believe anyone would agree to give one person power of ownership, power of decision-making, and 100 to 1000 times more income than all other contracting parties.

Marx also argued that contradictions within the capitalist system create crises which will lead to its collapse. Capitalism's "blind drive" for profit leads to overproduction; the markets cannot absorb all the products; cutbacks create unemployment; competition drives smaller capitalists out. Improved technology is introduced to save costs, but this increase in "constant" capital lowers the profit rate since only human labor produces surplus value. This shift swells the numbers of a reserve army of unemployed, but this also enables owners to hire workers at lower wages and for new expansion to occur. The recurrence of these crises with ever greater impact, however, will eventually lead workers to revolt and to overthrow capitalism.

Critics of Marx argue that he has been disproved by history. The working class has not become increasingly poorer. Recessions, perhaps, but no major crises have occurred in recent decades; capitalism clearly has not collapsed. Neo-Marxists have responded again in varying ways to these criticisms. While some still believe in the inevitable collapse of capitalism, others speak rather of inevitable socio-economic conflicts and ever-latent crises. Thus Samir Amin contends that while capitalism is "in decay," its contradictions may never lead to its collapse or socialist revolution. The Western capitalist world may simply continue to decay much as Rome did centuries ago.[110] Ernest Mandel argues that capitalism has been able to replace more severe crises with recessions because social legislation, such as unemployment compensation and welfare, has had a "dampening" effect abating what would have been severe crises a century before.[111]

Paul Sweezy sees monopoly capitalism as "stagnationist"; its need to maintain monopoly prices dictates a policy of slowing down and regulating the expansion of productive capacity.[112] Mandel, on the other hand, explains monopoly capitalism by cycles of expansionist periods followed by stagnationist ones, though with the cycles lasting far longer than in Marx's time.[113] Erik Olin Wright provides a helpful summary of current Marxist theories of accumulation and crises. He discusses four different "schools" of Marxist thought: (1) those who see the "declining rate of profit" as still operative; technology and investment in constant capital negates any rise in the rate of surplus value which can only come from living labor; (2) those who hold that "underconsumption" is the real cause of crisis; there is not a sufficient consumer market to absorb all the surplus; too many are too poor to buy; (3) those who attribute crises to the "profit squeeze"; the profit rate falls because of union demands for constantly escalating wages, though unemployment and consequent job insecurity can cause a relaxation of this squeeze; (4) those who argue that state expenditures create a decline because money from taxes does not make the surplus productive; but others argue that the state can indirectly create an increase in the rate of surplus value to offset a decline of profit rate.[114]

Finally, since the next chapter deals with Latin America, it would be worth noting at least the work of André Gunder Frank and Samir Amin in addressing the problem of underdevelopment and its relation to imperialism.[115]

Notes

1. See Ernest Mandel, *An Introduction to Marxist Economic Theory* (New York: Pathfinder, 1970) as an introduction. For further study see Paul Sweezy, *The Theory of Capitalist Development* (Oxford University Press, 1942) and his *Marxist Economic Theory*, 2 volumes (New York: Monthly Review, 1968). See Erik Olin Wright, *Class, Crisis and the State* (London: NLB, 1978) for a discussion of contemporary positions in neo-Marxism; and Assar Lindbeck, *The Political Economy of the New Left* (New York: Harper & Row, 2nd ed., 1977).

2. Daniel Bell and Irving Kristol, eds., *Capitalism Today* (New York: Basic Books, 1970) includes several essays in defense of capitalism. See also Milton Friedman, Ayn Rand, and others in *Views on Capitalism,* ed. Richard Romano and Melvin Leiman (Beverly Hills, Calif.: Benziger, Bruce & Glencoe, 1975 edition). See also Michael Novak, *The American Vision, An Essay on the Future of Democratic Capitalism* (Washington, D.C.: American Institute for Public Policy Research, 1978).

3. V. I. Lenin, *Selected Works in Three Volumes,* Vol. I. For a study of Lenin and Hobson on imperialism, see Irving M. Zeitlin, *Capitalism and Imperialism, An Introduction to Neo-Marxian Concepts* (Chicago: Markham, 1972), chapters 6 and 7.

4. John Kenneth Galbraith, *The New Industrial State* (New York: Signet, 1967). Galbraith developed five major theses in the book about the new industrial system in which large corporations exerted a dominant influence. He argued: (1) that the new system has replaced market economy with long-range planning; (2) that industrial power now rests in the hands of a complex technostructure of executives and experts and no longer with individual owners; (3) that growth and not profit-maximization is now the key motivating force; (4) that the state now plays a key role in regulating the economy; (5) that control by bureaucratic technostructures characterizes socialism and capitalism alike. Marxists took strong exception to (2) and (3).

5. Richard J. Barnet and Ronald E. Müller, *Global Reach: The Power of the Multinational Corporations* (New York: Simon and Schuster, 1974), p. 269.

6. Zeitlin, *Capitalism and Imperialism,* p. 36.

7. Markley Roberts, "The Concentration of Economic Power," in *AFL-CIO American Federationist,* May 1975.

8. Douglas F. Dowd, *The Twisted Dream, Capitalist Development in the United States Since 1776* (Cambridge, Mass.: Winthrop, 1977, second edition), pp. 76–77.

9. Barnet and Müller, *Global Reach,* pp. 235ff, and Markley Roberts, "The Concentration of Economic Power." See also John A. Sonquist and Thomas Koenig, "Interlocking Directorates in the Top U.S. Corporations," in *The Insurgent Sociologist,* Vol. V, No. III, Spring, 1975, pp. 196–229.

10. Barnet and Müller, *Global Reach,* p. 245.

11. Michael Harrington, *The Vast Majority, A Journey to the World's Poor* (New York: Simon and Schuster, 1977), p. 23.

12. Barnet and Müller, *Global Reach,* p. 17.

13. Ibid., p. 26.

14. James O'Connor, *The Fiscal Crisis of the State* (New York: St. Martin's Press, 1973), p. 6.

15. Ibid., Chapters 4 and 5 on social investment and consumption; Chapter 6 on social expenses.

16. Robert McNamara, "Address to the Board of Governors" of the World Bank, Nairobi, Kenya, September 24, 1973, p. 10. See also his address of September 26, 1977, where he speaks of 700 million seriously malnourished and the hundreds of millions for whom development has failed.

17. Harrington, *The Vast Majority,* p. 104.

18. Cited in Carl Oglesby and Richard Shaull, *Containment and Change* (London: Macmillan, 1967), p. 67.

19. Harrington, *The Vast Majority,* pp. 23, 45. See also S. M. Muller et al., "Does the U.S. Economy Require Imperialism?" in *American Society, Inc., Studies of the Social Structure and Political Economy of the United States,* ed. Maurice Zeitlin (Chicago: Rand McNally, 1977, 2nd ed.), pp. 294–306.

20. Paul Sweezy, *Modern Capitalism and Other Essays* (New York: Monthly Review Press, 1972), p. 18.

21. Ibid., p. 20.

22. Eduardo Galeano, *Open Veins of Latin America, Five Centuries of the Pillage of a Continent,* trans. Cedric Belfrage (New York: Monthly Review Press, 1973), p. 23.

23. Ibid., pp. 30–68.

24. Ibid., p. 50.

25. Ibid., pp. 72–75.

26. Frances Moore Lappé and Joseph Collins, *Food First, Beyond the Myth of Scarcity* (Boston: Houghton Mifflin, 1977), pp. 78ff.

27. Ibid., pp. 182–83. See also Harry Magdoff, *The Age of Imperialism, The Economics of U.S. Foreign Policy* (New York: Monthly Review, 1969) pp. 99–100.

28. Lappé and Collins, *Food First,* p. 157.

29. Ibid., pp. 36–37.

30. Ibid., p. 82.

31. Ibid., pp. 42–43.

32. Cited by Denis Goulet, "World Interdevelopment: Verbal Smokescreen or New Ethic?" in *Overseas Development Paper* 21, March 1976, p. 13.

33. Sweezy, *Modern Capitalism,* pp. 22–23.

34. John Gerassi, *The Great Fear in Latin America* (New York: Collier-Macmillan, 1968 revised), p. 370.

35. Lappé and Collins, *Food First,* pp. 194–98.

36. Ibid., pp. 255–56.

37. John K. Galbraith, "The Defense of Multinational Companies," in *Harvard Business Review,* March-April, 1978, pp. 83–93.

38. *Statistical Abstract of the United States, 1978* (Washington, D.C.: U.S. Bureau of the Census), p. 465. See also Robert Plotnick and Felicity Skidmore, "Progress Against Poverty: 1964–1974," in *American Society, Inc.,* p. 129.

39. *American Society, Inc.,* p. 63.

40. *Statistical Abstract, 1978,* pp. 475–76.

41. In addition to articles in *American Society, Inc.,* Ferdinand Lundberg, *The Rich and the Super Rich* (New York: Bantam, 1968), Morton Mintz and Jerry S. Cohen,

America, Inc., (New York: Dell, 1971), and *Poverty in American Democracy, A Study of Social Power,* from The Campaign for Human Development (Washington, D.C.: United States Catholic Conference, 1974). This last work, coordinated by Frederick J. Perella, Jr., covers most of the issues discussed in this section.

42. *Statistical Abstract, 1978,* p. 452, and on poverty, p. 465.

43. Lester C. Thurow, *Generating Inequality, Mechanisms of Distribution in the U.S. Economy* (New York: Basic Books, 1975), pp. 6, 10.

44. From Leo Huberman and Paul M. Sweezy, *The Introduction to Socialism* (New York: Monthly Review, 1968), p. 47.

45. Barnet and Müller, *Global Reach,* p. 292, and note, p. 458.

46. C. Wright Mills, *The Power Elite* (New York: Oxford University Press, 1969 reprint), p. 111.

47. Lundberg, *The Rich and the Super-Rich,* pp. 43, 935–36.

48. See Frank Ackerman et al., "The Extent of Income Inequality in the United States," in *The Capitalist System,* ed. Richard Edwards, Michael Reich, and Thomas Weisskopf (Englewood Cliffs, N.J.: Prentice Hall, 1972). Ackerman's study of 1962 income distribution showed the poorest one-fifth receiving less than 5 percent of the gross income and the wealthiest one-fifth receiving 45.5 percent. Income distribution *after* taxes remained at under 5 percent for the poorest group and the richest one-fifth still received 43.7 percent (p. 210).

49. Edward Fried et al., "Tax Reform," in *Principles of Microeconomics, Readings, Issues, and Cases,* ed. Edwin Mansfield (New York: W.W. Norton, 1974), pp. 141–42.

50. Ibid., p. 145. See also Barnet and Müller, *Global Reach,* notes pp. 457–58.

51. Philip Stern, *The Rape of the Taxpayer* (New York: Random House, 1973): on the millionaires, p. 68; on loopholes as welfare, pp. 5ff.

52. Paul Sweezy, *The Theory of Capitalist Development* (New York: Oxford University Press, 1942), pp. 11–15, and Chapter II.

53. Michael Harrington, *The Twilight of Capitalism* (New York: Touchstone, Simon and Schuster, 1976), p. 112.

54. On the transition from a production-oriented society to a consumer-oriented one, see Amitai Etzioni, "The Search for Political Meaning," in *The Center Magazine* 5, 2 (March-April, 1972), pp. 2–8. See also Daniel Bell, *The Cultural Contradictions of Capitalism* (New York: Basic Books, 1976), Chapter 1. And on changes in business ideology see Gerald F. Cavanagh, *American Business Values in Transition* (Englewood Cliffs, N.J.: Prentice-Hall, 1976).

55. See, for example, Fred D. Reynolds and William D. Wells, *Consumer Behavior* (New York: McGraw-Hill, 1977).

56. On "false needs" see Herbert Marcuse, *One Dimensional Man: Studies in the Ideology of Advanced Industrial Society* (Boston: Beacon, 1964), Chapter 9, pp. 225–46.

57. Barnet and Müller, *Global Reach,* pp. 172–84.

58. See "Why It is Called the 'Me' Generation," in *U.S. News & World Report,* March 27, 1978, pp. 40ff. Also Christopher Lasch, *The Culture of Narcissism* (New York: Norton, 1978).

59. Daniel Bell, *The Cultural Contradictions of Capitalism,* p. 25.

60. Seymour Melman, *The Permanent War Economy, American Capitalism in Decline* (New York: Touchstone, Simon and Schuster, 1974), pp. 137–39.

61. Ibid., p. 21.

62. Ibid., pp. 43–44.

63. Ibid., p. 51.

64. Ibid., pp. 200–02.

65. Ibid., p. 144.

66. Ibid., pp. 161–62.

67. Ibid., p. 164.

68. Ibid., p. 141.

69. O'Connor, *The Fiscal Crisis of the State,* pp. 154–57.

70. Kenneth Keniston, "The Alienating Consequences of Capitalist Technology," in *The Capitalist System,* pp. 269–73. See also Herbert Gintis' article on alienation which follows Keniston's in the same volume.

71. Harry Braverman, *Labor and Monopoly Capital, The Degradation of Work in the Twentieth Century* (New York: Monthly Review, 1974), pp. 31–39. See also Stanley Weir, "U.S.A.: The Labor Revolt," in *American Society, Inc.,* pp. 437–51?.

72. Cited by Braverman, *Labor and Monopoly Capital,* pp. 112–18.

73. Ibid., p. 149.

74. Ibid., pp. 321–35. Braverman acknowledges that the Soviet Union has not organized its work processes much better, but he attributes this failure to retreat from socialist objectives and not to inevitability (pp. 14–16).

75. Tibor Scitovsky, *The Joyless Economy, An Inquiry into Human Satisfaction and Consumer Dissatisfaction* (New York: Oxford University Press, 1976).

76. Nicos Poulantzas' *Classes in Contemporary Capitalism,* trans. David Fernbach (London: NLB, Verso edition, 1978), is an important neo-Marxist work. Erik Olin Wright, *Class, Crisis and the State* (London: NLB, 1978) takes up Poulantzas' analysis and offers his own. Wright finds Poulantzas' criteria for the "working class" so restrictive that only 20 percent of the labor force in the United States would be included. Wright's criteria would include as workers the large, white-collar, "new petty bourgeoisie." See his Chapter 2, pp. 53–54 especially.

77. Harold L. Wilensky, "Class, Class Consciousness, and American Workers," in *American Society, Inc.,* pp. 450–62. Wilensky argues that in the United States "a clearly defined working class no longer exists, if it ever did," p. 450.

78. John Kenneth Galbraith, "What Ever Happened to Class Struggle?" in *American Society, Inc.,* pp. 463–69. The quotation is on p. 465.

79. John C. Leggett, *Class, Race, and Labor; Working-class Consciousness in Detroit* (New York: Oxford University Press, 1968). Leggett found class consciousness among Detroit workers in the 1960s still strong, especially among unionized Blacks (Chapter 5). Richard F. Hamilton and James Wright, "The Transformation of the Class Struggle," in *American Society, Inc.,* pp. 470–79, also found it strong among *lower*-class workers.

80. O'Connor, *The Fiscal Crisis of the State,* Chapter 1.

81. James Boggs, *Racism and the Class Struggle* (New York: Modern Reader, 1970) sees white workers as a class above Blacks, pp. 97–98.

82. On Engels' view on women's liberation through socialism see *The Woman Question: Selections from Marx, Engels, Lenin, Stalin* (New York: International Publishers, 1970), pp. 10–11. Juliet Mitchell, *Woman's Estate* (New York: Pantheon, 1971) discusses both the "radical" feminist perspective which argues that male domination preceded capitalism and therefore must be the first to go, and the "socialist"

perspective which gives primacy to the economic restructuring of society. She concludes that both perspectives are needed (p. 95). See also Barbara Sinclair Deckard, *The Women's Movement: Political, Socio-economic, and Psychological Issues* (New York: Harper & Row, 1975), Chapter 14.

83. *Statistical Abstract, 1978,* p. 452.

84. Deckard, *The Women's Movement,* notes that in 1969 women comprised only 3 percent of all lawyers, 1 percent of all engineers, 2 percent of all business executives, 0.5 percent of all architects, pp. 113–14.

85. Tucker, *The Marx-Engels Reader,* 2nd ed., p. 475.

86. David Gold, Clarence Y. H. Leo, and Erik Olin Wright, writing for the *Monthly Review,* October–November, 1975, distinguished three main trends in current Marxist views of the state. The "instrumentalist" view studies the ties between the ruling class and the state. The "structuralist" view, reflected in the writings of Nicos Poulantzas and the Althusserian school, stress the functions which the state fulfills in behalf of the capitalist system. Whether members of the dominant ruling class occupy government positions themselves is not seen as essential. The "Hegelian-Marxist" view stresses ideology and consciousness.

In an article on "Modes of Class Struggle and the Capitalist State," in *Kapitaliststate,* Nos. 4–5, Summer 1976, Gosta Esping-Anderson, Roger Friedland, and Erik Olin Wright offer a somewhat different classification. They distinguish the popularly-held "pluralist" view of the state, the "instrumentalist" view, the "structuralist" view, and a "political class analysis" view. They classify the writings of James O'Connor and Claus Offe under the last head, contending that the structuralist view of the Althusserians takes too little account of conscious will and action. To avoid overcomplicating the issue, and since O'Connor himself writes of the state as a "structure" and of its structural functions, we have retained "structural" as a designation for his approach.

Ralph Miliband, *The State in Capitalist Society* (1969) and *Marxism and Politics* (1977) is generally labelled an "instrumentalist." G. William Domhoff, cited below, rejects this designation given to his works.

87. G. William Domhoff, *Who Rules America?* (Englewood Cliffs, N.J.: Prentice Hall, 1967), pp. 97–99, 105–7.

88. Cited in *The Detroit Free Press,* Parade section, May 23, 1976, p. 4.

89. Ibid. See also Richard Zweigenhaft, "Who Represents America?" a study of the 92nd Congress, in *The Insurgent Sociologist,* Vol. V., No. III, Spring, 1975, pp. 119ff.

90. G. William Domhoff, *The Higher Circles* (New York: Random House, 1971). Paul Sweezy, *Modern Capitalism,* pp. 97–99, and other Marxists had argued that Domhoff's earlier work, *Who Rules America?* had exposed only a "power elite" but not a ruling class. Non-Marxist critics, on the other hand, argued that the presence of upper class members in key positions did not prove that they exercised predominant power. Domhoff sought to answer both sets of criticism in *The Higher Circles.* He attempted to show that the upper class is a ruling class, and in answer to Marxist critics he distinguished between the wealthy upper class and a power elite composed of members from this class *and* higher level employees in institutions controlled by them (pp. 106–7).

91. The three studies cited are by Laurence Shoup, Diana Roose, and Beth Mintz respectively, in a special issue of *The Insurgent Sociologist,* ed. Domhoff, Vol. V., No. III, Spring, 1975.

92. James O'Connor, *The Fiscal Crisis of the State,* p. 69. But as noted in note 86, some would distinguish O'Connor's position from the French structuralists.

93. Ibid., pp. 105–6.

94. James O'Connor, "The Private Welfare State," in *The Poverty of Progress,* ed. Milton Mankoff (New York: Holt, Rinehart and Winston, 1972), pp. 99ff.

95. Michael Harrington, *The Twilight of Capitalism* (New York: Touchstone, Simon and Schuster, 1976), p. 224.

96. Ibid., pp. 226–27.

97. Dowd, *The Twisted Dream,* pp. 177–78.

98. Harrington, *The Twilight of Capitalism,* Chapter 10.

99. Charles Lindbloom, *Politics and Markets, The World's Political-Economic Systems* (New York: Basic Books, 1977), p. 171.

100. Ibid., pp. 172ff.

101. Ibid., p. 176.

102. Ibid., p. 195.

103. Ibid., pp. 195, 214.

104. Ibid., p. 356.

105. Alexander Balinky, *Marx's Economics* (Lexington, Mass.: D. C. Heath, 1970), Chapter IX.

106. Ernest Mandel, *An Introduction to Marxist Economic Theory,* pp. 25ff. His explanation of the theory of surplus value is quite clear.

107. Wright, *Class, Crisis and the State,* pp. 114–19.

108. Harrington, *The Twilight of Capitalism,* pp. 108–19. Marx is often accused of oversimplifying problems and reducing them to one factor. But, says Harrington, Marx *deliberately* oversimplifies at the outset. He begins with simple models to focus on certain features of the capitalist system. He does not intend to describe reality in all its complexity at the outset, but to move from the simple to the more complex, including more elements of reality as he proceeds. Far from changing his mind in Volume III, Marx began his investigations with the more complex reality described there and worked "backwards" to the simpler starting points of Volume I. In *presenting* his ideas Marx goes from the more simple or "abstract" to the more complex or "concrete." At no time does Marx intend labor theory to function as a quantitative measure of real-world prices. Marx doesn't even treat prices in Volume I, and he uses different models to conclude to "average rate of profits" as the measure of prices. By transforming natural resources into social products labor does constitute the source or substance of wealth; but it is not the measure of the price of commodities.

109. Anthony Cutler et al., *Marx's 'Capital' and Capitalism Today* (Boston: Routledge and Kegan Paul, 1977).

110. Samir Amin, "Toward a Structural Crisis of World Capitalism," in *Socialist Revolution,* No. 23, 1975, p. 40.

111. Mandel, *An Introduction to Marxist Economic Theory,* p. 65.

112. Sweezy, *Modern Capitalism,* p. 8.

113. Mandel, *An Introduction,* pp. 55–56. Mandel's *Late Capitalism,* trans. Joris De Bres (London: NLB, Verso Edition, 1978), develops his thesis in much greater detail.

114. Wright, *Class, Crisis and the State,* Chapter 3, pp. 124ff.

115. André Gunder Frank, *Latin America: Underdevelopment or Revolution* (New York: *Monthly Review,* 1970); Samir Amin, *Unequal Development, An Essay on the Social Formations of Peripheral Capitalism,* trans. Brian Pearce (New York: Monthly Review Press, 1977). And for an overview of theories on imperialism, see Tom Kemp, *Theories of Imperialism* (London: Dobson, 1967).

Chapter 5

Liberation Theology in Latin America

The impact of Marxism on Christianity has affected Churches throughout the world. But nowhere has its influence been felt more than in Latin America, where theology and debates over the mission of the Church nearly always involve some confrontation with Marxist thought. For more than a decade now the "theology of liberation" has dominated theological reflection in Latin America. Much of the interest generated by the Episcopal Conference of Latin American Bishops which met in Puebla, Mexico, in early 1979, and by Pope John Paul II's addresses preceding the conference, centered on how they might affect the views and concerns of liberation theology.

Supporters of liberation theology have hailed it as a model for all theological thought, as the first really serious effort by theologians to face the most pressing of human needs from an experiential basis, using a scientific analysis as their guide. The same supporters welcome it as an end to the hegemony of Western Europe in theology. Critics, on the other hand, charge that it is unrealistic and uncritical in its adoption of Marxist and socialist views, or that it manipulates the gospel to justify a priori political options.

The present chapter is an attempt to explain the main ideas of liberation theology, to note where Marxism plays some role in their formulation, and to attempt some evaluations. The main features of liberation theology are grouped under four headings: method/praxis; political and ideological critiques; new awareness/new biblical perspectives; the role of the Church. But first it may be helpful to provide some background which helps to explain liberation theology.

Background

Liberation theology addresses itself to a dramatically serious problem, to conditions of massive, desperate poverty and often to conditions of political oppression which block efforts and hopes for change. A visitor to Latin America may see many signs of growth and affluence, skyscrapers and luxury hotels, brilliant architectural projects in places like Brasilia (capital of Brazil),

172

gracious haciendas and luxuriant groves. But these benefit only a few. Behind these lie the bedrock poverty, malnutrition, illiteracy, and shabby housing which characterize the lot of the vast majority of Latin American people.

Conditions in Latin America

In almost every nation of Latin America 5 percent of the population controls 80 percent of the wealth. The overwhelming majority of the populace are completely landless. Most work for practically nothing. Brazilian sugar cane workers make about two dollars a day. Near Recife in Brazil a father picks corn and cotton for rich landowners to support his family on 65 cents a day. In Caracas, Venezuela, slum dwellers spend six hours a day commuting to work. Foreign investors, at the same time, amass profits to be transferred to affluent owners in other countries. United States investors buy up 60 million acres of Amazonia in Brazil.

Most people in Latin America go hungry. An estimated two-thirds of the population are undernourished. One half of Bolivia's children suffer from malnutrition and consequent brain damage. A study of one small town in northeastern Brazil showed 76 percent of all children under five to be seriously malnourished. Children in the slums of crowded cities roam streets in search of fresh garbage; children in impoverished rural areas eat clay when rice and beans run out. In the Andes of Peru and Bolivia natives chew cocoa leaves to stave off the pain of hunger.

In the villages of Bolivia peasants live in mud huts together with pigs and chickens. In Lima, Peru, over half the population are squatters. Nearly one-half of the people in Latin America suffer from some infectious or deficiency disease; few receive any medical care. Three-fourths of the people in some countries are illiterate. But when peasants in El Salvador and Brazil or workers in Bolivia or Peru demand fair rights, their efforts are crushed by force.

These are but brief descriptions of very desperate conditions.[1] Without them the whole issue of liberation theology could seem to be only an academic problem. It is not, for it concerns the response and responsibility of the Church in the face of such conditions.

The special situation of the Church in Latin America, especially the Catholic Church, must be taken into account, for it differs considerably from situations in the United States and Europe where religion is a more private affair. Measured in terms of Mass attendance, the significance of the Church in Latin America may not seem great. But the faith still plays an important cultural role in the life of the people. Moreover the Church is seen as the only major institution still free and strong enough to promote change. For centuries the Catholic Church played a very conservative role in Latin American society, but significant and often very dramatic changes have occurred over the last fifteen years. Bishops, as well as priests, religious, and lay people, have engaged in the struggle against injustice. Bishops have been jailed, kidnapped, and beaten; priests have been killed for their efforts to defend the rights of the poor. Conservative and even reactionary elements in the Church still remain strong; radicals threaten to polarize the Church from the other side; moderates try to steer between them. The tensions within the Church over responses to socio-political issues underlie much of the controversy about liberation theology and create significant differences within the movement itself.

The Influence of Paulo Freire

Many of the changing attitudes within the Church in Latin America grew out of commitments on the part of many priests and religious to become more actively involved with the poor and to help them become more conscious of their rights and dignity as human beings. While no single person can be credited with stimulating this change, the work and writings of Paulo Freire played a significant role both in influencing this new involvement and by providing ideas on "praxis" which would become pivotal in the method of liberation theology.

Freire wrote of the *Pedagogy of the Oppressed*. The oppressed who concerned him were the millions of illiterate peasants and urban dwellers of Latin America whose illiteracy locked them into a dehumanized "culture of silence." Overcoming illiteracy usually suggests teaching the poor or underprivileged to read and write in order to obtain better jobs or to enjoy the world of books. Freire approached the problem differently, for he saw illiteracy as affecting the entire self-image of the poor and their very possibility of full human development. As a child in Brazil during the great depression of the 1930s Freire had himself experienced how hunger and poverty created listlessness and apathy toward learning. At age eleven he vowed to fight against such conditions. He fulfilled his vow by organizing literacy campaigns in northeastern Brazil, campaigns which came to an end when he was jailed after the military coup of 1964.

His arrest and imprisonment make evident that his literacy campaign was viewed as a political threat. Indeed it was. But not because he "indoctrinated" the peasants with revolutionary ideas. His views on the dignity of each human person militated against such indoctrination. What did make the method revolutionary was that through it the poor came to a new awareness of themselves, began to look critically at their situation, and to recognize the possibilities of changing it.

Freire called this process "conscientization" (*conscientização*). It meant learning to perceive social, political, and economic contradictions and taking action against the oppressive elements of reality.[2] Awakening the consciousness of the poor does risk unleashing aggression and anger. But to give way to this fear only confirms the status quo and implies that it would be better for the poor not to recognize their oppression. They must pass through a stage of wanting to dominate, as they have been dominated, before they recognize what true liberation means.[3]

The oppressed must liberate *themselves*. On this point Freire insists. The oppressed have too often been victims of "false generosity," of people wanting to do good for them. "A real humanist can be identified more by his trust in the people, which engages him in their struggle, than by a thousand actions in their favor without that trust."[4] The self-liberating work of the oppressed does not mean others should not become involved. In fact Freire insists that the fundamental role throughout the history of the struggle against oppression has been carried out by members of the oppressing class who have gone over to the side of the oppressed. But too often in doing this they bring their class prejudice with them. They do not have confidence in the people's ability to think and act for themselves. The temptation to think and act *for* the poor is strong. The poor tend to be fatalistic ("What can I do?"), to be self-deprecating ("I'm not good for anything"), to be dependent ("You explain it; you know"). A revolutionary leader who accepts these feelings tends to use "propaganda" to convince the poor—the very method of the oppressors.

Freire's views on education build on the implications of this stance. He challenges a "banking concept of education" which treats the learner as a passive, empty container to be filled with the teacher's superior knowledge.[5] He proposes instead a "problem-posing" pedagogy which opens up the possibility for the oppressed to find their own answers to their own questions, to express their own needs and views. Freire elaborates on this method in discussing the role of generative words and themes, and of "decoding." The method enables the oppressed to speak their own "word," to name the world and to change it, for there is no word without praxis.

The notion of "praxis" is central to Freire's method and thought. True liberation can only be achieved through human beings who make their own history.[6] Praxis is the practical activity essential to transforming the world, but it also builds on theory and calls for changes in theory. While Freire's concept of praxis clearly echoes Marx's dictum that "men make their own history," it contrasts sharply with Lenin's insistence that revolutionary theory must be brought "from without." Freire acknowledges that revolutionary leaders are needed to help oppressed people construct a theory of liberating action. But it must be *their* theory, their word.[7] Freire warns that leftists can be as guilty of manipulating people as rightists. This occurs especially with "sectarians" who consider anything that is not their truth as a lie, who suffer from the absence of any doubt about their position.[8]

In articulating his own principles of liberation, Freire laid the groundwork for the method to be adopted by liberation theologians, a method that begins with commitment and praxis. How liberation theology conceives this praxis will be an important consideration. But several other points of emphasis in

Freire appear in liberation theology as well: the unmasking of false percep-
tions of the world, the centrality of political domination as the major problem
of Latin America, violence as initiated by the oppressors, and liberation as
restoring humanity to the oppressors as well.

Political Theology in Europe

The relation of European political theology to liberation theology is a
controversial issue. Many liberation theologians studied in Europe. Many
theological ideas enunciated by Jürgen Moltmann and Johannes B. Metz are
taken up by liberation theology: God is revealed *in* history and promises a
new future; the future God promised is a "new heaven *and* a new earth"; the
realization of this future calls for active collaboration of Christians in an effort
to transform the world; the Church must act for the sake of the world, not for
its own interests; the Church must become "an institution of social criticism"
confronting injustice in the world.[9] But if similarities exist, liberation theologians believe that their method of doing theology is quite different from that
of European political theology. They see liberation theology as more
grounded in concrete praxis and experience, more specific in its analyses of
socio-political conditions, and more committed to action.[10] Whatever link
may have existed at the outset, liberation theology quickly developed its own
distinctive character based on Latin American experiences, and it was from
within the Latin American Church that it received the impetus it needed for
growth.

The Medellín Conference

In the late summer of 1968, the Second General Conference of Latin
American Bishops (CELAM) met in Medellín, Colombia, to address major
issues related to the mission of the Church in Latin America. The bishops'
very use of the term "liberation" proved important. Before 1965 the term
"liberation" was not widely used. Reference more often was made to the need
for "development." But as Latin Americans began to realize that they were
"being *kept* in a state of underdevelopment' by their dependence on foreign
capital, use of liberation language became more pronounced.[11] Liberation
theology itself was still in a formative stage, so the Medellín conference did
not address itself to the emergent movement itself. But it did give prominence to the idea of liberation both as a socio-political term and as a theological one.

In addressing the issue of "Justice" the bishops charged that the misery
which besets large masses in Latin America was an "injustice which cries to
the heavens."[12] God intended that all should share in the goods of the earth,
and God sent his son "that he might come to liberate" all people from the
slavery to which sin had subjected them, from hunger, misery, oppression,

and ignorance.[13] The bishops attacked, as an erroneous concept of private property, a view which identifies a business with the owners of capital. In an authentically human economy a business is a community of persons, and persons cannot be the property of an individual, a society, or a state.[14] The bishops warned against Marxist systems which tend toward totalitarian concentration of state power, but they encouraged the awakening of social consciousness in all strata of society. They affirmed: "The Church—the People of God—will lend its support to the downtrodden of every social class so that they might come to know their rights and how to make use of them."[15]

In addressing "Peace" the bishops decried the extreme inequality that exists between social classes.[16] They attacked international imperialism and placed the principal guilt for the economic dependence of Latin American countries on foreign monopolistic powers.[17] They warned against the use of violence but recognized that situations of injustice were so grave as to constitute "institutional violence."[18] In speaking of "Poverty of the Church" they called for solidarity with and commitment to the poor.[19]

If the documents fell short of what some may have hoped for, they affirmed many of the points liberation theology would stress: poverty and oppression as major pastoral concerns, the biblical grounds for speaking of "liberation," the recognition of foreign imperialism and economic dependency as root causes of Latin American poverty, commitment to solidarity with the poor, and the need to denounce injustice and oppression.

Method and Praxis in Liberation Theology

Gustavo Gutiérrez's *A Theology of Liberation* was published in 1971 and appeared in English translation two years later. It remains the best known work in liberation theology and the best overall statement of its position. The exposition which follows most often uses Gutiérrez's work as a starting point and relates other liberation theologians to issues he discusses. The general plan of his book, moreover, reveals an inner dynamic which can be summarized and used as an initial overview of the method underlying liberation theology.[20]

1. *Commitment to Praxis:* Liberation theology begins with a commitment to live the gospel, by sharing in the lives and struggles of the poor, and by striving with them to bring about the changes needed to liberate them.

2. *Critical Reflection* (Political and Ideological Critiques): This praxis, this practical effort to live out the gospel, leads one to critical reflection. It leads one to look for the root causes of poverty and oppression, and to question the whole prevailing socio-economic system. It leads one also to question and criticize the way in which the Church has operated and expressed itself, in its theology, its social teachings, and its pastoral ministry.

3. *New Awareness/New Biblical Dimensions:* Out of this same praxis comes a newness of faith, the discovery of God's liberating power and the implica-

tions of this for understanding the faith. This discovery enables one to see Christian faith in a whole new light, to experience it with the eyes of the poor, and to recognize the promise it holds.

4. *The Role of the Church:* This new understanding of the faith leads to a new understanding of the Church and what its role should be in the given historical situation of Latin America.

These four headings will serve as the main divisions of the chapter, with "method" considered especially in conjunction with commitment to praxis.

The Method of Liberation Theology

Method is the most important feature of liberation theology and the key to understanding it. Gutiérrez's first chapter deals explicitly with method. But, as the brief summary above may suggest, method provides the key for understanding the whole of liberation theology. Gutiérrez defines liberation theology as "a critical reflection on Christian praxis in the light of the Word."[21] While this first section deals explicitly with method it is worth repeating that the whole of liberation theology is rooted in its methodology.

Theology, Gutiérrez begins, is an effort to understand the faith. In early centuries of the Church it was essentially a meditation on the Bible, a wisdom geared toward spiritual growth. It borrowed Platonic categories which emphasized contemplation and the life of the soul over the concerns of this life. From the twelfth century on, theology began to establish itself as a "science," as a systematic effort to unite faith and reason. Liberation theology brings a new methodology by beginning with critical reflection on praxis. Theology in the past stressed understanding the truths of revelation. Liberation theology emphasizes "doing the truth," first being actively engaged in living out the gospel and then, in the light of this experience, reflecting upon it. For liberation theology, doing the truth (orthopraxis) is far more important and far more consistent with the gospel than simply assenting to the truth (orthodoxy).

> The Christian community professes a "faith which works through charity." It is—at least ought to be—real charity, action, and commitment to the service of men. Theology is reflection, a critical attitude. Theology *follows*; it is the second step.[22]

The emphasis on "critical" reflection means that one must examine the Church's principles and attitudes, and one's own. The "reflection" starts not as theology did in the past with revelation and tradition, but with the questions which the present situation and history pose. In short, liberation theology offers not so much new themes as a new way of doing theology, a way that begins with commitment to praxis.

Praxis as a Starting Point

The three elements of Gutiérrez' definition—(1) critical reflection, (2) on Christian praxis, (3) in the light of the Word—are not separable in practice. But for the sake of explaining liberation theology it may be helpful to deal with them separately. Any truly human action is a thoughtful action. The notion of "praxis" implies this. Praxis is not action alone separated from thought or theory, but action guided by thought. Thought directs actions. But praxis involves a constant re-thinking of attitudes and theory, and a re-direction of actions on the basis of this re-thinking.

The idea of praxis, as Gutiérrez observes, has origins in Christianity itself. God's revelation and God's presence in the world call for a response. The response is not just understanding truths revealed but a commitment to live the faith.[23] From St. Paul and St. Augustine, through St. Ignatius's "contemplation in action," and into Vatican II's theology of the "signs of the times," the importance of Christian praxis has been stressed. The influence of Marxist thought, with its focus on praxis geared to the transformation of the world, has helped theology to recognize the importance of understanding faith in the light of human praxis in history. Liberation theology thus begins with commitment to praxis, with a conviction that theology can only be truly done through efforts to live the faith together with the poor who constitute the vast majority of Latin American people, and to reflect with them on the liberating hopes revealed by God.[24]

By beginning with praxis, liberation theology distinguishes itself from traditional theology in three ways. First, liberation theology begins with a situation rather than beginning with the Bible or with Church dogmas as traditional theology did and still does. Juan Luis Segundo stresses this difference. Traditional theology, and most theology even in the present, moves from theological truths to applications of these in the world. Since Christianity is a biblical religion, this way of doing theology focuses first on the Bible itself; reinterpreting the Bible in the light of the present comes after this. The traditional method uses sciences which help scholars to understand the past, for example, the study of ancient languages and literary forms. Liberation theology, in contrast, begins with situations in the present. In Latin America this means especially beginning with the actual political-economic situation of the vast majority of its people. Liberation theology considers social sciences which explain the present situation as more important than sciences which look only to the past, for understanding the Bible. The liberation theologian suspects, moreover, that all ideas, including theological ones, are intimately bound up with existing social situations so that theology cannot be studied or carried out autonomously.[25]

Second, liberation theology contends that theological truth cannot be attained through study alone but only through commitment and active engagement with others in an effort to transform the world. The very purpose of knowledge is to transform the world. Hugo Assmann insists that the task of transforming the world is so intimately linked to the interpretation of the world, that the latter is seen to be impossible without the former. "Reflection ceases to have a world of its own and becomes simply a critical function of action; its world and its truth are experience itself, and there is no more flight to a verbal world decked with ontological considerations that reflect man's inability to deal with the real problems."[26] Or in the words of Rubem Alves, "Truth is the name given by the historical community to those actions which were, are, and will be effective for the liberation of man."[27]

Third, liberation theology holds that theology can never be independent of praxis. It is precisely a critical reflection *on* praxis. The praxis it addresses is not primarily one's personal actions or commitment but the collective praxis of society, of the Church, of groups engaged in bringing about change. It reflects critically on past praxis, especially on the ways in which Christians and the Church have looked upon their faith and the world. But, as Alfredo Fierro observes, it is also a reflection geared to some subsequent praxis. "It gathers in the more vital concrete experiences of collective activity and explores their dynamic thrust into the future."[28]

Some Comments about the Use of Praxis

Since praxis is a central concept in both liberation theology and Marxism, some effort at evaluating its use may be helpful before proceeding to the next major section. Liberation theology begins with critical reflection on praxis. One of the most significant contributions of liberation theology is its efforts to see and experience faith "from the eyes of the poor" and to do this by a commitment to work with them for change. This starting point is important not only for the light it sheds upon Christianity but also because it constitutes a new strategy of social change for the Church, an effort to work from the bottom up.

Two concerns about the use of praxis, however, should be voiced. First, the caution noted by Paulo Freire comes into play. Not to work politically with the poor would mean that one believes that they are contented to be poor and oppressed, or that they can liberate themselves without any outside help, or that moral appeals to the wealthy and powerful will bring about change. But working with the poor always risks the danger of imposing political views on them, or raising their consciousness as to what concerns they "should" have and what tactics they should follow.

Dick Howard, writing on *The Marxian Legacy,* makes an important distinction between two senses of praxis. He speaks of theory *for* practice and of a theory *of* practice. Lenin, he says, tends to be a representative of the first, and Antonio Gramsci of the second.[29] In the first sense Marxism is viewed as a theory brought in by avant-garde leaders to guide workers. In the second sense Marxism is an expression of the workers' own praxis, of their own struggles and strategies. The first view, as I see it, runs the risk Freire addressed of imposing a theory, of viewing praxis as an effort to inculcate in others definite views on correct tactics and solutions. To the extent that it sees these tactics and solutions as already proven by past experience or authority, it can also negate the very meaning of praxis which involves a constant re-thinking of positions in the light of experience.

Several liberation theologians have drawn similar distinctions. Gutiérrez insists that liberation theology's purpose is not to elaborate an ideology to justify positions already taken; it does not purport to be a Christian ideology of revolution.[30] Enrique Dussel warns that absolutizing any one political project is anti-Christian.[31] Juan Carlos Scannone insists that the historical praxis of liberation theology must concern the praxis of *all* Latin American peoples and not the praxis of an avant-garde.[32]

A second concern about the use of praxis deals with recognition of its limits. Reflection on praxis can be immensely insightful and fruitful; it is indispensable for planning strategies and tactics of social change. But praxis of itself does not point to or prove any one correct line of action. Praxis is not a final criterion of truth, for the praxis itself must be evaluated. The history of Marxism and of political movements in general shows that different groups and factions, even when they work for change within the same historical situation, arrive at very different and conflicting views as to what strategy or tactics are called for. The failure of some tactic may "prove" to one group that the tactic won't work and to another that only the timing and organization of it was wrong. Groups and individuals who worked to achieve socialism in Chile reached very different conclusions on the basis of the praxis. But this difficulty points only to the limits of praxis; it does not affect the importance and inherent values of praxis as a starting point

Critical Reflection: Political and Ideological Critiques

Several years ago Gutiérrez described his own experience when he began to work with the poor. His personal account shows in very concrete terms how a commitment to the poor through praxis leads from awareness of situations to critical reflections about the entire political-economic system and about the need for a new Christian approach to political action. He said, in summary form:

> I discovered three things. I discovered that poverty was a destructive thing, something to be fought against and destroyed, not merely something which was the object of our charity. Secondly, I discovered that poverty was not accidental. The fact that these people are poor and not rich is not just a matter of chance, but the result of a structure. It was a

structural question. Thirdly, I discovered that poor people were a social class. When I discovered that poverty was something to be fought against . . . it became crystal clear that in order to serve the poor, one had to move into political action.[33]

A Political-Economic Critique of "Development"

Experiencing the poverty and oppression of those who constitute the vast majority in Latin America led Gutiérrez and many others to look for the structural causes of these conditions. It led especially to a critical re-examination of the models and policies of "development." Most countries in Latin America had been looked upon as "underdeveloped" in contrast to the rich developed nations of the United States and Western Europe. The developed countries were thus held up as models—culturally and socially as well as economically—of the path that underdeveloped nations must take. The 1950s and 1960s were to be "decades of development" in which Latin American countries would follow the lead of wealthier nations. Latin America would learn from their technology, their efficiency, their political reforms, and be helped by their aid to "catch up."

Developmental policies, Gutiérrez judged, had obviously failed in Latin America. Not only did poverty and oppression continue but the gap between the poor countries of the world and the rich had widened. More importantly it was becoming increasingly clear that the continuing misery in Latin America was in great part *caused* by the dependency which developmental policies encouraged. The people of Latin America were realizing that their own development would come about only through a struggle to break the domination of rich countries and their own native oligarchies. True development would come only through the struggle for liberation.[34]

On this basic point liberation theologians appear solidly in agreement. Development models had failed; new directions which could liberate Latin America from economic dependency had to be followed. Hugo Assmann lists a series of successive frustrations which led to complete disillusionment with development: the failure of the Alliance for Progress; the imperialist control of organizations such as the Agency for International Development (AID) which were supposed to help development; the failure of Latin American countries to make even modest demands heard at international meetings; the militarization of the continent and structures of repression supported by the CIA; the massive influx of foreign capital and control.[35]

José Míguez Bonino makes two additional points about dependence and development. First, he reminds us that dependence is not a new fact. Spain looked to Latin America to provide its gold and silver centuries ago, just as Western Europe and the United States now look to Latin America for coffee, copper, tin, and bananas. Second, development even where apparently successful does not mean better conditions for the mass of the population. By 1970 Brazil could boast a high rate of growth in its GNP. But 41.6 percent of the total Brazilian industry was in foreign hands. Increased production did not benefit those in need; the purchasing value of salaries had fallen 23.5 percent. The Brazilian population was simply a reserve of cheap labor for multinational corporations, with the government, army, and police simply acting as wardens.[36]

The conviction that reformist, developmental policies had failed, and that a more radical liberation from systems of economic dependence and oppression was needed, was the conclusion from historical praxis which most determined the political direction of liberation theology. It was this fundamental conviction about the situation in Latin America which has led some liberation theologians to speak out for the value of Marxist analysis. Marxism, says Míguez Bonino, "offers a scientific, verifiable, and efficacious way to articulate love historically."[37]

The Issue of Marxism as a Scientific Analysis

The use of Marxist analysis by Christians in Latin America, and claims that Marxism is scientific, have provoked a great deal of controversy. Some effort at appraisal of these issues may be useful at this point, though the appraisals may only add to the controversy. Two different questions might be asked. How much is liberation theology's praxis and call for liberation based on Marxist analysis? Does Marxism qualify as a scientific analysis and program of action?

In response to the first question, three different points might be made. First, liberation theology itself contains relatively little socio-economic analysis as such, at least judged by books and articles published in English. Jürgen Moltmann raises this point as a criticism, saying that for all its stress on the necessity of socio-economic analysis of conditions in Latin America, liberation theology itself carries out very little of such analysis.[38] But do theologians need to become economists to stress the importance of such analysis? I think not. Liberation theology's praxis *is* grounded on the conviction that development has failed and that the problem of dependence is basic. As Segundo Galilea observes, liberation theology is rooted in three assumptions about Latin America: that the vast majority of Latin Americans live in a state of underdevelopment and unjust dependence, that in Christian terms this constitutes a "sinful situation," and that Christians have a duty in conscience to commit themselves to overcome this situation.[39]

Second, if the first assumption noted by Galilea is taken as Marxist, then the bishops of Latin America can also be accused of subscribing to a Marxist analysis. The bishops at Medellín characterized the situation of Latin American countries explicitly as one of "dependence." After addressing the oppressions that arise from internal colonialism, they spelled out various aspects of the dependence created by external neocolonialism: one-crop dependencies and depreciation of the value of raw materials in relation to manufactured goods; the flight of economic and human capital out of Latin America; tax evasions by foreign companies and loss of their dividends; progressive debt. The bishops concluded, moreover, that the "principal guilt for economic dependence" rested with imperialistic monopolies.[40] The more recent Puebla documents, if less forceful, still point to "dependence," to "the presence of multinational conglomerates," and to "economic systems that do not regard the human being as the center of society" as some of the underlying roots of poverty and underdevelopment.[41] North American critics may feel that imperialism and capitalism are made the scapegoats of all Latin America's problems. But convictions about the fundamental causes of underdevelopment in Latin America come not from Marxists alone. They are widely held, and the last chapter attempted to show the reasons for these convictions. Even an archcritic of liberation theology, Bishop Alfonso López Trujillo, affirms: "We are convinced that capitalism is a human failure."[42]

Third, liberation theologians have not, as a group, made Marxism an exclusive or necessarily privileged tool of analysis. Gutiérrez makes no direct mention of the need for Marxist analysis in his A Theology of Liberation, though he does stress the importance of class struggle analysis. None of the thirteen authors in Frontiers of Theology in Latin America speaks of Marxism as an essential tool for analysis. It may be, as John Coleman contends, that many liberation theologians simply identify social science analysis with Marxism.[43] But direct references to Marxist analysis occur much less frequently than one would be led by critics to expect, and references to Marxism tend to be qualified when they are made.[44] On the other hand, given liberation theology's conviction about underdevelopment, and given the pervasiveness of Marxist ideas in Latin America, one could hardly analyze the problems of Latin America without at least implicit use of Marxist ideas.

Is Marxism scientific? There are certainly strong grounds for suspicions of such a claim. Classical Marxism proclaimed itself to be a "scientific socialism." Under the umbrella of science were included the atheistic-materialistic worldview of Marxism, its discovery of dialectical "laws" governing nature and history, and the historical inevitablity of socialism. What had been clearly philosophical principles of dialectical thinking in Hegel became scientific laws in Marxism, with all events in nature and history schematized under these laws. Numerous critics of Marxism have charged that this classical view of Marxism contains an amalgam of metaphysical and ideological elements that do not qualify as scientific. They charge that Marxism used the prestige of science to cloak its political goals.[45] Critical Marxists (see Chapter 2) have also challenged the exaggerated claims of scientific objectivity made by classical Marxism. But many of the continued claims on behalf of Marxism as a science *are* made in the name of classical Marxism since it remains strong in the dominant Marxist tradition.

Many neo-Marxists, following Althusser, distinguish between Marxist ideology and its scientific method. But even this distinction needs to be examined. Let us assume that the Marxist method of analysis can be separated from its worldview, that the social sciences in general can be called scientific, and that Marxist methodology has a rightful place within the social sciences. The first assumption will be examined more carefully in Chapter 7, but my own use of certain aspects of Marxist analysis in the last chapter implied such a separation. This same use implied that Marxism does provide a fruitful and systematic method of socio-economic analysis which justifies calling it, along with many other sociological and economic methods, scientific. But the mere use of a method does not guarantee scientific conclusions. Most today would accept economics as a legitimate social science. But that alone tells us little about a specific study or analysis. Economic analysis can be snoddy and amateurish or highly professional. Even recognized professional competence does not guarantee conclusions because of the assumptions that often govern a given study. Many certainly recognize the competence, but dispute the conclusions, of Milton Friedman's analyses based on a free-market, competitive capitalism model. So, too, Marxism may indeed be a useful tool of analysis, but every specific analysis must be evaluated on its own merits. The use of a Marxist method of analysis does not prove that Marxism in general provides scientific facts or conclusions. Hence it means very little to say Marxism is scientific.

Tactics, strategy, and plans for building a socialist society lie outside the realm of science. Politics, as Gramsci noted, is an "art." Tactics, strategy, and plans can *build* on scientific analysis, but they involve political skills, utopian hopes, and value judgments that do not belong to science.[46] Míguez Bonino's quotation, that Marxism offers a scientific, verifiable way to articulate love historically, suggests that Marxist tactics and plans are scientific. Its *analysis* may be scientific, but analysis only points up what is wrong. The great fear of critics is that Marxism, while calling itself a science, will become a religion, with its whole program embraced uncritically and unreservedly. But to reject all forms of Marxist *analysis* could turn the Church away from necessary investigations into the structural causes of poverty and oppression, and hence away from social change itself. What is needed, it seems obvious to me, is a critical use of Marxist analysis with an awareness of its assumptions and limits.

Ideological Critique of Church Doctrines

The criticism of development as a model for dealing with political-economic problems in Latin America led also to criticism of prevailing Christian attitudes and Church teachings as they relate to these problems. The Church, Gutiérrez contended, has considered the "spiritual life" more important than politics. When it has addressed political life, the Church's doctrines have tended to be humanistic rather than scientifically grounded analyses. Personal and conciliatory aspects of the gospel message have been stressed rather than political and conflictual dimensions.[47]

How has the Church conceived of its relationship to the political world? In the long age of "Christendom" rulers and ruled all shared the same faith. Since this no longer prevails Gutiérrez focuses rather on prevailing Church views which he found symbolized in Jacques Maritain's espousal of a "New Christendom." This view separates the temporal and the spiritual, the laity and the clergy. The laity work within the temporal, political world to transform society; the Church and its priests provide principles and inspiration but are not to become directly involved in politics. This approach fails, says Gutiérrez, because the Church *is* linked to political power in the world whether it thinks it is or not. The supposed autonomy of the Church conceals the real political option of a large sector of the Church, namely, its support of the established order.[48]

From a Protestant background, José Míguez Bonino offers a similar critique of how churches in Latin America have related to the political world. During the Spanish Colonial period the Catholic Church allied with aristocratic landowners, though the Church's role was always subordinate since it depended for protection of its own interests and property on the landowning class. Neocolonial Christianity in Latin America reflected the Protestant spirit, and in fact Protestantism made its entry into Latin America in the late nineteenth-century. New national leaders, the growing class of business entrepreneurs, and the liberal intelligentsia, all felt at home with a Protestant ethic that stressed democracy, political freedoms, and reform. The Catholic Church found itself still clinging to its traditional allies and alienated from the peasants, the emerging working class, and from liberals and the intelligentsia as well. The Church's efforts to "catch up" in the twentieth century were reflected in its support of Christian Democratic parties.[49]

Juan Luis Segundo has developed the most systematic ideological critique of the Church and its doctrines. His methodology, which employs a "hermeneutic circle," is spelled out in the first chapter of his *Liberation of Theology*. He defines the hermeneutic circle as "the continuing change in our interpretation of the Bible which is dictated by the continuing change in our present-day reality, both individual and societal."[50] This means that each new reality obliges us to interpret the word of God afresh, to change reality accordingly, and then go back and reinterpret the word of God again.

We have already seen how Gutiérrez found that a new experience of the poor and their situation led him to criticize both the developmental approach to social change and Church views on politics. Segundo uses the concept of "suspicion," of suspecting society's influence on theology, as part of the process leading to new awareness and new political and theological views. First, new experience of reality leads one to ideological suspicion; second, this ideological suspicion leads one to question the whole ideological structure of society, including theology. Thus, for example, new experience of poverty and oppression leads one to suspect that the traditional view, which opposes political involvement by the Church, serves as a political support for the status quo. This suspicion leads one to examine critically the whole domain of theology and Church practices: the sacraments, pastoral ministry, practices of piety, etc. Third, a new experience of theological reality leads one to exegetical suspicion; fourth, this exegetical suspicion leads one to a new way of interpreting scripture.[51] Thus, for example, a new experience of the liberating power of God leads one to suspect scriptural interpretations which have stressed only charity and not justice as the message of the Bible, and which link salvation to life hereafter and not to human liberation from oppression. This supicion opens one to a whole new understanding of scripture: to God revealing himself in history on the side of the poor, to the centrality of justice in both the Old and New Testaments, to the promises of a new heaven and a new earth.

Segundo's methodology touches on the whole scope of liberation theology. Our emphasis in this section is on his second step, his ideological critique of theology. His approach quite clearly draws upon Marx's insight that the superstructure of a society reflects its economic base. Dominant political ideas, religious ideas, philosophical ideas, and moral values to a great extent reflect the ideas and values of the dominant social class. But Marx failed, says Segundo, to complete the hermeneutic circle. Marx saw *only* the ideological elements in religion. He failed to appreciate the positive values and potential of religion and consequently he did not go back to religion to interpret it anew.[52]

Numerous examples could be given of how ideology infiltrates into Church doctrines and practices. The very idea of God became deformed. Early Christianity recognized an immanent God who is "before us" (the Father), "with us" (the Son), and "within us" (the Holy spirit). But Greek and Western thought made God transcendent and impersonal. The doctrine of the Trinity tells us that God is a community, this is a politically significant mystery which can point to what human society should be. But the Trinity became interpreted in a way that placed God in an eternal world apart.[53]

The Eucharist must be examined to see the influence of ideology in its interpretation and use. The Eucharist is viewed as a symbol of the unity of the Church. But there is no real unity in the world; the real world is marked by conflict and class antagonisms. By masking this fact the Church only reinforces divisions by not dealing with them. The spirituality of the Church likewise shows the influence of ideology. It stresses reconciliation and peace as gifts of the Spirit, and often offers only prayer as a recourse to the poor and oppressed. The Church has lacked a spirituality of Liberation.[54] Finally, the pastoral life of the Church can and does have this same effect of confirming the status quo. By giving priority to the internal life of the Church, to traditional catechetics and liturgical change, and by failing to recognize the primacy of politics in the real world, the Church permits the present system to continue without being challenged.

Some Comments on the Ideological Critique

Church teachings and practices have been used, consciously or not, as an "ideological screen" in support of the established order.[55] Social teachings on "the natural order" of classes, preaching aimed at teaching the poor to be patient and content with their lot, stress on peace and reconciliation and avoidance of conflict, all have had the effect of legitimizing prevailing systems. The charge that liberation theology simply reduces the faith to ideology does not square with efforts of Segundo and others to "complete the circle," to return to the faith with new understanding and love. But every *use* of ideological critique does not thereby become justified. Conducting a school, hearing confessions, visiting the sick could all be judged as justifying the status quo by one who believes that all Church efforts should go into organizing workers or peasants. When political groups want a particular strategy followed, almost any teaching or practice of the Church which does not favor this strategy can be "unmasked" as ideological. Some revolutionary Christian socialists in Chile did, it seems to me, use an exaggerated ideological critique to attack bishops for not supporting a very specific and very questionable revolutionary strategy (see the next chapter).

The issue of whether the Church can and should speak out on the issue of socialism versus capitalism will be discussed later in the chapter. But the whole issue of the Church and politics, and priests involved in politics, goes far beyond the question of Marxism and Christianity. Any attempt to resolve it with a few brief comments would be wholly inadequate.[56]

New Awareness/New Biblical Dimensions

The critique of development policies and the critique of ideological elements in Church doctrine supportive only of reformism led liberation theologians to a new awareness. Authentic liberation, Gutiérrez claimed, could only come to Latin America only through a liberation from domination exercised by the great capitalist countries and their domestic allies who control the national power structure. Such a liberation would require creating an entirely new kind of society. It would mean being open to socialism; it would mean learning from Marxism about structural causes and from Paulo Freire about conscientization.[57] It would also require the active participation of the oppressed. "It is the poor who must be protagonists of their own liberation."[58]

This new awareness led to the discovery of new dimensions in scripture about God's liberating power, and to new convictions about the role of the Church. Liberation, Assmann noted, means more than just freedom or improvement. It implies a judgment on, a condemnation of, the present state

of affairs. It is a word of confrontation and conflict. It expresses a new
historical awareness among Latin American peoples, and awareness that they
are not just insufficiently developed but dominated and oppressed peoples.[59]
But with this new consciousness of oppression came also a new way of
experiencing God and understanding Christian faith.

What in the Bible and Christian faith speaks to hopes of liberation from
conditions of oppression and bondage?[60] Four related biblical themes recur
most often in liberation theology as a response to this question: God as
liberator, with the Exodus as a special prototype; God's command to "do
justice," reflected in the denunciations of the prophets; Jesus, liberation and
the Kingdom of God; Jesus and the confrontations in his life which gave a
"political dimension" to his actions. These four themes will serve as a basis for
discussing new bibilical dimensions in liberation theology.

God as Liberator: Exodus

Through the influence of Greek philosophy on Christianity, God came to
be thought of as eternal, unchangeable, and outside of human history. Theology consequently said little about God's role in history apart from the one
moment of the Incarnation. Recent biblical scholarship, however, has placed
great stress on God's part in history, noting that God revealed himself only
gradually over a period of time and by entering into human history. Thus the
expression "the God of Abraham, Isaac, and Jacob" communicates this sense
of God gradually revealing more of himself to successive generations in the
course of Israel's history. He reveals himself by acting in history to bring
salvation.

God initiates human history by his gift of creation. He saves humanity from
destruction by floods when he appears to Noah; he promises to make
Abraham the father of a new nation; through Joseph he acts to spare the
descendants of Abraham from starvation; through Moses he liberates the
Israelites from slavery in Egypt and leads them to the promised land. Thus, as
Gutiérrez observes, "biblical faith is, above all, faith in a God who reveals
himself through historical events, a God who saves in history."[61] The salvation which God brings, moreover, is not just the salvation of the soul in a life
hereafter. As these historical events manifested, God acted to affect the lives
of persons on earth, to free them from hunger and misery, to liberate them
from Egyptian oppression, to bring them to a promised land.

The Exodus, especially, provides liberation theology with a striking
paradigm of God's liberating power. The Exodus out of Egypt molded the
consciousness of the people of Israel and revealed God's power to them.[62] It
showed that God's actions takes place *in* history and *as* history, and it showed
the political character of this history, for it embraced the total life of the
people.[63] The Exodus liberated the Israelites physically from the bondage of

Egypt.[64] The Exodus speaks to the present situation of Latin America for it reveals that God works in history and not outside it, and that God works to liberate the oppressed in the fullest political sense of the word.[65]

God's Demand: "Doing Justice"

God identifies with the poor and oppressed. To be a Christian one must share in this love. Love of God and love of neighbor, especially love of the poor, cannot be separated.[66] The central mystery of our faith is that God shared our humanity, so that every person must be seen as the living temple of God. The parable of the last judgment in Matthew 25 summarizes the very essence of the gospel message. Christ is to be found in the hungry, the thirsty, the naked. "Whatever you did for the least of my brethren you did unto me."

God's identification with the poor, however, is not just a question of charity but of justice. The prophets make this point clear: to know the Lord is to do justice. Míguez Bonino cites Jeremiah 22:16, in which Josiah is praised for doing justice: "He judged the cause of the poor and the needy; then it was well. Is not this to know me? says the Lord." Hosea 4:1–2 makes the same point by equating lack of knowledge of God with failure to do justice.[67]

José Miranda's *Marx and the Bible* provides a detailed study of this identification of knowledge of God and doing justice. Miranda argues first of all that Western translations of the Bible, since the sixth century A.D., robbed biblical texts of their force. What the Hebrew text intended to connote as "justice" the translations rendered as "almsgiving." Thus deeds we have come to consider works of charity or supererogation were in the original Bible texts called works of justice.[68]

Miranda's central theme is that one cannot claim to know Yahweh except by doing justice. To know Yahweh is to achieve justice for the poor. Miranda insists, moreover, that the Bible does not just mean that justice is one sign or manifestation of knowledge of God. It is *the* way. Citing another biblical scholar, H. J. Kraus, he concludes: "Amos, Hosea, Isaiah, and Micah know only one decisive theme: justice and right."[69] In the view of the Bible, Yahweh is the God who breaks into human history to liberate the oppressed. "I, Yahweh, have called you to serve the cause of justice . . . to free captives from prison and those who live in darkness from the dungeon" (Isa. 42:5–7). Or again in Exodus 6:3, God says, "Say this to the sons of Israel, 'I am Yahweh *and therefore* I will free you of the burdens which the Egyptians lay on you. I will release you from slavery to them."[70] Liberation flows from his very nature.

Miranda believes not only that injustice is denounced by Yahweh but that his justice is "fiercely punitive against the oppressors," that it is for their injustice that Yahweh defeats nations for Israel.[71] But it is likewise Israel's own injustices that are the direct cause of its rejection by Yahweh. Thus we read in Micah 3:9–12: "Now listen to this, you leaders of Jacob, rulers of

Israel, you who loathe justice and pervert all that is right; . . . because of this, since the fault is yours, Zion will be ploughed like a field."[72]

In short, justice is decisive for God. One cannot claim to know, love, or worship God except through doing justice.

Jesus and Liberation: The Kingdom of God

Jesus proclaimed the coming Kingdom of God. He preached primarily not about himself or even about God but about the Kingdom. Jon Sobrino writes: "The most certain historical datum about Jesus' life is that the concept which dominated his preaching. the reality which gave meaningfulness to all his activity, was 'the kingdom of God.' "[73]

To understand the import of the term "Kingdom of God," says Sobrino, we must understand what it meant to the people of Israel. They had suffered the destruction of the northern and southern kingdoms, the Babylonian captivity, and had failed to achieve national self-determination after these. But the prophets held out to them the promise of liberation, of a Messiah who would fulfill their hopes. This salvation was viewed as something radically new. Thus Yahweh announced: "Lo, I am about to create new heavens and a new earth; the things of the past shall not be remembered or come to mind. Instead there shall always be rejoicing and happiness in what I create" (Isa. 65:17). Jesus shared that prophetic vision and understood his task of proclaiming the Kingdom in that context.[74]

The Kingdom comes as a grace, it is due to God's initiative. But it is a salvation and liberation expressed in deeds. Jesus equates "proclaiming God" with "realizing God's reign in practice." His deeds, his healings. his driving out of demons, his raising to life, are signs of the coming Kingdom. They also show that Kingdom means transformation of a bad situation, of an oppressive situation. The Kingdom must overcome sin, not merely personal sin but sin in its social and collective dimensions, in groups that oppress and the structures they represent.[75]

It is not enough, however, to know what the Kingdom of God meant in Jesus' time. It must be grasped in the light of present experience. Today in Latin America, Leonardo Boff asserts, the Kingdom expresses a people's utopian longing for liberation from everything that alienates them: pain, hunger, injustice, death.[76] But it also conveys the absolute lordship of God who will carry out this liberation. Jesus proclaims that the Kingdom will no longer be utopian but the real fulfillment of happiness for all people. This Kingdom of God is not only spiritual but also a total revolution of the structures of the old world; it is this world transformed and made new. The cross symbolizes the suffering that unjust structures can impose on the world. The resurrection is an experience of liberation not only for Jesus but in every instance where elements of oppression are overcome and new life breaks through. If the Church is to be the bearer of the Kingdom, then demands of liberation are not only political demands but demands of the faith.[77] On this last point Gutiérrez writes: "To place oneself in the perspective of the Kingdom means to participate in the struggle for the liberation of those oppressed by others. That is what many Christians who have committed themselves to the Latin American revolutionary process have begun to experience."[78]

Jesus and Conflict: The Political Dimension

Many Christians, Gutiérrez observes, take for granted that Jesus was not interested in political life, that his mission was purely religious. To look for the characteristics of a contemporary political militant, he continues, would be to misrepresent his life and witness. He rejected the narrow nationalism of the Zealots and their belief that they could realize the Kingdom through their own efforts alone. He opposed all political-religious messianism which did not respect the depth of the religious realm and the autonomy of political action. He attacked instead the very foundation of injustice and exploitation, the disintegration of community. In doing so his actions took on a very definite political significance. He confronted the major power groups of his society. He called Herod a "fox"; he denounced the hypocrisy and legalism of the Pharisees; his teachings threatened the privileged position of the Sadducees; and he died at the hands of political authorities.[79]

Several other liberation theologians argue for the political dimension of Jesus' life by focusing on his confrontations and conflicts with authorities. Ignacio Ellacuria contends that Jesus lived in a highly politicized atmosphere in which all he did necessarily carried political implications.[80] His criticisms interfered with the whole socio-political power structure. In criticizing the Scribes and Pharisees he was attacking their monopoly over the faith and consequently He undermined the power base of the priestly class. He also threatened the power balance between the Jewish nation and the Romans. His condemnation of wealth carried the same political implications. Míguez Bonino adds that the universality of Jesus' love cannot be interpreted as a compromise with or acceptance of evil, and that he was *rightly* accused of taking the side of the oppressed against the constituted religious and political authorities.[81]

Sobrino emphasizes the targets of Jesus' denunciations. If Jesus does not speak in contemporary terms of unjust structures or institutions, his denunciations are almost always *collective*. They are aimed at the Pharisees because they pay no attention to justice, at the legal experts because they impose intolerable burdens on the people, at the rich because they refuse to share their wealth with the poor, and at the rulers of the world because they govern despotically. The anathemas are also directed against abuse of power, be it religious, intellectual, economic, or political.[82]

In a powerful chapter on the death of Jesus, Sobrino argues that the crucifixion can only be explained as the historical consequence of Jesus' life and preaching of the Kingdom. Jesus proclaimed a God of liberation, a God concerned about human life and dignity, a God whose love is so deeply affected by all that is negative that *he suffers* from the death of his Son and from human suffering. But this God whom Jesus proclaimed conflicted with the God of religion, the God of external rituals and temple worship, the God in whose name priviliged classes subdue others. Jesus was charged with blasphemy for proclaiming such a God, but he suffered the punishment imposed on political agitators (crucifixion) rather than the punishment dealt out to religious blasphemers (stoning) because his denunciations challenged every claim to power which does not embody God's love and truth.[83]

Jesus seems clearly to have renounced the use of violence in his own defense or as a means of confronting injustice. He drove money changers out of the temple. He did not, however, use or condone violence against persons. But given the violence of oppressive conditions in Latin America would not revolutionary violence be justifiable? Liberation theologians do not deal with this issue as often as one might expect. Gutiérrez, in *A Theology of Liberation*, speaks often of oppressive institutional violence in Latin America and of the necessity of class struggle to oppose it. But he does not discuss to any extent a recourse to revolutionary violence. Some liberation theologians have affirmed non-violence as an essential Christian stance on liberation. Leonardo Boff affirms that the power of God, to which Jesus bore witness, is love. "Such love rules out all violence and oppression, even for the sake of having love itself prevail." The apparent efficacy of violence does not manage to break the spiralling process of violence.[84] Segundo Galilea argues that liberation from violence, both from institutional violence and from subversive violence, is one of the most important tasks confronting Christianity. He holds that liberation theology and Christianity "tell us that violence cannot be overcome with purely human means or with other forms of violence."[85]

Juan Luis Segundo, on the other hand, believes that Jesus' message of non-violence is not a matter of faith but an ideological stance taken in a particular historical context. The Israelites felt that God commanded them to exterminate their enemies; Jesus insisted on love and nonresistance to evil; each ideology had its own historical function to carry out. What theology must do is decide what ideology is needed in the light of the present situation of socio-political oppression in Latin America. Since it would be unrealistic to look centuries back to biblical situations for an answer, the best approach would be to ask: "What would the Christ of the Gospels say if he were confronting our problems today?"[86]

Some Comments about Biblical Perspectives

Critics of liberation theology charge that it oversimplifies the biblical message of the faith and tends to reduce it to politics with a definite ideological thrust.[87] Their criticisms might be grouped and considered under three charges: that liberation theology reduces faith to politics, that it interprets political dimensions of the gospel one-sidedly, overemphasizing human efforts, and that it uses scripture to justify its own political positions.

Liberation theology is criticized for reducing faith to politics. Liberation theologians *do stress* the political dimensions and political implications of scripture because they see Latin America's most urgent problems as bound up with politics. But stress cannot be equated with denial of all other aspects. A theologian who writes on prayer is not accused of ignoring marriage. More qualifying statements within liberation theology might have averted some of the criticism. Segundo, for example, makes a claim for liberation theology which could be used as an objection to the response that it only stresses the political. He writes: "Liberation is meant to designate and cover theology as a whole" and it is "the only authentic and privileged standpoint for arriving at a full and complete understanding of God's revelation in Jesus Christ."[88] The fact that he moves on to discuss the political problem of socialism versus capitalism as a test of theology might add to the impression that liberation theology deals only with politics. But Segundo does not say that *politics* is the privileged standpoint or covers theology as a whole; he says that *liberation* is. Liberation has a much fuller meaning than political action. Certainly other liberation theologians in the same volume of *Frontiers of Theology in Latin America* quite clearly take liberation in a broad sense and say explicitly that politics is only one dimension of the faith.[89]

The second objection raised against liberation theology is that when it treats the political dimension of the Bible it gives a one-sided and oversimplified interpretation, and it overstresses human activity in achieving liberation. Some liberation theologians have presented one-sided interpretations of biblical passages. Miranda's *Marx and the Bible* falls into this. His major thesis that justice is the prevailing theme of scripture has been supported by other scripture scholars.[90] His book, moreover, contains a powerfully moving call to justice. But Miranda also makes strong, sweeping statements that do present only one dimension of the biblical message. He claims, for example, that the justice proclaimed by Isaiah is "fiercely punitive against oppressors," without mentioning numerous passages that extol God's great mercy.[91] He claims that not even the anarchist Bakunin made assertions more subversive of the law than St. Paul, overlooking Paul's admonitions that slaves obey their masters and wives their husbands.[92] Phillip Berryman, in an otherwise very positive presentation of liberation theology, comments on the extreme form of Miranda's arguments.[93] And as the title of the book would suggest, Miranda often does impose a Marxist framework on the Bible.

Biblical passages have many dimensions and hence lend themselves to different interpretations. The sources most often cited by liberation theologians could be used to show that liberation does *not* come through struggle and oppression. If the Exodus account serves as a paradigm of liberation, it is not an example of overthrowing oppressors. The Jews fled Egypt; they did not overcome their oppressors and establish a new social order in Egypt. Yahweh told them that it was not because of their efforts, but because of him, that they were liberated. They struggled and fought wars to gain possession of the promised land, but not against oppressors over land they could claim was due to them in justice. Yahweh told them: "It is not for any goodness of yours that Yahweh gives you this rich land to possess, for you are a headstrong people" (Deut. 9:6). Similarly, when the prophets denounced injustice they did not call for collective political action but for conversion of the powerful and wealthy. They insisted moreover that only God could provide true justice (Isa. 1:24ff.; Exod. 3:7–9). Neither did Jesus organize the masses to overthrow unjust structures.

These examples, however, do not negate the central claims made by liberation theology that God acts in history to bring human, physical liberation and that he defends the poor and denounces injustice. The examples only serve to illustrate Segundo's argument about the distinction between faith and ideology. These central claims of liberation theology pertain to faith; how they were acted upon in biblical times was conditioned by cultural ideologies. If exact imitation of what the prophets did or what Jesus did is made a matter of faith, then few of the institutional ministries of the Church could be justified. Jesus never started a school or built a parish church; nor did he instruct his apostles to do so. The essential thing is to discover and act upon the spirit and intention that underly God's revelations and Jesus' actions. Dorothy Soelle articulates this well:

> Social awareness of transformation cannot and need not be justified biblically. . . . It is not a matter of compiling in a biblistic sense materials pertaining to the political activity of Jesus and using them to establish whether or not he was a revolutionary. The main thing is not to describe his concrete behavior and to imitate it, but rather to discern the intention or tendency of that behavior and to realize anew his goals in our world.[94]

Leonardo Boff's essay on "Christ's Liberation via Oppression" complements what has already been said about the meaning, spirit, and tendency of Jesus' words and behavior. Jesus preached good news to the poor and was born and lived among them; he denounced injustice; he put human good above legalism when he healed on the Sabbath; he died for values he refused to compromise. Yet at the same time he forgave and he maintained a deep love for every person and respect for each person's liberty.[95] To combine the strength to oppose and overcome injustice with a love that is forgiving is, I believe, to live with the spirit of Jesus. Combining these, moreover, could be the distinctive contribution of Christianity to human liberation.

The third criticism raised against liberation theology is that it uses theology to justify political positions already taken. A criticism often heard about liberation theology is that it identifies God's will and Marxist socialism: it identifies the poor with the proletariat, prophetic denunciation with Marxist critiques of capitalism, God's liberation with socialist revolution, and the Kingdom of God with a new socialist society. But if liberation theology made no effort to correlate the poor of the Bible with the poor in Latin America, and injustice denounced in the Bible with contemporary injustices, it would lose all meaning. The very purpose of liberation theology is to relate the word of God and historical praxis.[96] The issue is whether liberation theology determines in advance what it will find in praxis by adopting only Marxist categories. If the summaries we have given on biblical perspectives accurately reflect liberation theology as a whole, the identification of biblical and Marxist categories is *not* characteristic. Opponents of liberation theology, Galilea observes, often fail to distinguish between liberation theology as such and political documents published by revolutionary Christian groups. Some forms of liberation theology, he acknowledges, do tend to be "ideologized" and to rely on Marxist categories, but this current is limited and not representative of liberation theology as a whole.[97] To his remarks could be added those of other liberation theologians who criticize the "absolutizing" of any one ideological position.[98]

Quite often it is the opponents of liberation theology who read into theological statements a Marxist-Leninist identification. Bishop Alfonso López Trujillo's *Liberation or Revolution?* exemplifies this tendency. The book cover, not inappropriately in light of its tone, presents the title in dripping paint to suggest bloodshed. Where liberation theologians speak of the political dimension in Jesus' mission, López Trujillo treats them as militant proponents of violent revolution. "Is Christ a Zealot who seeks radical change by means of violence. . . . Does He impatiently seek the 'Kingdom,' and does He want to speed his mission by means of violence?"[99] In short, where facile identifications of liberation and Marxism are made, they are most often the products of opponents, or of militant political groups using liberation theology, not from within liberation theology itself.

A way of reading liberation theology more sympathetically, while at the same time testing the basic faithfulness of liberation theology to scripture, would be to list points that they hold and ask: "which of these should be *denied?*" Could any of the following be judged contrary to faith or scripture?

> God reveals himself in history.
> God desires the full human freedom of his people, at every level of their life.
> God reveals a very special concern for the poor and is angered by injustice done against them.
> Jesus sought to bring God's liberating power and justice to all.
> Jesus identified in a very special way with the marginal people of society, the outcasts, the poor.

Jesus denounced those who placed burdens upon the poor and who placed legalism (law and order) over human need.

Jesus sought to "break the power of evil and sin" in the world.

Jesus' actions were seen as a threat to those in positions of power.

A similar set of statements could be drawn up to reflect the role of faith in the present as expressed in liberation theology. Which of these should be denied?

The issue of poverty and oppression is the gravest problem facing the great masses of people in Latin America.

Without denying the value of other ministries, primary importance should be attached to the work of helping the poor.

The poor of Latin America are the landless peasants, the marginal people in the barrios of the city, the underpaid, underemployed, or unemployed workers.

In Latin America capitalism has failed to serve the common good, and developmental policies have not succeeded in bettering the situation.

These failures suggest the need for a more profound analysis of causes, using the best tools available from the social sciences.

The Church should be willing to evaluate its own social teachings to see if they are adequate to the present situation.

Some Church teachings may reflect cultural attitudes or "ideologies."

To work directly with the poor is certainly consistent with the spirit of Jesus and the mission of the Church. It might prove more effective for social change than educational work with upper and middle classes, a work which seems to have had very limited success in changing conditions in Latin America.

Working with the poor and striving with them for liberation can lead to a very enriching and new understanding of the faith.

In its concern for the poor and for ending injustice the Church should be willing to take stands, even if this involves conflict with some of its own members, for example regarding land reform.

It may be argued that this list of statements, and other efforts made to strike a balance, are out of harmony with liberation theology which concerns itself with praxis and the process of liberation, not with theological propositions. But an important political issue is involved, namely, whether liberation theology wants to build support for its positions within the institutional Church.

The Role of the Church

In *A Theology of Liberation* Gutiérrez stressed the changes that must occur within the Church itself. The Church, and in particular the bishops, must fulfill a role of prophetic denunciation of the grave injustices rampant in Latin America. This role would in itself place the Church in conflict with those who wield power. The Church should also undertake a "conscienticizing evangelization," helping people to become aware of the liberation proclaimed by Jesus. The Church must examine its own poverty, its own structures, and the lifestyle of its clergy.[100] Two particular political issues emerged in liberation theology regarding the stance of the institutional Church. The first is stressed most by Gutiérrez: the Church should opt to struggle with the poor. The second has been raised by Segundo: the Church should opt for socialism. A third issue should also be considered in this section regarding the very nature of the Church and who constitutes the Church.

Opting to Struggle with the Poor

Gutiérrez argues strongly that the Church should opt to be on the side of the poor. But opting to be on their side means being *against* their oppressors. This raises a critical issue of "unity" within the Church. The Church has always thought of its mission as universal, as embracing and unifying all men and women of every class. Vatican II called the Church a "visible sacrifice of saving unity," a sign of "the unity of all mankind" and "the universal sacrament of salvation." The Eucharist symbolizes this unity. The problem is that this unity is unreal; it does not reflect political reality. Too often the Church is tied to a social order which pits the powerful against the weak.

> The protection which the Church receives from the social class which is the beneficiary and the defender of the prevailing capitalist society in Latin America has made the institutional Church into a part of the system and the Christian message into the dominant ideology. Any claim to noninvolvement in politics . . . is nothing but a subterfuge to keep things the way they are.[101]

The issue is not whether the Church should use its influence in Latin America. Its influence is there. The issue is whether it should continue to be used in support of the existing order or against it. Church influence, Gutiérrez insists, should be used to *denounce* the present order and to criticize itself as a part of that order; in its evangelizing it should also *announce* what should be. This does not mean reducing the Gospel to political consciousness but simply that the Gospel as a message of total love "has an inescapable political dimension."[102]

The most troubling question of all, Gutiérrez recognizes, is class struggle. Humanity is in fact divided into oppressors and oppressed, into antagonistic social classes. How can one relate universal charity and the unity of the Church with this social reality? To speak of class struggle is not to advocate its creation but to recognize it as an existing fact. Advocating class struggle means working to eliminate a situation in which there are oppressed and oppressors. To build a just society necessarily implies an active and conscious participation in class struggle. To deny class struggle is to put oneself on the side of the dominant sectors. Neutrality is impossible. The universality of Christian love is an abstraction until it becomes a political reality. Love does not mean avoiding confrontations. In fact one loves oppressors by liberating them from their inhuman condition as oppressors. Thus class struggle does not mean hatred but "effective combat." Unity is not something given; it is a process, the result of overcoming all that divides people. The Church must opt to struggle with the poor against their oppressors so that true unity may be realized.[103]

Opting for Socialism

Can and should the Church declare itself in favor of socialism? If concentration of ownership in the hands of foreign monopolies and a domestic oligarchy is seen as a fundamental cause of poverty and oppression in Latin America, should not a clear option be made in favor of socialism? Segundo argues that the Church, or more accurately theology, must be able to choose socialism over capitalism. He counters two objections to such a decision. The first is a pragmatic refusal by the Church to make such options on the grounds that politics lies outside its proper sphere and that it opts only for Christ. Underlying this pragmatic response Segundo sees the Church absolutizing religious values and relativizing all political values. He contends that it would be more evangelical to view the attainment of a truly liberated society as an absolute value, and religious institutions, dogmas and sacraments as having only a relative value. The second objection comes from European political theology which claims that the Church, in light of its transcendent mission, should reserve judgment on all political and social systems refusing to absolutize any of them.[104]

Segundo argues that a choice between socialism and capitalism can and should be made. By socialism he means "a political regime in which the ownership of the means of production is taken away from individuals and handed over to higher institutions whose main concern is the common good."[105] He asserts that the prophets and Jesus made bold political decisions, not by applying theological criteria, but by a sensitive, direct response based on evaluations of the here and now. Christian theology must do the same by confronting a decision for socialism.[106]

Gutiérrez clearly calls for the creation of an entirely new social order and he names socialism as the most fruitful and far-reaching approach to liberation. But he is more cautious in speaking of socialism than Segundo. He contends that there is no monolithic orientation in the liberation movement, that liberation "can" mean taking the path of socialism, but that the ambiguities of the term socialism require the use of cautious language and careful distinctions.[107] In another place he argues that the message of liberation "is not identified with any social form, however just it may appear to us at the time."[108] Raul Vidales, in discussing Gutiérrez's views, claims that "the critical function of theology keeps the Christian permanently disestablished and, while urging him to commit himself to liberation, maintains him in a situation and attitude from which he can relativize systems."[109]

Socialism seems clearly to be a preferential option among liberation theologians and the direction many liberation movements take. But how qualified or unqualified this option should be remains an issue.

The Nature of the Church

When Gutiérrez wrote A Theology of Liberation much of his discussion of what the Church should do referred to the institutional Church, its bishops and clergy in particular. But he placed great stress on the "conscientization" mission of the Church, its need to become directly involved with the poor, and the importance of the poor themselves becoming makers of their own destiny. In calling for this he was describing a process that was already underway within the Church in Latin America and one that gained great momentum in the course of the 1970s. By the end of the decade some 100 thousand base communities (comunidades de base) had emerged with a membership of over seven million, with Brazil having the largest number of groups. While priests have generally acted as catalysts in their development, the communities have assumed their own dynamism and lay leadership. Comprising groups of a few dozen peasants and workers they meet to discuss the Bible in the light of their own social reality.[110] But even these base communities are only one expression of a Church in which the poor are seen, not as recipients of the Church's pastoral care, but as the people of God, active in shaping the future of the Church and their own lives. With this change has come theological reflection on the relationship between the official, hierarchical Church and the Church of the people.[111] The Puebla conference, as will be seen, both approved of base communities and concerned itself with their unity in the Church.

Segundo's views on the Church should be mentioned though they stem from a different problematic than the one just noted. The issue he addresses is what the Church should be and who should be called true Church adherents. The Church, Segundo believes, should be made up of those willing to take seriously the demands Jesus makes on his disciples. The Church should not minimize its requirements, as it now does, to include as many people as possible. Rather it should recognize that only a small number can successfully carry out the Church's mission of justice and love.[112] Only a minority can respond effectively to the raising of consciousness. Only a minority "revolutionary vanguard," as Lenin recognized, can resist mass tendencies to accept immediate gains and work instead for long-range goals. As the gospel attests:

"Many are called and few are chosen." The Church should be comprised of a minority ready and able to transform society.[113]

Comments on the Role of the Church

This evaluation will focus only on the issue of opting for socialism. The final pages of this chapter will take note of the "option for the poor" made by the Latin American bishops at Puebla; Chapter 8 will discuss in some detail the issue of class struggle. Earlier evaluations in this chapter of praxis should suggest what my views would be on Segundo's "vanguard" conception of the Church.

Can and should the Church in Latin America opt for socialism? The Church could and should, I believe, call for an end to the *monopolization* of land and of commercial enterprises by a small wealthy elite. The Church could also acknowledge as an ideal a type of democratic, mixed-economy socialism consistent with human dignity and freedom, and consistent as well with the development of its own social teachings. But the Church should not and morally cannot opt in advance for any form of socialism without knowing the direction it might take. The official Church has suggested long-range options in the past. Under Pius XI it proposed the idea of "corporatism." But it had to reject corporatism in the form it took under fascism. This very example provides an initial reason why I feel that Segundo's *way* of proposing the "either-socialism-or-capitalism" option is not a good test of theology. He defines socialism as a political regime "in which ownership of means of production is taken away from individuals and handed over to higher institutions whose main concern is the common good," and capitalism as a political regime in which ownership is "left open to economic competition."[14] His definition would rule out a land reform movement in which every family might own and be able to cultivate its own farm. Handing over ownership to higher authorities, on the other hand, could mean exclusive control and major profits going to a small government elite. The added phrase "whose main concern is the common good" would seem to counter such a possibility, but to use it as a norm is to introduce into the definition the very reserve and relativism Segundo argues against. The Church, and every moral agent, should exercise a "reserve" in deciding whether a concrete, actualized system does or does not serve the common good. The Church should not hold out for an unattainable ideal; it must be part of historical praxis; it does have to make here-and-now decisions to support a certain direction or not. But it is the very concreteness of these decisions that requires openness to new possibilities and rules out either-or decisions made in advance.

Toward the Future

When the third General Conference of Latin American Bishops (CELAM) met in Puebla, Mexico, January 27–February 13, 1979, there were fears that the bishops would go back on the stands they had taken at Medellín ten years before, that liberation theology might be condemned in some way, and that all use of Marxism would be forbidden. The Secretary General of CELAM, Bishop Alfonso López Trujillo, did indeed try to promote a document and to select delegates with a view to clamping down on the liberationist trend which had grown strong since Medellín. Pope John Paul II's opening address, which the press reported as saying only that "Jesus was not a revolutionary" and that "the Church's mission is not political," did not bode well for liberation theology.[115] But the Puebla Conference proved to be a stand-off between radical-progressive and conservative-reactionary forces. The socio-economic analyses and the theological perspectives enunciated at Puebla lacked the forcefulness of Medellín. But concern for injustice and liberation language continued to be used. No explicit discussion was taken up in the documents about liberation theology as such. But the concept of "integral liberation," of a liberation that embraces the political, spiritual, and personal, emerged as a key notion.[116] The most positive aspects of the Puebla Conference, from a liberation viewpoint, were the declaration of a preferential option for the poor and the approval and encouragement of base communities.[117] Gutiérrez was quoted as saying that the future of these communities was more important than liberation theology itself. By not condemning every form and every use of Marxism the Puebla Conference may have left some openings. But its explicit references to Marxism were all negative. It noted the distinction between Marxist analysis and Marxist ideology only by way of warning against their close link. It condemned "classical Marxism" as an inadequate view of human beings and it rejected "Marxist collectivism" along with the ideologies of capitalist liberation and "national security."[118]

Liberation theologians themselves made a decision which may turn out to be as important as anything they have written. They decided to work with bishops at the conference rather than waiting to criticize Puebla documents or to write their own alternative documents. Though not able to work within the conference, the theologians made themselves available to bishops who consulted with them, passed documents out to them, and used their suggestions. The final documents fell short of their hopes, but they showed themselves to be theologians "of" and "in" the Church. This has, I believe, important political significance, for it broadens their support within the Church. Hierarchical support, it might be added, has proved important also to activist priests and religious, for it provides some protection against government efforts to silence them.

When liberation theology first emerged, Gutiérrez could write, "In Latin America we are in the midst of a full blown process of revolutionary ferment."[119] Ferment produces fervor, and much of the criticism directed against liberation theology in its early years was a reaction to this fervor. It called for "critical" reflection, but seemed to evoke uncritical adherence to its own ideas. But the ferment subsided. Revolutionary hopes were sometimes tragically crushed, as in Chile where an entirely new relation between Marxism and Christianity might have emerged. Liberation theology has had to speak, in recent years, of a theology of captivity and suffering as well as of liberation. But it has grown broader and richer in the process. If it once seemed to be a new "fad" in theology, it is proving itself to be a very deep-rooted expression of the hopes and struggles of Latin American peoples.

This chapter began with a question about the relationship between Marxism and liberation theology. Actual references to Marx or to Marxist writings are relatively infrequent in liberation theology. Liberation theology is not grounded in Marxism. It is grounded in the experiences of the peoples of Latin America and in faith reflection. The pervasiveness of Marxist thinking in Latin America does affect liberation theology. It uses Marxism "heuristically," that is, it takes certain insights from Marxism and uses these to gain insight both into situations in Latin America and into the faith. It draws especially upon Marxist insights into the relation of theory to praxis, the political-economic causes of underdevelopment, and the relation between ideology and social structures. But all of these have Christian counterparts as well: commitment to living the faith and reflection on religious experience; biblical denunciations of injustice; criticisms of the Church in every age for failing to act on justice demands. Conditions would have demanded this kind of reflection and action whether Marxism existed or not. If Marxism often engenders uncritical acceptance, nearly every liberation theologian cited in this chapter—Gutiérrez, Segundo, Assmann, Míguez Bonino, Galilea, etc.—includes some criticism of the use of Marxism. And, if Galilea's assessment is correct, those who rely heavily on Marxist categories constitute a limited current within liberation theology.

The fact that Latin America has contributed to the Church an important group of theologians is significant in itself, for it constitutes a cultural liberation of the Third World from the hegemony of European and North American theology. Moreover efforts have been made within the United States to learn from the method of liberation theology. In August 1975, Latin American theologians, North American theologians, and laity representing many diverse racial and ethnic groups in the United States, met in Detroit to discuss the process of theologizing by beginning with situations. Their talks and papers were published as *Theology in the Americas*.[120] In June 1978, a second "Theology in the Americas" conference was held in New York. Whether liberation theology will significantly affect theological reflection outside Latin America remains uncertain, but it has already profoundly changed Church attitudes and Church praxis there.

Notes

1. The description of conditions in Latin America given here is drawn from (1) the first in a series of articles by R. C. Longworth and Ronald Yates on "South America '78," in *The Chicago Tribune,* Sunday January 22, 1978, Section 1, p. 16; and José Míguez Bonino, *Revolutionary Theology Comes of Age* (London: SPCK, 1975), pp. 22–23. Míguez Bonino's work was also published in the United States as *Doing Theology in a Revolutionary Situation* (Philadelphia: Fortress, 1975).

2. Paulo Freire, *Pedagogy of the Oppressed* (New York: Seabury, 1974), p. 19. For more on Freire see Denis Collins, *Paulo Freire: His Life, Works and Thought* (New York: Paulist, 1978).

3. Freire, *Pedagogy of the Oppressed,* p. 30.

4. Ibid., p. 47.

5. Ibid., p. 58ff.

6. Ibid., p. 119.

7. Ibid., pp. 126, 185.

8. Ibid., p. 23.

9. See Jürgen Moltmann, *Theology of Hope,* trans. James W. Leitch (London: SCM Press, 1967), and his *Religion, Revolution, and the Future,* trans. M. Douglass Meeks (New York: Charles Scribner's Sons, 1969); Johannes B. Metz, *Theology of the World,* trans. William Glen-Doepel (New York: Herder and Herder, 1969).

10. See the criticism of European political theology by Hugo Assmann, *Theology for a Nomad Church,* trans. Paul Burns (Maryknoll, N.Y.: Orbis, 1976), Chapter 1; and by Enrique Dussel, "Domination-Liberation: A New Approach" in *The Mystical and Political Dimension of the Christian Faith,* Concilium 96, ed. Claude Geffré and Gustavo Gutiérrez (New York: Herder and Herder, 1974), pp. 34–56. This volume will be referred to hereafter as: Concilium 96.

11. See Assmann, *Theology for a Nomad Church,* pp. 45–46.

12. Medellín documents, in Joseph Gremillion, ed., *The Gospel of Peace and Justice* (Maryknoll, N.Y.: Orbis, 1976), "Justice," No. 1, p. 445.

13. Ibid., No. 3, p. 446.

14. Ibid., No. 10, p. 449.

15. Ibid., No. 20, p. 453.

16. Ibid., "Peace," No. 3, p. 455.

17. Ibid., No. 9, p. 457.

18. Ibid., Nos. 16–19, pp. 460–61.

19. Ibid., "Poverty of the Church," No. 7, p. 473.

20. Gustavo Gutiérrez, *A Theology of Liberation,* trans. and ed. Sister Caridad Inda and John Eagleson (Maryknoll, N.Y.: Orbis, 1973). Gutiérrez is a Peruvian diocesan priest who developed many of these theological ideas in interchange with students and other laity. The summary we have given corresponds roughly to the following chapters of his book: Method/Commitment to Praxis, Chapter 1; Critical

Reflections/Political and Ideological Critiques, Chapters 2 and 6 on Latin America, Chapters 4 and 5 on the Church; New Awareness/New Biblical Dimensions, Chapters 6 and 7 on new awareness, Chapters 9, 10, 11 on the biblical, The Role of the Church, Chapter 12 (and 7).

21. Ibid., p. 13.

22. Ibid., p. 11.

23. Ibid., pp. 6ff.

24. In his essay, "Liberation Praxis and Christian Faith," in *Frontiers of Theology in Latin America*, trans. John Drury, ed. Rosino Gibellini (Maryknoll, N.Y.: Orbis, 1979), Gutiérrez also explains the method of liberation theology and he describes the "journey" which led many Latin American theologians to the conviction that theology must begin with praxis. This book, with essays by thirteen liberation theologians and a helpful appendix with biographical data on each of them, is perhaps the best single volume of selections available.

25. Juan Luis Segundo, S.J., *The Liberation of Theology*, trans. John Drury (Maryknoll, N.Y.: Orbis, 1976), pp. 7–8.

26. Assmann, *Theology for a Nomad Church*, p. 74.

27. Alves is cited by Assmann, *Theology*, p. 76.

28. Alfredo Fierro, *The Militant Gospel, A Critical Introduction to Political Theologies*, trans. John Drury (Maryknoll, N.Y.: Orbis, 1977), p. 183.

29. Dick Howard, *The Marxian Legacy* (N.Y.: Urizen Books, 1977), p. 44. In explaining Howard's distinction I may have drawn the line between Lenin and Gramsci more sharply than he does. On Gramsci's views see my own Chapter 2.

30. Gutiérrez, in *Frontiers of Theology in Latin America*, p. 22; and also his introduction to *A Theology of Liberation*, p. ix.

31. Enrique Dussel, in *Frontiers of Theology in Latin America*, p. 212.

32. Juan Carlos Scannone, in ibid., pp. 216–17. Also in the same volume, Assmann warns against an elitist praxis but he believes the praxis of the poor is often far more radical than that of liberation theologians, pp. 135–36.

33. Gutiérrez's experiences are recounted by José Míguez Bonino in a statement for *Theology in the Americas*, ed. Sergio Torres and John Eagleson (Maryknoll, N.Y.: Orbis, 1976), p. 278.

34. Gutiérrez, *A Theology of Liberation*, pp. 26–27.

35. Assmann, *Theology for a Nomad Church*, pp. 49ff.

36. Míguez Bonino, *Revolutionary Theology Comes of Age*, pp. 27–28.

37. José Míguez Bonino, *Christians and Marxists: The Mutual Challenge to Revolution* (Grand Rapids, Mich.: Eerdmans, 1976), p. 115.

38. Jürgen Moltmann, "On Latin American Liberation Theology," in *Christianity and Crisis*, March 29, 1976, Vol. 36, No. 5, pp. 57–63.

39. Segundo Galilea, "Liberation Theology and New Tasks Facing Christians," in *Frontiers of Theology in Latin America*, p. 167.

40. See Medellín Documents, "Peace," No. 9, p. 457, in Gremillion, *The Gospel of Peace and Justice*.

41. *Puebla and Beyond* (Maryknoll, N.Y.: Orbis, 1979), Final Document, nos. 64 and 66.

42. Bishop Alfonso López Trujillo, *Liberation or Revolution?* (Huntington, Indiana: Our Sunday Visitor, 1977), p. 101.

43. John A. Coleman, "Civil Religion and Liberation Theology in North America,"

in *Theology in the Americas*, p. 133.

44. For example, Assmann opposes any kind of "schematic Marxism" and stresses the imperfection of scientific tools of analysis, in *Frontiers of Theology in Latin America*, p. 147. Galilea, in the same volume, argues that the fact of dependence is not tied to a Marxist theory of dependence, p. 167.

45. See Max Eastman, *Marxism: Is it Science?* (New York: W.W. Norton, 1940), pp. 53–54, and Michael Polanyi, *Personal Knowledge* (New York: Harper Torchbooks, 1964), pp. 227ff. To these one could add the works of John Plamenatz, Karl Popper, H. B. Acton and others.

46. See Phillipe Warnier, *Marx pour un chrétien* (Paris: Fayard-Mame, 1977). Warnier defends the use of Marxist analysis as scientific but argues that subjective factors, such as humanistic and moral values, are all involved in the political use of Marxism. See his Chapter 5, "Le Marxisme, une fausse science?" and also Chapters 4 and 7.

47. Gutiérrez, *A Theology of Liberation*, p. 49.

48. Ibid., p. 65.

49. Míguez Bonino, *Revolutionary Theology Comes of Age*, Chapter 1.

50. Segundo, *The Liberation of Theology*, p. 8.

51. Ibid., p. 9. The examples used to illustrate his four points are my own.

52. Ibid., pp. 16–17.

53. Segundo, *A Theology for Artisans of a New Humanity*, Vol. III (Maryknoll, N.Y.: Orbis, 1974), pp. 98ff. For a study of Segundo's thought see Alfred T. Hennelly, S.J., "Challenge of Juan Luis Segundo," in *Theological Studies*, March, 1977, Vol. 38, No. 1, and Hennelly's *Theologies in Conflict: The Challenge of Juan Luis Segundo* (Maryknoll, N.Y.: Orbis Books, 1979).

54. On the spirituality of the Church see Segundo Galilea, "Liberation as an Encounter with Politics and Contemplation," in Concilium 96, pp. 19–33.

55. See Míguez Bonino, *Christians and Marxists*, Chapters 3 and 4.

56. The Puebla Conference tried to resolve the issue of the Church and priests in politics by distinguishing between politics in a broad sense of seeking the common good along the lines of certain moral norms, and the pursuit or exercise of political power based on some party ideology. The latter form of "party politics" is said to be properly the realm of lay people. See *Puebla and Beyond*, Final Document, Nos. 521–24. Pastors and priests are told that they must be concerned with unity and that they should divest themselves of every partisan political ideology that might condition their attitudes, ibid., Nos. 526–27.

A better distinction, I believe, could be drawn between the Church or priests taking positions on specific issues and on party politics, though the Church itself has not always observed this line in its opposition to Communist parties. Since the leaders, the policies, and the actions of a political party or movement change constantly, it does not seem that the Church should ever attempt a general endorsement. The bishops' concern for unity, on the other hand, serves as a poor criterion for political judgment. Support for the right of workers to organize, for land reform, for racial integration, and opposition to almost any injustice, will nearly always involve conflict with Church members who disagree or whose interests are at stake. Yet the Church should be called upon to speak on such issues.

57. Gutiérrez, *A Theology of Liberation*, pp. 83ff.

58. Ibid., p. 113.

59. Assmann, *Theology for a Nomad Church*, pp. 49ff.

60. See Jon Sobrino, S.J., *Christology at the Crossroads*, trans. John Drury (Maryknoll, N.Y.: Orbis, 1978), p. 35. See also Leonardo Boff, "Christ's Liberation via Oppression," in *Frontiers of Theology in Latin America*, pp. 100ff.

61. Gutiérrez, *A Theology of Liberation*, p. 154.

62. See Assmann, *Theology for a Nomad Church*, p. 66, and Rubem Alves, *A Theology of Human Hope* (Washington, D.C.: Corpus Books, 1969), p. 89.

63. See Míguez Bonino, *Revolutionary Theology Comes of Age*, pp. 134–35.

64. Fierro, *The Militant Gospel*, pp. 140ff.

65. Assmann, *Theology for a Nomad Chruch*, p. 35.

66. See Sobrino, *Christology at the Crossroads*, pp. 169ff. and 204f.

67. Míguez Bonino, *Christians and Marxists*, pp. 31–33.

68. José P. Miranda, *Marx and the Bible: A Critique of the Philosophy of Oppression*, trans. John Eagleson (Maryknoll, N.Y.: Orbis, 1974), pp. 14–15.

69. Ibid., p. 46.

70. Ibid., pp. 78–79.

71. Ibid., p. 83 and 121.

72. Ibid., p. 165. In Scripture see also Amos 4:1–3, and Hosea 10:13.

73. Sobrino, *Christology at the Crossroads*, p. 41.

74. Ibid., pp. 43–44.

75. Ibid., pp. 50ff.

76. Leonardo Boff, "Salvation in Jesus Christ and the Process of Liberation," in *Concilium* 96, pp. 81–88.

77. Ibid., p. 88. Opponents of liberation theology have accused it of identifying the Kingdom as something human activity alone can achieve. Boff clearly does not, p. 89.

78. Gutiérrez, *A Theology of Liberation*, p. 203. Also on the distinction noted above between the Kingdom and human efforts, pp. 227, 231.

79. Ibid., pp. 225ff.

80. Ignacio Ellacuría, *Freedom Made Flesh*, trans. John Drury (Maryknoll, N.Y.: Orbis, 1976), pp. 31ff.

81. Míguez Bonino, *Revolutionary Theology Comes of Age*, pp. 121–24.

82. Sobrino, *Christology at the Crossroads*, p. 53.

83. Ibid., pp. 204ff. On God suffering, pp. 225–26.

84. Boff, in *Frontiers of Theology in Latin America*, p. 120.

85. Galilea in ibid., "Liberation Theology and New Tasks Facing Christians," p. 175.

86. Segundo, *The Liberation of Theology*, pp. 116–17. See also Míguez Bonino, *Christians and Marxists*, p. 124, who comments only briefly on the question of violence by saying that if socialist revolution involves violence a Christian should be concerned with keeping it at a minimum.

87. See the criticisms of the International Theological Commission, "Human Development and Christian Salvation," in *Origins*, November 3, 1977, Vol. 7, No. 20. As an advisory group to the pope, the Commission's criticisms of "some forms" of liberation theology constituted the most formal critique. The criticisms focused chiefly on biblical interpretations which were found oversimplified. The Commission itself was criticized for not including a liberation theologian in its deliberations. Clark H. Pinnock, "Liberation Theology: The Gains, the Gaps," in *Christianity Today*, January 16, 1976, Vol. XX, No. 8, is critical of liberation theology

88. Segundo, in *Frontiers of Theology in Latin America,* p. 241.

89. Gutiérrez, ibid., insists that Christian liberation is not restricted to political liberation, but stresses its universality and transcendence, p. 128, pp. 107–8; see also Vidales, pp. 35–36 and Galilea, pp. 169–70.

90. See, for example, John R. Donahue, S.J., "Biblical Perspectives on Justice," in *The Faith That Does Justice,* ed. John C. Haughey, S.J. (New York: Paulist, 1977), p. 68.

91. Miranda, *Marx and the Bible,* p. 83.

92. Ibid., p. 187.

93. Phillip Berryman, "Latin American Liberation Theology," in *Theology in the Americas,* pp. 71–73.

94. Dorothee Soelle, *Political Theology,* trans. John Shelley (Philadelphia: Fortress, 1974), p. 64.

95. Boff, "Christ's Liberation via Oppression," in *Frontiers of Theology in Latin America,* pp. 100–131.

96. See Raul Vidales, in *Frontiers of Theology in Latin America,* p. 41.

97. Galilea, in ibid., pp. 169–70.

98. In *Frontiers of Theology in Latin America,* see Gutiérrez, p. 22; Vidales, p. 47, Joseph Comblin, p. 76, Dussel, p. 212, Scannone, pp. 218, 221.

99. López Trujillo, *Liberation or Revolution?,* pp. 16–17.

100. Gutiérrez, *A Theology of Liberation,* pp. 101–19.

101. Ibid., pp. 265–66.

102. Ibid., p. 270.

103. Ibid. pp. 275–78.

104. Segundo, "Capitalism Versus Socialism: Crux Theologica," in *Frontiers of Theology in Latin America,* pp. 242–46. An earlier version of Segundo's article appeared in Concilium 96.

105. Ibid., p. 249.

106. Ibid., pp. 253–56.

107. Gutiérrez, *A Theology of Liberation,* pp. 90, 111.

108. Gutiérrez, "Liberation, Theology and Proclamation," in Concilium 96, p. 74.

109. Raul Vidales, "Some Recent Publications in Latin America on the Theology of Liberation," in Concilium 96, p. 129.

110. Alan Riding, "Latin Church in Siege," in *The New York Times Magazine,* May 6, 1979, p. 40.

111. See Ronaldo Muñoz, "The Function of the Poor in the Church," and Hubert Lepargneur, "The Problem of Poverty and How the Church Can Help," in *The Poor and the Church,* ed. Norbert Greinacher and Alois Müller (New York: Seabury, 1977), pp. 80–88 and 89–96 respectively.

112. Juan Luis Segundo, *The Community Called Church* (Maryknoll, N.Y.: Orbis Books, 1973), pp. 82–83.

113. See Segundo, *The Theology of Liberation,* Chapter 8.

114. Segundo, in *Frontiers of Theology in Latin America,* p. 249. In addition to the arguments I have given in the chapter, I would also dispute Segundo's absolute-relative distinction. The Church may put an absolute value on the spiritual, in the very general sense of the total spiritual development of a person. But it reserves and relativizes in the spiritual realm just as it does with the political. It condemns false mysticisms, improper liturgies, invalid baptisms, etc. It may be that the Church, by its

actions, has not given equal importance to the general value of transforming society. But the terms of comparison should be a general value with a general value or a specific spiritual option with a specific political option. Segundo compares a general value, i.e. "the spiritual" with a specific option, i.e., socialism.

115. Pope John Paul II, in his address to the bishops at Puebla, insisted that the conception of Christ as "a political figure, a revolutionary, as the subversive from Nazareth" does not tally with the Church's catechesis. (See *Puebla and Beyond*, the pope's Opening Address, I, 4, p. 60.) Gutiérrez, as noted in the chapter, reaches a similar conclusion while defending the political "dimension" in Jesus' life. The pope also insisted that the mission of the Church "is religious in character, and not social or political," ibid., III, 2. But press releases failed to complete his sentence which said that the Church "cannot help but consider human persons in terms of their whole being," which the pope then illustrated with the parable of the Good Samaritan. In subsequent addresses in Mexico the pope made clear that he wanted to be linked to the cause of the poor and to speak on behalf of those who were exploited harshly.

116. "Integral liberation," the bishops said, involves liberation *from* all forms of bondage, from personal and social sin and from everything that tears apart the human individual and society. It is also liberation *for* progressive growth in communion with God and other human beings. Liberation affects all dimensions of life—social, political, economic, cultural (*Puebla and Beyond*, Final Document, Nos 480ff.). The bishops rejected violence and the dialectics of class struggle (ibid., No. 486).

117. The bishops devoted a long section to a "preferential option for the poor" in which they called for conversion of all sectors of society to solidarity with the poor and the poor Christ (*Puebla and Beyond*, Final Document, Nos. 1134–65). They did not include suggestions for opting for struggle *against* oppressors.

The bishops strongly affirmed the growth of base communities (Base-level ecclesial communities, or CEBs), calling them the "hope of the Church" (*Puebla and Beyond*, Final Document, Nos. 617ff., especially No. 629 and also No. 96).

118. The bishops named "classical Marxism" as an inadequate view of human beings, for it reduces human nature to the economic (*Puebla and Beyond*, Final Document, No. 313). And in discussing ideologies in Latin America they rejected "Marxist collectivism" and its dialectics of class struggle (ibid., No. 542). The bishops mentioned that some distinguish between Marxist analysis and Marxist ideology. But they noted the distinction for the sake of reiterating Paul VI's warning that it is dangerous to ignore the fact that analysis and ideology are closely linked. The bishops also warned of the risk of ideologizing theological reflection by basing it on a praxis that has recourse to Marxist analysis (ibid., Nos. 543–45).

119. Gutiérrez, A *Theology of Liberation*, p. 89.

120. The issue of the relevance of Marxism to the United States emerged often in the first Theology in the Americas conference. No one sought to defend capitalism or deny the perceptiveness of Marxist analysis. But various groups at the conference argued that the oppression they faced could not be reduced to economic oppression. Racism and sexism, for example, have their own distinctive roots. Hence, in contrast to Latin America, there was no single U.S. experience to build upon. See Gregory Baum's evaluation of the conference, in *Theology in the Americas*, pp. 399ff.

Chapter 6

Chile under Allende
and Christians for Socialism

The election, in September 1970, of Salvador Allende Gossens as President of Chile, opened a dramatic moment in the history of socialism and in the relationship between Marxists and Christians. It marked the first completely free election of a Marxist head of government committed to a transformation of the existing economic system. It also marked the first Marxist government to receive significant support from some Christian groups and to have relatively cordial relations with the hierarchical Church. But in the years which followed the Church experienced considerable tension within its own ranks, reflecting divisions within the country as a whole. Three years after Allende came to power his socialist regime ended, the victim of a swift and ruthless military coup.

The Allende experiment raised many questions. Could it have succeeded? Why didn't it? From different perspectives came very different answers. Right-wing opponents took Allende's fall as proof that Marxism cannot win sufficient support to carry out socialism democratically. Revolutionary Marxists were confirmed in their judgment that only by arming the people and seizing power can socialism be assured. Some observers felt that Allende himself lacked the decisiveness needed for the job. But many who strongly supported Allende's effort felt that it could have succeeded had it not been for the special obstacles created by U.S. interventions, right-wing subversive efforts, and left-wing pressures to force the pace of socialization. While this chapter will include some reconstruction of the Allende years, it will not attempt to answer the questions posed above. Its primary focus will be rather upon the Marxism-Christianity issue. What stance did the Church take toward the Allende government? Why did rifts develop within the Church and could they have been avoided? How might the Allende years contribute to a new understanding of Marxism-Christianity? The chapter is divided into three main parts: a recounting of the Allende years and the attitude of the official, hierarchical Church toward his government; a study of the Christians for Socialism movement in Chile and its interactions with the hierarchy; a brief look at the international Christians for Socialism movement which grew out of the Chile Experience.

Chile and the Catholic Church under Allende

Chile was in many respects uniquely suited to undertake a democratic path to socialism and to test Marxist-Christian relations in a new way. If Chile suffered from many of the same socio-economic problems endemic throughout Latin America, it also had a long democratic tradition and one of the most progressive Churches in Latin America. To delve deep into Chile's past for background would take us too far afield, but it may be helpful to reconstruct briefly the situation prior to Allende's election.

Chile Prior to 1970

Under the leadership of Eduardo Frei the Christian Democrats won the elections of 1964. The Christian Democrats had been formed by Catholic intellectuals nearly thirty years before to provide an alternative to the dominant, conservative National Party. They won support from Chile's middle class which, unlike other Latin American countries, constituted nearly 30 percent of the population. They sought through reforms to create a fairer distribution of wealth in Chile. The upper 5 percent of the population, most typically large landowners, had annual incomes of $50,000 to $200,000, while Chilean peasant families tried to live on $200–300 a year.[1] Ten percent of the population owned 86 percent of all arable land; Frei initiated land reforms to break up large estates and distribute land among poor peasants.

Frei sought also to nationalize Chile's copper industry, the major source of income from exports. But he contracted to do so by buying back part ownership in mines owned by U.S. companies.[2] Copper mining had become a major industry in Chile since the mid-nineteenth century. Britain was the first foreign power to draw profits from copper, but by 1914 United States firms had gained control of Chile's copper industry. U.S. firms also gained a monopoly on the production of electricity, telephone services and railroad operations. In 1971 the Chile Copper Corporation claimed that the four biggest U.S. mining companies had, over a sixty-year period, taken out of Chile wealth to the value of $10.8 billion dollars. This amounted, they said, to more than Chile's GNP over its entire four-hundred-year history.[3]

The Catholic hierarchy quite clearly supported the Christian Democrats, though they resisted pressures to make specific endorsements of any party or candidate. In contrast to more conservative hierarchies in other parts of Latin America, the Chilean bishops were socially minded. Two years before Frei's election they issued a pastoral letter calling for land reform and reform of business and government structures.[4] The Church established research centers which contributed ideas to the Frei government. The Belgian Jesuit Roger Vekemans, who would emerge in the 1970s as the arch-opponent of liberation theology, served as a special advisor to Frei.[5]

U.S. liberals also supported Frei's efforts, viewing the Christian Democrats as an alternative to Marxist revolution. A charge was later made, in 1973, that the U.S. had dispatched nearly $20 million and sent one hundred CIA and state department agents to help Frei win the 1964 election against Allende. Frei denounced the accusation as totally unfounded.

The Frei government spoke of creating a "communitarian" society and encouraged popular participation in politics. But the expectations created by promises of reform led to disillusionment, especially when a workers' demonstration against pay cuts and a ban on strikes was quelled by force and seven protesters died. Youth groups reflected the first signs of disunity in the Christian Democratic Party. In 1968 a group of Christians, including seven priests, took over the Santiago Cathedral in the name of the people. A "Young Church" movement resulted.[6] It denounced the structure of power, domination and wealth with which the institutional Church was too often allied. It demanded that the hierarchy prove its concern for justice with deeds, and added demands that priests be allowed to marry and that Church authorities be selected democratically. The nucleus of this "Young Church" group formed, in 1969, the Movement for Unified Political Action (MAPU) to bring the Church more in line with the workers' movement and Marxist parties.

A growing number of priests became politically radicalized. Many had made the decision to live with the poor, to share their life and to work in their organizations. These priests of the *"poblaciones"* in Chile lived an experience quite similar to that of worker priests in France after World War II. They began to experience the "institutionalized violence," the insecurity and hunger of the poor. They felt reformism had failed and they began to look toward Marxist socialism as the only solution.[7]

This shift away from Christian-Democratic reformism and toward Marxism was reflected in a conflict which developed in 1968 at ILADES, a Jesuit institute founded to relate social sciences and the social doctrine of the Church to Latin America.[8] Its director, French Jesuit Pierre Bigo, had gained renown for his work *The Social Doctrine of the Church*. The assistant director, Gonzalo Arroyo, S.J., would become the leader of the Christians for Socialism four years later. The conflict arose when Bigo rejected an article on problems of development as being too Marxist. In the ensuing conflict a new temporary director was named, the bishops withdrew support from the project, Arroyo and many others resigned, and Bigo was reinstated. Bigo argued that the new trend was too Marxist and contradictory to Church doctrine. Arroyo argued that Christian thinking on socio-political problems should not be identified with the Church's traditional social doctrine. It contained too many ambiguities, did not really address the problems of Chile, and was being used to justify one political position, viz., the Christian Democrats. Bigo claimed the institute's study should be objective and neutral. Arroyo claimed it should maintain an "advocacy" stance. This conflict may explain in part the heavy stress placed on the critique of "Social Christianity" (the social doctrine of the Church) by the Christians for Socialism in subsequent years.

The Chilean hierarchy, even during the Allende years, identified more comfortably with the stance of the Christian Democrats. But most did not wish to rule out the possibility of Catholics collaborating with Marxists. When asked, in 1968, whether Catholics in Chile could cooperate or participate in Marxist organizations, ten Chilean bishops responded affirmatively, six others hedged but were open to it as a possibility, and only four were clearly opposed.[9] In a pastoral letter of 1969, which drew sharp criticism from the right, the bishops affirmed the desire of Catholics for "profound social transformation" and praised "the sharp sensitivity" of certain radical priests and Catholics whose ideas carried both a promise and a risk.[10] Prior to Allende's election, right-wing groups wanted Cardinal Raúl Silva Henriquez of Santiago to speak out publicly against Allende. Instead the Cardinal appeared on television six weeks before the election and declared that the Church was not linked to any system or political party and that its mission required the Church to be nonpartisan.[11]

Allende's Election and Initial Success

Allende came to power in the elections of 1970 as the leader of the Popular Unity (UP), a coalition of six political parties, including his own Socialist Party and the Communist Party. Allende had helped to establish the Socialist Party as a Marxist party independent of Moscow, and he had been the leading contender in the previous two presidential elections. In 1970 he won with 36.2 percent of the vote as opposed to 27.8 percent for Radomiro Tomic of the Christian Democrats and 34.9 percent for former president Jorge Alessandri, running as an Independent. Plurality victories were not uncommon in Chile. Alessandri won in 1958 with only 31.6 percent of the vote. But the lack of a majority vote would be used later against Allende to argue that he never had the popular support of the nation. The Christian Democrats agreed to ratify the election in Congress if Allende agreed to certain democratic guarantees and constitutional reforms. The Congress officially elected Allende on October 24. Allende pledged that his new government would be a multi-party government, a nationalist, popular, democratic and revolutionary government that would move toward socialism.[12]

Allende faced difficult odds from the outset. Right-wing groups within Chile planned to do all possible to disrupt his efforts, and U.S. business interests sought first to block his election and then to bring about his downfall. Washington columnist Jack Anderson, in March 1972, would make public ITT documents which revealed that company's efforts to protect its $153 million telephone enterprise by exerting pressures on the State Department, the CIA, and U.S. Ambassador Edward Korry to intervene against Allende.[13] U.S. Senate investigations would later verify the substance of this and many subsequent allegations. Throughout the months prior to the 1970 election ITT looked for ways to stop Allende from being elected. John McCone, former director of the CIA and consultant to ITT, met with Henry Kissinger and CIA director Richard Helms in mid-1970 to offer the government $1 million from ITT to help block Allende's election. A working relationship developed between ITT's William Merriam and William V. Broe, the CIA's director of clandestine operations in Latin America. When Allende was elected, an ITT memo of late September 1970 revealed a plan suggested by Broe to induce economic collapse in Chile. Another memo in September noted that President Nixon had given the green light to U.S. Ambassador Korry to do everything possible short of military intervention to defeat Allende. After ITT property was expropriated a year later, in September 1971, a new eighteen-point plan was developed by ITT to assure the collapse of Allende.[14] Suggestions included fostering discontent in the Chilean military, cutting off bank loans, withholding the shipment of spare machine parts, and slowing trade between the U.S. and Chile. The White House denied ever seriously considering the plan, but it seemed at times almost a script for what did occur.

1. Initial Victories: 1970–71. Allende scored a number of triumphs nevertheless in his initial year in office. He launched a campaign to distribute free milk to Chilean children, nearly half of whom were undernourished. He inaugurated measures to improve dramatically the medical care available to the poor. A people's health train with doctors, dentists, and pharmacists gave free treatment during a thirty-five-day tour of the southern provinces.[15] Bus fares were reduced for the poor; land for use as vacation resorts was awarded to poor schools and labor councils.

But the fundamental task of socialism was to make Chile's basic resources its own by putting an end to foreign ownership and control. This meant nationalization of key industries; smaller private enterprises Allende wished to encourage. Initial steps involved taking over the administration of two firms controlled by U.S. interests: Nibsa, a plumbing and heating fittings manufacturer, and Alimentos Purina, a manufacturer of animal and chicken feed.[16] An existing labor law, which allowed for federal intervention to protect worker interests, provided legal sanction for the initial expropriations. But a constitutional amendment was needed to legalize nationalization of the copper industry. Since the copper industry accounted for 80 percent of Chile's export earnings, this constituted the major step toward making Chile the owner of its own basic wealth. Three U.S. firms would be affected: Anaconda, Kennecott, and Cerro. Banks also were nationalized; other large companies were bought out, "requisitioned," or put under national management. Allende stressed, however, that small private industries would be encouraged to expand their production. More than 30,000 companies were to remain in private hands. Only plants with capital of more than $1 million could expect expropriation, and then only if they were judged monopolistic or unproductive.[17]

Land redistribution had also been a socialist priority. The Agricultural Minister announced government plans to expropriate all farms of more than 80 hectares. But Allende also sent a bill to Congress to check illegal seizures of farms. Leaders who organized seizures would be imprisoned.[18] Land reform was an especially volatile issue. Wealthy land owners, 4.4 percent of the rural population, owned 80 percent of the total farm land. Half of the peasant population worked as wage laborers or share-croppers. Another 25 percent owned tiny plots insufficient to feed a single family.[19] Some land reform had been attempted by Frei, but only one-tenth of the peasants had received land before 1970.

For the first year the gains were impressive. The GNP rose 8.5 percent; unemployment dropped from 8 percent to a record low of 3.8 percent; the workers' share in the national income rose from 51 percent to 59 percent. Municipal elections showed 51 percent for the Popular Unity.[20] Some socialist goals had failed to pass in Congress, such as Allende's plan for "people's tribunals" and his bill to create a unicameral assembly to replace the two-house Congress.[21] But Congress did vote unanimously in favor of nationalizing the copper industries. Some serious strikes had occurred, some manifest discontent certainly existed, and the assassination of General René Schneider by right-wing militants proved ominous. But overall the first year of Allende's rule, through most of 1971, could be judged quite successful.

2. The Catholic Church's Stance: 1970–71. What can be said of the Church's stance during this time? Jaime Rojas and Franz Vanderschueren describe the relationship of the Catholic hierarchy to the Allende regime under three different "modalities": friendly support, especially in the first year; constructive criticism, especially in the last year; political mediation during crises, in the last two years.[22] In all aspects of protocol the bishops dealt with the Allende government as they had with previous regimes. Relations with the government most often devolved upon Cardinal Silva. On inauguration day the Cardinal led the traditional prayer of thanksgiving, the *Te Deum.* Allende later remarked, in an interview with Regis Debray, that he looked on this act by the Cardinal as 'most significant and profound" and as an indication of the changing attitude of the Church.[23] At the celebration of May Day, 1971, organized by the Marxist-led Trade Union Center, Cardinal Silva again made an official appearance. Soon after Allende took office the Cardinal declared that "there are more evangelical values in socialism than in capitalism."[24] When Castro visited Chile at the end of 1971 the Cardinal met with him. These actions were widely interpreted as symbolic acts of legitimation for the government. As such they made the Cardinal the target of attacks from the right.

As for Allende's nationalization of copper and other industries, Cardinal Silva said that the process had been "constitutionally impeccable," that the action was in harmony with the United Nations' principle that every country has the right to reclaim its basic resources.[25] For his part, Allende fully respected not only freedom to worship but freedom of religions to propagate their views and to conduct schools. Religious freedom never became an issue. A stir would be created in March 1973 when the government proposed a unified school plan, but even this move was not interpreted, except by the right-wing, as an effort to impose atheistic-materialistic ideology.

In April 1971, the Catholic bishops of Chile formulated an important pastoral document on socialism. They referred to it as a "working paper" and entitled it "Gospel, Politics, and Various Types of Socialism."[26] The bishops accepted the Allende government as the legitimate expression of a democratic vote and they promised to collaborate in its efforts to serve the people of Chile and promote justice. But the bishops expressed warnings because of the Marxist inspiration of Chile's socialism. The potential dangers they noted in Marxism were its atheistic worldview and values, its exaggerated claim to be scientific, its economic reduction of consciousness, and the fact that Marxism in other countries had led to totalitarian regimes which repressed human rights. But the bishops also recognized capitalism as destructive of human values and they felt that special conditions in Chile could make its socialism different from previous Marxist ones. The fact that socialism had come about through a democratic process was especially encouraging. Much would depend, said the bishops, on the democratic maturity of the people, the effort of Christians, and the openness and critical spirit of the Marxists themselves toward their own system.

The bishops allowed for Christian participation in Marxist parties but spelled out three criteria for making a mature political opinion:

> (1) A Christian must choose that model or political party which has the greatest possibilities for opening a passageway in the history of Chile at this moment to the liberating force of the resurrection of Christ. (2) The person must intensify his or her gospel commitment so as to be able to critique and re-evaluate permanently the political option that has been chosen. (3) Each person must know the risks which a particular political option will entail and assume this commitment only if the good to be achieved outweighs the evil that could occur, and if the person has the capacity of overcoming the dangers involved.[27]

The Church itself, the bishops continued, should always be nonpartisan and not endorse any specific party or program. This also held for priests and religious who could hold their own personal political option but should not engage in partisan politics. The bishops concluded the document saying that the Chilean Church would cooperate with the Marxist government by supporting all that is liberating in the process towards socialism, and by opposing all that could enslave people.[28]

Juan Luis Segundo, in his *Liberation of Theology*, quite unfairly represents the bishops' position when he says that their 1971 letter affirms "that in Chile socialism is not a real alternative to the existing capitalist system."[29] His own footnotes quote the bishops as saying something quite different. They said rather that the opposing alternatives of capitalism and socialism are ' not the only possible ones" and that there are many forms and degrees of both. They do say, in reference to past experience, that "the concrete embodiments of Marxist socialism" thus far cannot be accepted as an authentic alternative to capitalism.[30] But they also go on in the letter to affirm that Chilean socialism could be different, given the democratic process which accompanied it.

A group of eighty priests, meeting at the same time as the bishops, issued a declaration in strong support of socialism. Their declaration would be the first step toward the formation of a Christians for Socialism movement the following year. The "Group of 80" declaration came before the official promulgation of the bishops' letter. But tension would soon arise because of the conflicting approaches the two groups took toward socialism. The priests felt that the Church, while nonpartisan in respect to specific political parties, should clearly opt for socialism at this juncture in Chilean history. The third criterion set down by the bishops for making a political option, especially the demand that a person have the capacity of overcoming the dangers involved, would be sharply criticized by pro-socialist Catholics as "stacking the deck" against any option for Marxist socialism. But the controversies between the bishops and the Christians for Socialism will be studied in much more detail later in this chapter.

Growing Crises and Military Overthrow

Pressures from external and internal sources created mounting problems for Allende as he began his second year in office. Leftist critics perhaps too facilely blame the United States for all the problems in the Third World. But whatever degree of importance one might assign them, United States' policies did significantly affect Allende's efforts. In a television interview in May 1977, David Frost confronted former President Richard Nixon with alleged charges that he had ordered the CIA to try to prevent Allende's election, that the United States had cooperated in efforts to assassinate General Schneider, that the CIA had spent some $8 million between 1970 and 1973 to aid Chilean opposition groups in subverting Allende's plans, and that financial pressures were exerted to cripple Chile's economy. Without responding directly to these charges Nixon argued that he had seen

Allende's government as a threat to national security on the grounds that Allende was cooperating with Castro. Nixon cited a visitor who remarked to him: "If Allende should win the election in Chile, and then you have Castro in Cuba, what you will in effect have in Latin America is a Red sandwich, and eventually it will all be Red." Nixon admitted that the United States had put economic squeezes on Chile, but claimed that domestic problems in Chile, not U.S. intervention, led to Allende's downfall.[31]

1. The Impact of U.S. Policies on Chile. ITT led in the efforts to thwart Allende, but soon found support in the copper companies which Chile had expropriated. Several months after their nationalization Allende announced that the U.S. copper companies would receive no compensation for their loss. Defending his action in a speech to the United Nations on December 4, 1972, Allende argued that U.S. copper companies actually owed Chile money because the excess profits they had made in preceding years far exceeded their estimated worth. A reasonable margin of profit, said Allende, would be 12 percent. But Kennecott had made an average annual profit of 52.8 percent from 1955 to 1970, including a 205 percent profit rate in 1968. Anaconda during the same period averaged 21.5 percent in profits, as opposed to 3.5 percent from their investments elsewhere. Over the past forty-two years, Allende charged, they had taken more than $4,000 million in profit out of Chile from an initial investment of $30 million.[32] Allende also charged the United States with creating an economic blockade against Chile and that pressure from U.S. interests was responsible for cutting off lines of bank credit to Chile. Kennecott had retaliated by attempting to block payments to Chile for copper sold in France and Germany.[33] But the greatest impact was felt by Chile in its unsuccessful efforts to gain bank loans and credit.

In August 1971, the U.S. Export-Import Bank (EXIMBANK) rejected a Chilean request for $21 million in loans to purchase Boeing jets, on the grounds that the issue of Chile's compensation for U.S. copper companies was not resolved. In October, U.S. Secretary of State William Rogers told representatives of six major U.S. corporations in Chile that the United States would take steps to cut off all aid to Chile.[34] In December 1972, Chile's Finance Minister charged that in 1970 Chile could call on lines of credit totalling $219 million, but this had fallen to a mere $32 million due to pressure from international banking organizations. In the seven years before 1971, he said, Chile had received more than $1 billion from the World Bank, the Inter-American Development Bank (IDB), and the Agency for International Development (AID). But Chile had not received a single credit from any of these organizations in more than a year and credits worth $205 million were being held up.[35] A precipitous drop in the world price of copper during 1971, from 68 cents a pound to 49 cents, further intensified Allende's financial problems.[36]

2. Internal Unrest and Conflict. Internal dissension became manifest toward the end of Allende's first year in office and continued to mount as time went on. Much of it arose out of the middle class. In December five thousand women joined in "the march of the empty pots" to protest food shortages and a visit by Fidel Castro. Police intervened when leftist groups confronted the marchers. Opposition forces comprised a majority in Congress and they succeeded in passing an anti-socialist bill in February 1972. It prohibited government expropriation of businesses without specific authorization of Congress. In April, a crowd estimated at 200,000 rallied in Santiago to protest food shortages.[37]

Opposition from the left also intensified. The Movement of the Revolutionary Left (MIR) followed the Leninist view that revolutionary socialism could not be achieved without "smashing the state machine." Socialism could not depend on constitutional means since the bourgeois state was created to protect capitalist interests. The MIR therefore stressed, and organized, direct takeovers of land and factories by peasants and workers. They believed also that seizure of power ultimately had to come through armed struggle.[38] The far left pressured Allende to move more quickly and to change the political structure to enable more radical change to occur. But when they led the populace to create a "popular assembly" in Concepción, Chile's third largest city, Allende denounced their action. Only with increased stress on "popular mobilization" in 1973, however, did direct opposition to government policies become more frequent on the left.

As early as the summer of 1971 Allende ran into conflicts with workers also, especially those already in higher pay brackets. Throughout his years in power Allende could count on the poorest sectors of the country to respond most favorably to the "spirit" of socialism, to participate in planning, and to recognize the need for increased efforts at work. Some unionized workers in copper and coal mines, in contrast, tended to view the government simply as a new owner.[39] In the summer of 1971 localized strikes by coal miners and copper miners forced pay raises of 40 percent and 43 percent respectively.[40] Broadcasting workers at all of Santiago's radio stations struck for pay raises in December. Bus drivers and personnel of the state rail agency went out on separate strikes in July 1972. Shopkeepers, service personnel and professional groups went on strikes at different times when they saw their own interests threatened. Truckers provoked a serious crisis when they went out on strike in October 1972, for food distribution relied heavily on them. Most truckers were owner-operators of their own trucks. They needed spare parts which U.S. firms would no longer supply; they had to compete as well with new fleets of diesel-powered trucks. Accusations were made both after this strike and again in July 1973 that right-wing and U.S. money had subsidized the truckers' strike.

Allende faced pressures on all sides. But the view, often fostered in the U.S. press, that his government had only minority backing, misrepresented popular feelings. Tomic of the Christian Democrats had proposed his own version of socialism in the 1970 election. Hence the initial vote for Allende and Tomic combined, constituted a significant majority of 64 percent for socialism. Moreover, in the March 1973 elections the Popular Unity increased its plurality to 44 percent, with Allende's own Socialist Party showing the greatest gains. A survey, commissioned by an opposition journal, *Ercilla,* in September 1972, indicated that while high income people were nearly unanimous in feeling essential goods were harder to buy, 75 percent of low income people felt they were easier.[41] The fact that food consumption had increased 27 percent in one year suggests that the poor were certainly better off.

But in January 1973, food distribution rules had to be enforced to combat inflation and the growing black market.[42] Members of the far right Fatherland and Liberty were arrested in May on charges of an alleged plot against the government. While a majority of workers stayed on the job, a strike at the El Teniente copper mine caused copper exports to be halted. The strike continued for seventy-four days before the walkout ended in July. Professionals, teachers, physicians, and nurses struck in support of the copper miners and to protest the government's economic policies.[43] The cost of living had risen a record 238 percent in the twelve months ending in May.

An attempted military coup was thwarted in June. An Allende aide was assassinated in July. Truckers went on strike again; violence grew; the government requisitioned trucks used by strikers. In August, Allende's staunchest military defender, General Carlos Prats, resigned as defense minister and army commander-in-chief. The cabinet was shuffled again. The Christian Democrats called for new elections. But on September 11 the armed forces and national police moved in, and after heavy fighting seized control of the government. Allende was killed, and with him died democracy in Chile and the first democratically elected Marxist government.[44]

3. The Catholic Church and its Growing Tensions. Divisions within the Church itself became more pronounced as crises increased for Allende. Some bishops and priests had been anti-Marxist from the outset. Fr. Raul Hasbun used Catholic television to criticize Allende—a fact which contradicts reports that Allende suppressed freedom of the media[45]—and in 1973 he began to attack the government as "totalitarian Marxism." Rightist Catholic school teachers permitted students to take off class to join in anti-Allende demonstrations. Many pro-socialist Christians, on the other hand, moved closer to the MIR position and promoted popular mobilization and seizures of power.

Some Catholics had protested sharply, in the early months of the Allende government, when superiors of five religious congregations offered to cede some of their schools to the government. But the first open criticism by the Catholic hierarchy came in March 1973 when the government proposed a "National Unified School" system. The government shelved the plan when they met with opposition, although the episcopate only criticized parts of the plan without rejecting it totally.[46] In July 1973 the bishops issued a statement deploring the deteriorating economic and political situation in the country. Even this letter made an effort not to fix blame, but it was taken as a criticism of the government.

For the most part, the Catholic hierarchy, and Cardinal Silva in particular, sought to mediate crises to the extent they could. Allende met with religious leaders on several occasions to get their suggestions and win their support. During the October crisis of 1972 the bishops issued a declaration saying that they believed the great majority of the Chilean people were in favor "of the continuity of the Constitution and respect and obedience to legitimate authority" and that "the process of change tending toward the liberation of the poor from all injustice and poverty should continue."[47] Most often the messages of the Cardinal and the bishops stressed peace, dialogue, and the avoidance of violence. Three weeks before the coup, Cardinal Silva invited Allende and the president of the Christian Democrats to his residence in what became the last formal effort to bridge the gap and to save the government. Through all three years religious freedom and rights never became an issue.

Christians for Socialism:
Ideological Struggle within the Church

In discussing Marxism-Christianity in Chile, most of the focus thus far has been upon relations between the official, hierarchical Church and the Allende government. That they could cooperate and respect each other constituted a major breakthrough in Christian-Marxist relations. The stance of the official Church was made clear on several occasions: the Church is nonpartisan in respect to political parties and systems; it can support the Allende government because it won office fairly through democratic process. The bishops had also set down rules for priests and religious to follow. They could personally opt for one political position or another, though they must be especially self-critical if the option is for Marxist socialism; they were not to act politically in the name of Christianity or of the Church.

For many priests and religious in Chile this stance proved distressing and unacceptable. Many had lived and worked with the poor and experienced with them the hopes generated by socialism. They drew upon liberation theology and the concerns expressed at Medellin. They became convinced that socialism in Chile expressed God's own liberating action in behalf of the poor. They felt not only called personally to work for the new socialist society, but they believed that the official Church should give its support by opting expressly in favor of socialism so that the moment of liberation would not be lost.

This section of the chapter thus deals with the conflict which developed between these two positions, a conflict which remained unresolved. The account which follows says little about the important relationships which developed between priests and the poor they sought to serve, though it was these relationships which gave rise to their position. It likewise says little about the right-wing Christian groups who criticized the hierarchy for not opposing Allende and condemning Marxist socialism. It should also be made clear that the amount of attention given to pro-socialist Christians and their relations to the hierarchy in this chapter does not mean that their interaction greatly influenced events in Chile. Many, on the contrary, would argue that their roles were quite insignificant given all the political-economic factors at work during these years. But for our purposes, in studying the relation of Marxism/socialism to Christianity, the problems raised by this confrontation are important.

"Declaration of the 80"

In April 1971 a group of eighty priests, native Chileans and missionaries, met to reflect on the significance of Allende's socialism in the light of their Christian faith and the bishops' documents of Medellín. Invited to be with them was the liberation theologian Gustavo Gutiérrez. At the conclusion of their sessions they issued a declaration in the press which forcefully stated the conclusions they had reached. They found the working class with whom they lived and worked suffering from malnutrition, lack of housing, unemployment, and with little hope for educational or cultural development. The cause of this situation was clear: "It is the capitalist system, resulting from domination by foreign imperialism and maintained by the ruling classes of this country."[48] With accession of the People's Government there was now hope. Socialism could pave the way for a new economy and generate new values leading to fellowship and new dignity for each worker. They continued:

> We feel committed to the process that is now under way and we want to contribute to its success. The underlying reason for our commitment is our faith in Jesus Christ, which takes on depth and vitality and concrete shape in accordance with historical circumstances. To be a Christian is to be in solidarity, in fellowship, with other human beings. And at this moment in Chile fellowship means participation in the historical project that its people have set for themselves.[49]

They went on to declare that they saw no incompatibility between Christianity and socialism, quoting Cardinal Silva, "There are more evangelical values in socialism than there are in captialism."

The group saw a need for breaking down the mistrust that exists between Christians and Marxists. They accepted collaboration with Marxists in constructing a new socialist society. This collaboration, they felt, would be facilitated to the extent (1) that Marxism is used as an instrument for analyzing and transforming society and (2) that Christians purify their faith of all that prevents real and effective commitment. This commitment, in turn, meant supporting the measures aimed at social appropriation of the means of production—nationalization of mineral resources, socialization of banks, expansion of agrarian reform. Moreover, the people would have to be mobilized to combat former owners who will resist losing their ownership and privileges. While admitting that not all was necessarily positive in Chilean socialism, the priests insisted that "criticism should be formulated from within the revolutionary process, not from outside it."[50] They concluded that they, as priests, like each and every Christian, must do what they can to make their own modest contribution.

Responses to the Declaration

The rector of the Catholic University of Santiago, Beltran Villegas, SS.CC., responded to the declaration three days after its publication and the Chilean bishops responded a few days after that. Their criticisms expressed many of the same reservations noted in the last chapter in regard to liberation theology. Villegas, as a theologian, focused his concerns on the tendency to identify theological perspectives and faith commitment with specific political options. The bishops expressed this concern as well but, as Church rulers, they reacted most strongly to what they viewed as priests claiming to speak in the name of Christianity.

1. *A Theologian Responds.* Villegas agreed with the Group of 80 that capitalism had proven to be inhuman and execrable, that a socialist regime could be more respectful of human dignity, and that Christians could work with Marxists to help create a new society. But Villegas also noted points in the declaration that disconcerted him. First, he was disturbed that they had made a personal political option into an objectively "theological" position. Solidarity with other human beings is an essential Christian message, but working to promote Chilean socialism is a personal translation of this, not a universal duty incumbent on all Christians.[51] Second, Villegas questioned their adoption of a Marxist class-centered outlook. A Christian may use Marxist analysis, but neither its scientific validity, nor its separability from an atheistic Marxist worldview, are universally clear and self-evident. And the Marxist stress on the proletarian class as the exclusive bearer of humanity's future does not dovetail with Jesus' concern for the poor. All people, rich and poor, are called to be saved. Finally, Villegas recognized the priests' right to opt *personally* for social transformation through class struggle, but not their right to do so "as priests" or to designate any one option as "Christian."[52] Despite the criticisms Villegas concluded his response by expressing his admiration, respect, and friendship for them.

2. *The Bishops Respond.* The Chilean bishops, in their response, first enunciated several general statements about the role of the Church in respect

to politics and about Marxism in Chile.[53] They were points which their pastoral letter on the "Gospel, Politics, and Various Types of Socialism" developed in much greater detail. The mission of the Church is to proclaim and live out the gospel. The Church itself is not tied to any political system, nor does it have the competence to pronounce on specific solutions of a political or economic nature. The Church should, on the other hand, denounce whatever might delude and enslave people, and it must promote those things which would safeguard the dignity of the human person. Marxist socialism poses legitimate questions because its concrete embodiments in history have led to denials of human rights, though the same is true for embodiments of the capitalist system. In respect to the government of Chile, its legitimacy should be respected, and its efforts to eliminate poverty and fashion a more human society should be supported, but this support should include serious-minded criticism.

The bishops then addressed the declaration of the 80. "Like any citizen, a priest is entitled to have his own political option. But in no case should he give this option the moral backing that stems from his character as a priest."[54] Priests should, therefore, abstain from taking partisan political positions in public. To act otherwise would be to revert to an outdated clericalism. "If the political option of the priest is presented as a logical and inescapable consequence of his Christian faith, as it was in this case, then it implicitly condemns every other option and it is an attack on the liberty of other Christians."[55] Priests should not put themselves at the service of any ideology or human faction, but should be heralds of the gospel.

The bishops then affirmed that the situation created by the declaration did not affect their esteem for the priests in question, nor diminish their high regard for the work of these priests among the working class. They concluded with renewed hope "in the liberating presence of Christ" so that his activity in behalf of the poor might be supported in love.

3. An Appraisal of the Interchange. Within the Group of 80's initial declaration and the responses of Villegas and the Chilean bishops are contained nearly all the major issues which would trouble the Church in Chile from then on and which continue to create tensions in Latin America. Neither side sought to defend capitalism; both expressed commitment to liberation of the poor. At issue were (1) how qualified or unqualified should support of the socialist experiment be; (2) to what extent the efforts to create a new socialist society could be identified with "God's liberating action"; (3) to what extent and in what form should priests be involved in politics. All of these emerged as issues in Chapter 5 on liberation theology, but some additional reflections on them in the Chilean context may be worth considering.

Both sides could make a reasonable case for their positions. Socialism, as the priests saw it, offered a unique opportunity to end the great injustice created by monopolistic ownership on the part of wealthy landowners and foreign companies. To repeat constant warnings about the possible dangers of Marxist socialism could only weaken the unified effort needed to build a new society and strengthen the hand of those who wanted to subvert it. The Church had traditionally proclaimed its opposition to socialism; public declarations by priests in favor of socialism were needed to offset this. Marxist socialism, as the bishops saw it, offered both a promise and a risk. To ignore the risk, given the past history of Communist regimes, would be irresponsible. Christians can never give unqualified approval to any system. They should support it to the extent that it promotes justice and the common good, and stand in criticism to the extent that it does not. For priests to say that they speak for God or for Christianity in affirming any socio-political movement or system can never be justified. (Whether the priests actually did this in the declaration needs to be questioned.)

While these differences were very real, the expression of them tended to be exaggerated. Had the priests expressed more qualifications—that they spoke for themselves only, that they recognized certain risks but felt these had to be taken, etc.—they could have dissipated many of the criticisms made of their declaration. On the other hand, both Villegas and the bishops failed to note the qualifications that *were* expressed. Throughout the declaration one finds personal, qualifying phrases repeated: "It is clear to us," "we feel committed," "we do not see any incompatibility," "we say at this moment," "we support measures."

Nowhere in the declaration do the priests *say* that all Christians must be socialists, that workers alone reflect the poor with whom Jesus identified, or even that God's liberating action was now manifest in Chilean socialism. They declare that the reason for *their* commitment is *their* faith in Jesus Christ. They do say that "to be a Christian is to be in solidarity" and that this means "participation in the historical project that its people have set for themselves." But this is nearly as general as the bishops' reference to "the Liberating presence of Christ in the midst of the historical process through which we are now living." The declaration does link God's commitment to the history of human beings with the present. But the connection is again made in very personal and general terms: "and we say that at this present moment loving one's neighbor basically means struggling to make the world resemble as closely as possible the future world that we hope for and that we are already in the process of constructing." In short, many of the criticisms aimed at the declaration were based on interpretations *read into* the declaration.

These reflections significantly affect the issue as to whether the priests were speaking "as priests" and in the name of Christianity, or only as private citizens. Certainly the distinction is difficult to draw. As Villegas noted, a statement by eighty priests draws attention and carries weight that a similar declaration by eighty laypeople would not. In some cultures, moreover, some people may tend to accept whatever a priest says as "gospel truth." But an entirely different dynamic might have developed had the bishops and other critics recognized the declaration as a personal statement and had they simply insisted that all future statements make clear the personal nature of political options.

Considerable attention has been given this first brief exchange because it serves as a paradigm of the conflicts that arose in Chile and which continue to trouble the Church. A basic difference did divide the pro-socialist priests and the bishops, centered on the issue of how partisan or nonpartisan the Church should be. As time went on the priests would grow more insistent that there is no middle ground between socialism and capitalism. They would publicly criticize the a-politicism of the episcopate and challenge any statement that reflected the reformist stance of the social teachings of the Church in the past.[56] Both priests and bishops, on the other hand, did make continued efforts to keep lines of communication open. But this initial exchange established a pattern on both sides which made mutual understanding more difficult, a pattern of "reading into" statements interpretations which only accentuated points of opposition.

The Founding of Christians for Socialism, 1972

In the early part of December 1971, a group of priests from various countries in South America met in Chile to plan a convention of Christians who regarded socialism as a necessary precondition for a just and human society. The group met also with Fidel Castro who encouraged them by recognizing Christians as "strategic allies." Castro laid stress on "popular mobilization" during his visit to Chile, which some Chileans took as a criticism of Allende. His comments on a democratically-elected socialist government as an alternative to guerilla warfare were taken, in turn, as a criticism of the MIR. The group formulated a "draft agenda" for the convention and invited Cardinal Silva to be a patron.

1. **Cardinal Silva's Reactions to the Convention Agenda.** The Cardinal's initial response, in March 1972, was sharply critical of the draft agenda for the proposed convention. "From my study of this document I am convinced that you are going to hold a political meeting and that your aim is to commit the Church and Christians to the struggle on behalf of Marxism and the Marxist revolution in Latin America. As you see it, Marxism is the one and only way to liberate man."[57] He criticized the agenda on several points: for proposing groups of "committed Christians" with no reference to the Church; for proposing a narrow formula of revolution as the only way to liberation; for reducing Christianity to revolutionary class struggle; for reducing theology to ideology; for reducing Christianity to one dimension, the socio-economic; for reducing Christianity to something purely sociological.

The Coordinating Committee responded to the Cardinal's letter two weeks later.[58] They admitted that the draft agenda gave a one-sided picture of Christian thought, but that was because it focused only on the socio-economic. They had no intention of denying what had been omitted, viz., many other aspects of the faith. They then responded in detail to each of his criticisms.[59] Their responses were aimed primarily at showing that their stress on political implications of the faith did not amount to "reduction" of the faith to politics.

In April 1972, the Cardinal wrote again to the Committee. He accepted the substance of their responses as "being quite positive" and he noted that many of their remarks had clarified their position a great deal. He felt, however, that their responses included unjust criticism of his own dealing with them, for example, that he had made personal charges against some of them and that he objected to their working for liberation of the Chilean people. He concluded with a prayer that his fears about the convention would not prove correct and that it might represent a step forward in the liberation activity of Christians in Latin America.[60]

In an "authorized summary" published the same month, the points on which Cardinal Silva *agreed* with pro-socialist priests became more evident. He felt that liberal capitalism, based on an unrestricted quest for profit, was an outdated system responsible for many of the problems affecting Chile. He agreed that most in Latin America probably desired some type of pluralistic and democratic socialism, and that if people opted for this, the Church would have no difficulty in accepting it and collaborating with it. He recognized that class struggle was a social reality, that Christian thought had been influenced by capitalist structures and ideology, that some features of Marxism could be used in analyzing society, and that priests and laity should organize to study problems and explore new solutions.[61] His differences would continue to focus on public involvement of priests, especially to the extent that they appeared to speak in the name of Christianity and to accept Marxist socialism without being critical of its risks.

2. The 1972 Convention: Chile's National Report. Christians for Socialism marked its formal beginnings as an international group with the convention of April 23–30, 1972, in Santiago. Some four hundred delegates from various countries attended. Among them were Bishop Méndez Arceo of Cuernavaca, Mexico, and liberation theologians Gustavo Gutiérrez and Hugo Assmann. The majority of delegates were priests, but some Protestant ministers and many lay people were also present. The convention began with national reports, including ones from Peru, Puerto Rico, and Cuba. But the major report came from Chile itself.

Part I of the Chile report was basically a political analysis. It described the "failure" of the Christian Democrats from 1964–70 and the new "Chilean way" to socialism begun in 1970. It noted the achievements of the Popular Unity government and responded to criticisms against it. It observed that because of the long dominance of bourgeois ideology many segments of the proletariat and peasantry still lacked socialist consciousness. The report argued that opposition to the government would only be resolved to the extent that organized labor and the people are "mobilized politically to defend what they have won and to move on towards the full takeover of power so that the transition to socialism becomes irreversible."[62] Hence they insisted that socialism be constructed from the grass-roots up.

Part II of the report dealt with "The Christian Element in the Present Historical Process." It offered first a "typology" of different political parties of Christians, a typology already noted in discussing liberation theology. "Christian Conservatism" represented the old order dominated by landowners and the upperclass who were in power when independence was won from Spain. "Christian Reformism" or Social Christianity was led by intermediate classes but used by the dominant class. This reformism drew its initiatives from the Church's social teachings which were infected by bourgeois ideology and offered only moralistic criticisms of social injustices while upholding capitalism. The Christian Democrats marked the culmination of this reformism which still characterized the position of most Christians. "Revolutionary Christianity" had recently emerged as a third type. Its advocates are still a minority and they are subject "to pressure and to subtle but effective persecution by their hierarchical officials and their communities," but despite this many have discovered evangelical Christianity and the "combative face of Jesus Christ."[63]

The main thrust of this report then dealt with a critique of reformist Social Christianity as contrasted to Revolutionary Christianity. The Chilean Christians for Socialism obviously felt that continued Catholic allegiance to the Christian Democrats represented the major obstacle to the acceptance of their own views.

First, the report noted the differences in starting points of these two movements. Social Christianity draws upon a long tradition of the social doctrine of the Church. These social teachings of the Church have progressed in recent years but are still read from a reformist perspective. Pope Paul VI's *Octogesima Adveniens* (1971), the report adds, represented an advance not reflected in the Chilean pastoral letter of the same year. Revolutionary Christianity has as yet no history but is being formed through contact with peasants and workers and use of Marxist analysis.[64]

Second, Social Christianity and Revolutionary Christianity are distinguished by two different types of logic. In the logic of Social Christianity, theory is fashioned prior to the concrete praxis of history. It moves deductively from first principles to conclusions without history entering in at all. Revolutionary Christianity, in contrast, uses a historical, dialectical logic established by Hegel and Marx. It starts with conflict as a basic fact in human relationships and reflects on human praxis in response to conflict. Thus while Pius IX condemned Communism in principle as intrinsically evil, and while Chilean bishops set down conditions and warnings about the risks of Marxism, the logic of Revolutionary Christianity operates differently. Warnings about the dangers of Marxism reinforce fears and restrain people from taking risks, even though the bishops also condemn the dehumanizing effects of capitalism. Revolutionary Christianity recognizes that every solution entails risks, but risks and dangers cannot be avoided. ' If we are confronted with a fire, there is not a great deal of room for deliberation. The task confronting us is to put it out. Nor do we have much choice in picking our risks."[65] The Christian revolutionary knows that Marxism has operated from an atheistic, materialistic philosophy, and that this had serious repercussions in the Soviet Union. But the revolutionary also knows that the future will take the form given it by those who actively shape it and consequently is willing to accept the risks entailed and to make every effort to transform them into a new form of the Spirit's presence.

Third, two types of social consciousness also mark the difference between Social Christianity and Revolutionary Christianity.[66] Social Christianity proposes reforms and "appeals" to business and political leaders to bring about change. It appeals to justice, peace, humanism, universal charity, and universal solidarity, and it opposes egotism, injustice, and violence. Its social consciousness, in short, is ethical consciousness. Revolutionary Christianity recognizes that ethics cannot be treated separately from socio-economic structures which condition it. Christian thought and practices contain ideological elements which need to be "unmasked." Traditional Christian thought rejects "class struggle" as generating hatred, but it does not recognize that conditions create hatred, that the "have-nots" experience hatred when they are oppressed. Traditional Christian thought celebrates the Eucharist as a symbol of unity. But unity does not exist; it has to be constructed. What Christians have looked for in Marxism is a strategy; it cannot be an exact science because it operates in the realm of liberty; but it can ascertain definite trends in society.[67]

Part III of the national report from Chile offers certain guidelines for action: love of neighbor concretized in commitment to the working class and its historical project of socialism; mobilization of the people toward a utopian goal of total liberation, to create "a new heaven and a new earth"; the development of a new revolutionary consciousness to divert people from the ideology of Social Christianity. The ideological battle is of primary importance. The Church and the sacraments cannot be allowed to serve the interests of a minority capitalist class. Christians for Socialism have no desire to create a political movement of their own, nor to form a front in opposition to their communities or hierarchy. But with Che Guevara they do believe that "when Christians dare to give full-fledged revolutionary witness, then the Latin American revolution will be invincible."[68]

A final document summarized the positions taken at the convention: the need for socialism, the impossibility of any middle ground between capitalism and socialism, the impossibility of neutrality in the class struggle, a return to the wellsprings of Marxism and a criticism of traditional Marxist dogmatism, the need for priests to take on political responsibility, the recognition of socialism as the only acceptable option, the need to identify and unmask ideological justifications that are supposedly Christian, etc.[69]

3. *The Chilean CFS: Intensified Radicalization.* At a national meeting of the Christians for Socialism (CFS) in November 1972, Secretary General Gonzalo Arroyo defined three essential objectives of the group: (1) Political efficacy—the need for clear awareness of tendencies in the present situation, those which contain revolutionary potential and those which risk a retreat to reformism or fascism. CFS is not aligned with any one specific political party, but each member should have a militant commitment. (2) Specific ideological struggle—the need to unmask the use of Christian values to defend a bourgeois social order, to unmask the monolithic and apolitical nature of the Church which favors reformist Social Christian positions, to prepare Christian communities to do political analysis. (3) Construction of a new experience in faith—new forms of living the faith and of celebrating the Eucharist, replacing symbols impregnated by the dominant ideology. Arroyo insisted, however, on remaining within the Church and not breaking with the hierarchy, with a view towards a new Church more centered in the base community.[70]

At the same meeting Diego Irarrazaval delivered a speech entitled "What Is to Be Done? Christians in the Socialist Process." The task, he insisted, was a revolutionary one, one that begins with the historic situation not with Christianity or theology. This revolutionary task was the very site for encounter with God. God manifested his presence in the struggle of the people. Irarrazaval's speech criticized Christian reformism and pointed to specific instances where the "bourgeois ideology" of the Church was manifest—in the bishops' stand on Church schools and their calling for "peace" rather than support of the people in the October strikes. Irarrazaval insisted that one could not construct a "Christian socialism" because the impetus for socialism came from the working class, not Christianity.[71] He criticized the hierarchy for accepting the Popular Unity government only because it was democratically elected. The bishops failed really to support the revolutionary process as such for "they do not support popular power against the State and the bourgeois order, they do not support the revolutionary taking of power by the working class and its vanguard."[72] He likewise criticized popular religious piety, for example, praying to the Virgin Mary, which separates the people from the struggle. "We have discovered that the kingdom of God is the reward of those who struggle for liberation. We have the attitude that the reign of justice and brotherhood will come because the struggle of the oppressed progresses towards that end."[73]

By 1973 nearly 300 priests, pastors, and religious throughout almost all the provinces of the country had some connection with the group. Its membership represented very diverse views on socialist tactics. But according to Rojas and Vanderschueren the group as a whole continued to move toward the far left wing of the Popular Unity without breaking from it, and its positions on several issues and events placed it in opposition to leaders of the Popular Unity government.[74]

The Bishops' Prohibition of Involvement in Christians for Socialism

For the Chilean bishops the strain of relations with the Christians for Socialism had reached a breaking point. At their plenary session in April 1973, they discussed the whole theological and pastoral question of priests and religious in politics. They concluded that priests and religious should be prohibited from belonging to the Christians for Socialism. But they agreed to postpone any statement until they could formulate a doctrinal statement explaining their reasons. The definitive document was ready in the middle of August, but final approval came only on September 13—two days after the fateful military coup which overthrew Allende. Only the executive committee of the episcopal conference met in September, and the document prohibiting the CFS might never have become public had not the secretary of the episcopal conference, Bishop Carlos Oviedo, acted on his own to send out the document.[75] If this last comment is accurate, Segundo is again quite unjust when he observes that "when their partisans were being persecuted and sometimes killed in the streets, the Chilean bishops were meeting to make some final observations on the 'Christians for Socialism' movement and to condemn them."[76]

The declaration of the bishops contains a brief statement about the positive contributions of the CFS movement: motivating Christians to engage in problems of social justice, contributing a keen sense of the socio-economic factors which condition moral and spiritual life, a revitalization of theology by contact with historic problems of the day, etc. But overall the declaration is quite negative. The document is lengthy. But since most of the criticisms have already been expressed in earlier statements of the bishops, a relatively brief summary should suffice.

1. They (CFS) reduce Christianity to one dimension, namely politics. "In the view of the Church held by this group we see an obsessive and exaggerated emphasis on the socio-political realm, and a strong tendency to reduce the whole dynamism of the Church to this one dimension."[77] They would like to reduce the Catholic faith and the Church's dogma and morality to Christian commitment to liberation understood in an increasingly temporal and materialistic sense.[78] Charity, the kingdom, the sacraments, conversions, are all interpreted to refer to social classes, political parties, or groups.[79]

2. They use the gospel to espouse one particular political option. "They end up concluding that their option is a perfect expression of the gospel message and consubstantial with Christ's manifestation in the world."[80] The primary and essential mission of the Church, it would seem to them, is to mobilize the masses in favor of one specific type of revolution.[81] They make membership in the Church conditioned upon a political option. Love of the

poor is equated with the adoption of a revolutionary stance in favor of one social class against another, an outlook dictated by Marxist analysis.[82]

3. They reduce all other Christian views to bourgeois ideology. They maintain that "the hierarchy is putting itself in the service of the bourgeois ideology and its class interests, and is therefore an ally and defender of the oppressive structures of capitalism."[83] Their use of a Marxist-Leninist method reduces the religious life of humanity to an ideology reflecting class struggle. Where religion claims to be apolitical, this method sees only alienation or complicity with dominant social groups. They reduce the struggle between good and evil to class struggle, though no group is the clear and simple embodiment of good and evil.[84] They readily accept Marxism's criticism of religion, but do not undertake any in-depth criticism of the postulates of Marxism to which they accord the label of indisputable science.[85]

4. They claim to speak for true Christianity and the true Church. "Thus this group inevitably ends up by somehow 'sacralizing' its own cause and making it a Church within the Church—or rather the 'true Church,' a new sect, only marginally associated with the hierarchical ties of the ecclesial community." Its Secretariat exercises a kind of teaching function parallel to that of the bishops. "It feels obliged to dictate what the stance of Christians should be vis-à-vis this or that given situation or problem."[86] If the group seeks to form a front for penetrating into the Church and converting it to a political force from within and tying the Church to a specific program of social revolution, it should state this openly and not regard itself as an ecclesial group.[87]

In the light of these charges the bishops then prohibited priests and religious from belonging to CFS and from carrying out the kinds of activity denounced in the document.

The Aftermath: Some Critical Reflections

The military junta which seized power in September 1973 enforced its rule swiftly and ruthlessly. Thousands were executed, imprisoned, tortured, or expelled. Thousands more lost jobs. Scores of priests fled the country or were deported. Strikes that had severely impaired Allende's government met with quick solutions under the junta—strike leaders faced execution or imprisonment. All political parties, including the Christian Democrats, would be suppressed. Chile's long democratic tradition came to an end and remained suppressed in the years which followed. The Catholic hierarchy, its leftist critics charged, not only failed to protest the illegal seizure of power but accorded the junta the same symbolic acts of legitimation, such as public Masses and prayers of thanksgiving, that they had given to democratically elected governments. Gonzalo Arroyo argued that the bishops' actions after the takeover lent support to the thesis that institutionalized churches and religions are integral parts of the overall socio-economic system, and that the

Church had given up even its reformist stance and reverted to a conservative and regressive position.[88] Supporters of the hierarchy would answer that their acceptance of the military junta was dictated by concerns about deteriorating conditions and growing anarchy in the final months of Allende's rule, and that their strong protests against violations of human rights since that time reflect their true stance. In any case, our concern here is not with the Church in Chile at present, but with the divisions within the Church during the Allende years.

Any effort at assessing the actions of the Christians for Socialism and their relation to the hierarchy faces two serious objections. First, perhaps no outsider, no one who did not live through the events and know all the interplay that occurred, should attempt to assess what happened. Leftist Christians may especially resent criticisms coming from a North American who was "outside the revolutionary process." Second, even those directly involved tend to assess what happened in terms of their own prior convictions. Hence, as noted at the beginning of the chapter, anti-Marxists "learned" from the experience of the Allende years that Marxist socialism creates more ills than it solves. The far left learned that socialism can only succeed by armed struggle and complete seizure of power. Moderate, pragmatic socialists learned that socialism must proceed more gradually, that gains must be consolidated, and the middle class won over. The following reflections are thus offered with some misgivings, and with an awareness that the pragmatist position just noted influences the judgments made. The reflections focus, however, on the ideological struggle within the Church rather than on the political situation as a whole.

In an introduction to the many documents in *Christians and Socialism*, a Chilean priest "very closely connected" with the movement wrote in retrospect:

> The Christians for Socialism realize that they were impatient, eagerly seeking radical solutions. They sometimes made hasty judgments, issued unfair denunciations, and fell into errors of interpretation. Their statements and declarations were published in the heat of a political and ideological debate that had gone on uninterruptedly for three years in Chile. They contained prophetic intuitions, but they also lacked doctrinal precision and were often ambiguous and incomplete. . . . They did not intend to break with the past, with the hierarchical Church and other Christians. . . . They also realize that they were not critical enough towards developments and activities within the Popular Unity coalition.[89]

How much this reflects the attitude of most who were involved in the Chilean CFS would be difficult to assess. But to the extent it does, some of the criticisms which follow may be self-criticisms by members themselves.

The situation in Chile did not, indeed, lend itself to carefully balanced statements and decisions. Ideally, decision-making should involve a thorough study of data and critical evaluation of possible solutions before action is taken. Such a process is not likely to occur when a potentially satisfying course of action risks being lost, if it is not acted upon immediately. Or in the Chilean CFS's own words: "If we are confronted with a fire, there is not a great deal of room for deliberation." The CFS spoke, moreover, in a political language. Their statements were "calls to action," words intended to evoke and strengthen commitment, not nuanced and self-critical reflections more attainable in less pressured times. At times, the bishops and other critics "read into" their statements more than they had said. In their response to Cardinal Silva the CFS did add nuances and qualifications which their original statements may not have contained. The source of conflict, therefore, should not be laid solely on the CFS. They did, nevertheless, expressly undertake an "ideological struggle" and the strategy used does need to be questioned.

Rojas and Vanderschueren, whose overall account of the CFS is generally quite favorable, criticize them on two points particularly. First, they failed to achieve a massive ideological change among Christians because they did not take sufficient account of the middle class, "the world of practicing Christians," and they did not recognize that the Christian Democrats enjoyed significant electoral support among many social classes. Second, they failed to win over more of the lower classes because the poor lacked any deeply rooted revolutionary tradition, and also because the lower classes were accustomed to looking to the hierarchy for leadership. Allende, these authors note, looked also to the hierarchy rather than to CFS who could have helped him build a bridge to the Christian masses.[90]

But what of the CFS's ideological struggle in relation to the hierarchy? On a psychological level their criticisms can be easily understood. But it is difficult to see what they stood to gain from public criticisms of the hierarchy and uncompromising attacks on the Church's past social teachings. The bishops' nonpartisan stance had been a helpful factor in Allende's election, and he seemed satisfied with their neutrality. Bishops are loyal to Church teachings, and documents in Vatican II and at Medellín had stressed the nonpartisan position the Church should take in respect to politics. To win the support of bishops and other Catholics who felt loyal to the Church's tradition one might appeal to the most progressive statements in the Church's social teachings and build upon them. But simply to identify this tradition with the Christian Democrats for the sake of condemning it could only create opposition. The bishops had given implicit support for socialism by respecting the legitimacy of Allende's government, by defending his nationalization of the copper industry, by calling for peace and the continuation of his regime. Yet they were accused of opposing it because they did not identify with strategies of the far left aimed at popular seizure of power. CFS spokespersons did indeed reduce God's will not only to socialism but to specific tactics of the far left.

What was the strategy of the CFS in respect to the Church itself? One explanation would be that it was a conscious effort to split the Church, to "de-legitimize" the hierarchy by identifying them with pro-capitalist rule so that the masses would lose all confidence in their leadership. Such a tactic has been used against "ruling elites" by leftist groups in the past. But such an explanation runs counter to the CFS's efforts not to break with the hierarchy, to answer the Cardinal's objections, and to remain a group of "loyal dissent." Another explanation would be that they hoped to win over the hierarchy to their position. But the open criticisms noted above could hardly hope to achieve this. A more plausible explanation is that they did not "plan" opposition to the hierarchy but fell into it when their own positions were challenged and criticized. The initial "Declaration of the 80" contained no direct criticism of the hierarchy. But following the unfortunate dialectic of most arguments, charges and counter-charges created feelings which made effective dialogue increasingly difficult.

The CFS set as guidelines for action: political efficacy or working for revolutionary socialism, ideological struggle or working to change consciousness in the Church, and the construction of a new faith experience. The first objective may indeed have justified class struggle. Class struggle as a model for changing consciousness in the Church needs to be questioned. It is one thing to win over bishops and other Christians to a recognition of bourgeois ideological elements in the faith; it is another to accuse them of supporting bourgeois positions which justify oppression. Unless one somehow envisions the "overthrow" of the hierarchy, persuasion rather than class struggle would seem the more realistic tactic within the Church.

How consciousness can be changed *within* the Church is thus an important issue raised by the experience of the Church during the Allende years. Arturo Gaete, in his essays on the Church's social doctrine noted in Chapter 3, offers a concrete example of a "dialogical" approach to consciousness changing. He makes the same point the Chilean CFS wished to make, the need for new models of socio-economic thought in Christianity. But he does so by praising the achievements of the social encyclicals, noting the legitimate values they sought to preserve, but pointing beyond them as well. The decision of liberation theologians at Puebla to influence the bishops' declarations rather than waiting to oppose them offers another important example of such an approach.

But again, in defense of the Chilean CFS, they were not permitted the time needed to approach ideological issues with calm reflection. The situation was urgent, the moment opportune. For the first time the poor began to experience the possibility of overcoming their poverty and oppression, to experience hope in the future, and to feel a sense of dignity and pride. Priests, religious, and laity experienced this with them and sought to help them make it a lasting reality. Whatever criticisms are made should not offset esteem for what they strove to achieve.

Christians for Socialism Internationally

Spurred by the Chilean experience and by growing opposition to capitalism, together with the conviction that it cannot be reformed, Christians for Socialism groups have developed throughout the world. Many groups explicitly identify themselves as CFS; others go by other names. Membership figures are not documented and would be difficult to estimate. People with CFS orientation certainly number in the thousands and perhaps hundreds of thousands in Latin America, and thousands do belong to CFS groups in Italy. Smaller CFS groups exist in Holland, Belgium, Spain, and other European countries. France has many pro-socialist Christian groups, but they were slow to create Christians for Socialism as such. Many of the "Catholic Left" in England, already pro-socialist in the 1960s, have moved to affiliation with CFS. Groups exist in many African and Asian countries as well. From a recently formed group in Ireland to a small group on the island of Mauritius, CFS has established itself in many parts of the world. It maintains communication between groups through an international bulletin, *Liaisons Internationales*.

A first international conference of CFS was held in Quebec in April 1975.[91] It undertook a political analysis of transnational capitalism and of the struggles for liberation against capitalism. It reflected also on the growing struggle between "a popular and proletarian Christianity" and dominant bourgeois ideology. It studied the world's economic crisis and the hunger, unemployment, and oppression left in its wake. It found the most basic cause of this crisis in capitalist world expansion, with power concentrated in large corporations most of which operate out of the United States. The final document of the conference makes no explicit reference to Marxism, but both the analysis and the language of the document clearly reflect its influence. The document reads like a manifesto. Its heavy use of Marxist rhetoric and its unqualified identification of theological perspectives with the struggle for socialism leave it open to the same criticsms made of Chilean CFS statements.

As the Chilean CFS and proponents of liberation theology had done, the Quebec document locates Christian faith in the context of the struggle to liberate oppressed peoples from capitalism. It sees "the revolutionary task" as the place where faith attains its full growth. It sees the poor themselves as bearers of the good news of liberation. Their praxis is a subversive praxis which seeks a new earth; conversion means to overcome one's own complicity in oppressive structures and to challenge them. "Moreover, and above all, if we say we are Christian, it means to open ourselves to the burning question of the needs of the popular struggle. This political and spiritual rupture is the presence of the resurrection, the passover of freedom and the experience of the new life according to the Spirit."[92] The document then challenges the silence and subservience of most churches in respect to capitalism, their legitimizing of capitalism by stress on purely spiritual concerns and by their claims to be non-political. The declaration calls for a "new kind of Christianity," tied to the interests of the working class, as an alternative to a Christianity allied ideologically and structurally to the still dominant system of capitalism.

CFS continued, in some countries, to clash with the hierarchy. The bishops of Ecuador, in September 1976, condemned the movement. They made explicit reference to the Quebec document, calling it an incoherent mixture of the Bible and revolutionary praxis, and charged that CFS had assimilated not only the vocabulary, but the tactics and part of the ideology of Marxism. In November 1976, sixty-five bishops in Colombia issued a similar condemnation, rejecting claims that Marxist analysis is scientifically valid and separable from its atheistic ideology.[93]

A few bishops, on the other hand, have been openly supportive of and even involved in Christian socialist efforts. In most countries the hierarchy has simply avoided taking any stand on CFS. Much of the conflict in Chile, and subsequently in some other Latin American countries, stemmed from the fact that the CFS group was strongly identified with priests. Hence the authority issue, of priests speaking in the name of the Church, came to the forefront. In countries such as Italy where the laity predominate in CFS groups, or in countries such as Holland which have ecumenical memberships, the bishops-versus-priests conflicts are much less focal. But there are also countries in which priest groups do exist, such as O.N.I.S. in Peru, where relations with the hierarchy are better due both to greater openness on the part of the bishops and less public criticism of the Church on the part of the priests.

Christians for Socialism is not a political party. This point had been made by the Chilean CFS, it was repeated by the Italian CFS,[94] and has become a general, operative principle. They do stand for socialism, but members work through a variety of different political commitments. Groups, and individuals within groups, range considerably in their stances, from militant Marxist-Leninists to pacifist social-democrats. They do not attempt to develop a common strategy, even within small groups. Their goal is rather to reflect on their common Christian faith in the light of a commitment to socialism. This commitment, too, differs in intensity. Some see their faith as lived out precisely in the struggle for socialism; others may be little more than study groups with some effort to act on their reflections.

CFS does not have its own plan for socialism. It recognizes the secular nature of political options and believes that the poor and the working masses must themselves provide the project for social change. Some have accepted Marxist strategy and goals uncritically and their attitudes of certitude can alienate those who might otherwise be supportive. But others have recognized the need to criticize dogmatic appropriations of Marxism, to be critical of their own attitudes, and to value what the Christian heritage can bring to socialism.

A United States movement of Christians for Socialism developed in 1974. It first called itself American Christians Toward Socialism (ACTS), but in 1978 took on the name of Christians for Socialism in the United States. Some of the initial members had come out of the Chile experience; many had direct experience in Latin America or contact with those who had; still others came to socialism through U.S. anti-war or civil rights movements in the 1960s. The same range of socialist positions, noted above, also characterize U.S. members. Full members are expected to participate actively in the life of the group and to make some financial contribution to local and national efforts. Some groups include associate members. Group functions include theoretical study, reflections of members' lives and engagement in the political and ecclesial arenas, and celebration together. By the end of the 1970s membership nationally had grown to about three hundred with chapters in Detroit (the national office), Chicago, Washington, D.C., New York, Iowa, Wisconsin, and California (which has the largest membership).

Christian groups working for socialism and Christian advocacy of Marxist ideas will certainly continue into the 1980s. The experiences of the 1970s, beginning with Chile, proved that Christians can work with Marxists and that Christians and Marxists do share in a common hope for society. The experiences also showed that Christian advocates of Marxism can fall under the same criticisms levelled at Marxists. Marxism can evoke a passionate conviction in its adherents that they alone possess the right program for society. Christian Marxism can evoke this same conviction. Most of the criticisms aimed at CFS (e.g. seeing its political option as the only truly Christian one) had this tendency in mind.

But the experiences of the 1970s have also brought maturity and growth to Christians involved in Marxist/socialist movements. As with liberation theology, the use of Marxist ideas has become more self-critical. The greatest contribution Christians might make to Marxism would be to show that dedicated action can be combined with an openness and sensitivity to other views and other persons.

Notes

1. Gary MacEoin, *No Peaceful Way: Chile's Struggle for Dignity* (New York: Sheed and Ward, 1974), p. 35.

2. Ibid., pp. 50ff.

3. Ibid., pp. 37–38.

4. T. Howland Sanks, S.J., and Brian H. Smith, S.J., "Liberation Ecclesiology: Praxis, Theory, Praxis," in *Theological Studies*, Vol. 38, No. 1, March 1977, p. 22.

5. Jaime Rojas and Franz Vanderschueren, "The Catholic Church of Chile: From 'Social Christianity' to 'Christians For Socialism'," in *The Church and Politics in Latin America* (Toronto: Latin American Research Unit, LARU), Vol. 1, No. 2, February 1977, pp. 15–18, on these centers and Vekemans' role.

6. Ibid., p. 23.

7. Ibid., pp. 21–22.

8. *Social-Activist Priests: Chile*, "The Crisis of ILADES" (Washington, D.C.: LADOC, Latin American Documentation, USCC, n.d.), Keyhole series, No. 5, pp. 9–18.

9. Thomas G. Sanders and Brian H. Smith, "The Chilean Catholic Church During the Allende and Pinochet Regimes," in *Fieldstaff Reports* (New York: American Universities Field Staff, Inc., West Coast South America Series), Vol. xxiii, No. 1, March 1976, p. 5.

10. Lester A. Sobel, ed., *Chile & Allende* (New York: Facts on File, Inc., 1974), p. 25.

11. Sanders and Smith, "The Chilean Catholic Church," pp. 6–7.

12. Sobel, *Chile & Allende*, pp. 32–33.

13. Ibid., pp. 116–21; and MacEoin, *No Peaceful Way*, pp. 63ff.

14. Ibid., pp. 75–77; and MacEoin, *No Peaceful Way*, p. 65.

15. North American Congress on Latin America, *New Chile* (New York: NACLA, 1972), p. 21.

16. Sobel, *Chile & Allende*, p. 37.

17. Ibid., pp. 78–79.

18. Ibid., p. 50.

19. NACLA, *New Chile*, p. 66. The *New Chile* estimation of land ownership, 4.4 percent owning 80 percent, is obviously more severe than the 10 percent owning 86 percent figure cited earlier by MacEoin.

20. Paul Sigmund, "Three Views of Allende's Chile," in *Chile: Politics and Society*, ed. Arturo Valenzuela and J. Samuel Valenzuela (New Brunswick, N.J.: Transaction Books, 1976), pp. 121–23.

21. Sobel, *Chile & Allende*, pp. 41, 45.

22. Rojas and Vanderschueren, in *The Church and Politics in Latin America*, pp. 34ff.

23. Regis Debray, *The Chilean Revolution, Conversations with Allende* (New York: Vintage, 1971), p. 96.

24. Rojas and Vanderschueren, in *The Church and Politics in Latin America*, p. 36.

25. Quoted in MacEoin, *No Peaceful Way*, p. 89. If most of the chapter focuses on the Roman Catholic hierarchy and later on the predominately Catholic Christians for Socialism, it should be noted that Protestants, who comprise 10 percent of the Chilean populace, also played a role. MacEoin, pp. 18, 109, includes some brief account of their involvement.

26. The 1971 document was published by La Conferencia Episcopal de Chile, "Evangelio, politica y socialismos," in *Documentos del episcopado: Chile, 1970–1973*, ed. Carlos Oviedo Cavada (Santiago: Ediciones Mundo, 1974). The document is summarized and discussed in Sanks and Smith, "Liberation Ecclesiology," pp. 25ff. Their articles serve as the basis for my own treatment of the document.

27. Quoted by Sanks and Smith, "Liberation Ecclesiology," pp. 26–27, from *Documentos*, pp. 90–91.

28. Sanks and Smith, "Liberation Ecclesiology," p. 27. See also Rojas and Vanderschueren, in *The Church and Politics in Latin America*, pp. 28–29.

29. Juan Luis Segundo, S.J., *The Liberation of Theology*, trans. John Drury (Maryknoll, N.Y.: Orbis, 1976), pp. 130–31.

30. Ibid., p. 152.

31. Nixon interview excerpted in the *New York Times*, Thursday, May 26, 1977, p. 40.

32. In addition to the speech of Allende before the General Assembly of the United Nations, December 1972, the impact of U.S. policies on Chile is discussed by Maurice Zeitlin and Richard E. Ratcliff, "The Concentration of National and Foreign Capital in Chile, 1966," and by Elizabeth Farnsworth et al., "The Invisible Blockade: The United States Reacts," in *Chile: Politics and Society*, pp. 297ff. and pp. 338ff. respectively. See also *New Chile*, pp. 27–44.

33. Sobel, *Chile & Allende*, pp. 92, 111.

34. Ibid., p. 61. On the cutback in loans from world banks see also MacEoin, *No Peaceful Way*, pp. 95–99.

35. Sobel, *Chile & Allende*, p. 94.

36. Ibid., p. 58.

37. Ibid., pp. 78–83.

38. NACLA, *New Chile*, pp. 143–49.

39. On worker responses and attitudes, see Arturo and Samuel Valenzuela, "Political Constraints to the Establishment of Socialism in Chile," and James F. Petras, "Nationalization, Socioeconomic Change and Popular Participation," in *Chile: Politics and Society*, pp. 1ff. and pp. 172ff., respectively.

40. Sobel, *Chile & Allende*, p. 54.

41. "¿Qué piensan los Chilenos hoy?" in *Ercilla*, no. 1039, September 5, 1972, p. 10.

42. Sobel, *Chile & Allende*, p. 109.

43. Ibid., pp. 125–28. MacEoin, *No Peaceful Way*, p. 147, points out that 70 percent of the copper workers at El Teniente stayed at work and that the U.S. press greatly distorted the strike by saying that nearly all the workers had gone on strike.

44. Sobel, *Chile & Allende*, pp. 130–41.

45. See MacEoin, *No Peaceful Way*, pp. 112–17, on freedom of the press during the Allende years.

46. Rojas and Vanderschueren, in *The Church and Politics in Latin America,* p. 37.

47. Ibid., p. 39.

48. John Eagleson, ed., *Christians and Socialism* trans. John Drury (Maryknoll, N.Y.: Orbis, 1975), Document 1, p. 3.

49. Ibid., pp. 3–4.

50. Ibid., p. 5.

51. Ibid., p. 8. Document 2. Since Villegas does not explicitly identify their option with promoting Chilean socialism one might charge that I am "reading into" his statement (a criticism I later make of him). But it seems clear that this is what he intends.

52. Ibid., p. 11.

53. Ibid., pp. 12–15. Document 3.

54. Ibid., p. 14.

55. Ibid.

56. Rojas and Vanderschueren, in *The Church and Politics in Latin America,* p. 45.

57. Eagleson, *Christians and Socialism,* p. 41. Document 4, is the "draft agenda" for the proposed convention; Document 5 is an episcopal memo about the convention; Document 6 is the letter of invitation to Cardinal Silva; Document 7, cited here, is Cardinal Silva's initial response to Gonzalo Arroyo on the draft agenda.

58. Ibid., Document 8, pp. 48–51.

59. Without detailing all of the Committee's responses to the Cardinal, some of the most significant points might be noted. In response to the objection that they proposed "a narrow formulation of revolution as the only way," the committee argued that considering other options would split forces. They recognized the temptation of viewing Marxism as a cure-all, but believed that its methodology, "more than any other," spotlighted the interrelated character of the factors blocking liberation. They do not hold that the proletariat *coincides* with the poor of the gospel, but they see a "dovetailing" of both if the gospel is to be interpreted in a modern context, pp. 52–55. To the objection that they "reduce" Christianity to politics, they distinguish between theological language, which the Cardinal uses, and sociological or political terms, which they are using, pp. 55–58. They do not deny the values of a sense of sin, of prayer, etc., but they are stressing the political, pp. 58–60.

60. Ibid., Document 9, pp. 62–63.

61. Ibid., Document 10, pp. 64–66.

62. Ibid., Document 11, Part I, pp. 69–82, quote on p. 79.

63. Ibid., Part II, pp. 82–91, quotes on pp. 90–91.

64. Ibid., pp. 91–95.

65. Ibid., p. 98.

66. Ibid., pp. 101–10. One could certainly argue with the report's description of the two types of logic operative in Catholic social thought and in Marxism. The strongest criticism made of Marxist methodology, reflected especially in Stalin's formulation of it, is that *it* operates deductively, establishing dialectical principles and then basing conclusions on these.

67. Ibid., pp. 111–12.

68. Ibid., pp. 112–18, quote on p. 118.

69. Ibid., Document 18, pp. 160–75. Documents 12–17 contain national reports from Peru, Puerto Rico, and Cuba, an inaugural address by Arroyo, an address by

Bishop Méndez Arceo, and a message to the convention by Allende.

70. Rojas and Vanderschueren, in *The Church and Politics in Latin America*, pp. 44–45.

71. Diego Irarrazaval, "What Is to Be Done? Christians in the Socialist Process?" (New York: Church Research & Information Projects [CRIPS], 1975), p. 13.

72. Ibid., p. 17.

73. Ibid., p. 25.

74. Rojas and Vanderschueren, in *The Church and Politics in Latin America*, pp. 45–46.

75. Ibid., p. 47, and also Sanks and Smith, "Liberation Ecclesiology," pp. 31–32.

76. Segundo, *The Liberation of Theology*, footnote 2, p. 152.

77. Eagleson, ed., *Christians and Socialism*, Document 19, p. 189.

78. Ibid., p. 192.

79. Ibid., pp. 202–3.

80. Ibid., p. 184.

81. Ibid., p. 200.

82. Ibid., p. 205.

83. Ibid., p. 190.

84. Ibid., pp. 194–95.

85. Ibid., p. 214.

86. Ibid., p. 215.

87. Ibid., pp. 216–17.

88. Ibid. (Document 20), p. 231.

89. Ibid., Introduction, p. ix.

90. Rojas and Vanderschueren, in *The Church and Politics in Latin America*, pp. 46ff.

91. International Conference of Christians for Socialism, Quebec, April 13, 1975 (New York: Church Research & Information Projects [CRIPS], 1975).

92. Ibid., No. 17.

93. On the condemnations from Ecuador and Colombia see *Latinamerica Press*, January 27, 1977, p. 4, and January 13, 1977, pp. 5–6, respectively.

94. A report from a September 1973 meeting in Bologna, Italy, which drew over two thousand people, can be found in *Options for Struggle, Three Documents of Christians for Socialism* (New York: Church Research & Information Projects, CRIPS, 1974), esp. pp. 38–39.

PART III

AN APPRAISAL OF OBJECTIONS
TO MARXISM

Chapter 7

Atheism and Materialism

Those who contend that Marxism and Christianity are incompatible and even contradictory need raise only one obvious issue—atheism. Marx, Engels, Lenin, Mao Tse-tung and all the great Marxist leaders have been atheists. All seem, moreover, to have considered atheism intrinsic to Marxist socialism. How, then, can the issue even be open for question?

Once again the meaning of "Marxism" comes into play. Those who insist that Marxism means what "most Marxists have held" will argue that Marxism is a total "worldview" in which atheism and materialism are integral, essential parts. Those who contend, on the other hand, that Marxism is essentially a "method of analysis" and a program for achieving socialism may argue that the link between socialism and atheism stemmed from past historical conditions rather than from any inner logic.

Are atheism and materialism essential to Marxism? Are they critically important, intrinsic components of Marxism, or are they historically conditioned factors not really essential to the achievement of Marxist socialism today? Most of this chapter will be devoted to an investigation of the sources of Marxist theory, viz., Marx, Engels, Lenin, to discover why they advocated atheism and why they linked it with socialism. But one is tempted to say that the only really important question is what Marxists *today* hold. Still more important is the *attitude* they bring to religion. A militant atheism, hostile to religion, obviously poses a great threat to Christianity. A tolerant atheism, respectful of those with religious beliefs, creates a very different situation. The same certainly holds true for Christianity. An "inquisitional" Christianity seeks to crush out all who do not accept the true faith; an "ecumenical" Christianity engenders a very different climate. But attitudes are themselves influenced by tradition, so the sources of Marxist atheism and materialism merit investigation. This chapter traces back and evaluates different types of atheism within Marxism: the humanistic atheism of the young Marx, the ideological atheism of Marx and Engels historical materialism, the scientific atheism and materialism of Engels, and the militant atheism of Lenin.[1] It will then take note of reappraisals of Marxist atheism by recent critical Marxists.

Humanistic Atheism: The Young Marx

In considering Marx's own atheism, two features stand out. First, Marx became an atheist *prior* to becoming a socialist. At the outset, then, his reasons for atheism were independent of his advocacy of socialism. If atheism and socialism came to be inseparably linked, they were not intrinsically connected to begin with. Second, Marx's statements on atheism are nearly all concentrated in the 1840s, in the early period of his life. He devoted very little energy to atheism in later years. This certainly reflected the conclusion he reached early in his career that economic conditions lay at the root of society's ills, with religion being only a symptom of the problem. It may also suggest that Marx had such a disdain for religion that he did not consider it worth his energy.[2] Whatever the reasons, he gave little stress to militant atheism as his career progressed. In his early years, however, religion was a frequent target for attack.

The dominant thrust of the humanistic atheism of the young Marx can be simply put: *Religion is servility and submission to authority*.[3] To be fully human one must assert one's own freedom and self-determination, and be guided by reason alone. Freedom versus servility, reason versus authority, these are the issues that most shaped the young Marx's atheism. How these were spelled out in his early writings will be the focus of this section, but a brief recounting of his early years will help to set the scene. Some points noted in Chapter 1 will be repeated.

Biographers offer little help in determining at what point exactly Marx became an atheist and whether he underwent any inner struggle in the process. Marx was born a Jew, with rabbis on both sides of the family among his descendants. But discrimination against Jews in Germany led Marx's father to convert to Protestantism. Marx himself was baptized a few years later. There is little indication, however, that religion played any significant role in the young Marx's life.

When Marx completed his secondary studies at Trier in 1835, one of his exam papers dealt with "The Union of Believers with Christ According to John 15:1–14." In the essay Marx asserts that history proves the necessity of union with Christ. The unrest, the superstitions, and the egoism of pagan peoples show that human beings need a higher truth and light, namely Christ, if they are to attain true perfection. Whether this essay reflected the personal convictions of Marx at this stage, or whether he simply wrote to fulfill a school requirement cannot be very well determined. Certainly never again would he write as he did in this essay: "In union with Christ, therefore, we turn above all our loving eyes to God, feel the most ardent thankfulness towards Him, sink joyfully on our knees before Him."[4]

Another exam essay, "Reflections of a Young Man on the Choice of a Profession," suggests a rather impersonal view of God, who is referred to throughout as "the Deity." The essay also reveals Marx's emerging humanism and his disdain for anything that degrades humanity. A profession should be chosen which assures us the greatest worth, one based on ideas of whose truth we are thoroughly convinced. "But worth can be assured only by a profession in which we are not servile tools, but in which we act independently in our own sphere."[5]

Whatever the level of belief Marx may have had at Trier, he ended his university years at Berlin as a very convinced atheist. The Young Hegelians had challenged Hegel's views on religion. Ludwig Feuerbach's *The Essence of Christianity* (1841) is most often cited as the forerunner of Marx's atheism. Feuerbach argued that God is simply an abstraction, a human projection. Human beings, in earlier times, projected their fears of nature and personified the sun and the sea as gods. Now they project their own human attributes of reason, love, and power into an imagined God. By attributing to an imaginary God the powers which really belong to the human species as a whole, humans alienate themselves and deprive themselves of a sense of their true worth.

While Feuerbach's analysis, together with the writings of Bruno Bauer, influenced his views, Marx went back to the writings of Greek materialists to state his own case for atheism. In his doctoral dissertation (1841) on Greek philosophy he affirmed sharply that philosophical reason must act freely, unshackled by religious beliefs and authority. In a foreword to his dissertation, a foreword which alarmed even Bruno Bauer by its boldness, Marx proclaimed that philosophy must answer its adversaries with the cry of Epicurus:

> Not the man who denies the gods worshipped by the multitude, but he who affirms of the gods what the multitude believes about them, is truly impious. Philosophy makes no secret of it. The confession of Prometheus: 'In simple words, I hate the pack of gods' is its own confession, its own aphorism against all heavenly and earthly gods who do not acknowledge human self-consciousness as the highest divinity. It will have none other beside; . . . it responds again, as Prometheus replied to the servant of the gods, Hermes: 'Be sure of this, I would not change my state of evil fortune for your servitude. Better to be the servant of the rock than to be faithful boy to Father Zeus'.[6]

For Marx the issue was clear. One must choose humanity or God, reason and freedom or servility and submission to religion.

In notes and appendices related to his dissertation the same conviction was reaffirmed. Comparing the contributions to society of religion and of reasoned philosophy, Marx asserted that "the former has been only the hotwater bottle for some individual souls while the latter has been the animating spirit of world-historical developments."[7] Marx felt that the proofs for the existence of God were really only explanations of human self-consciousness. Whatever one conceives as real takes on a reality for that person, whether it is the Christian God, Moloch, or the Delphic Apollo.[8]   For a time Marx considered editing a journal of atheism with Bruno Bauer. He turned his attention instead to broader political issues. Where Marx did treat of religion in his articles of 1842, still prior to his advocacy of communism, his attack was upon the idea of a "Christian state." The fact that the Prussian King, Frederick Wilhelm IV, claimed that he was God's representative on earth and demanded that his "children" trust him must certainly have confirmed Marx's view of religion as servility and submission to authority. But he also found the very concept of a "Christian state" to be a contradiction. A state should be based on reason; Christianity demands a faith that relinquishes reason. Tertullian grasped the true essence of Christianity when he said: "It is true because it is absurd."[9] Christianity stands contradicted by the practical, political life of Christians themselves:

> Does not every moment of your practical life give the lie to your theory? Do you consider it wrong to go to court if you are cheated? But the apostle writes that this is wrong. Do you offer your right cheek if you are struck on the left, or do you not bring legal action for assault? Yet the gospel forbids that. . . . Are not most of your legal proceedings and the majority of civil laws concerned with property? But you have been told that your treasures are not of this world.[10]

By the fall of 1843 Marx had come to realize that religion should not be the main focus of his criticism. Religion was only a symptom of what was wrong, not the basic cause. If earlier he had argued that reason and not Christianity should guide the state, he now contended that separation of Church and state would still not bring true human emancipation. Religion and human emancipation are contradictory notions. One cannot be religious and truly free at the same time. The very fact that religion could continue to exist in a political democracy, such as the United States, proved that political freedom does not bring true freedom.

> But since the existence of religion implies a defect, the source of this defect must be sought in the nature of the state itself. We no longer take religion to be the basis but only the manifestation of secular narrowness.[11]

The "Jewish Question," from which this quote is taken, reveals one additional element in Marx's humanistic atheism. Socialism places great stress on community and social relationships. As Marx moved toward a revolutionary socialism his condemnation of religion struck at religion as "egoism." Christianity as an official state religion at least gave the illusion of a common bond between people. With separation of Church and state religion manifested its true nature as a private, egoistic concern. The so-called "Rights of Man" declared by the French Revolution and the American Constitution—the right to property, the right to security, the right to religious freedom—only protect and reinforce selfish interests. They are rights of "the egoistic man, the man withdrawn into himself, his private interest and his private choice, and separated from the community as a member of civil society."[12]

Marx's attitude toward religion from this point on can be seen in the first words of his "Toward the Critique of Hegel's Philosophy of Law: Introduction": "For Germany the criticism of religion has been essentially completed, and criticism of religion is the premise of all criticism."[13] As a defect or alienation that keeps people from attaining true human freedom, religion must be criticized. But Feuerbach and Bauer had successfully unmasked religion on an intellectual level. The criticism of religion must now go deeper, to the basic economic causes which underlie the human misery of which religion is merely a manifestation. This insight laid the groundwork for historical materialism and for the ideological atheism we will consider next. But a final citation from the essay quoted above neatly summarizes the humanistic atheism of Marx's early years while at the same time pointing to his new orientation:

> The criticism of religion ends with the doctrine that man is the highest being for man, hence with the categorical imperative to overthrow all conditions in which man is a degraded, enslaved, neglected, contemptible being. . . .[14]

For Marx personally, then, atheism was an essential point, but initially unrelated to the achievement of socialism. If to be a Marxist means to subscribe to what Marx personally held, then it would seem that a Marxist must be an atheist. If, on the other hand, to be a Marxist means to use his method of analysis for attaining socialism, then Marx's personal atheism would hardly seem essential. By way of analogy, one does not need to subscribe to Freud's atheism to do Freudian psychoanalysis. One might argue polemically, moreover, that if freedom of human reason from authority was the basic point of Marx's humanistic atheism, then his criticism might be directed more today against submission to Communist Party rule and authority.

How valid is Marx's humanistic critique of religion? From the account in Chapter 3 of the Church in the nineteenth century, it should be evident that paternalism and insistence on submission to authority have been too often characteristic of the Church. Even at present many "fallen-away" Christians would agree with Marxists who deny that religion and humanism are compatible. They have experienced religion as something which engenders fear of God, guilt for sins, submission to rules, and individualistic piety, rather than as something which enriches them as human beings. But countless other Christians have experienced religion as something which does enrich and ennoble them. They experience faith in Jesus and in God's power as sources which enable them to love more deeply, to act more justly and courageously, and to live more freely and hopefully. They would reject, therefore, the "human-freedom-or-submission-to-God" dichotomy which Marx proposed. Contemporary theology, influenced perhaps by Marxist criticisms, places great stress on becoming more fully human, and this is reflected even in popular catechisms.[15] Whatever the failures may be in practice, many Christians today experience the message of Christ as a call to be more fully human.

Ideological Atheism: The Historical Materialism of Marx and Engels

The critique of religion most associated with Marxism can be simply put: *Religion is simply a reflection of human misery and an ideology which impedes social change.* "Ideological" atheism may not be a totally adequate term to describe this ground for atheism, but the substance of the critique will hopefully become clear. Marx came to the realization, in 1843, that the problem of human emancipation lay at the level of civil society.[16] Political changes, even political revolutions, were inadequate. The economic structure of civil society had to be radically transformed. Economic causes were primary; all other causes were secondary. This insight created a shift in Marx's approach to atheism. Religion remained an alienation, a degrading servility which had to be overcome. But intellectual criticism alone would not eliminate it. Feuerbach had failed to recognize this and consequently his critique of religion fell short. Taking note of Feuerbach's position but going beyond it, Marx wrote:

> The basis of irreligious criticism is: Man makes religion, religion does not make man. And indeed religion is the self-consciousness and self-regard of man who has either not yet found or has already lost himself. But man is not an abstract being squatting outside the world. Man is the world of men, the state, society. This state and this society produce religion, which is an inverted consciousness of the world because they are an inverted world. . . . Religious suffering is the expression of real suffering and at the same time the protest against real suffering. Religion is the sigh of the oppressed creature, the heart of a heartless world, as it is the spirit of spiritless conditions. It is the opium of the people.[17]

Men and women must become conscious of the fact that religion is an illusory solution to human problems, a drug used to escape from suffering. But criticism alone will not cause religion to disappear; religion is only a manifestation of a deeper problem. The socio-economic conditions which cause misery, and hence the need for religion, must be abolished.

Marx's conviction that religion will disappear once socio-economic conditions have been humanized is forcefully stated in the *1844 Manuscripts*.[18] Not only will religion disappear but atheism itself will no longer be required. The very purpose of atheism is to negate God in order to assert human dignity. Once a new socialist society has been achieved even atheism will be superfluous. Human self-consciousness will be the expression of positive, healthy conditions. There will be no need to deny God's existence; the idea of God will have no more meaning or function for healthy, self-affirming human beings in a truly human, socialist society.

Were this line of argument the only grounds for Marx's atheism a rapport with Christianity might certainly be found. Both Christians and Marxists want a truly human society; both groups could concentrate on attaining it. If *then* religion disappears, Marx will have been proved right. It simply did reflect human misery. If religion remains, then Christians can claim that it expresses something much deeper and more positive about human existence.[19]

But Marx's atheism contains more. As noted already, Marx viewed religion itself as an alienation, as a degrading servility. He also viewed it as an obstacle to social change. The writings of Marx and Engels on historical materialism thus contain two different, if interrelated, approaches to religion: (1) religion is a reflection of the economic structure of society and hence of secondary importance; (2) religion is an ideological force which tends to justify the status quo and impede change, and hence it needs to be criticized. The first approach, as will be seen, continues to receive more emphasis, but both arguments can be found in Marx's and Engels writings.

The German Ideology (1845), which set down the basic premises of the materialist view of history, stresses religion as a mere reflection of socio-economic conditions. How people produce, their mode of production, is the primary factor in history and the shaping of society. Politics, religion, and ideology are secondary. Consciousness does not determine life, but life determines consciousness. "Morality, religion, metaphysics, and all the rest of ideology and their corresponding forms of consciousness no longer seem to be independent."[20] But idealist historians fail to recognize the determinative causality of economic forces. They accept the illusion that epochs are determined by political or religious motives which in reality are only manifestations of real, economic motives.[21] "In every epoch the ideas of the ruling class are the ruling ideas, that is, the class that is the ruling material power of society is at the same time its ruling intellectual power."[22] Religious views change to accommodate the views of the ruling class. Thus the *Communist Manifesto* treats changes in Christianity as reflections of changing class dominations.

When the ancient world was in its last throes, the ancient religions were overcome by Christianity. When Christian ideas succumbed in the eighteenth century to rationalist ideas, feudal society fought its death battle with the then revolutionary bourgeoisie. The ideas of religious liberty and freedom of conscience merely gave expression to the sway of free competition within the domain of knowledge.[23]

Engels developed this relationship between religion and modes of production in several of his later writings. In its origins, Engels wrote, "Christianity was preceded by the complete collapse of ancient 'world conditions' of which Christianity was the mere expression."[24] Christianity itself then likewise changed "with every new phase of these world conditions." The clergy in the Middle Ages gained a monopoly over intellectual education and politics, hence the class struggle against feudalism took the form of attacks against the Church.[25] The Protestant Reformation marked the first stage of the bourgeoisie's rise to power.

If revolutionary struggle once assumed the form of religious conflicts, religion in the nineteenth century played only a reactionary role. For Marx, it would seem, religion had been on the side of reaction throughout its history. In 1847 he delivered a scathing denunciation of Christian "social principles" in answer to those who believed their development would put Communists to silence.

> The social principles of Christianity have now had eighteen hundred years to develop and need no further development by Prussian consistorial councillors.
>
> The social principles of Christianity justified the slavery of Antiquity, glorified the serfdom of the Middle Ages and equally know, when necessary, how to defend the oppression of the proletariat, although they make a pitiful face over it.
>
> The social principles of Christianity preach the necessity of a ruling and an oppressed class, and all they have for the latter is the pious wish the former will be charitable. . . .
>
> The social principles of Christianity preach cowardice, self-contempt, abasement, submission, dejection, in a word all the qualities of the *canaille;* and the proletariat, not wishing to be treated as *canaille,* needs its courage, its self-feeling, its pride and its sense of independence more than its bread.
>
> The social principles of Christianity are sneakish and the proletariat is revolutionary.
>
> So much for the social principles of Christianity.[26]

Marx's humanistic atheism also shows itself here again. Religion, for Marx, is simply cowardice, abasement, and submission.

In one of his few later writings which treat religion, Marx describes it as an obsolete social force which continues to vegetate long after the basis of its existence has rotted away. But it tries to summon all its strength for one final stand before its "agony of death." Thus in England, in a "conspiracy of the Church with monopoly capital," the Church attempted to enforce Sunday closing laws.[27]

Marx and Engels both recognized the ideological uses of religion in behalf of the status quo. But they were confident that as conditions changed under socialism religion would vanish. Religion as a mere "reflection" of human conditions is the most recurring image in their writings. Thus Marx wrote in *Capital, I:* "The religious world is but the reflex of the real world." The ancient worship of nature reflected a low and narrow stage of productive power; Christianity, especially Protestantism, fits capitalist society. "The religious reflex of the real world can, in any case, only then finally vanish, when the practical relations of every-day life offer to man none but perfectly intelligible and reasonable relations with regard to his fellowmen and to nature."[28]

Engels wrote in a similar vein in *Anti-Dühring.* "All religion, however, is nothing but the fantastic reflection in men's minds of those external forces which control their daily life, a reflection in which the terrestrial forces assume the form of supernatural forces."[29] At first, it was forces of nature which were reflected, then later social forces which dominate people's lives. Once social forces have been brought under the domination of society religion itself will vanish "for the simple reason that then there will be nothing left to reflect."[30]

If the account given thus far in this section accurately summarizes the writings of Marx and Engels, one tentative but important conclusion can be drawn, one to which we will return later in the chapter. Their historical materialism places little stress on "militant" atheism. They denounce religion but they do not call for combat and struggle against religion. They are convinced that religion is simply a reflection of unhealthy conditions and will vanish when those conditions change. Never, to my knowledge at least, do they declare "war" on religion or single it out as a dangerous enemy to be opposed. But we will return to this point later.

The Marxist analysis of religion would be incomplete, moreover, if only the negative functions of religion were noted. Some present-day Marxists and Christians have argued that Marx's expression, in 1843, that religion is "the *protest* against real suffering" shows that he recognized the potential of religion as a stimulus for social change.[31] Given the context of this phrase—religion is then called "the sigh of the oppressed creature" and the "opium of the people"—and given Marx's consistently negative views in other writings, it is difficult to see more intended than an *impotent* protest against suffering.

Engels, on the other hand, did very clearly recognize the revolutionary power of Christianity, at least in earlier stages of its history. Writing "On the

History of Early Christianity" Engels goes so far as to compare it to the socialist movement of the working class in his day:

> The history of early Christianity has notable points of resemblance with the modern working-class movement. Like the latter, Christianity was originally a movement of oppressed people: it first appeared as the religion of slaves and emancipated slaves, of poor people deprived of all rights, of peoples subjugated or dispersed by Rome.[32]

Early Christianity, moreover, embraced socialism. It did not sustain socialism, according to Engels, because it looked to a heaven or millennium beyond rather than to a transformation of this world. But the spirit of early Christianity and modern socialism have much in common. Engels quotes Renan approvingly: "If I wanted to give you an idea of the early Christian communities, I would tell you to look at a local section of the International Working Men's Association."[33]

Engels found in the Book of Revelation a picture of "real genuine early Christianity."[34] The Book of Revelation, said Engels, contained little of dogma. The Trinity was unknown to it; there was no trace of original sin. It contained the revolutionary idea of Jesus sacrificing himself for others, but the Book's own author was unaware that he represented a religion which was to become one of the most revolutionary elements in the history of the human mind. The Book of Revelation contained neither the dogma nor the morality of later Christianity "but instead a feeling that one is struggling against the whole world and that the struggle will be a victorious one." This eagerness for struggle and a certainty of victory, Engels added, are totally lacking in Christians of today and are to be found now only among socialists. Like socialism, Christianity was originally a mass movement. The first Christians were recruited from among the lowest strata of people, as becomes a revolutionary element. They realized, too, that the kingdom of God and the New Jerusalem could be conquered and opened only after arduous struggle with the powers of hell.[35]

Early Christianity was not the sole example of revolutionary Christianity for Engels. In his *The Peasant War in Germany* Engels described in detail the revolutionary Christianity of Thomas Münzer in the sixteenth century, and he praised the courage and endurance of the Anabaptists in their struggle.[36]

While these were judgments on Christianity's past history and while Engels gave little indication that religion could play an active, progressive role in the future, he does implicitly affirm an important point. Religion is not by its very nature passive and an impediment to change. It can be a stimulus to action, even to revolutionary action. At least some Marxists have come to recognize this point. This conclusion, combined with critical Marxism's recognition that religion and other elements of the superstructure cannot simply be "reduced" to economic conditions, could lead to a reappraisal of the need for ideological atheism in Marxism.

Many Christians, on the other hand, have acknowledged that the Marxist ideological critique of religion has often been justified.[37] Religion has served to pacify the masses and to justify the status quo. It has allied itself with reactionary ruling classes; it has preached resignation and submission to the poor.[38] The Bible itself denounces those who practice injustice while claiming to worship God. But again, ideological use or abuse of religion should not be equated with the very nature of religion.

Scientific Atheism and Philosophical Materialism: Engels

To understand Marxist atheism fully one must take into account the deep conviction, especially evident in Engels, that history was moving irresistibly forward and upward. He shared the belief of many in the nineteenth century that history meant progress. From a radical Hegelian perspective this meant that Christianity, once a positive, progressive "moment" in history now had become anachronistic and obsolete. From a perspective of the French Enlightenment this meant that reason and science were sweeping away the superstitions of religion and metaphysics. The radical Hegelian view was evident in Engels' historical materialism. The Enlightenment view seems clearly to have influenced Engels' writings on science and religion.

Engels sought constantly to identify Marxism as a science. Marx, he claimed, had discovered "the great laws of motion in history." Engels himself attempted to show that the same materialism and dialectics which explain history explain nature and all of reality as well. Marxism thus provided a total scientific view of the world. *Religion is an unscientific, superstitious view of the world.* Engels' scientific atheism took two main approaches: (1) to show the triumph of science over religious belief, and (2) to show that philosophical materialism, viewed dialectically, is the necessary basis for all science.

The Triumph of Science over Religion

Regarding the triumph of science over religious superstition, it is important to recall a major problem which confronted Christianity well into the present century—the apparent conflict between new scientific discoveries and literal interpretations of the Bible. Galileo's theory of the solar system conflicted with a biblical view about the earth as the center of creation, and specifically with the biblical account of the sun "standing still" at the battle of Jericho. Theories about the origin of the universe out of nebular gasses over billions of years conflicted with the story of God's creation in six days. Darwin's theory of evolution seriously threatened the idea of God's special creation of Adam and Eve.

These conflicts played a significant role in Engels' scientific atheism. From letters that Engels wrote in his youth, it becomes evident that rationalist criticisms of the Bible instilled doubts in him which led him eventually to abandon his faith. His letters to his friend Friedrich Graeber in 1839 reveal the tension Engels experienced between scientific rationalism and his Protestant faith. "I cannot understand how the orthodox preachers can be so orthodox since there are some quite obvious contradictions in the Bible." "I cannot understand how one can still try to maintain literal belief in the Bible or defend the direct influence of God, since this cannot be proved anywhere."[39]

For a time Engels struggled to sustain his faith against the doubts raised by rationalism. "Tears come into my eyes as I write this. I am moved to the core, but I feel I shall not be lost; I shall come to God, for whom my whole heart yearns."[40] But rationalism won out and the writings of Feuerbach brought the final death blow to Engels' religious beliefs. An interest in science and a conviction that science confirmed materialism led Engels, in the later years of his life, to return to the issues of science and religion which troubled his youth.

In an introduction to *Dialectics of Nature,* Engels chronicles the triumph of science over religion, a triumph which he felt proved dialectical materialism. Modern science, Engels observes, began at the time of the Reformation. New worlds were being discovered; new modes of production were developing. The static world of the Middle Ages came to an end. "The dictatorship of the Church over men's minds was shattered."[41] Natural science developed in the midst of the general revolution and was itself thoroughly revolutionary. Science also had its own martyrs. Servetus and Giordano Bruno were burned at the stake by Church authorities. Copernicus, if only from his death bed, threw down the gauntlet to ecclesiastical authority. The emancipation of natural science from theology had begun.

Science then made great strides through the discoveries of Newton, Descartes, Kepler, and others. But science still clung to the view of the absolute immutability of nature. Newton tried to keep the idea of God with the postulate of a divine first impulse. Immanuel Kant made the first breach "in this petrified outlook on nature," when he postulated a theory which later scientists would prove: the existence of nebular masses as the starting point of the universe. Geology began to point to the evolution in time of plants and animals. In 1842, the epoch-making discovery of the "transformation of energy" confirmed that matter in motion explains physical change. Darwin proved the evolution of the human species. The cell was shown to be the constituent element of all organisms.[42]

Science, says Engels, can now explain the origins of the human species and the development of thought without reference to God. The use of the hand as a tool and an erect gait distinguished the human from the ape and laid the basis for the development of articulate speech. The natural sciences confirm dialectical materialism for they require the principle of matter in constant motion. "But the motion of matter is not merely crude mechanical motion, mere change of place, it is heat and light, electric and magnetic tension, chemical combination and dissociation, life and, finally, consciousness."[43] In short, science has driven out religious explanations of the universe and of human origins and has replaced them with a dialectical materialist view of all reality.

Materialism as a Basis for Science

The second aspect of Engels' scientific atheism, to show that science confirms and is based upon a dialectical, materialist view of nature, is already woven into his account of the triumph of science over religion. But in other writings Engels explicitly spells out what he believes to be the necessary philosophical foundations of science. The "paramount question of the whole of philosophy," says Engels, is "the question of the relation of thinking to being, the relation of spirit to nature." The question, which is primary, spirit or nature, can be sharpened into this: "Did God create the world or has the world been in existence eternally?"[44] In the work just cited, on Ludwig Feuerbach, Engels moves away from this latter question and focuses on the epistemological issue of the relationship between thinking and being. But in *Anti-Dühring* he takes up the question of the existence and nature of the world.

"The real unity of the world consists in its materiality," and this is proved "by a long and protracted development of philosophy and natural science."[45] Kant's theory of nebular mass at the beginning of the universe, the transformation of energy, the cell, Darwin's theory of evolution, all point to materialism. What needs to be answered, in Engels' mind, is how to explain motion and development in the universe—"how we are to get from absolute immobility to motion without an impulse from outside, that is, without God."[46]

Traditional materialists had no answer, for they conceived of matter at rest, and they thought of motion in a mechanical way which required a first impulse. For Engels the answer is simple enough and provided by a dialectical perspective. "Motion is the mode of existence of matter. Never anywhere has there been matter without motion nor can there be. . . . Motion is therefore as uncreatable and indestructible as matter itself."[47] The inner tension and dynamics of matter itself suffice to explain motion and change. The development and growth of all living organisms proceed from the capacity of the cell to change. Changes in inorganic nature—mechanical force, heat, electricity, chemical energy—are different forms of manifestation of universal motion. The origin of plant, animal, and even human life is explained by a long process of evolution from a few unicellular germs which in turn arose from protoplasm or albumen generated by chemical means.[48]

All of nature, then, can and should be understood as matter in motion. The history of society in all its branches, and the totality of all sciences which deal with the human, need to be explained by the same basic principle. Marx had proved that history and society are governed by "general laws of motion," with material forces as their base.[49] All of our thought processes likewise flow from a materialistic, dialectic base. For mind is a product of matter, and our concepts derive from a material base as images of real things. The dialectic itself becomes "merely the conscious reflex of the dialectical motion of the real world."[50] Thought and consciousness are products of the human brain and man himself is a product of nature; "whence it is self-evident that the products of the human brain, being in the last analysis also products of Nature, do not contradict the rest of Nature but are in correspondence with it."[51] Nature, history, and thought are thus all embraced in one materialistic "science" of all reality.

Engels thus carried Marxism far beyond its critique of capitalist society and made it a total worldview, atheistic and materialistic at its very core. By linking natural sciences to the Marxist analysis of society, he conferred on Marxism all the prestige of the former. In so doing, however, he not only created a seemingly impassable gulf between Marxism and Christianity but he also engendered a raft of problems for Marxism itself. To cite but one example: If dialectical materialism determines the very principles of scientific method and is not just a philosophy of science, how does one explain that science in the Western world has operated without it?

Had Engels written only about the history of science and its conflicts with religion, the problem today would be much less troublesome. While some atheists today would still argue that science and religion are incompatible, and some Christian fundamentalists still reject any scientific theory that contradicts the Bible, the issue of science versus religion has ceased to be a major pre-occupation for scientists or Christians. Theologians now recognize that the Bible was never intended to teach "science." It was meant to convey religious truths and it used language and images of its time to convey these. The book of Genesis does not reveal *how* God created the world and humankind but simply *that* God did. Material reality *is* the basis of science. Perhaps Christians should develop greater interest, as Teilhard de Chardin did, in the evolutionary process of the material world. But science and philosophy of science are distinct. Most contemporary philosophers, outside the Marxist-Leninist tradition, would view Engels' statements about the indestructibility of matter in motion as metaphysical judgments which lie outside the realm of science itself.

The Many Meanings of "Materialism"

The issue of materialism, however, raises even more fundamental questions about the compatibility of Marxism and Christianity. As Engels presents Marxism, philosophical materialism is the basis for all its theory, including historical materialism. From this perspective, then, one cannot separate the Marxist "method of analysis" from its philosophical foundations. Hence, it would seem, one cannot use a Marxist method without being a materialist and hence an atheist.

The problem with this conclusion revolves around the term "materialism." The word "materialism" provides the connecting link between the Marxist investigations of history, nature, and thought. One would assume a consistent use of the term. But in fact the word "materialism" changes its meaning from one sphere to another. In the Marxist view of history, materialism refers to material, economic forces or modes of production. In its view of nature, materialism refers to "matter in motion" as a basic ontology. In its view of knowledge, materialism stands for an epistemological realism. The enemy, "idealism," stands in the first case for those who think ideas determine history; in the second case for those who think God or Hegel's Absolute Spirit created the world; in the third case, for those who hold that ideas are simply constructs of reality.

Even these distinctions, however, are oversimplifications. The Marxist theory of knowledge, in Engels and Lenin, asserts three very different theses: that the world is objectively real and not a product of the mind; that the world is knowable; that ideas are "copies" of reality. On this basis most Catholic Thomists would qualify as "materialists" on the first two points.

Marx himself is not without blame for the ambiguities which revolve around the term "materialism." In *The Holy Family* he characterized as materialist several very disparate positions in the history of philosophy: Descartes' physics based on the mechanical motion of bodies, the French Enlightenment's this-worldly interests, Francis Bacon's use of an inductive scientific method, empirical sense knowledge, and Helvetius' recognition of the influence of environment on human development.[52] It is significant that it is this last example, and not ontological materialism, which Marx singles out as the connecting link between materialism and socialism. "If man is shaped by his surroundings, his surroundings must be made human."[53]

Engels' efforts to explain materialism, in *Ludwig Feuerbach*, only compound the problem. He claims that "the relation of thinking and being" is the great basic question of all philosophy.[54] But under the heading of this *one* great basic question of philosophy he treats the question of the existence and immortality of the soul, the existence of God, and then as "another side" of the same question, the problem of the objectivity of our knowledge. He then equates two very different questions as to whether we can know the real world and whether we can produce a correct *reflection* of reality. He concludes that the dialectic itself is merely the conscious reflex of the dialectical motion of the real world, and hence that Marxism can claim objective knowledge of laws that govern both history and nature.[55] But short of a mechanistic, linear causality which would claim to reduce all human behavior and thought to observable molecular interactions in nature—a view Engels would have rejected—it is difficult to ascertain any logical inner connection between the many different problems lumped under the general term "materialism."

But is Marx's method of analyzing society and history bound to philosophical materialism? Certainly it came to be linked *ideologically* with materialism in the dominant Marxist tradition. But is there any inner logic which binds them together? Apart from the ideological connection it is difficult to see what the origin of the universe or the existence of a soul has to do with an analysis of capitalism. Many critical Marxists and Marxist scholars have certainly challenged Engels' contention that the dialectic is "merely the conscious reflex of the dialectical motion of the real world." Alfred Schmidt, in *The Concept of Nature in Marx,* argues strongly for the "non-ontological character of Marx's materialism." Marx was not a metaphysician; his goal was not to replace Hegel's World Spirit with a material World Substance. His interest, Schmidt maintains, was in the world *as mediated* by human subjects. He never treated nature as dialectical in itself as Engels did. Marx's dialectic is the interaction of human beings shaping the world and being shaped by it.[56] This stress on the dialectic as interaction also contradicts a "reflection theory" of knowledge. Schmidt contends: "Marx did not see in concepts naively realistic impressions of the objects themselves, but rather reflections of the historically mediated relations of men to these objects."[57] The dialectic of Marx is not a mere reflex of reality; it is not even a "law" for history. It is an historical method.[58]

Z. A. Jordan, in *The Evolution of Dialectical Materialism,* and many critical Marxists noted in Chapter 2, agree in dissociating Marx's historical method from Engels' dialectical materialism.[59] Fr. Gustav Wetter likewise concludes that historical materialism "is in no sense necessarily allied to philosophical materialism." One could adopt historical materialism, he observes, without even knowing dialectical materialism.[60]

When Marx used "materialism" to describe his method of analyzing society, he used it to speak of the "material" activity of labor, the production of "material" goods, and of "material" or economic forces as primary factors in history. But such a use of the term materialism does not necessitate a philosophical materialism which reduces consciousness to being a product of matter. One *could* postulate, as Catholic scientist-theologian Teilhard de Chardin did, an evolution of consciousness through the growing complexity of matter. One *could* postulate, as Engels did, that the initial productive acts of primitive human beings took place unconsciously at first and then caused consciousness to develop. But the very nature of production, and certainly work as we know it in history, would seem to require consciousness as an essential element. The very act of using a tool is a conscious act, for it involves grasping a relationship between the tool to be used and the work to be done. The satisfying of material needs, which Marx called the first historical act, was of *conscious* needs. Even if one does accept the primacy of productive activity, consciousness plays a constitutive role in that activity. To that extent "consciousness *does* determine life." In short, one could hold with Marx's "materialism" that economic forces are the most influential in shaping society and history without reducing human behavior to a mere "reflex" of material conditions.

Materialism in Respect to Human Dignity, Morality, and Freedom

Many Christians feel that a materialist view of human nature is destructive of human dignity, morality, and freedom. Given the already ambiguous meanings of materialism any fully adequate response to this would be lengthy and difficult. But some clarifications can perhaps be made. Assuming Engels' philosophical materialism, some Christians would argue that a view which considers human persons as nothing more than complex natural organisms, and which fails to recognize them as "made in the image and likeness of God," deprives individuals of their dignity. Other Christians, perhaps citing Lenin's comment that "morality is subordinated to the interests of the proletariat's class struggle,"[61] see Marxism as destructive of all true morality. Still others, focusing on Marx's own sense of materialism which views human beings and human nature itself as shaped by society, feel that Marxism negates freedom. But the major problem, it can be argued at the outset, lies not so much with any of these as it does with the attitudes and interpretations of Marxist leaders or rulers toward these materialist views. The paragraphs which follow will explain this contention.

Far from denying human dignity, Marx and Engels envisioned socialism as a restoration of dignity. Moral indignation against the degradation of workers in the capitalist system inspired their efforts. Contempt for what they considered the servility and submissiveness engendered by religion gave rise to their atheism. Christians may rightfully feel that religion, as Jesus intended it, enhances human dignity and that the transcendent value of human existence is lost without it. But even in practice, among ordinary citizens of Communist countries, it would be hard to show that respect for human dignity has been lost. Great stress, in fact, is placed on human equality and solidarity. One might indeed argue that the very values embodied in Marxist socialism come out of the Judaic-Christian tradition. Evidence would seem to indicate that the peoples of Communist countries, though educated in philosophical materialism, are no less respectful of others than the peoples of countries where Christianity is practiced. The problem lies, therefore, not with the consequences of a materialist philosophy as such, but with rulers who insist that only such a philosophy is correct and who violate the human dignity of those who believe otherwise by suppressing or restricting their expression of differing views.

A similar statement might be made of morality. Marx and Engels criticized "bourgeois" morality and rejected *as a method* an analysis of society based on moral values. But their very effort to establish socialism would make little sense if the values it represented, such as equality, mutual cooperation, and self-actualization, were not esteemed. Again in practice a high degree of "moralism" can be found among the peoples of Communist countries. Thus, Eugene Kamenka finds stressed in the Soviet Union such values as devotion to country, dedication to work, self-sacrifice for others, family love, and honesty.[62] These values undoubtedly function as a support for the existing social order, but they do provide a basic morality. On the part of rulers, on the other hand, the subordination of morality to class struggle can and has been used to justify ruthless executions, torture, and labor camps. But the cruelty of ruthless leaders serves as a poor measure of morality. One would hardly want to judge Christianity by the Inquisition, by Christian overseers of Nazi prison camps, or by Christian military who carry out tortures in Chile and Brazil.

The issue of freedom raises a special problem because it is linked more closely to a Marxist view of human nature. When Marx wrote, in *The German Ideology,* predicting what communist society would be, he spoke in terms of "individuals" controlling their work and their lives, not of persons subordinated to society.[63] But he also believed that human nature depends on society. Change conditions in society and the very nature of persons within that society will change. Donald Munro argues that Marx also recognized certain "static" or fixed traits in human nature, growing out of basic human needs. But the Soviet concept of human nature, Munro claims, ignored the static elements. It viewed human beings as passive reactors to the environment and sought aggressively to mold them into new social beings. The Chinese Communist view of human nature, he observes, goes even further. The person is defined by society and hence the strong efforts in China on education and thought reform.[64]

Perhaps more than any other aspect of Marxism this view of the malleability of human nature, which has led to Party and state attempts at social engineering, stands in conflict with Christian views. Underlying both the Christian and the Western democratic tradition of human nature is a view of the human person as having a private self with a dignity, freedom, and rights not dependent on society or the state. When Catholic social encyclicals speak of the danger of "the absorption of the individual by society," and when Protestant theologians criticize the locating of social evil exclusively in social conditions, they are addressing this point. This objection in no way eliminates the need for changing social structures. Oppressive socio-economic conditions are destructive of human life and dignity; healthy, just conditions are essential to human development. This change, many would argue, is what a true socialism could achieve. The objection focuses rather on the danger of a Communist party controlling society in order to shape the values, needs, and nature of the individuals under them.

Militant Atheism: Lenin

Whether Marxism is essentially atheistic or not may ultimately be less important than the question of the extent of its militancy against religion. A Marxist or Marxist party may espouse an atheism totally hostile to religion or give little weight to atheism and be even respectful of the beliefs of others. Marxism would appear to be a very militant atheism both in theory and practice. But the evidence from Marx's and Engels' later writings suggest otherwise. While they both remained convinced atheists, what they said or failed to say about *tactics* in respect to religion is highly significant. Both were convinced that religious belief would soon be anachronistic. Science was already displacing religion on an intellectual level; with socialism and the overcoming of social alienation it would vanish completely. Consequently the socialist movement should concern itself with its primary task, to overcome the prevailing capitalist system.

The young Marx did indeed speak of the criticism of religion as "the premise of all criticism," but his later writings said little about the need to "combat" religion or to struggle against it. He did criticize the Gotha Program of the German Social-Democrats for their inclusion of "freedom of conscience." The Workers' Party should have recognized, said Marx, "that bourgeois 'freedom of conscience' is nothing but the toleration of all possible kinds of religious freedom of conscience, and that for its part it endeavors rather to liberate the conscience from the witchery of religion."[65] But one such statement hardly constitutes a militant atheism.

Engels, for his part, warned against tactics that stress a war on religion. He criticized the Blanquists and Bakuninists for being too radical on atheism. He claimed that for most German Social-Democrat workers and for many French workers atheism had already outlived itself. These workers had purely and simply finished with God. The Blanquists' and Bakuninists' desire to abolish God by decree could only be counter-productive. Persecution only promoted undesirable convictions. "This much is sure: the only service that can be rendered to God today is to declare atheism a compulsory article of faith and to outdo Bismarck's *Kirchenkulturkampf* laws by prohibiting religion generally."[66] Likewise in *Anti-Dühring* Engels criticized Dühring for calling for the abolition of religious worship. Religion will vanish when the conditions which cause it have been overcome, said Engels. "Herr Dühring, however, cannot wait until religion dies this, its natural, death. He proceeds in more deep-rooted fashion. He out-Bismarcks Bismarck, he decrees sharper May laws not merely against Catholicism, but against all religion whatsoever; he incites his gendarmes of the future against religion, and thereby helps it to martyrdom and a prolonged lease of life."[67] Thus, neither the later Marx nor Engels called for a militant atheism, and German Social-Democrats left religion as a "private matter" in respect to party membership.

A more hostile and militant atheism did, however, arise with Marxism, and Lenin bears much of the responsibility for its development. With Lenin a significant shift in language and attitude occurs. In some respects his approach to religion seem quite similar to Marx and Engels'. His writings on religion constitute only a very small portion of his voluminous output. He cautions about tactics which would make religion a primary target and lose allies for the revolutionary struggle. "We shall always preach a scientific outlook," Lenin writes, "but this does not mean that the religious question be given a prominence which it does not deserve.'[68] Lenin notes Engels' condemnation of the Blanquists and Bakuninists, and he quotes Engels' criticism of Dühring. But having cautioned against the use of inflammatory tactics, he moves on in each case also to condemn "opportunism" and to insist that religion cannot be a private affair for Party members and that religion must be combatted.[69]

Lenin considered religion socially harmful. If he agreed in theory that religion would inevitably disappear, his great stress on ideological struggle carried over into his views on religion. He showed little interest in probing into the nature of religion and was impatient with attempts to revise the Marxist critique of religion.[70] His view of religion was quite simple. Religion originated in superstitious fears of nature, and is perpetuated by the oppression of social forces. It is used by the exploiting class to justify their rule and to drug the exploited masses into submission. Writing on "Socialism and Religion" (1905) Lenin asserted:

> Religion is the opium of the people. Religion is a kind of spiritual gin in which the slaves of capital drown their human shape and their claims to any decent human life.[71]

But in "Attitude of Workers' Party towards Religion" (1909) the phrase "opium of the people" takes on a much stronger sense.

> Religion is the opium of the people—this dictum of Marx's is the cornerstone of the whole Marxist view on religion. Marxism has always regarded all modern religions and churches and all religious organizations as instruments of bourgeois reaction that serve to defend exploitation and to drug the working class.[72]

This very switch in emphasis in the use of the word "opium," from an escape which the oppressed feel they need (Marx) to a drug foisted on them by exploiters (Lenin) puts religion into much sharper conflict with Marxism. Lenin does not hesitate to draw the consequences.

> Marxism is materialism. As such, it is as relentlessly hostile to religion as was the materialism of the Encyclopaedists of the eighteenth century or

the materialism of Feuerbach. This is beyond doubt. . . . We must combat religion—that is the rudiment of *all* materialism, and consequently of Marxism.[73]

Lenin does go on to say that the dissemination of atheist views is not the chief task of Marxism. Atheistic propaganda must be subordinated to its basic task—the development of the class struggle of the exploited masses against the exploiters.

But again the language of Lenin's utterances on religion manifests not merely disdain but detestation. "Every religious idea, every idea of god, even every flirtation with the idea of god is unutterable vileness . . . it is vileness of the most dangerous kind, 'contagion' of the most abominable kind."[74] The more progressive and enlightened the religion, the more dangerous it was in Lenin's eyes. Filthy deeds and acts of violence are far less dangerous "than the subtle, spiritual ideas of a god decked out in the smartest 'ideological' costumes." The Catholic priest who seduces young girls is far less dangerous than a democratic priest who preaches the creating of god.[75] In Tolstoy, says Lenin, one finds at times a ruthless criticism and a sober realism, but at other times "we have the preaching of one of the most abominable things on earth—religion, the endeavor to replace priests officially appointed by priests who are priests by moral conviction, i.e., the cultivation of the most subtle, and therefore particularly disgusting, clericalism."[76]

"Unutterable vileness," "one of the most abominable things on earth," Marxism as "relentlessly hostile to religion"—the language of Lenin clearly reveals his attitude and it very explicitly excludes the possibility of a positive attitude toward a more progressive religious view. But the statement which would most profoundly influence future Communist Party policy came in Lenin's "Socialism and Religion":

> We demand that religion should be a private affair as far as the state is concerned, but under no circumstances can we regard religion as a private affair as far as our own party is concerned. . . . We demand the complete separation of the church from the state in order to combat religious darkness with a purely ideological, and exclusively ideological, weapon, our printed and oral propaganda. One reason why we have founded our league, the Russian Social-Democratic Labour Party, is just to wage such a fight against all religious stultification of the workers. For us therefore the ideological fight is not a private affair but a general affair of the Party and the proletariat.[77]

The German Social-Democrats had agreed to leave religion as a private affair even for party members. They had not formed in order "to wage a fight" against religious beliefs. Lenin's formula changed this and the change had profound implications. That a political party should be able to propagate ideas, including atheism, is one matter. But once in power in Russia the Communist Party became *the* expression of the interests of the people. Atheism thus became not merely a Party ideology, but a "state ideology." Freedom of worship could be proclaimed but atheism became the ruling ideology of a Soviet society directed by the Party. Separation of church and state took on a very different meaning from the form it assumed in Western Europe and the United States. In one of the last articles he wrote, Lenin continued to insist on the need for the untiring efforts of militant atheistic propaganda.[78]

In fairness to Lenin, one might cite various historical conditions that influenced his judgment on religion. The Czarist regime was thoroughly reactionary and repressive and the Russian Church was closely allied to the regime; "Socialism and Religion" was written at the height of revolutionary ferment in Russia (1905); some Bolsheviks before the Revolution seemed to be despairing of success and turning to religion as a solace; religious beliefs were often mixed with pure superstition.[79] But whatever the qualifying circumstances may have been, Lenin did influence Marxism toward a far more militant approach to religion.

Atheism in Practice: The U.S.S.R. and Eastern Europe

The Bolsheviks took power in Russia on November 7, 1917. They immediately nationalized all land, including all the property holdings of monasteries and churches, and soon after passed a divorce law and laws on marriages, births, and deaths, taking jurisdiction out of the hands of the Church. The official decree separating Church and State came on January 23, 1918. It proclaimed that "every citizen may profess any religious belief, or no belief at all" and that "free performance of religious rites is permissible." But other stipulations proved ominous. Authorities were to see that religious rites did not "disturb public order" and no one could refuse to perform his or her duties as a citizen on the basis of religious beliefs. The Church and religious were to be subject to rules concerning private associations. They had no right to own property; they no longer possessed "the rights of judicial persons."[80]

Interpretations of the decree and additional decrees restricted religion still more. Churches could be used for secular and even anti-religious purposes. Priests and clerics were disfranchised and not allowed to join trade unions or work for state enterprises. Their children were barred from schools above the elementary grade. The initial decree allowed religion to be taught privately; a decree of June 13, 1921, prohibited religious instruction anywhere to groups of persons below the age of eighteen.[81] The program of the Communist Party, March 1919, made the aim of the Party quite explicit: "The aim of the Party is finally to destroy the ties between the exploiting classes and the organization of religious propaganda."[82]

Patriarch Tikhon denounced the government decree of separation. Resistance to the liquidation of church property and confiscation of church treasures led to resistance and violence. Scores of priests and laypersons were charged with counter-revolution which led to some executions and imprisonments.[83] Twenty-eight bishops and more than one thousand priests of the Orthodox Church had perished in these conflicts by 1923.

Intensive atheist propaganda was ordered by the Congress of the Communist Party in April 1923. A "League of the Godless" was formed to assist the Party's work of anti-religious propaganda. Atheism became an integral part of the educational system. In 1927 Stalin declared: "The Party cannot be neutral towards religion, and it conducts anti-religious propaganda against all religious prejudices because it stands for science, whereas religious prejudices run counter to science." Communists who hinder the full development of anti-religious propaganda, said Stalin, should be expelled.[84]

The Church negotiated a kind of "modus vivendi" under Metropolitan Sergei in 1927. The years which followed were marked by intermittent periods of intensified anti-religious propaganda and returns to accommodation. Jews and other minority religious groups often faced the most serious restrictions.

Communist takeovers in Eastern Europe and China after World War II followed the patterns of the Soviet Union. Church associations were dissolved, Church property was confiscated, and schools were nationalized. Attempts were made to divide the Church from within by creating schismatic, "progressive" Churches and by creating antagonisms between bishops and clergy and between clergy and laypeople. In Czechoslovakia, thousands of priests were arrested and charged with spying, terrorism, and collaboration with the Nazis during World War II. By April 1951, three thousand of the country's seven thousand priests were estimated to be in jail or otherwise kept from their ministry.[85] In Hungary, in one night, June 9, 1950, nearly one thousand priests, nuns, and monks were seized and taken to concentration camps. All but four of the 67 religious orders in the country were dissolved and the monks and nuns given three months to return to civilian life.[86] The trial and forced confession of Cardinal Joseph Mindszenty symbolized Communist persecution of religion everywhere. From China, escaped and deported missionaries told stories of mock trials, executions, imprisonment, and torture.

Hostility, however, does not develop without cause. The Church itself shared the blame for much of the hostility generated against it. In some countries it possessed large land holdings and allied itself with reactionary governments to protect its own interests. Too often it put its own security and prestige ahead of concerns for social justice. Communism often was, in John Bennett's words, "a judgment upon Christians and churches."[87] Unquestionably, too, the Churches did oppose the new socialist regimes and Communist rulers did have to deal with the Church as an "enemy force."

Communist opposition to religion, on the other hand, did not simply stem from the opposition it met in trying to establish socialism. It brought with it a total worldview in which atheism was considered essential to society. It sought to fashion a "new man," to break down traditional belief systems and to replace them with a new one.[88]

Concluding Reflections and New Developments

This chapter has attempted to argue that there is no essential, necessary connection between atheism/materialism and Marxist socialism. Most Marxists, on the other hand, have traditionally viewed atheism as essential and Marxist-Leninist parties historically became quite militant on this point. What has been in the past, however, need not dictate the future. The history of the Church itself should be proof of that. The tortures of the Inquisition, executions and imprisonments of non-believers, the imposition of one belief on all, rigid dogmatism—all these are part of the Church's own past record. Only two decades ago Protestants still feared what a Catholic president might mean for the United States.

Suspicions of Marxists offering an "extended hand" of friendship are not without warrant, given the history of Communism. But projections from the experience of the past can be so strong that any change is ruled out a priori. If past history "proves" that Marxism is intrinsically atheistic and intolerant of religious belief, then past history also proves that Catholicism is intrinsically absolutist and intolerant of religious beliefs other than its own. Attitudes do change. Many Catholics, including the hierarchy, truly believe themselves to be not simply tolerant of other views but deeply respectful of them. To rule out, *a priori,* the possibility of similar attitudes in Marxists can hardly be justified.

In a final analysis, the key issue is not whether atheism is theoretically essential to Marxism but the *attitude* of Marxists toward those with religious belief, and vice versa. Intolerant attitudes produce persecutions; respectful attitudes produce a climate where collaboration is possible. So the more basic question becomes how to evaluate Marxist "attitudes" toward Christians, and Christian attitudes toward Marxists. Generalizations at this level are impossible. Each situation needs to be evaluated on its own merits.

Where Communism is already in power, atheism as a state ideology tends to prevail. But wide differences exist in the degree of religious liberty allowed. At one extreme is Albania, which in September 1967 closed every religious institution and declared itself "the first atheist state in the world." The churches in Poland and the German Democratic Republic, on the other hand, enjoy more rights and privileges and are relatively independent.[89] Both countries went through an initial phase of great conflict. Churches in both countries still experience tension and far more restrictions than in most Western countries. But accommodations have been achieved and some Christians are active in government legislative bodies. The Catholic Church in Poland has actually shown a considerable increase in the number of priests, parishes, monks, and nuns, and it has today a much larger organizational structure than in pre-war years.[90] More than 90 percent of the Polish population still maintain at least nominal allegiance to the Church, and a 1970 survey of some high schools showed 62 percent of the students as adherents of the Catholic Church.[91] But much of this strength was developed through a struggle to preserve the faith in the face of government opposition.

Historical conditions which prevailed in Russia and post-war Europe may no longer prevail today. The U.S.S.R. served as *the* model for Communism in post-World War II takeovers and the Bolshevik attitude to religion was embraced. Separation of Church and state, which in many Western countries had been realized through liberal demands, had not been obtained in the Soviet Union and other Eastern European countries. Many in the Church hierarchy were aristocrats or allied with the ruling class. Hence socialist demands were linked to liberal demands for separation. Little dialogue between Christians and Marxists had ever occurred. They viewed each other simply as enemies. Marxists could justly claim that the churches were a counter-revolutionary force opposed to socialism.

In countries where socialist movements are pressing for change today the situation is often quite different. Tensions certainly still exist. But much greater interaction between Christians and Marxists has taken place. Often the tension and conflict appear within the Church itself, between Christians still hostile to or fearful of Marxism and those advocating socialism. Generalizations at this level fail also. In Italy, Berlinguer has disavowed atheism as a constituent element of Party ideology. Extensive interchange between Christians and Marxists, between Party and Church officials, has occurred. In France, the Party still retains an official atheistic ideology, but it disavows all anti-religious propaganda. Nor can one simply identify the Communist Party and Marxism in France; many French Marxists are aligned with the Socialist Party. In Latin America, the varieties of Marxist groups and strategies, the differing attitudes of Church officials toward socialism, the extensive interaction of Christians and Marxists, would make any concrete assessment tendentious. Chilean socialism under Allende, as we have seen, held the promise of a very different Christian-Marxist experience. The purpose here, however, is not to attempt assessments of Marxist attitudes in all parts of the world, but to suggest that these attitudes are a far more determining factor than the past history of Communism. The assessment is not unilateral either. Marxists have had good reasons for doubting the commitment of Christians to social change. Their attitudes, moreover, have often been shaped by Christian anti-Communism. Their attitudes toward Christianity will be greatly affected by Christian attitudes toward them. Openness to Marxism and Marxists runs the risk of being taken in and manipulated. A closed attitude risks confirming the traditional Marxist opposition to religion, but more importantly it risks losing possibilities for the creation of more truly democratic, just societies.

For the United States, the issue of atheism seems almost irrelevant. For the most part, atheism is simply ignored as an issue in most scholarly Marxist journals. On purely pragmatic grounds, any effort to build atheism into a socialist ideology would be suicidal. Surveys show 94 percent of U.S. Americans believing in God and 54 percent attending Church on a monthly or more basis. Separation of Church and State was achieved at the outset in the United States and can hardly be made a socialist issue. To attack religion as "superstition" will hardly be convincing to tens of millions of highly-educated Christians. Criticisms of the lifestyle of clergy, the tax exemptions of churches, their financial holdings, or of the status quo attitudes of Church officials, can hardly qualify as grounds for mass adherence to atheism. If a socialist movement is to develop in the United States, it will have to harness, and not alienate, religious sentiment.

Attitudes change slowly. For the most part, with the exception of such phenomena as priest-workers in France, no widespread reevaluations of Marxism and Christianity developed until the 1960s when churches began to question more deeply their commitment to transforming the world. The Marxist critique of religion has spurred reexamination of Church doctrines and practices, as we have noted in earlier chapters and sections of this chapter.

Marxist Reappraisals of Religion

From the Marxist side have come reevaluations of the nature and function of religion. Most have come from individual "critical" Marxists, though some practical inroads have been made on the dominant Marxist tradition. Ernst Bloch certainly stands at the forefront of Marxist efforts to reappraise religion. His writings significantly influenced the development of a "theology of hope" by Jürgen Moltmann, Johannes Metz, and other Christian theologians. Beginning with his writings at the end of World War I on the spirit of utopia and the political-religious radicalism of Thomas Münzer, and culminating in his major work on *The Principle of Hope,* the question of messianic hope preoccupied Bloch. The new, the future, and dreams of hope Bloch saw as essential to both Marxist and Judaic-Christian thought. With its strong emphasis on deterministic, economic factors, Marxism often lost sight of its own inherent utopian tendency and of the desires which underlie all movements that strive to transform the world.[92] What distinguished Judaism and Christianity from other religions was that their founders were historical figures; their God acted in history and upon history. Moses led his people out of Egyptian enslavement toward a promised land; Jesus challenged the existing social order and gave the poor new hope for a coming kingdom. With Christianity, religion emerged as an "explosively posited messianism" with the promise of a new world.[93] Bloch criticized the accommodation of the Church to the existing political world, but saw the revolutionary spirit of Christianity kept alive by figures like Joachim di Fiore and Thomas Münzer.

Bloch remained an atheist. In place of God he put a void, an open space, the pull of the future. But he retained from religion its depth of hope and promise of a kingdom.[94]

Rudolf Siebert has made a study of several critical Marxists (the early Lukács, Max Horkheimer, L. Kolakowski, and others) who have undertaken reappraisals of religion.[95] A re-examination of Hegel's dialectical explanation of religion has been one source of new insight. Hegel asserted that the ground of religion is not humanity's feeling of "negation," the suffering, fears, and sense of powerlessness which traditional Marxism gave as the basis for religion. Religion arises rather from a "negation of the negation," from a conscious reflection which enables human beings to *overcome* their fears.[96] These critical Marxists offer several important distinctions about religion. While they still question the objective reality of God, some recognize the positive, subjective basis of religion with its longing for universal justice, love, solidarity, and freedom. While they challenge ideological uses of religion, they also recognize the relative independence of religion from social conditions. Not every concept of God is ideological; something of religion remains after it has been de-ideologized.[97] Horkheimer distinguishes good, progressive religion and evil, reactionary religion.[98] Kolakowski draws a distinction between "priests" and "jesters." He claims that Communist societies as well as churches have their "priests" who defend the status quo of existing institutions. Both Communism and Christianity need "jesters" to criticize them from within.

Milan Machovec, in *A Marxist Looks at Jesus*, goes much further. Drawing upon contemporary biblical scholarship he offers a deeply sympathetic portrayal of Jesus. Machovec challenges dominant Marxist views about Christian faith. Jesus, he says, did not encourage flight from the world and escape from misery, but offered hope for its transformation.[99] Jesus' teachings on love of enemies and renunciation of violence are wrongly understood if taken as a submission to oppression. Jesus uncompromisingly resisted evil wherever he found it, but he insisted that *how* one confronts evil is important.[100] Machovec argues, moreover, that Marxists should themselves seriously reflect on the question of the "means" used to fight evil since Marxists have at times abused their power.[101] The message of Jesus, Machovec concludes, cuts across all worldviews and ideologies. Jesus did not propound an ideology. He was concerned with human beings, with their victories and failures, their love and pain, their despair and unconquerable hope.[102]

Roger Garaudy, once a leading theoretician in the French Communist Party, has fallen from prominence since his expulsion from the Party in 1970. But his remarkable evolution from a Stalinist Marxism to advocacy of a "Christian Marxism" merits some mention. The writings of Teilhard de Chardin and the "open" Christianity of Karl Rahner and other contemporary theologians first led Garaudy to re-evaluate Marxist opposition to Christianity. In his *From Anathema to Dialogue* (1966) Garaudy felt that these new currents in Christian theology had affirmed the value of work and efforts to transform the world, and as such made Christianity far more compatible with Marxism. He recalled the writings of Engels which recognized the revolutionary element in Christianity. Christianity as an institution, he noted, has often supported the status quo and as an ideology it has preached resignation. But Christianity is also a faith which *stands up to the world*.[103]

In his *The Alternative Future* (1972) Garaudy took a far more dramatic step. He called for the rejection of a positive atheism which excludes God from the world. "Marxism," he said, "can only be the authentic breaker of chains if it can include this Christian insight, the divine element in man."[104] With Bloch, Garaudy stresses this principle of hope as the foundation of both a true Marxism and Christianity. Like Machovec, Garaudy insists that the *means* one uses to achieve revolutionary change must be consistent with the society desired. "One cannot first conquer power and change structures by any and all means, and then, from the height of the conquered power, bestow liberty."[105]

But the most remarkable conclusion drawn by Garaudy concerns his own inner transformation. After forty years of believing his militancy as a Marxist was incompatible with Christian faith he feels now that they are one.

> It is an overwhelming experience when a man who has professed himself an atheist for many years discovers that there has always been a Christian inside him. It is overwhelming to accept responsibility for such a hope.[106]

To conclude that Garaudy's experience is indicative of any widespread change occurring among Marxists would be quite misleading. The great majority of Marxists remain convinced atheists and most of their parties retain atheistic materialism as an official worldview. Perhaps few have even entertained the idea of reevaluating religion. Most Marxists, Machovec observes, bring a burden of prejudice to the question of Christianity. Most have felt that the radical rejection of Christianity is part of the "sacred heritage" of Marxism, a judgment based on clear memories of the reactionary and anti-social role of the Church in the nineteenth century and continued at times in the present.[107] The weight of tradition lies heavy on both Christians and Marxists. But it is historical tradition far more than any inner logic which has linked Marxist atheism and socialism together.

Notes

1. The division of the types of Marx and Engels atheism was suggested by Gustav Wetter's "Evangelisation und Marxismus," in *Evangelisation,* ed. M. Dhavamony, S.J. (Rome: Universita Gregoriana, 1975), pp. 381–404. Other divisions could obviously be made. Thus, for example, Philippe Warnier, in *Marx pour un chrétien,* distinguishes seven different types of Marxist atheism, pp. 87f.

2. Nicholas Lobkowicz stresses Marx's disdain for religion in "Karl Marx's Attitude Toward Religion," in *The Review for Politics,* Vol. 26, No. 3, July 1964.

3. On this central thesis of Marx's humanistic atheism Giulio Girardi writes: "The denial of God is a condition of the very possibility of the affirmation of man." Girardi, *Marxism and Christianity,* trans. Kevin Traynor (New York: Macmillan, 1968), p. 26. Quentin Lauer stresses the same point: "Marx was an integral humanist who saw supreme value in man, and only in man. . . . Marx is not out to get rid of God; he is out to free man—not to free him from God but from himself and from his enslavement to religion, which is his own creation." Quentin Lauer S.J., "The Atheism of Karl Marx," in *Marxism and Christianity,* ed. Herbert Aptheker (New York: Humanities Press, 1968), p. 54.

4. Marx, *Collected Works,* Volume I (New York: International Publishers, 1975), p. 638.

5. Ibid., p. 7.

6. Ibid., pp. 30–31.

7. Easton, *Writings of the Young Marx,* p. 58. From notes on "Platonism and Christianity," related to his doctoral thesis.

8. Ibid., pp. 64–66. From a note on "Reason and the Proof of God."

9. Ibid., p. 117. From "The Leading Article in No. 179 of the *Kölnische Zeitung.*"

10. Ibid., p. 126.

11. Ibid., p. 222. From Marx's "On the Jewish Question."

12. Ibid., p. 237.

13. Ibid., p. 249. From "Toward the Critique of Hegel's Philosophy of Law: Introduction."

14. Ibid., pp. 257–58. Marx's italics are omitted.

15. A contemporary Catholic catechism for adults, *The Teaching of Christ,* ed. Ronald Lawler, OFM Cap, and others (Huntington, Indiana: Our Sunday Visitor, 1976), affirms: "Christ teaches men how to live on earth in a genuinely human way. The Catholic faith does not lead men to be less human, but to be more human. . . . (Christ) makes men more human by enabling them to draw on the resources of God. . . . He calls men to become fully human" (p. 32). The catechism unfortunately reflects a continued lack of sensitivity to the problem of male sexist language in the Church, but it does indicate the effort to show that Christianity accepts humanistic goals.

16. Marx's first real exposition of a materialist view of *history* came with *The German Ideology* in 1845. But insights into the effect of economic conditions on

religion and politics can be found clearly in his writings in 1843–44.

17. Easton, *Writings of the Young Marx*, p. 250. From "Toward the Critique of Hegel's Philosophy of Law: Introduction." In calling religion a general ground of "consolation and justification" Marx also notes the ideological function religion plays in preserving the status quo (ibid.). For Marx's position on religion vis-à-vis Feuerbach see also his 4th Thesis on Feuerbach, ibid., p. 401.

18. Ibid., p. 314. From Marx's essay on "Private Property and Communism" in the *1844 Manuscripts*. The same concluding passages of this essay also reassert Marx's humanistic atheism. "A being only regards himself as independent when he stands on his own feet, and he stands on his own feet only when he owes his existence to himself" (ibid., p. 312). "If I attribute my life to a creator, I become dependent and my life is not my own."

In this passage Marx also lays the basis for scientific atheism. He challenges the very notion of creation. "Who created the first human being and nature as a whole?" is a false question. It *assumes,* says Marx, the non-existence of the world at some point in time, whereas science is quite capable of explaining the formation and development of the earth as a self-generative process (ibid., p. 313).

19. Herbert Aptheker, a U.S. Marxist, makes this point in "Marxism and Religion" in *Marxism and Christianity,* which he also edited, p. 39.

20. Easton, *Writings of the Young Marx,* p. 415. From "The German Ideology."

21. Ibid., p. 433.

22. Ibid., p. 438.

23. In Marx and Engels, *On Religion* (New York: Schocken Books, 1964, fifth printing, 1974), p. 88.

24. Ibid., p. 94. From Engels' "Review of G. Fr. Daumer's *The Religion of the New Age.*"

25. Ibid., p. 99. From *The Peasant War in Germany*, Chapter 2.

26. Ibid., pp. 83–84. From Marx's "The Communism of the Paper *Rheinische Beobachter.*"

27. Ibid., pp. 127–28. From "Anti–Church Movement—Demonstration in Hyde Park."

28. Ibid., pp. 135–36. From *Capital,* I.

29. Ibid., p. 147. From *Anti-Dühring.*

30. Ibid., p. 149.

31. Thus Herbert Aptheker writes that "Marx emphasizes the protest potential of religion, he emphasizes its beauty, and its source of refreshment," in *Marxism and Christianity,* p. 33.

32. Marx and Engels, *On Religion,* p. 316. From "On the History of Early Christianity."

33. Ibid., p. 318. For similar statements about the spirit of early Christianity see also Engels on "Bruno Bauer and Early Christianity," ibid., pp. 194–204, and on "The Book of Revelation," ibid., pp. 205–12.

34. Ibid., pp. 325–34. From "On the History of Early Christianity."

35. Ibid., p. 336.

36. Ibid., pp. 109ff. From *The Peasant War in Germany.*

37. See, for example, José Míguez Bonino's critique of the use of religion as an "ideological screen" to support the status quo, in his *Christians and Marxists: The Mutual Challenge to Revolution* (Grand Rapids, Michigan: Eerdmans, 1976), Chapters

3 and 4. Míguez argues that the Bible itself contains a powerful criticue of the ideological uses of religion, of religion used as an excuse for injustice. Another example would be George Hampsch's criticism of triumphalism and moral imperialism in the Church. Hampsch, "The Practice of Freedom" in *Marxism and Christianity*, ed. Aptheker, pp. 122–42.

38. How justified Marxist criticisms have been of the ideological use of religion can be exemplified by a quotation from a nineteenth century Catholic journalist converted from Protestantism. Were it not that he intended his words quite seriously the quote would appear almost a caricature of the attitude Marx attacked: "Christianity in the Church takes hold of the poor. To them the Gospel is especially preached. It limits and regulates their desire for temporal comfort. It teaches them resignation, submission to Providence, not as vague powerless sentiment, but as a positive duty. . . . Christianity diverts their attention from their weary life in this world, its privations, its suffering. . . . Life on earth is short, but the future life is eternal." G. D. Wolff, "The Danger of 'Socialist Communism,'" in *American Catholic Social Thought on Social Questions*, ed. Aaron I. Abell (Indianapolis: Bobbs-Merrill, 1968), p. 66.

39. Marx and Engels, *Collected Works*, Volume 2, Engels: 1838–1842. The quotes are from letters to Friedrich Graeber in 1839, p. 426 and p. 457, respectively.

40. Ibid., p. 461.

41. Frederick Engels, *Dialectics of Nature* (Moscow: Progress Publishers, 1934, 4th printing 1966), p. 21.

42. Ibid., pp. 25–30.

43. Ibid., pp. 36–37.

44. Frederick Engels, *Ludwig Feuerbach and the Outcome of Classical German Philosophy* (New York: International Publishers, 1941, fifth printing 1967), p. 21.

45. Frederick Engels, *Anti-Dühring, Herr Eugene Dühring's Revolution in Science* (New York: International Publishers, 1939, new printing 1966), p. 51

46. Ibid., p. 68.

47. Ibid.

48. Engels, *Ludwig Feuerbach*, p. 46.

49. Ibid., pp. 47–49.

50. Ibid., p. 44.

51. Engels, *Anti-Dühring*, pp. 42–43.

52. Karl Marx and Frederick Engels, *The Holy Family or a Critique of Critical Critique* (Moscow: Foreign Languages Publishing House, 1956), pp. 159–75.

53. Ibid., p. 176.

54. Engels, *Ludwig Feuerbach* p. 20.

55. Ibid., pp. 44–48.

56. Alfred Schmidt, *The Concept of Nature in Marx* (London: NLB, 1971), pp. 30–35, 61, 79.

57. Ibid., p. 111.

58. Ibid., p. 167.

59. Z. A. Jordan, *The Evolution of Dialectical Materialism* (London: Macmillan, 1967), Chapter 1, and "Is Marx a Materialist?" pp. 50–57.

60. Gustav Wetter, S.J., *Soviet Ideology Today*, trans. Peter Heath (London: Heinemann, 1966), p. 185. Many Marxists would obviously dispute these conclusions which dissociate Marx from Engels' dialectical materialism. See, for example, Donald Weiss, "The Philosophy of Engels Vindicated," in *Monthly Review*, January 1977, pp.

15–31. Weiss argues persuasively that Engels was not a "reductionist," but he does not really address the charge that Engels made Marxism into an ontology.

61. From Lenin's "The Tasks of the Youth Leagues" (1920) in V. I. Lenin, *Selected Works in Three Volumes,* Volume III (New York: International Publishers, 1967), p. 468.

62. Eugene Kamenka, *Marxism and Ethics* (London: Macmillan, 1969), pp. 60ff.

63. Easton, *Writings of the Young Marx,* pp. 460–69, from *The German Ideology.*

64. Donald J. Munro, *The Concept of Man in Contemporary China* (Ann Arbor: University of Michigan Press, 1977), pp. 11–19.

65. Tucker, *Marx-Engels Reader,* 2nd ed. p. 540. From Marx's *Critique of the Gotha Programme* (1875).

66. Marx and Engels, *On Religion,* p. 143. From Engels on "Emigrant Literature."

67. Ibid., p. 149. From *Anti-Dühring.*

68. V. I. Lenin, *Selected Works,* Volume XI (London: Lawrence and Wishart, 1939), pp. 661–62. From "On Socialism and Religion" (1905).

69. Ibid., pp. 664ff. From "Attitude of Workers' Party Toward Religion."

70. See Bohdan R. Bociurkiw, "Lenin and Religion," in *Lenin: The Man, The Theorist, The Leader. A Reappraisal,* ed. Leonard Shapiro (New York: Praeger, 1967), p. 108.

71. Lenin, *Selected Works,* XI, p. 658.

72. Ibid., p. 664.

73. Ibid., p. 666.

74. Ibid., pp. 675–76. From "Letters to Maxim Gorky."

75. Ibid., p. 676.

76. Ibid., p. 682. From "Leo Tolstoy as a Mirror of the Russian Revolution."

77. Ibid., pp. 659–60. From "Socialism and Religion."

78. V. I. Lenin, *Selected Works in Three Volumes,* III. "On the Significance of Militant Materialism" (1922), pp. 662–70.

79. See Aptheker in *Marxism and Christianity,* p. 35.

80. *The Russian Revolution and Religion.* A Collection of Documents Concerning the Suppression of Religion by the Communists, 1917–1925. Trans. and ed. Boleshaw Szczesniak (Notre Dame, Ind.: University of Notre Dame, 1959), pp. 34–35.

81. Robert Conquest, *Religion in the U.S.S.R.* (New York: Praeger, 1968), p. 14.

82. *The Russian Revolution and Religion,* p. 49.

83. Conquest, *Religion in the U.S.S.R.,* p. 15.

84. Ibid., p. 19.

85. Gary MacEoin, *The Communist War on Religion* (New York: Devin-Adair, 1951), p. 55.

86. Ibid., pp. 134–35.

87. John C. Bennett, *Christianity and Communism Today* (New York: Association Press, 1948, fifth printing 1970), p. 3.

88. See J. M. Bochenski, "Marxism-Leninism and Religion," pp. 1–17, and David E. Powell, "Rearing the New Soviet Man," pp. 151–70, in *Religion and Atheism in the U.S.S.R. and Eastern Europe,* ed. Bohdan R. Bociurkiw and John W. Strong (Toronto: University of Toronto, 1975).

89. Ibid., Gerhard Simon, "The Catholic Church and the Communist State in the

Soviet Union and Eastern Europe," pp. 190ff. This same volume also contains essays on specific countries in Eastern Europe.

90. Ibid., pp. 214–15.

91. Ibid., pp. 192, 214.

92. Ernst Bloch, *Man on His Own, Essays in the Philosophy of Religion,* trans. E. B. Ashton (New York: Herder and Herder, 1970), p. 39.

93. Ibid., pp. 150–52.

94. Ibid., pp. 220–21.

95. Rudolf Siebert, "The New Dimension in Western Marxism," in *Horizons,* in two articles: (1) Vol. 3, No. 2, 1976, pp. 217–36, and (2) Vol. 4, No. 1, 1977, pp. 43–59.

96. Ibid., first article, p. 229.

97. Ibid., pp. 231–32.

98. Ibid., second article, p. 52.

99. Milan Machovec, *A Marxist Looks at Jesus* (Philadelphia: Fortress, 1976), pp. 84–89.

100. Ibid., pp. 108–9.

101. Ibid., p. 33.

102. Ibid., p. 204.

103. Roger Garaudy, *From Anathema to Dialogue,* trans. Luke O'Neill (New York: Herder and Herder, 1966), p. 115.

104. Roger Garaudy, *The Alternative Future: A Vision of Christian Marxism,* trans. Leonard Mayhew (New York: Simon and Schuster, 1972), p. 80.

105. Ibid., p. 182.

106. Ibid., p. 177.

107. Machovec, *A Marxist Looks at Jesus,* p. 19.

Chapter 8

Property, Violence, Class Struggle, Democracy

Most of the major objections to Marxism can be summarized under the heading of "the means it uses." Many Christians recognize the legitimacy of the criticisms which Marxists make of the prevailing capitalist economic system. They agree that something needs to be done to overcome the injustices and inequality which so dehumanize society. But they fear that the Marxist remedy, because of the means it employs, may be worse than the problem it sets out to cure. They fear that the ideology of atheism and materialism, with which Marxism has traditionally identified, will be imposed and freedom of religion lost. Some feel that the primary tenet of Marxism, the abolition of private property, takes away a basic natural right. Many believe that Marxist revolutionary tactics will engender far more evil than the good they hope to achieve. Appeals to revolutionary violence seem completely opposed to the Christian message. Class struggle would appear to contradict Jesus' command to love one's enemies. Perhaps most especially the Marxist-Leninist tradition of the "dictatorship of the proletariat" raises serious misgivings about the achievement of a more human society through Marxist socialism. Socialism holds out an ideal of a socio-economic system in which people work more cooperatively together and share more equitably, but also one in which *they* control the means of production and hence are more free. The history of Communist nations, however, too often reveals power in the hands of a party elite or state bureaucracy which "absorbs the individual" and brings less human freedom rather than more.

The problem of atheism and materialism has already been addressed. These other objections to Marxism need now to be considered. One chapter, one person's views, can hardly resolve them all. But a perspective can perhaps be established from which to evaluate them more fully. Such a perspective is the intended aim of this chapter.

The Right to Private Property

Socialism, Pope Leo XIII declared in *Rerum Novarum* (1891), is manifestly against justice. "For every man has by nature the right to possess property as

278

his own" (RN, n. 5). If this objection to socialism still holds, then all other ideological questions about the compatibility of Christianity and Marxism, or of Christianity and any form of socialism, would be useless exercises. In Catholic social thought, moreover, the right to private property served not only as an objection to socialism but as a fundamental first principle. Hence, the importance of this issue, which deals more with Church teachings on property than with a reappraisal of Marxist thought. It should be stressed, however, that the Marxist critique focuses on private ownership of "means of production" (of factories, land and natural resources) rather than on owner-ship of one's own home and consumer goods.

From another perspective, the issue of the "right" to private property has lessened in importance. Official Catholic teachings on property have under-gone a notable change since Leo XIII (see Chapter 3); in Protestant theology the right to property never played quite so central a role; the concentration of production in the hands of large corporations or the state has also signifi-cantly altered the issue. But the issue should be addressed. An historical perspective reveals that early Christian attitudes toward property were quite different from views that came to predominate in recent centuries.[1]

The Biblical Tradition

What form property relations should take, whether ownership should be private or social, was not an issue for the people of Israel. But the *use* of property was a very grave and serious concern. God intended the goods of the earth for all people. Those who exploited the poor or simply showed no concern for the poor were denounced.

> Yahweh calls to judgment the elders and princes of his people: "You are the ones who destroy the vineyard and conceal what you have stolen from the poor. By what right do you crush my people and grind the faces of the poor?" (Isa. 3:14–15).
>
> Woe to those who add house to house and join field to field until everywhere belongs to them and they are the sole inhabitants of the land (Isa. 5:8).[2]

Right to possession always carried with it communal obligations. Mosaic legislation stipulated the use of property for the benefit of all. The harvesters were to leave some of their crop for the poor (Lev. 19:9–10; 23:22). The land should be given a rest every seventh year so that the poor, and even animals, might eat what grows wild on it (Exod. 23:10–11; Lev. 25:2–24).

Jesus denounced those who piled up riches (Matt. 6:24; 19:23–36; Luke 12:13–21; 16:19–31); he blessed the poor (Luke 6:20–26); he proclaimed his mission on behalf of the poor and downtrodden (Luke 4:18); he claimed that final judgment on one's life would depend on the response one had given to the needy (Matt. 25:31–46).[3] It can be argued that none of these biblical references constitutes a case against private property, but only against its abuse. They do, however, establish a basic norm for evaluation of property systems: their ability to care for the needs of all, including the most destitute.

The early Christian community formed a "communist" society.

> The whole group of believers was united, heart and soul; no one claimed for his own use anything that he had, as everything they owned was held in common. . . . None of their members was ever in want, as all those who owned land or houses would sell them, and bring the money from them, to present it to the apostles; it was then distributed to any members who might be in need (Acts 4:32; 34–35).

The early Church Fathers made much of this example. Later commentators, on the other hand, tended to discount it since it was a voluntary system of communal ownership. Some would even use the fact that communal owner-ship soon disappeared to argue that socialism doesn't work. But it remained in the Christian tradition, nevertheless, as an ideal of what human relation-ships should be in respect to earthly goods.

The Church Fathers

Far from justifying private property as a "natural right," the Church Fathers viewed it as a necessary evil. God had created the goods of the earth for all to use, and God's original plan for the world in the Garden of Eden intended equality and communal sharing. Private property came as a result of the fall, as a consequence of human sinfulness. Communal ownership was "natural"; private property was only a "convention" needed in the light of original sin.[4]

Clement of Alexandria, around A.D. 200, set down a principle to which nearly all the early Church Fathers subscribed: God intended the goods of the earth for all; no one should live in abundance while others are in need. The Fathers of the fourth and fifth centuries went further: private property is not according to nature; no one can rightly claim possessions as "mine."[5] St. Basil, who distributed all his own possessions among the poor, chastised the rich: "Tell me, what is yours? Where did you get it and bring it into the world?" The rich preempt what is common to all. "If only each one would take as much as he requires to satisfy his immediate needs and leave the rest to others who equally needed it, no one would be rich—and no one would be poor." St. Jerome claimed that all riches came from injustice, that the rich person is either an unjust person or the heir of one. St. Ambrose insisted:

> Nature has poured forth all things for men for common use. God has ordered all things to be produced, so that there should be food in common to all, and that the earth should be a common possession for

all. Nature, therefore, has produced a common right for all, but greed
(*usurpatio*) has made it a right for a few.[6]

The Church Fathers viewed the early Christian community at Jerusalem as
an example of God's plan for property relations. St. Cyprian, in the third
century, explained that the practice of the early Church was an example of the
universal rule according to which the whole human race ought to share
equally in the goods of the world. Chrysostom, Jerome, and Augustine
viewed it, if not as a rule, at least as an ideal to be followed.[7]

Gratian's *Decretum* (about 1140) embodied the theory that according to
nature all property was common, and this view was made a part of the law of
the medieval Church. But Gratian also stated rules for the acquisition of
property. Private property had become a fact of life. Commentators thus
began distinguishing between different kinds of natural law to prove that
private property was legitimate and not simply an institution based on sin.
The authority of Aristotle's writings gave weight to arguments for private
property. Scholastic philosophers who preceded St. Thomas Aquinas had
already concluded that private property was a natural and good institution.[8]

St. Thomas Aquinas

The question of private property played a rather small role in the overall
philosophy of Aquinas. But his ideas on property laid the groundwork not
only for nineteenth and twentieth century Catholic thought, but for the
Protestant and secular thought of the post-medieval period as well. His
legitimation of private property as part of the natural law was itself quite
natural for that period of history. Even from a Marxist perspective private
property "fit" naturally into the undeveloped means of production of that
period. From a Christian perspective, however, the important question is *how*
Aquinas dealt with the question of property and whether his arguments
remain still applicable many centuries later.

St. Thomas does not make the right to private property a fundamental
principle of his socio-political thought. He treats it only by way of example in
distinguishing different senses of the natural law and in discussing the morality of theft. He knew that some Church Fathers had claimed that "the
possession of all things in common" was a matter of natural law. He thus first
treats property in the *Summa* in the context of trying to defend the natural law
as unchangeable.[9] Christians had come to accept laws permitting private
ownership. It would seem that this either violated the natural law as enunciated by the Church Fathers or that the natural law had changed. St. Thomas
responded by saying that certain changes can occur by way of "addition"
without fundamentally altering the natural law. Applying this distinction to
private property Aquinas said that ownership belongs to the natural law not
in any absolute sense or because 'nature inclines thereto," but because nature

does not oppose it as an addition. He makes the same case, unfortunately, for slavery. Thus he concludes that while possession of all things in common and universal freedom are general principles of the natural law, private property and slavery have been "devised by human reason for the benefit of human life." The law of nature was not changed by them, therefore, "except by addition."

He treats the issue of private property again in dealing with the problem of theft. He asks: "Whether it is lawful for a man to possess a thing as his own?"[10] The very question is significant, for again, far from treating ownership as a self-evident principle of natural law, St. Thomas had to argue that it was "not contrary" to natural law. He gives three reasons why he believes a person should have the power to procure and dispense of things, and hence to possess property as necessary for human life: (1) work is more likely to be carried out when persons labor for their own procurement rather than for the community; (2) order is better observed when each is responsible for certain things; (3) peace is better ensured if each person is content with his or her own things. At the same time Aquinas reasserts the older Church tradition regarding the use of possessions: "In this respect man ought to possess external things, not as his own, but as common, so that, namely, he is ready to communicate them to others in need." Then, in discussing theft, Aquinas contends that it is not theft to take or use another's property in the case of extreme need.[11]

Several important conclusions might be drawn from St. Thomas' treatment of property. First, while he spoke of private property as natural, he did not speak of it as a natural "right" in the way Locke and later philosophers would do. Private property was not natural in any absolute sense or "because nature inclines thereto"; rather it was natural only "because nature did not bring with it the contrary." In speaking of private property as a "natural right" Leo XIII and Pius XI assigned to it a far greater weight than Aquinas did. Second, St. Thomas subordinated private property to the common good. He did this by making the lawmaker responsible for regulating private property for the common good, by stressing that external things are common as to their use, and by insisting that need for the support of life supersedes ownership. Third, his three arguments for private property (work, order, peace) were inductions based on experience, not deductions based on the very nature of the human person. His reasoning was based on a very concrete assessment of what social arrangements he felt best served the common good and the needs of all members of society in his day. The same type of reasoning might lead to a very different assessment about private property relations in today's society.

Much of the debate over private property in the later Middle Ages and into the Reformation revolved around the issue of church and state rights in respect to property. Luther attacked monastic property holdings for not being put to good use, but defended the principle of private property against the Anabaptists who wanted all property to be common. For Luther men and women were too depraved by the Fall to use reason or natural law to justify private ownership. But the biblical command not to steal proved that God intended private property.[12] The notion of "stewardship," on the other hand, became an important Protestant concept regarding the just use of property.

What the Reformation did influence was a more "individualistic" cast given to the theory of private property. Thus Richard Schlatter writes: "In the Protestant world God gives grace, not to a Church, but to individual Christians who then unite to form a Church; in the new political philosophy, God (or nature) gives rights, not to rulers, but to individuals who then proceed to create rulers."[13] John Locke developed what would become the classical liberal theory of this new philosophy in respect to property. "Life, liberty, and property" became a sacred trinity of natural rights—or, as a Marxist would contend, of bourgeois rights. Private property as a natural right became firmly embedded in Western thought.

The Papal Encyclicals

The evolution of Catholic social teachings on property has already been discussed in Chapter 3. But it may be helpful to conclude this section with a summary of the changes which have occurred in Catholic social teachings, beginning with Leo XIII's stress on the right to private property as a major argument against socialism, to more recent Church pronouncements which mark a return to the earlier Church tradition of the "universal purpose of all created things."

In *Rerum Novarum* Leo XIII called socialist proposals to eliminate private property "emphatically unjust" because they would rob lawful possessors and bring the state into a sphere not its own (RN, n. 3). Pope Leo also gave three positive reasons in defense of the right to property: human beings need stable possession of goods to provide for the future; the results of labor should belong to the one who has done the labor; fathers need to be able to provide for wife and children and be able to transfer what they have gained (RN, nn. 5–11).

What evaluative response might one give to these arguments today? Certainly the positive concern of the pontiff should be acknowledged. He justly sought to defend and protect what he felt was essential to human dignity and personal security. The danger that state control over property would also bring state control over the lives of individuals still remains a serious question. A strong case can be made for private property, moreover, where individuals do own their own business or land. Private ownership can engender a sense of responsibility, of achievement, of pride and security. But does capitalism really make possible such ownership for more than a privileged few? Marx and Pope Leo both agreed that the results of labor belonged to the laborer. Leo sought to defend private property on that score. But the images he used to describe the relation of work to property ownership suggest the small farmer-owner as his model rather than propertyless factory workers. Thus he spoke of the act by which a person "makes his own that portion of nature's field which he cultivates" and of "the soil which is tilled and cultivated," etc. (RN, nn. 7–8). Of the worker Pope Leo said that "if he lives sparingly, saves money, and invests his savings, for greater security, in land" he could own property and he should not be deprived of this "possibility" (RN, n. 4). The socialist critique argues precisely on this point, that capitalism *deprives* the great mass of workers of any real ownership and hence that they cannot attain the security and provision for the future which private property theoretically provides.

Pius XI, in *Quadragesimo Anno,* recognized that great masses of people were in fact propertyless and had little hope of owning any means of production (QA, nn. 59–60). His vision of a "corporatist" society was meant to provide a middle way between capitalism and a totally collectivist socialism. Had it ever come to fruition, other than in a corrupt fascist form, it might have provided a true alternative. Critics, however, point to the very practical problem which stands in its way, the unwillingness of owners to relinquish voluntarily their power or even a part of it.[14]

Pius XII's affirmation that the right of all persons to use material goods for their sustenance is prior even to the right of private ownership marked a turning point in the Church's teaching on property. Pope John XXIII repeated it and stressed the dignity of the human person, rather than the right to property, as the basic principle of Catholic social thought. Vatican II made no mention of the right to property and returned to the early Church Fathers' tradition which made the "universal purpose of created goods" the principal governing norm of property relations (*Gaudium et Spes,* n. 69). Pope Paul VI's *Populorum Progressio* likewise gave first place to the universal purpose of created things and reiterated that all other rights are subordinate to the right of every person to obtain what is needed for sustenance and growth (PP, n. 22).

A document by the Pontifical Justice and Peace Commission in 1977, entitled "The Universal Purpose of Created Things," summarized the new stance of the Catholic Church. The special issue it addressed was the question of "who owns the oceans?"[15] But the Commission used the occasion for a renewed reading of Catholic social teachings on property.

The Church's authentic doctrine, the Commission stated, is founded on "the first and guiding principle of the universal purpose of created things." Rights inherent in various types of property must be subordinated to this principle. Faced with a radical repudiation of the very purpose of private ownership the Church was led in the past to emphasize its value in order to safeguard freedom in the face of oppressive interference by the state. But many, including many Christians, retained only the Church's defense of their property and ignored the more fundamental principle of the universal purpose of created things. In speaking of a "natural right" to property, the Commission continued, the Church wished to assert a fundamental element *in each person* which allowed material goods to be appropriated. But the term "right to property" took on the culturally-conditioned sense of property holdings protected by law. The result has been that Church teachings have been used to justify existing property systems as natural in the sense of "permanent and inviolable." The Church's doctrine was intended rather to judge and adapt existing property relations in view of the human and social finality they ought to serve.

> The real question is thus the following: does the existing regime, and the development it is undergoing, still enable all men to exercise their "natural" (hence valid for all) right to have access in one form or another to some power over things, a power to be exercised in responsible freedom? Or, on the contrary, do the existing regime and its inner logic lead to the exclusion of the majority from such a perspective? And do they not lead, moreover, by a new abuse, to concentrate in the hands of a minority not only the responsibilities for property, but also all social and political powers?[16]

The Commission document lacks the status of an encyclical, but it does present itself as an official Catholic stance on property. It re-interprets the Church's traditional defense of private property and thereby sets down new norms from which to judge property systems. All persons have a natural right to the goods of the earth and should be able to exercise some freedom and control over the property on which they depend. Property systems which exclude the majority from free exercise of these rights are criticized. These norms of themselves do not resolve the capitalism-versus-socialism issue since both state socialisms and large-corporate capitalist systems in many countries have failed to live up to these norms. But the norms do set aside the "right to property" arguments which ruled out socialism from the outset. They leave open the possibility of a democratic socialism or of a more widely shared private ownership which could provide a freer access to the goods of the earth and greater control by individuals over their lives.

Violent Revolution

At first blush the reason for Christian opposition to Marxism on the score of violence would seem quite evident. Marxism advocates violent revolution; Christianity renounces violence as contrary to the message of Jesus; hence Marxism and Christianity are incompatible. Upon closer examination this dichotomy tends to fall apart, though certain serious issues do remain. It tends to fall apart because the Marxist tradition includes "peaceful" transitions to socialism, but more importantly because Christians have by no means resolved for themselves whether violence is ever justified. In fact, the more traditional Christian view has been that "under certain circumstances" violence may be justified. When terrorists are killed by police in order to save hostages, the Christian world does not cry out in outrage against this employment of violence. But the growth in recent decades of Christian groups strongly committed to non-violence has made the issue of violence a critical question.

The issue of violence, then, has become the focus of considerable debate *within Christianity* itself, apart from any evaluation of Marxism. This makes any effort to contrast Christian and Marxist views on violence exceedingly problematic. For a Christian pacifist the problem is not Marxism but violence itself. The use of violence on behalf of a Marxist revolution would be wrong but so, too, would be a violent revolution aimed at overthrowing a repressive Communist regime. Most Christians, on the other hand, tend to condone or at least accept violence under certain limited circumstances. Assuming this perspective for the moment, not as morally right but simply as a *de facto* attitude, will permit a better focus on Christian attitudes toward Marxist revolution.

What are most Christians who object to Marxist revolutionary violence really opposing? Is it violence itself? Is it revolution? Several historical examples suggest that it is neither. U.S. Americans celebrate with pride, and with little sign of moral misgivings, the signing of the Declaration of Independence which led to a revolutionary war. The sympathies of the Christian world went out to the Hungarians who attempted to overthrow their Communist government in 1956. The overthrow of Batista in Cuba in 1959 won general support and approval from Christians *until* Castro adopted a radical and eventually Marxist program after the overthrow.

The point of these examples should be clear. Apart from the pacifist position which is consistent in rejecting all violence, most Christians tend to justify some violent revolutionary actions. Thus their opposition to Marxism cannot be based simply on a rejection of violence *per se* or of revolution *per se*. Nor can it be argued that Marxist overthrows always involve more violence than others. The Bolshevik revolution involved very little violence. The provisional government surrendered almost without a fight. Eastern Europe fell to Communism without prolonged, violent struggle, thanks to the menacing presence of Soviet occupation armies. The Chinese Communist revolution, it is true, involved years of protracted warfare; but Chiang Kai-shek's nationalist armies fought the same protracted wars against the rule of despotic war lords.

Where then does opposition to Marxism really lie as regards violence? It would seem to be focused on the carrying through of the revolution, in the repression of counter-revolutionary forces *after* the overthrow. China proved to be the most extreme example, with hundreds of thousands, perhaps millions, of wealthy landowners brought to trial and executed.[17]

Cambodian Communists have carried out an even more ruthless elimination of "class enemies." In Russia, mass executions did not follow upon the Bolshevik takeover. However, the civil war which ensued did occasion repressive violence, and Stalin's forced collectivization of peasants and later Party purges brought violence to an extreme. Execution of political prisoners followed upon Castro's victory in Cuba.

These communist revolutions, on the other hand, were often fought against violent, repressive regimes. Czarist Russia shot down hundreds of peaceful demonstrators on "Bloody Sunday" (1905); it executed, imprisoned, and sent to Siberia its political opponents. Batista's regime was ruthlessly repressive; executions and imprisonments far exceeded Castro's actions.[18] If economic oppression serves as the main justification for Marxist revolution, it is frequently violent repression by the state which fuels the anger-provoking revolution. The very effort to encourage "reforms" in many Latin American countries brings down repression, executions, tortures, and imprisonment. In Chile it was not the Marxist regime of Allende which employed violence but the right-wing junta which overthrew it. But violence justified by pointing to the violence of one's enemies creates only a vicious circle of violence, not a more humane society.

How then does one take hold of the issue of violence? Two questions may help to focus on the problem of violence in reference to Marxism. First, does Marxist socialism necessarily imply violent revolution? Second, where violent overthrow of a regime appears to be the only recourse, can a Christian participate in a Marxist revolution or any other revolution?

Does Marxism Necessarily Imply Violent Revolution?

Certainly almost all Marxists would agree on the necessity of "revolution" on one level, namely, the radical transformation of society. Mere reforms of the capitalist system will not overcome its destructive consequences. But is *violent* overthrow of the old necessary to achieve a radical socialist transformation? Certainly Lenin argued that it was in *State and Revolution.*[19] Salvador Allende tried to prove that it was not, with his election in Chile in 1970, and Eurocommunists have committed themselves to a non-violent, parliamentary path to political power. Marx and Engels, as has been noted in Chapters 1–2, left an ambiguous legacy. At times they stressed the inevitability of violent revolution, but at other times they spoke of the possibility of peaceful transitions to socialism in England, the United States, and Germany.

One might certainly question, as Eduard Bernstein did, the influence of Hegel's dialectic on the Marxist tradition of revolution (see Chapter 2). The dialectical "laws" tend to inject a priori assumptions into the analysis of social change: that history develops through a process of "negations" and of "qualitative leaps" from one stage to another. The dialectic, viewed as an objective law, would seem to require a dramatic leap or negation, a violent revolution, for the transition from one economic stage to another. But what violent revolutions can be pointed to which marked the transition from ancient to feudal society? And what revolutions, other than the French Revolution and to a lesser extent the English revolution of 1688, can be shown to account for the transition of all Western countries from feudalism to capitalism? If one is to establish the necessity of revolution, it would have to be on grounds other than dialectical inevitability.

The major argument of many Marxist-Leninists would then be to point to experience. Only through violent revolution has Marxist socialism been able to come to power and stay in power. One might make exception for countries of Eastern Europe after World War II, but the presence of Soviet troops certainly influenced the outcome of elections. Allende did come to power by way of election, but his subsequent overthrow was a confirmation for many Marxist-Leninists of the necessity of armed force. The Eurocommunists have not succeeded in gaining power. Where Marxism has won power, in the Soviet Union, in China, in Cuba, in Vietnam, it has done so through revolution.

But this argument also needs to be examined. In the countries just mentioned, the possibility of a peaceful, legal transition to socialism had been shut off. Democratic structures did not exist. The same may hold true in some Third World countries today, but it is not true for advanced capitalist countries. The very possibility of change through elections, no matter how illusory one may judge bourgeois democracy to be, blunts revolutionary movements from developing as they did in countries where only revolution promised any hope of change. If experience is used as a criterion, then revolutionary strategies to achieve socialism have failed in capitalist countries of the First World. Given the long tradition of democratic structures in these countries, and respecting them, many Marxists in the United States and Europe see greater feasibility of achieving socialism through elections. Others, needless to say, would strongly disagree.

Where Violent Overthrow Appears To Be the Only Recourse,
Can Christians Participate in a Marxist Revolution, or Any Revolution?

Some countries, in the Third World particularly, face conditions in which a democratic transition to socialism, or for that matter even substantial reforms, seem remote possibilities. Hopes for revolution have likewise diminished as national security forces become more adept at crushing incipient movements. But assuming conditions that would make revolution a possibility, as occurred in Cuba, what are the moral considerations?

Christian attitudes on revolution range from strict non-violence, through violence under certain limited conditions, to justification of violent revolution as a Christian duty. Hence no one position represents *the* Christian view on violent revolution, even apart from considerations of a specifically Marxist revolution. On this last point it should be noted that in Nicaragua, the one country where revolutionary overthrow did occur in the late 1970s, the revolution was *not* Marxist inspired or led.

In Latin America, among those firmly committed to a radical transformation of society, Bishop Helder Camara stands as a symbol of non-violent resistance, while Camilo Torres died as a member of a guerrilla group. Bishop Camara based his non-violence stand on the beatitudes of Jesus.[20] Camilo Torres, a Colombian priest-sociologist, felt that only by revolution could the poor and oppressed of his country be freed. He joined a guerrilla group in the mountains of Colombia, where he was killed by government forces on February 15, 1966. He wrote explaining his decision: "I found that revolution is necessary in order to feed the hungry and give drink to the thirsty. . . . I believe that the revolutionary combat is a Christian and priestly combat. . . . It is the only way, in the concrete circumstances of our country, for us to love our neighbors as we should."[21]

Both Camara and Torres, however, are examples of personal decisions and callings rather than moral judgments on revolution as such. Bishop Camara also wrote: "I respect those who feel obliged in conscience to opt for violence, . . . those who have proved their sincerity by the sacrifice of their life. In my opinion, the memory of Camilo Torres and of Che Guevara merits as much respect as that of Martin Luther King. I accuse the real authors of violence."[22] As for Camilo Torres it is not clear whether he ever fought with the guerrillas or if he simply felt moved by conscience to be part of their movement. So we are left again with the question: "Can Christian participation in a revolution be justified?"

The principles of the "just war" theory may serve to give some focus to the issue, though attempts to apply the theory to modern nuclear warfare have brought it into disrepute and pacifists would again reject any justification of violence.[23] "Legitimate authority" and "just intentions or goals" are usually given as the first two principles of the theory. Legitimate authority in the case of war would mean that only duly constituted government officials can declare and conduct a war. A revolutionary movement, by its very nature, lacks recognized authority, but an effort can be made to discern whether it truly represents the aspirations of the majority of the populace and not those of an elitist group. Similarly, in reference to "just intentions or goals," leaders must be judged to be working for a more human society and not simply to gain power for self-seeking ends. Many critics of Marxist-Leninist movements would argue that while the masses do support revolutionary overthrow of the old they do not necessarily support the special Marxist "agenda" and ideology which leaders seek to impose after the revolution.

The revolution must also be a "last resort" when other non-violent means have been tried and are seen as offering no hope of success. Many in Latin America feel this point has been reached, that not even Christian-Democrat reform movements, which once offered some hope, have made any headway.

Obviously these criteria can never be proven to apply conclusively to a situation; one could always hold out for the possibility of other means succeeding. But they at least provide guidelines. The three other principles of the just war theory merit more detailed consideration: "just cause," "hope of success," and "the good to be achieved outweighs the bad that might result."

Is there "just cause" for revolution? Certainly if "taxation without representation" justified the American revolution, the poverty and oppression within many Third World countries would seem to justify revolution. On one point advocates of non-violence and of violence agree: violence already exists. Any revolutionary act would not be the initiation of violence but resistance to a systemic violence imposed by conditions of oppression and enforced by military and police in behalf of "national security." State authorities can speak more euphemistically of the need for "force" to maintain order, but it is violence to those who fall under it. A mining town in Peru is occupied by military forces when workers try to strike; the town's water and food supply is cut off to force an end to the strike. Peasants in El Salvador are shot for attempting to organize; priests are killed for assisting them. Arrest, imprisonment, and torture are meted out to those who try to organize peasants and workers in Brazil and Chile. Violence from above is a daily occurrence.

But it is not even this violence which most stirs revolutionary anger. It is the oppressiveness of economic systems which leave millions in dire poverty. As Bishop Camara stresses, in his *Spiral of Violence:* "It is common knowledge that poverty kills just as surely as the most bloody war." It leads to physical deformity, and to moral deformity when people must live without hope.[24] If a case can be made for violent revolution, the principle of just cause would be its strongest point.

Is there "hope of success"? For a time the Cuban revolution seemed to offer hope of successful socialist revolutions in other parts of Latin America. Today almost no strategy promises great hope. Revolutionary struggle did succeed in Nicaragua in 1979. But it did not trigger broad revolutionary hopes throughout Latin America. Revolutionary movements risk being decimated. Even efforts at piecemeal reform are often crushed also as subversive and Communist inspired. A non-violent movement would certainly win greater Christian support, but critics argue that a Gandhi or a Martin Luther King, Jr., would be swiftly eliminated by regimes insensitive to human dignity and the power of love.[25] These are mostly pragmatic considerations. Hope of success is a moral issue because violence in itself is an evil, and if its use does not lead to effective change it can hardly be condoned. Hence the moral outrage against terrorism. Hope of success must be based on a careful, concrete assessment of conditions in each situation.

Does "the good outweigh the bad?" Those who argue for non-violence make their strongest point in respect to this question. Whether the revolution be Marxist or otherwise the pacifist argues that violence can only beget more violence.[26] Those who use violence to attain revolution will use violence to retain their gains. Where violence becomes a strategy of social change bad effects will always outweigh the good. Those, on the other hand, who feel that revolution can be justified point to the example of Nicaragua where victorious forces ruled out vengeance and executions. One of the very goals of the revolution was to bring violence to an end.

There are great human costs both in allowing repressive conditions to continue and in attempting a revolutionary struggle to end them. But reduction and elimination of violence should itself be a goal.

From this last position the specific issue of Marxist revolution returns to focus. The most common fear expressed about a Marxist-Leninist revolution is that it may create a repressive rule in which any gains in social equality will be offset by loss of personal freedom. More on this important point will be taken up in the last section of this chapter. Defenders would snap back that only a privileged minority enjoy such freedom. Basic human needs for food, shelter, and jobs are denied the majority. This kind of debate clarifies very little. The tone of a movement and the attitude of its leaders may very well determine the degree of violence and repression a revolution might engender. A revolution led by people who stress, in anger, the destruction of the old system and the elimination of class enemies will most likely create a repressive regime. Those whose real and deep concern is for liberation of the poor and for a truly human society are more likely to be trusted in the reconstruction of a more just society. But the great risk of revolutionary movements is that the very process of radicalization produces an anger which can be very dehumanizing and create a spirit of revenge.

Jacques Ellul's treatment of violence has been criticized, with good reason, for caricaturing positions with which he disagrees and for giving too great a weight to human sinfulness and depravity. But his "Christian realism" does offer an important perspective for a Christian searching for a middle ground between facile justification of violence and complete non-violence. "Christian realism demands that a man understand exactly what he is doing, why he is doing it, and what the results of his doing [it] will be."[27] Violence can never be a good; it always remains contradictory to Christian life. Consequently, Ellul argues, a Christian "cannot participate in a movement that makes violence and men's anger a factor in its strategy nor can he credit an ideology that promises to establish a new order through violence."[28] Participation to end the suffering of others may lead a Christian to use violence, but it is used out of necessity, not as something God intends. Moreover, says Ellul, a Christian must "change camps" once the revolution is won. When the victors begin to oppress the former oppressors, the Christian must defend against this new oppression.[29]

None of these reflections really resolves the issue of violence, on which Christians themselves are divided. At best they can provide some guidelines for approaching the problem. The special problem with *Marxist* revolution concerns not so much the violence of revolutionary fighting, a violence common to all revolutions, but the aftermath of revolutionary victory. Critics fear that Marxist Party rulers will use the doctrine of "class struggle" to eliminate or repress large groups of former enemies, and that in the name of the "dictatorship of the proletariat" they will determine and then impose by force the socialist measures the masses are expected to follow. But one can also envision a socialism growing out of revolution in which socialist measures are proposed democratically, with general participation in decision-making, and with a minimum of force used to maintain order. The next two sections have an important bearing on this problem.

Class Struggle

For many Christians the Marxist doctrine of class struggle constitutes a major block to any acceptance of Marxism. Jesus taught love of enemies; class struggle makes enemies of an entire group. It would divide Christians against each other. With other Marxist doctrines, the question of whether they were essential to Marxism became crucial. Class struggle, however, quite clearly belongs to the very essence of Marxism. It cannot be explained away as not really from Marx or as no longer relevant. Christian advocates of Marxism, however, feel that class struggle is not incompatible with Christianity. They feel that the Church should accept it as a reality and opt to be with the poor in this struggle. Hence the best method of evaluating this issue may be to contrast traditional and radical Christian attitudes toward class struggle. The descriptions which follow are very generalized and oversimplified statements of the two positions, used simply to point out the issues involved.[30]

The traditional view: God intended different classes to work together in harmony. Every effort should be made to reconcile their hostilities toward each other. Christianity teaches us to "love your enemies and do good to those who hate you." To urge class struggle is to spur hatred and greater antagonism. The mission of the Church should be one of "reconciliation." It should opt for methods that will bring different classes and peoples together. Pope Leo XIII certainly espoused this view but it continues, in more nuanced forms, as the position of many theologians and Church hierarchy.

The radical pro-Marxist view: class struggle is a social fact. Marxism did not create class struggle. It simply recognizes it as a fact and attempts to overcome it. It is the capitalist system which generates antagonisms by creating a division between owners and workers. Reconciliation and love are desirable goals but they can never be achieved under a capitalist system which is built upon class divisons. Marxism does not create feelings of hostility; they are there already. It shows rather how divisions and antagonisms in society can be overcome. The Church cannot be neutral in the class struggle. It should opt to be on the side of the poor and the oppressed. Not to opt in their favor is to support the status quo.

Before considering some of the criticisms raised against both of these positions, a distinction should be made about the use of the term "class struggle." Class struggle can mean a social reality, the object of the Marxist method of analysis. Class struggle also means a strategy of social change, a means of overcoming class divisions. Failure to distinguish between these two meanings often obfuscates the issue. Use of this distinction, on the other hand, provides a base for evaluating the traditional and radical Christian positions. Some of the criticisms leveled at both positions have already been noted in other chapters, but they are brought together here in relation to the question of class struggle.

Class Struggle as a Social Reality and Object of Marxist Analysis

The traditional Christian view can be faulted for failing to recognize sufficiently that social problems have *structural* causes. The early social encyclicals assumed a natural, hierarchical order of social relations: rulers and subjects, rich and poor, owners and workers. Church teachings stressed the harmony of interests that should prevail within this order. From this perspective the Church viewed social problems as the failures of individuals to accept their respective responsibilities and duties within this order of things. The greed and avarice of owners, the impatience of workers, were cited as causes of conflict. Moral appeals were thus made for a return to the teachings of Christ and of the natural law.

This approach contains an important truth. Attitudes are important. No society can be truly human until personal responsibility for the common good and concern for others prevail. But structures engender attitudes, as studies of instutional racism have made clear.

While the Church has come to recognize that God did not intend class distinctions as part of the "natural order" of things, it continues to address "appeals" to the wealthy and powerful, appeals which suggest a lack of awareness of the structural causes of conflict. Ownership and control of means of production create conflict. Monopolization of economic power engenders a logic of its own; maximization of profits flows not from the greed of a few individuals but from the system itself. The very goals of a monopolistic capitalist *system* tend to negate the efficacy of appeals, even when directed to people of very good will.

Mutual appeals to both owners and workers, moreover, assume some equality of power. Trade unions may have created some semblance of balance in the United States, but the great majority of the poor in the world, including the marginal and unemployed in the United States, have no trade-off power at all. An appeal for "reconciliation" makes sense at an interpersonal level when two people of equal standing are involved. Christian radicals are correct, however, when they recognize at a societal level that insistence on reconciliation serves as an ideological support for the rich and powerful who dominate in their relations with workers and the poor.

The radical, pro-Marxist view, on the other hand, faces a different type of criticism. The recurring criticism of the radical Marxist analysis of class struggle usually fastens on one objection: Marxist analysis oversimplifies. It reduces a very complex set of class divisions to two antagonists, capitalists and workers. It reduces an even more complex set of causes for social conflict to one cause, class struggle. Marx's *solution* to the problem of class struggle has been especially criticized. He underestimated the drive for power in human nature and he consequently overestimated the capacity of a socialist economy to eliminate conflicts and to change human nature. But Marx's analysis of class conflict was not quite as simplistic as critics often make it appear. In the nineteenth century, class conflict *was* often quite patent. Strikes and efforts to unionize were met with police force, and class awareness was heightened by a long European tradition of social classification by estates Moreover Marx deliberately used a simplified "model" of analysis to which more concrete and complex divisions could be added. He focused on the two classes *most* significant for explaining social change at his point in history. Marx's own historical analyses of class struggles in France and Germany display a very nuanced awareness of divisions within classes, as Irving M. Zeitlin has shown in *Marxism: A Re-examination.*[31]

What of the use of Marxist class analysis today? Certainly there are many critical Marxists who clearly recognize the complexity of social classes and other social factors operative in advanced, technological societies (see Chapters 2, 4). But oversimplified uses of class analysis are certainly prevalent also. Marxism is not just a scientific method of analysis used by social scientists. It is also a revolutionary movement and an ideology. Greatly simplified conclusions can replace careful analysis and become the basis of programs of action. Oft-repeated formulas too often serve in place of nuanced critical analysis. While it is true that no social theory can ever take into account every complexity and that at some point theory must lead to concrete action, a program of action should be based on the best, most searching and self-critical analysis possible, freed from a priori convictions. And this has often not been the case with popularized Marxist analysis.

Class Struggle as a Strategy for Social Change

The Marxist analysis of class struggle leads naturally to a program based on this analysis. The capitalist system creates class conflicts; the conflicts can only be eliminated by changing the system itself. But to bring about this change workers must be conscious of themselves as a "class." They do this by becoming more aware of their common interests and concerns, but above all by recognition of their common enemy—the capitalist class. Marx felt that objective conditions of oppression would inevitably create this class consciousness. Lenin put more stress on Party leadership in "raising consciousness" of workers. In either case, Marxists view class struggle as a strategy to heighten workers' awareness of the capitalist class as an enemy to be overcome.

To encourage and even provoke conflict, to target on one group as a class enemy to be overthrown, such a strategy would seem contrary to the great Christian commandment of love. Certainly it is an emotional issue in many parts of the Christian world. But much of the emotion stems from the fact that the "mode" of class struggle is left undefined both by Marxists and their critics. It can signify anything from organizing unions to assassinations.

The traditional Christian view quite clearly opted for a "reconciliation and harmony" model of social change over a "conflict and class struggle" one. Certainly reconciliation and harmony are to be preferred *if* they can be effective. But Jesus d d not eschew conflict when he attacked the hypocrisy of the Pharisees, and the Church has itself used conflict-provoking tactics as a method, in fact if not in theory. It has attacked many forces in the world as "enemies," including Communism itself. Church efforts to end racial discrimination and Church efforts to oppose abortion have generated sharp conflict. The Church has, moreover, involved itself in class struggles. Too often in the past its efforts to "keep the peace" meant pacifying the poor. But Church leaders have shown willingness also to opt for the poor in their struggles. When bishops in Brazil or El Salvador defend the rights of peasants to organize, when priests and bishops in Peru defend workers in their right to strike, when the U.S. bishops in Appalachia, in a 1975 pastoral letter, attacked mining corporations for their policies, and when Church groups gave support to the United Farm workers, the Church took sides in class struggle.

Why, then, does the call by radical Christians for the Church to opt for the poor in their class struggle evoke such strong negative reactions? Some reactions can be written off as a defense of the status quo. But the expression and practice of class struggle create real and serious problems. If class struggle includes morally acceptable tactics, it has also been used to justify atrocities. Stalin's elimination of the "kulak" class in Russia and Chinese Communism's mass executions of rich peasants stand as examples. Quite clearly no Christian means to advocate this. But class struggle, left unqualified, is a blank check which no Christian should be expected to sign.

The traditional objection to a strategy of class struggle is that it "stirs up hatred." The radical response sometimes given is that the hatred and hostility are already there. As they stand neither position gives the whole picture. Stirring up conflict against a common enemy can be done without hatred and as a morally acceptable tactic. Saul Alinsky used conflict tactics, "deliberately rubbing wounds," to arouse urban communities in the United States to action. But he won Church support once it was shown that he did not incite people to act beyond what they recognized as legitimate means. No Christian, on the other hand, should be expected to endorse the sentiments of Che Guevara when he upheld "hatred as a factor in struggle; intransigent hatred for the enemy, which impels one to exceed the natural limitations of the human being and transforms him into an effective, violent, selective and cold killing machine."[32]

One may certainly object that Christian advocates of Marxism certainly do not approve all possible tactics of class struggle without qualification. Nor does Che Guevara speak for all Marxists any more than Pinochet in Chile speaks for all Christians. But the failure at times to express qualifications and to distinguish morally acceptable from unacceptable forms of struggle underlies some of the tension created by the issue. Lenin's comment that "morality is subordinated to the interests of the proletariat's class struggle" may give an unfair picture even of Marxist-Leninist views on morality.[33] But for Christians moral considerations must be expressly normative. Revolution is not an end in itself. Even Camilo Torres' decision to join in revolutionary combat had love and justice as normative values: "It is the only way . . . for us to love our neighbors as we should." Morality is not subordinate to class struggle. Where the need to struggle is posed there must also be a demand that the struggle be human. Thus René Coste writes: "A Christian practice of class struggle will not be Christian unless it recognizes the primacy of love and, to that extent, it will not be Marxist."[34] (Here, too, one might certainly question the assumption that Marxists never act out of love.)

If this book were written in Europe or Latin America where class awareness is much more heightened, a much more detailed consideration of class struggle would be called for, and in Latin America of revolutionary violence as well. In the United States class struggle remains a relatively unused concept and revolutionary violence only a remote possibility. For most U.S. Americans the questions and difficulties most often raised in respect to Marxist socialism are those which will be considered in the following pages.

Democracy or Dictatorship?

In the United States at least, the strongest objection to Marxism is that it would bring the loss of political freedoms which Americans cherish. "Capitalism unquestionably has its faults, but Marxist socialism would be far worse. Communism is totalitarian and destructive of human freedom." This criticism needs to be addressed. At times it is extended to all socialism which is seen as bureaucratic government control over society. But this latter objection will be considered in the next chapter; this final section will deal only with the Marxist tradition.

Dominant Marxism: "A Totalitarian Temptation"?

Some readers may feel that too little criticism has been made of Marxism as it has worked out in practice in Communist nations. "By its fruits you shall know it" and Communism hardly fulfills the lofty norms of an ideal society by which it judges capitalism. Some Marxists, on the other hand, may feel that the book contains too much criticism already, given the heavy anti-Communist bias already existing in the United States. Admittedly an effort has been made to distinguish Marxism in theory from Communism in practice because of the all too prevalent dichotomy: "choose Communism or capitalism, the Soviet Union or the United States." But the criticism of Marxism as actualized in Communism does need to be faced, especially the charges of those who see Marxism leading "inevitably" to loss of political freedom.

Jean-Francois Revel's *The Totalitarian Temptation* provides a fairly recent example of such criticism. His quarrel is with movements and nations which have attempted to achieve socialism based on Marxist-Leninist-Maoist models. He accepts the values of socialism and sees the world evolving toward socialism in one form or another. But he believes that true socialism must be democratic and that the main obstacle to true socialism is not capitalism but Communism.[35]

First of all, Revel challenges Leftist hopes that Communism will evolve toward democratic pluralism. He sees no evidence that this will ever happen.

> The distinctive characteristic of communism, its very reason for being, is to eliminate the possiblity of any challenge to its rule, thus to deny to the people, and indeed to the ruling minority itself, any opportunity to change their minds, once the regime is in power.[36]

In a democratic, pluralistic system rulers pay for their mistakes by being voted out of office. In the Communist system the people pay for mistakes with a tightened grip of the government over them.

Second, Revel believes that all Communist states are Stalinist. If special historical conditions are used to explain away Stalin's rise to power, they fail to explain the pervasiveness of Stalinism wherever Communism exists. Stalinism results not from special historical conditions but from the logic of believing in an abstract model of society whose truth is accepted as proven once for all, and which is then imposed and used to justify the ruling power.[37] Revel thinks that an "unofficial Stalinism" often prevails in Third World countries because they view as a lesser evil any movement which will destroy the prevailing old system.[38]

Third, Revel attacks Leftists in developed countries for excessive criticisms of capitalism based on comparisons of capitalism to an "ideal" socialism rather than to actual Communist systems. Unemployment is criticized in capitalist countries, but not the artificial full employment of Communist countries where productivity has dropped as low as one-sixth of that in capitalist ones. Wage levels also are considerably lower in Communist countries.[39]

Fourth, Revel contrasts the power groups in democratic and communist countries. The free state, he notes, was born out of the idea of the separation of mutually restricting powers—the executive, legislative, and judiciary. The economic power of the business firm, union power, media power, military power, and technological power have multiplied these divisions and freed society from guardianship of the state. The totalitarian state, when it fails to satisfy the needs of the society it rules, must constantly reinforce its hold over all these powers.[40] True socialism, Revel concludes, can only come about by outgrowing, not destroying, capitalist civilization and by preserving its two most positive features, its capacity to produce and its political, individual and cultural freedoms.[41]

Communism: A Different Form of Democracy?

Two possible Marxist responses might be given to the criticisms raised by Revel and many others. The first would be to defend the achievements of existing Communist nations. The second would be to recognize the validity of the criticisms and to explore the possibility of Marxism leading to a more democratic socialism. The first approach will be noted in this part, and the second in the concluding part of this chapter.

To write off Communist nations simply as failures or as providing neither freedom nor justice—as Revel charges—can hardly be warranted. They have achieved both economic freedom from insecurity and justice goals, including democratic participation at the level of work especially. Critics often judge Communist economies by standards of the United States or Western Europe. But Communism should be judged by its own starting points in industrially backward countries. Khrushchev's boast that the Soviet Union would surpass American industrial output by the 1970s was not realized; the gap has widened in recent years. But the Soviet Union has grown into a major industrial power, and for a twenty-one year period (1950–71) its total output of goods and services increased 213 percent compared with only 108 percent in the United States.[42] If significant wage differentials still exist, the Soviet Union has achieved a significant degree of economic equality by eliminating wealth gained simply through investment.[43] It has also guaranteed medical care for all and security for its older citizens.

By U.S. standards the People's Republic of China is still a very poor country. But judged by its own situation prior to 1950 or judged by conditions in many other poor countries, its successes have been striking. Almost all foreign observers who have been to China in recent years agree that the average Chinese citizen lives substantially better than at any time before the Communists came to power.[44] Basic human needs have been met. The people are better fed, better educated, better cared for medically. Many observers of Cuba would make the same argument, at least for the poorer half of society. For many millions of desperately poor people in the world the achievement of such freedom from want must certainly outweigh concerns about freedom of the press or the right to vote. The most basic democratic freedom, some would argue, is the right and opportunity to be able to meet basic human needs.

The truly classless society may still be a distant vision in Communist countries, but Mao Tse-tung proved remarkably successful in inculcating a sense of equality among the Chinese people.[45] *Time* magazine may write it off as a "dank, Orwellian passion for proletarian ideology,"[46] and controlled thought-reform did indeed account for some of the results, but Mao succeeded in gaining mass support and mass participation in building up a new China. Economist John Gurley, some years ago, raised an interesting and important issue about Mao's approach to the economy in contrast to the underlying assumptions of capitalism.[47] Capitalism, Gurley noted, uses the best. It looks for the most skilled workers available, the most ideal locations, the best managerial expertise. Efficiency results, but so does an ever-widening gap between the gifted and the disadvantaged. Mao, on the other hand, quite deliberately built "on the worst." He gave top priority to raising the level of the populace as a whole. By developing the skills of the poorest, all would advance together. Human development was given priority over efficiency. But in the long run Mao believed that productivity would also be greater. Many capitalist critics are cynical about any incentive system other than individual material gains. But economists evaluating Mao's efforts believe he was able to stimulate productivity through social incentives.[48] China's new "modernizations," on the other hand, may confirm critics in their "realistic" pragmatism concerning incentives.

One may still object that whatever economic achievements have been gained, they have come at the cost of political freedom. The Communist Party has sole and uncontested power. But there does exist in Communist countries a form of democratic participation lacking in capitalist countries where ordinary workers rarely get elected to any office and have little say about the productive process. Factory workers and peasants do get elected, in Communist countries, to legislative offices at local and national levels. In China, if pressure to maintain the "correct" line of thought and action comes from the top down, popular participation in policy formulation and implementation is also strongly promoted. A good deal of self-determination is permitted for production teams and discussion of policy decisions at the commune level. The motivational factor of self-reliance of smaller groups appears to have played a very significant role in the Chinese economy.

Most U.S. Americans and Western Europeans may look at these achievements and still feel that the losses in democratic freedoms are far too high a price to pay. But to many peoples of the Third World, who most often have little by way of democratic freedoms and even less for the fulfillment of basic needs, the achievements of China or Cuba can appear as great hopes. These hopes could be a "totalitarian temptation" and bring suffering rather than a hoped-for liberation. But if comparisons are to be made on the basis of actual practice and not just theory, it is capitalism and not Communism which lacks models for underdeveloped countries to follow. Taiwan and a few small countries may prove an exception; but the United States has shown little indication of wanting to support the Third World to the extent that it has Taiwan.

When one looks to the United States and Western Europe, however, the problem of freedom and democracy returns in force. Severe economic crises and collapses could conceivably turn their peoples away from concerns about democracy to sheer worry about survival. In the present, however, any system that would seem to portend a loss of democratic freedoms stands little chance of winning popular support. So the questions return. Can Marxism be the basis for a democratic socialism? Are Marxism and democratic freedom compatible?

A True Marxism: From Dictatorship of the Proletariat to Democracy?

Just as the humanism of the young Marx could be used politically to criticize existing Communist regimes, so too have efforts to prove Marx "democratic" been called upon to justify Eurocommunism and democratic-socialist movements. But while some blame Stalin, Lenin, or "objective conditions" for Communist failures regarding democracy, other critics of Marxism find the roots of totalitarianism in Marx's own thought. J. L. Talmon links Marx to a "totalitarian-democratic" tradition growing out of Rousseau, Robespierre, and French socialists.[49] Whereas liberal democratic thought builds on a politics of trial-and-error and the absence of coercion, totalitarian democracy rests on the assumption of a sole and exclusive truth. Talmon places Marx in the latter category because of his conviction that only proletarian socialism holds the truth. Karl Popper attacked Marx on similar grounds. Leszek Kolakowski traces the "Marxist roots of Stalinism" to Marx's insistence that human liberation demands social unity, a unity which Kolakowski contends can only be achieved by suppressing conflicts and dissent.[50]

Richard Hunt and Hal Draper have both written books to defend Marx as democratic.[51] Hunt finds both Marx and Engels consistently democratic. Even in their most revolutionary years they always envisioned "a kind of participatory democracy organized without any professional leaders or administrators at all."[52] Both Marx and Engels frequently stressed universal suffrage as essential to the goals of the proletariat.[53] Hunt also clarifies their criticisms of "bourgeois democracy." Bourgeois democracy in the mid-nineteenth century did *not* mean universal suffrage; often only the bourgeoisie and landowners could vote even where constitutional governments had been established. In France barely 3 percent of the adult male population met property qualifications for voting.[54]

Hunt likewise argues that Marx and Engels never embraced the idea of a "vanguard" party which would lead the revolution or organize a seizure of power. Nor did they ever advocate a "minority revolution." Marx sharply criticized Weitling, Willich, and Blanquists who called for immediate attempts to seize power without the assurance of mass support.[55] Far from defining a Communist Party as the leading force in the revolutionary struggle, Marx spent very few years within any party structure. The organizations which Marx and Engels did direct were, moreover, characterized by internal democracy.[56]

Hal Draper approaches the issue differently but makes a similar case for Marx's commitment to democracy. Earlier socialists did propose a socialism imposed from above. "Marx," says Draper, "was the first socialist figure to come to an acceptance of the socialist idea *through* the battle for the consistent extension of democratic control from above.'[57] Marx consistently defined socialism in democratic terms and democracy in socialist terms.[58]

But what of Marx's advocacy of a "dictatorship of the proletariat"? Hunt makes a very thorough investigation of Marx's use of this controversial expression, drawing upon an earlier study by Draper.[59] What we often take to be Marx's doctrine is the statement made by Lenin in *State and Revolution*. Lenin wrote:

> The proletariat needs state power, the centralized organization of force, the organization of violence, both for the purpose of *crushing* the resistance of the exploiters and for the purpose of *guiding* the great mass of the population—the peasantry, the petty-bourgeoisie, the semi-proletarians—in the work of organizing Socialist economy.
>
> By educating a workers' party, Marxism educates the vanguard of the proletariat, capable of assuming power and of *leading the whole people* to Socialism, of directing and organizing the new order, of being the teacher, guide, and leader of all the toiling and exploited in the task of building up their social life without the bourgeoisie and against the bourgeoisie.[60]

Was this Marx's conception of the dictatorship of the proletariat? Did he stress the need for "crushing" the bourgeoisie? More importantly did he conceive of it as a series of "tutorial" relationships: the masses led by the proletariat, and the proletariat in turn educated by a workers' party, by a vanguard which directs and organizes the new order? Hunt clearly thinks not.

Hunt draws up several arguments to show that Marx did not define dictatorship of the proletariat in the strong sense given the term by Lenin.

Hunt first notes that the term "dictatorship" historically meant a provisional government in time of emergency, and not a rule over the masses or denial of rights to opponents.[61] Hunt then stresses that among the millions of words written by Marx and Engels the term "dictatorship" is linked to rule of the proletariat in only eleven places. And these uses fell within three distinct periods: 1850–52, 1871–75, 1890–93. In the first period noted, Marx and Engels sought to establish a united front with Blanquists who viewed revolution as the work of a professional elite. Dictatorship of the proletariat became a *compromise* formulation with the last three words added by Marx and Engels to stress that rule must be by the workers as a whole.[62]

For nearly two decades after this initial use Marx and Engels never employed the term. They did so again after the Paris Commune (1871), again with a view to an alliance with the Blanquists. But the alliance was short-lived because the Blanquists would not recognize rule by the entire revolutionary class.[63] Moreover when Engels pointed to the Paris Commune as an example of what the dictatorship of the proletariat would look like, it was precisely the Commune's efforts to introduce universal suffrage and to create a popular democracy that had won Marx's praise.[64]

In only *one* locus does Marx suggest a specifically repressive mission for the dictatorship, and even this was conjoined to a defense of peaceful tactics.[65] It is this one reference to crushing the resistance of the bourgeoisie which Lenin used to define the repressive function of the dictatorship of the proletariat. Nowhere does Marx define the dictatorship as "guiding" the masses or speak of a vanguard party as "leading" them to socialism.

In notebooks on Bakunin, written by Marx in 1874–75, Marx defended his position that socialism would be democratic. When Bakunin asked if all forty million Germans would be members of the government, Marx answered: "Certainly, for the thing begins with the self-government of the communities." All of Bakunin's objections dealt with the possibility of one group dominating over others. All of Marx's responses were to deny this, and he explicitly rejected the idea that "learned socialists" would be used to educate or rule over the masses.[66]

Engels referred once more to the dictatorship of the proletariat in his critique of the Erfurt program (1891). He argued that a new society might grow peacefully out of the old in democratic countries like the United States, France, and Britain "where you can do whatever you want constitutionally as soon as you have the majority of the people behind you." In Germany, a democratic republic must be demanded: "If one thing is certain, it is that our party and the working class can only come to power under the form of a democratic republic. That is, indeed, the specific form of the dictatorship of the proletariat. . . ."[67] Political power, he added, must be concentrated in the hands of the popular representative body.

One could, then, find justification for a democratic socialism in the writings of Marx and Engels. The most serious criticism one could make of Marx is not that his social sm demanded totalitarian rule but that he failed to recognize, or at least to deal with, the problem of *political* power which would arise after a revolution.

More important than what Marx held—and this holds true for all the issues discussed in the last two chapters—is what Marxists today will say or do in respect to democracy. The Marxist-Leninist tradition has held the dictatorship of the proletariat to be an essential doctrine. One-party rule has characterized Communist nations, though they proclaim themselves democratic republics. But the issue of democracy has become a critical one even for Marxist-Leninists. Allende chose to win power in Chile through popular election. The Eurocommunist Parties have committed themselves to "the democratic road to socialism" as their one and only strategy. The term "dictatorship of the proletariat" has been dropped. They have insisted they will respect all democratic freedoms and pluralism of political parties, and will step down if voted out of office (see Chapter 2). Many critics of Marxism-Leninism remain suspicious of this new stance; many militant Marxists, on the other hand, see it as a retrogression to the old reformist strategy of the Social-Democrats; many socialists who consider themselves Marxists have long insisted on democracy.

The Eurocommunist Parties, if similar in their program, cannot simply be judged as the same. The Spanish Communist Party retained a Stalinist stance until the 1970s but has now become the most outspoken proponent of Eurocommunism. The Italian Communist Party has a history into which Eurocommunism fits more naturally. Gramsci insisted on the achievement of hegemony before a revolution could be successful; Togliatti followed his strategy with a more gradualist approach than Gramsci would have liked. The French Communist Party, though it dropped "dictatorship of the proletariat" in 1976 and committed itself to respect for democratic institutions, nevertheless arouses the most uncertainty. Etienne Balibar's *On the Dictatorship of the Proletariat* (1977) does not help to allay suspicions. Balibar is a leading Party theoretician and a former pupil of Althusser. He has questioned whether a Party congress *can* drop the expression "dictatorship of the proletariat." He insists that he is not affirming the idea of a repressive dictatorship; he maintains that the dictatorship of the proletariat does not refer to a "form" of government at all. Hence the dilemma "democratic rule or the Soviet model of single-Party domination won through violence" is a false one.[68] Balibar makes a strong effort to distinguish Lenin's views from Stalin's. But the conclusion he draws is still that one class must be the ruling class; hence there can only be either dictatorship of the bourgeoisie or dictatorship of the proletariat.[69] If the dictatorship of the proletariat is not a political form, Balibar gives little indication what political form it might take, nor does he discuss the issues of political liberties, party pluralism or other institutions associated with bourgeois democracy. His inclusion of Lenin's quote that dictatorship expresses "a relentless life-and-death struggle between two classes, two worlds, two historical epochs"[70] will hardly reassure those who question whether the French Communist Party would peacefully step down if voted out of office.

There is, on the other hand, an ever increasing number of Marxists in many parts of the world who would agree with Fernando Claudin that there can be no true socialism without democracy. Claudin was once a leading figure in the Spanish Communist Party. He recognizes that Party denunciations of political democracy and political freedoms, as being only bourgeois concerns, now make it difficult for the Party to identify itself as democratic.[71] Claudin rejects one-party rule and the claim of any party to be *the* representative of the working class. Not only must democratic structures developed under bourgeois capitalism be retained, but additional forms of democracy must be developed from the grass roots up.[72]

Studies, like those of Hunt and Draper, which try to prove Marx's concern for democracy, and affirmations, like those of Claudin, that socialism must be democratic if it is to be true to its purpose, do not thereby make Marxism democratic. The dominant Marxist tradition has not greatly respected democratic structures or concerns. The conviction that one Party "knows" what is best does create totalitarian tendencies, especially when an entirely new economic system must be initiated and sustained. But Communist practices in the past do not "prove" that Marxist socialism cannot be democratic. A practical decision about the attitudes of Marxist leaders and movements in regard to democracy, and an estimation of their flexibility and openness to different views, may be more important than "what Marxism teaches." More important still may be the extent to which real "hegemony" has been achieved (see Chapter 2 on Gramsci). To the extent that mass popular support for socialism already exists and socialist experiments have been tested, the need to impose or enforce socialism will diminish. To the extent that multiple democratic structures exist which enable masses of people to express their views and to exercise their power, the possibility of one Party's leaders being *able* to impose their rule will diminish. The issue whether socialism is desirable enough and feasible enough to achieve such support and hegemony, even in the United States, needs finally to be considered.

Notes

1. A lecture by Peruvian priest Ricardo Antoncich, S.J., on the Catholic Church and private property, proved helpful in studying this issue. A similar study by Ignacio Ellacuría, S.J., of El Salvador, "The Historicization of the Concept of Property as a Principle of De-ideologization," in *Estudios Centroamericanos*. September–October 1976, was also useful.

2. Biblical quotes in this section are from *The Jerusalem Bible*. Numerous other biblical denunciations of injustice toward the poor might be cited (e.g., Isa. 32:5–8, 58:6–7; Ezek. 18:10–13 22:29–31; Amos 2:6–7, 5 10–12; 8:4–10). Nancy Sylvester, IHM, "Church Perspective: How Private is Ownership?" in *Network Quarterly*, Vol. 6, No. 1, Winter 1978, includes numerous references to biblical sources and citations from early Church Fathers.

3. See Richard J. Cassidy on Jesus' stance regarding riches and the rich, in *Jesus, Politics and Society, A Study of Luke's Gospel* (Maryknoll. N.Y.: Orbis, 1978), pp. 25ff.

4. On the Church Fathers see Richard Schlatter. *Private Property: The History of an Idea* (New Brunswick, N.J.: Rutgers University Press, 1951), Chapter 3 and especially pp. 36–39. See also Frank Grace, *The Concept of Property in Modern Christian Thought* (Urbana, Ill.: University of Illinois, 1953), Chapter 2.

5. Schlatter, *Private Property*, p. 36.

6. Martin Hengel, *Property and Riches in the Early Church* (Philadelphia: Fortress, 1974), pp. 2–4 on St. Basil and St. Ambrose. Reference to St. Jerome (Carta 120) from Sylvester, in *Network Quarterly*.

7. *Schlatter, Private Property*, p. 39.

8. Ibid., pp. 42–46.

9. St. Thomas Aquinas, *Summa Theologica*, trans. Fathers of the English Dominican Province (London: Burns, Oates & Washbourne, 1927), I-II, Q. 94, art. 5, response to objection 3 Making the same distinction between "natural' considered absolutely and considered as an addition, Thomas argues that considered absolutely there is no reason a particular piece of land should belong to any one person; but considering its use and cultivation, it is commensurate that it belong to one person, II-II, Q. 57, art. 3. It should also be noted that Aquinas places responsibility on lawmakers for distributing and regulating private property for the common good, I-II, Q. 105, art. 2.

10. Ibid., II-II, Q. 66, art. 2.

11. Ibid., II-II, Q. 66, art. 7.

12. Schlatter, *Private Property*, p. 90.

13. Ibid., p. 125. To skim so quickly over four centuries does an obvious injustice to Protestant thought. A more adequate treatment can be found in Schlatter, *Private Property*, Chapters 5–6, and in Grace, *The Concept of Property in Modern Christian Thought*, Chapters 2 and 5.

14. See Grace, *The Concept of Property*, p. 139.

15. The text of the Commission document can be found in *Church Alert,* The Sodepax Newsletter, No. 18, January–March, 1978, pp. 14–17.

16. Ibid., p. 17.

17. Stuart Schram, *Mao Tse-Tung* (Baltimore: Penguin Books, 1966), claims that by official Chinese count in 1951 some 135,000 enemies of the revolution had been executed. Hostile estimates of the number range as high as 10–15 million. Schram himself estimates some 1–3 million were executed, p. 267.

18. John M. Swomley, *Liberation Ethics* (New York: Macmillan, 1972), citing a study by Paul Sweezy and Leo Huberman, estimates 20,000 killed under Batista and 700 executed after Castro took power, pp. 108–9.

19. *Lenin on Politics and Revolution,* pp. 186, 195.

20. Helder Camara, *The Church and Colonialism, The Betrayal of the Third World,* trans. William McSweeney (Denville, N.J.: Dimension Books, 1969), pp. 109–10.

21. Camilo Torres is cited in François Houtart and Andre Rousseau, *The Church and Revolution,* trans. Violet Nevile (Maryknoll, N.Y.: Orbis, 1971), p. 200.

22. Camara, *The Church and Colonialism,* p. 109.

23. J. G. Davies, *Christians, Politics and Violent Revolution* (Maryknoll, N.Y.: Orbis, 1976), pp. 168ff., uses the just war theory to discuss the issue of violence. His book provides a Protestant perspective on all the very complicated issues discussed in this section, and his bibliography gives some indication of how much has been written on the questions of violence and revolution. See also René Coste et al., *Guerre revolutionnaire et conscience chrétienne* (Paris: Pax Christi, 1964).

24. Helder Camara, *Spiral of Violence,* trans. Della Couling (Denville, N.J.: Dimension Books, 1971), pp. 25–26.

25. See Swomley, *Liberation Ethics,* on the principle of "hope of success," pp. 129–34. Swomley analyzes the reasons for Castro's success in Cuba in contrast to failures of revolutionary efforts in Bolivia, Argentina, and Peru.

26. I have not taken up the biblical argument for non-violence in Jesus' own behavior and his injunction to "turn the other cheek," because I do not believe these can be made into a social ethics. Taken literally, "turn the other cheek" would also rule out legal prosecution of criminals. On the other hand, the consequences of using violence, no matter how just the cause, should trouble the Christian conscience.

27. Jacques Ellul, *Violence, Reflections from a Christian Perspective,* trans. Cecelia Gaul Kings (New York: Seabury, 1969), p. 82.

28. Ibid., p. 134.

29. Ibid., pp. 138–39.

30. For a more detailed study of Christian views on class struggle see René Coste, *Les Chrétiens et la lutte des classes* (Paris: Editions S.O.S., 1975) and his *Analyse marxiste et foi chrétienne* (Paris: Ouvrieres, 1976). See also Miguez Bonino, *Christians and Marxists,* pp. 92ff. and 131ff. A lecture by Ricardo Antoncich was also used in drawing up this section.

31. Irving M. Zeitlin, *Marxism: A Re-examination* (New York: Van Nostrand Reinhold, 1967).

32. Cited by Davies, *Christians, Politics and Violent Revolution,* p. 175.

33. Lenin, *Selected Works in Three Volumes,* Volume III, p. 468.

34. Coste, *Analyse marxiste,* p. 211. His Chapter 5 is devoted to the issue of class struggle.

35. Jean-Francois Revel, *The Totalitarian Temptation,* trans. David Hapgood (Gar-

den City, N.Y.: Doubleday, 1977), p. 15.

36. Ibid., p. 27.

37. Ibid., pp. 41–53.

38. Ibid., p. 103.

39. Ibid., On unemployment, p. 167, on average wages, p. 195. In 1975, says Revel, the average wage in Hungary was $90 a month or one-third of the minimum wage in France and far below the U.S. poverty line.

40. Ibid., pp. 252–55.

41. Ibid., p. 285.

42. See "Can Russia Surpass America?" *U.S. News & World Report*, May 15, 1972, pp. 29–33.

43. See Alec Nove, *The Soviet Economy* (New York: Praeger, 1969, 2nd edition), pp. 27–28.

44. Barry Richman, *Industrial Society in Communist China* (New York: Random House, 1969), p. 913, concluded that few poor countries in the world have been as successful as China and that its citizens were substantially better off than they had been at any time prior to 1950. John K. Galbraith, *A China Passage* (New York: Signet, 1973), p. 104, concluded from his visit that China had devised a highly effective economic system. *Report From Red China*, ed. Frank Ching (New York: Avon, 1972), contains dozens of accounts praising the achievements of the People's Republic of China. *Time* magazine (January 1, 1979), pp. 32–33, took a dimmer view of China, commenting on the "seediness and poverty" of its city streets. But even *Time* correspondent Richard Bernstein admitted that there is strong evidence that the Chinese have an adequate diet, that most enjoy basic good helath and are adequately clothed.

45. On the striking sense of equality observed by at least one correspondent, see Seymour Topping, "Canton: A Society Transformed," in *Report From Red China*, p. 141 especially. On the challenge of Mao's efforts to Christianity see *The New China: A Catholic Response*, ed. Michael Chu, S.J. (New York: Paulist Press, 1977).

46. *Time* magazine, January 1, 1979, p. 16.

47. John W. Gurley, "The New Man in the New China," in *Center Magazine*, III, 3 (May–June 1970). See also Jack Gray, "The Economics of Maoism," in *China After the Cultural Revolution* (New York: Random House, 1970).

48. Richman, *Industrial Society in Communist China*, raises doubts about the ultimate effectiveness of incentives that neglect personal gain, but concludes that nonmaterial incentives have been highly effective in China, p. 817. On this point see also E. L. Wheelwright and Bruce McFarlane, *The Chinese Road to Socialism* (New York: Modern Reader, 1971), Chapter 8.

49. J. L. Talmon, *The Origins of Totalitarian Democracy* (New York: Praeger, 1960) and *Political Messianism: The Romantic Phase* (New York: Praeger, 1960).

50. Leszek Kolakowski, "Marxist Roots of Stalinism," in *Stalinism*, ed. Robert C. Tucker (New York: W. W. Norton, 1977). Karl Popper, *The Open Society and Its Enemies*, Volume II (Princeton, N.J.: Princeton University Press, 1971 edition).

51. Richard N. Hunt, *The Political Ideas of Marx and Engels, I: Marxism and Totalitarian Democracy, 1818–1850* (Pittsburgh: University of Pittsburgh, 1974). In Chapter 1 Hunt discusses Talmon's thesis. Hal Draper, *Karl Marx's Theory of Revolution, I: State and Bureaucracy* (New York: Monthly Review, 1977).

52. Hunt, *The Political Ideas of Marx and Engels*, I, p. xiii.

53. Ibid., pp. 217, 229, but also pp. 79–85 and passim.

54. Ibid., p. 134.

55. Ibid: Marx's criticisms of Weitling, pp. 156, 198, of Willich, p. 241, and of the Blanquists, pp. 251ff. Also for Marx's views on terrorism see pp. 198ff.

56. Ibid., Chapter 8.

57. Draper, *Karl Marx's Theory of Revolution*, I, p. 59. Draper projects three works on Marx, but even Part I is divided into two volumes. The first deals with Marx on democracy; the second deals with Marx's analysis of Bonapartist and Bismarckian states. In the second part Draper argues that "bourgeois rule" does not necessarily mean *direct* rule by bourgeois class members.

58. Ibid., p. 283.

59. Hal Draper, "The Dictatorship of the Proletariat," in *Marxism*, ed. Michael Curtis (New York: Atherton Press, 1970), pp. 285–96.

60. Hunt, *The Political Ideas of Marx and Engels*, I. pp. 341–42. Words underlined are my own emphasis. This quote can be seen in its context in *Lenin on Politics and Revolution, Selected Works*, p. 198. The words "crushing" and "suppression," it might be added, occur frequently in *State and Revolution*.

61. Hunt, *Political Ideas*, pp. 296–97

62. Ibid, p. 298

63. Ibid. pp. 307–11.

64. Ibid., p. 332. See Marx's views on the Paris Commune in Tucker, *Marx-Engels Reader*, 2nd ed., pp. 629–34.

65. Ibid., p. 315, cited from Marx's *Anarchism and Anarcho-Syndicalism*.

66. Ibid., pp. 319–28. Quote, p. 324. These notebooks on Bakunin came to light only in recent years.

67. Cited by Hunt, *Political Ideas*, p. 333.

68. Etienne Balibar, *On the Dictatorship of the Proletariat*, trans. Grahame Lock (London: NLB, 1977), p. 40.

69. Ibid., pp. 59–60.

70. Ibid., p. 146.

71. Fernando Claudin, *Eurocommunism and Socialism*, p. 97 and p. 77.

72. Ibid., pp. 124–29.

Chapter 9

Personal Reflections:
Marxism, Socialism, the United States

This final chapter will focus especially on the United States and on socialism. As items of public interest and debate in the United States neither Marxism nor socialism rates highly. Why this is so and whether it should be so needs to be discussed. The book as a whole undoubtedly reflects much of my own personal framework, in the questions asked, in points stressed, and in values that were normative in making assessments. But this chapter includes "personal reflections" as part of its title because it could otherwise read like a proposed strategy of social change for the United States. Any proposal of a strategy would have to be backed up with a much more in-depth study of social and political conditions in the United States and with long experience of full-time commitment to social and political action. These reflections may prove helpful, on the other hand, for individuals. Many U.S. Christians, I suspect, wrestle with the same feelings I find in myself troubled about massive poverty in the world and a vast number of social problems in this country; feeling guilty about living in relative affluence and about lack of greater political involvement, yet already pressed down by work and unsure where best to expend energy; convinced that significant and perhaps very radical social change is needed, but cautious when radical solutions are proposed. This chapter addresses this problem while making some final assessments about both Marxism and socialism. Before beginning with a discussion of the United States, however, some concluding reflections are called for regarding the whole issue of Marxism-Christianity.

A Concluding Reflection on Marxism-Christianity

The book attempted to offer a reappraisal of Marxism and Christianity. Those hoping to find black-and-white, yes-and-no answers in the book did not find them. Many assessments in the book ended with an "it depends." But the very nature of most controversial questions requires such an answer. The principal question of the book, "Are Marxism and Christianity compatible?", depends on the definition one gives to Marxism and what one holds as essential to Marxism. The dominant "classical" Marxism, with its atheistic worldview, is incompatible with Christianity and presents itself as such. Marxism viewed as a self-critical method of analysis is not incompatible. When tactics and strategies of social change are added on, Marxism may or may not prove incompatible. Socialist ideals of cooperation and sharing are certainly compatible with Christianity.

A major purpose of the book was to show that there are different interpretations of Marxism and hence different types of Marxists. Certainly we acknowledge the same of Christianity and Christians. Any book which claimed to explain what "Christians hold" or even "what Catholics hold" would demand frequent distinctions. Contemporary Roman Catholics disagree strongly at times with official teachings of the Church, for example on birth control, and they disagree with each other. Similarly, then, it is not possible to make unequivocal and universal judgments about Marxism and Marxists in general. This works two ways. One cannot judge all Marxism by classical Marxism; but neither can one assume a critical and open Marxism since classical Marxism clearly remains the dominant tradition.

Two very different kinds of appraisals were made in the course of the book. The first dealt with theory and past history. Some definite, if disputable, conclusions were reached. I argued, for example, that while Marx was personally an atheist, his atheism came prior to his advocacy of socialism and is not intrinsically connected with it. I argued also that Lenin's militant atheism played a far greater role in shaping Communist idology and practice. But these conclusions do not determine what individual Marxists or Marxist parties hold, and what they hold today is decisive in determining Marxist-Christian relations. The second kind of assessment made in the book dealt with specific movements, such as Christians for Socialism and Communist parties. Specific groups would require more careful study and more direct experience before any sound judgment could be made. Certainly the brief treatment given to Eurocommunist parties, for example, provides insufficient evidence for evaluating them.

One major issue did emerge in the course of writing the book. It provides, for me at least, an important criterion for judging Marxism and Marxists. The main distinction usually stressed in recent Christian discussions of Marxism is between Marxist analysis and Marxist ideology or worldview. A more important one, I believe, is between an open, self-critical Marxism and a closed, dogmatic Marxism. Marxist analysis can be open and creative; it can also be locked into a predetermined framework. The Marxist worldview can be proposed as a philosophy respectful of other views or it can be imposed as a state ideology. Many different objections have been made against Marxism—its worldview, its use of class struggle, etc. But one overriding issue kept returning in the papal encyclicals, in the views of Protestant theologians, in contemporary criticisms: the fear of Marxists "imposing" their worldview and their pre-determined plans on society, and doing so without ever doubting their certitudes. This fear is a legitimate one. Marxist regimes have a dismal record of imposing a social order and ideology rather than allowing people to express or develop their own hopes, plans, and worldviews. But this fear assumes that all Marxists think and act alike, and does not leave open the possibility of a critical Marxist movement leading to a truly liberated society.

Christianity, and the Roman Catholic Church in particular, has its own dismal record of dogmatism. But neither the stereotype "dogmatic" nor the stereotype "passive and subservient to the status quo" characterizes all Christians. Protestant theologian Reinhold Niebuhr accused Marxism of criticizing its enemies without ever subjecting its own views to criticism. But it is instructive that he made the same criticism of Roman Catholicism which, he contended, was impelled by its history and doctrine of grace "to claim unconditioned possession of the truth."[1] Catholics would acknowledge the truthfulness of his description as regards the past and perhaps as a continuing problem in the present. But they would challenge the assertion that Catholicism is "impelled" to such a claim on truth. Doctrines, of themselves, do not have inevitable consequences. But doctrines believed with a closed mind, and imposed as the sole truth, do. The power of a state to impose its ideology is certainly far greater than the power of a church to bind by conscience and guilt, but both threaten human freedom. Perhaps the link between official, closed systems of thought and loss of freedom in society cannot be proved as causal. But it appears to me a significant factor, and explains why so much emphasis has been put in this book on "critical" Marxism and critical use of Marxism.

Marxism in the United States

What role might Marxism play in the near future in the United States, and how might it contribute to Christian thought and action? Three different topics will be discussed: Marxist analysis, Marxist political parties, and Marxist socialism. The conclusions reached about each of these are quite different.

Marxist Analysis

The use of Marxist analysis, and interest in Marx and Marxism, has grown significantly over the last decade in the United States. Books on Marx and Marxism have proliferated over the last ten or fifteen years. Robert Heilbroner reviewed in one article a dozen new books on Marx for *The New York Review of Books*. He credits Marx with the discovery of a whole new mode of inquiry. Marx, says Heilbroner, was the inventor of critical social science, a new mode of inquiry comparable only to Plato's discovery of the mode of philosophical inquiry.[2] Charles Lindbloom makes a similar comment about Marx's importance: "Marx's comprehensive analysis of an entire social system and culture is a synthesis that no other social scientist has ever rivaled."[3]

Formal use of Marxist analysis may still appear only in radical journals of economics, political science, or sociology, but the number of such journals is significant: *New Left Review, Monthly Review, Telos, Review of Radical Political Economy, The Insurgent Sociologist, Politics and Society, Science & Society, Radical America,* and *Socialist Review* are but some. A new journal, *Marxist Perspectives,* offers a broad overview of Marxist cultural analysis. Scores of academic conferences are held each year in the United States on Marxist theory. Elements of the Marxist critique enter into most contemporary analyses of U.S. society, whether consciously noted or not. Conventional economists take Marxist economics more seriously. Paul Samuelson revised his much-used *Economics* textbook to include at least a discussion of Marxism.

Given the growing trend toward conservative politics in the United States, this growth in the use of Marxist analysis may seem surprising. But disillusionment with "liberalism" and government spending as a solution to socioeconomic problems has triggered not only conservative politics but also more radical analysis. Three factors have contributed to this growth of radical analysis: the activism and radical politics of the 1960s pointed to the need for more long-range analysis; the dominance of economic issues in the 1970s led specifically to more radical economic analysis; increasing awareness of world hunger and poverty stimulated research on their structural causes.

The special impact of the Marxist critique on world-wide Christianity has already been noted. Response to the Marxist critique of religion contributed significantly to new Christian attitudes. Recognition that Christianity must be this-worldly, that it must create community, that it must exist "for the sake of the world" and not simply for its own sake and growth, that it must involve itself with the poor, all these can be attributed in part to the challenge of Marxism. But the Marxist economic critique has also led many Christians to go beyond concerns for society to the recognition of structural and systemic causes. If this recognition has been far more pronounced in Latin America and other parts of the world, its effects can also be seen within the Church in the United States.

In 1975 twenty-six Catholic bishops in Appalachia wrote a powerful pastoral letter which reflects greater awareness of structural causes. One could hardly call the bishops Marxists, but the language of their analysis about the causes of the poverty and powerlessness in Appalachia is striking:

> The way of life which these corporate giants (i.e., coal companies particularly) create is called by some 'technological rationalization.' . . . Too often, however, its forces become perverted, hostile to the dignity of the earth and of its people. . . . The driving force behind this perversion is "Maximization of Profit," a principle which too often converts

itself into an idolatrous power. . . . It delivers up control to a tiny minority whose values then shape our social structures. . . . Great fortunes were built on the exploitation of Appalachian workers and Appalachian resources. . . . Meanwhile corporate profits for the giant conglomerates, who control the energy resources, keep on skyrocketing.[4]

The qualifying words "too often" distinguish the bishops' views from a Marxist analysis which would see corporate actions as the logical consequences of the system. But their statement of causes is significant.

Marxist analysis can be used simplistically; partial insights can be claimed as scientific conclusions. But what Marxist analysis offers is a way of viewing socio-economic problems "holistically," of seeing the interrelatedness of poverty, unemployment, consumerism, and powerlessness, by focusing on one central factor—the ownership and control of means of production. This type of analysis is greatly needed in efforts to create a more just society.

Marxist Political Parties

Marxist political parties, nearly all of them Marxist-Leninist, abound in the United States. Student activists of the 1960s and early 1970s brought a new influx of members into some older organizations and created new groups of their own. Leninism, with its stress on a unified, disciplined, vanguard party appealed to many youth who had found groups like the Students for a Democratic Society (SDS) too unstructured. Younger members often see themselves as the beginnings of the "revolutionary vanguard" called for by Lenin.[5]

The Communist Party USA (CP-USA) still remains the largest Marxist-Leninist party in the United States. But from a peak membership of 100,000 in the late 1930s it dropped below 10,000 in the 1950s when Communists suffered first from anti-Communist trials and hunts at home and then from disillusionment caused by revelations of Stalin's brutal purges and the Soviet Union's crushing of the Hungarian uprising. The 1960s did not help the Communist Party to recoup its losses because it was viewed by youth activists as having lost its revolutionary drive and as following a reformist strategy.

The Socialist Workers Party (SWP) began in the late 1930s as a Trotskyist movement, espousing Marxist-Leninist tactics but attacking the Soviet Union's deviations from revolutionary socialism. Through the formation of the Young Socialist Alliance (YSA) it did build on the youth movement of the 1960s. It appears to have moved toward a more parliamentary and reformist strategy in the late 1970s. Its membership is under 2000. The International Socialists (IS), a much smaller group centered mostly in the Midwest, grew out of a split with the Socialist Workers Party. Numerous other Marxist-Leninist groups could be mentioned: the Workers World Party (WWP), another splinter group from the SWP; the Progressive Labor Party (PL), formed originally by members of the CP expelled for ultra-leftism; the Revolutionary Communist Party (RCP), a Maoist group begun in the 1970s; Communist Party (Marxist-Leninist) in support of China; the Communist Labor Party (CLP), a small pro-Stalinist group with predominately Black membership. Most have membership of a few hundred or less.

As the origin of groups already mentioned may suggest, ideological differences have created a fairly constant pattern of factional disputes and splits. Student groups especially are prone to devote much of their energy to claims to represent "true" Marxism-Leninism and the "correct" strategy of social revolution. Thus, for example, the Trotskyist Organization USA publishes *Truth*. And the "truth" is that the Communist Party has betrayed the masses, the pseudo-Trotskyists of the Socialist Workers Party are liars and allied with Stalinism, the Pabloite deviationists have undermined the Fourth International, and SWP spokespersons have betrayed Marxism by speaking positively about religion.[6] This example may be an exaggerated one. But the tendency to fight over ideological differences makes it difficult to conceive how any large-scale, unified Marxist political party could develop in the United States. No "ideological" party has ever made great inroads in U.S. politics, much less divided groups which propose "revolution" under the banner of Soviet heroes and symbols.

Most Marxist political groups, I feel, tend to confirm stereotyped Marxism. But again exceptions should be made. I did not undertake to study each party. Such a study probably would show important differences, and this becomes more true in treating individuals. Certainly some leaders and intellectuals within the Communist Party USA and the Socialist Workers Party, for example, have critically re-examined their positions. One new movement, which perhaps belongs more to a discussion of socialism, certainly differs from others. The New American Movement (NAM), begun in the early 1970s and committed to democratic socialism, allows for very different ideological perspectives and uses a broad, critical Marxist analysis.

Marxist Socialism

A criticism of what is wrong with society does not imply a correct solution or plan for a new political-economic system. Marx was a critic, not a planner. Apart from the general principle that means of production should be socially and not privately owned, Marx gave little indication of how a socialist economy would operate. Apart from a few references to a transitional "dictatorship of the proletariat" and an eventual disappearance of the state, Marx said little about the political organization of a new system. Lenin, consequently had to face problems which Marx never even considered. Defending his New Economic Policy and the measure of state capitalism it necessitated, Lenin wrote in 1922: "It did not even occur to Marx to write a word about this subject; and he died without leaving a single precise quotation or irrefutable instruction on it. That is why we must get out of the difficulty entirely by our own efforts."[7]

Marx may have been correct in believing that any complete blueprint for a future society would be utopian. But by not foreseeing the vast number of political and economic problems that would follow upon a radical restructuring of society Marx proved even more utopian. Marxism can now draw upon the lessons learned from the experience of socialist countries which have made the transition from capitalism. Since Lenin led the Bolsheviks to victory, his tactics for achieving socialism still remain the most influential Marxist source. Mao Tse-tung, Fidel Castro, and others have developed their own innovations, but one Leninist feature characterizes Marxist socialism—single party rule. Hence most U.S. Americans, with strong feelings about democracy, are understandably dubious about looking to Marxism for a strategy and plan with which to transform society. Marxism may pose the right problem, but neither in Marx's theory nor in Leninist practice do we find a solution pointing to the kind of society the United States might ideally become. A great deal can be learned from innovative and inspiring features of Chinese, Cuban, and Yugoslavian socialism; much can be learned from Marxist theorists who have reflected on how to achieve a truly democratic socialism. But "learning from" is quite different from "looking to" Marxism for an answer. Marxism doesn't have the answer.

Socialism in the United States

The same question raised about Marxism in the United States might be asked about socialism. In what way does it and can it contribute to a more just and human society? The response will focus more or less on the same three aspects discussed under Marxism: socialism as a critique, as a political movement, and as a solution or plan.

Socialist Critique

In beginning with socialism as a critique, I do not mean to distinguish a socialist critique from a Marxist critique. Perhaps some distinction is possible; but they agree in recognizing the capitalist system as the fundamental problem. Where they often diverge is on questions of strategy and tactics. What I wish to emphasize is simply that I am convinced that socialism and Marxism both raise the right issue—ownership and control of the means of production. To spell out the critique in detail would be to repeat the whole of Chapter 4. The inherent "maximization of profit" drive has enormous consequences. As a consequence of cost-minimizing and efficiency, cities have been used and then left to decay when they no longer served as ideal plant locations. Massive unemployment, underemployment, and job insecurity have resulted. Control of the work process has created dehumanized work and alienated workers. Drive for profit has engendered a consumerism in which persons become objects to be manipulated by stimuli geared to play on hedonism and sexism. Distribution of profits creates great social inequality. Control of state power guarantees subsidy for capital accumulation and shifts social expenses from the economic sector to the state.

At this point, however, I would like to focus on one point—democracy. It is a critical point for two reasons: it is certainly the most cherished value in the U.S. American heritage; maintaining democracy is an argument often used against socialism and for protecting the system as it now is. Michael Novak, for example, defends capitalism in the name of democracy. He speaks of the U.S. political-economic-cultural system as "democratic capitalism." He argues that history proves that democracy without capitalism is difficult to achieve, and that nations which have leaped straight into socialism have failed to achieve democracy.[8] Novak is right that democracy and capitalism did develop together. They seemed even to complement each other in the early years of U.S. history when most settlers owned their own farms or businesses. But the situation is quite different today. Ownership of means of production is not widely distributed; it is highly concentrated in giant corporations; less than one of ten working U.S. Americans is self-employed. And the United States does have institutions of political democracy, so that any transition to a new economic system would have that tradition to build upon. At issue is whether monopoly capitalism supports democracy or whether in fact it undermines it. Is the very phrase "democratic capitalism," in reference to the present, even a contradiction in terms?

Democracy means that the people as a whole exercise sovereignty. Through universal suffrage, by majority vote, they can make decisions or select representatives to make decisions which affect their common good. Monopoly capitalism, as Charles Lindbloom has argued, does not fit well into this democratic process.[9] Executives of large corporations are responsible primarily to stock holders and not to the public. Yet their decisions affect the common good even more than government decisions do. They determine plant locations, jobs, wages, prices, profits, products, the work process. Whether cities decay or get rebuilt, whether housing is built for the poor or for higher income brackets, depends on their decisions. Yet the public has no say, no vote, in these decisions, nor on the people who make them. They cannot be voted out of office.

The economic power of large corporations prevails in government as well. Their investments determine productivity. Since the state is held responsible for the economic well-being of the country it cannot ignore their demands for subsidies and tax rebates. Moreover, the federal government itself draws its appointed officials chiefly from the upper class, and elected officials come predominately from higher income groups.

Large corporations greatly determine much of U.S. foreign policy. Government decisions about support or non-support of other nations are weighed in terms of business interests or business potential. This obviously affects seriously the democracy of the other countries involved as well.

Most of our natural resources belong to private corporations. We are perhaps fortunate that water remains, for the most part, a publicly controlled commodity. Oil is not, and it is not surprising that three of the largest multinational corporations in the world, with profits exceeding the GNP of many nations, are oil companies.

"Consumer sovereignty" is capitalism's own explanation of economic democracy. What is produced, how much is produced, what price is charged, are ostensibly determined by the free market. "Consumers vote with their dollars." Indeed they do, and a few customers with millions to spend on luxury items "outvote" masses of people whose dollars need to be spent on food and shelter. Democracy assumes one person, one vote. Consumer sovereignty allots votes according to income: a thousand votes to one, a single vote to others. The legitimacy of calling this system "democratic capitalism" needs to be challenged.

What I have done in this brief section on the socialist critique is summarize what I feel are the most legitimate and convincing arguments against contemporary capitalism. The critique, as I have presented it, is directed against *concentration* of ownership, not private ownership as such. Some socialists/ Marxists seem to argue as if private ownership by its very nature is alienating because it encourages individualism. I do not agree with this. American pride in the self-made person, and reward for personal responsibility hard work, and initiative, are not misplaced values, nor should they be equated with selfish individualism. Many parents have worked hard for the sake of their families, and have been generous and cooperative with others in the process. In pre-Civil-War America four of every five white U.S. Americans owned their own farm or business. Some grew wealthy by exploiting slaves or taking land from native Americans. But for a great many income resulted not from exploitation of others but from their own work, given a country that provided almost unlimited opportunities and resources for such initiative. There are still small businesspersons and farmers who reflect this tradition.

Socialists are correct, however, in recognizing that production has become increasingly socialized and ownership increasingly concentrated. Work today is a collective activity with hundreds and thousands involved in the same enterprise. A return to a more individual-based economy would be unrealistic. Hence the issue raised by the socialist critique returns. Should the ownership, control, and profits from these enterprises remain in the hands of a small minority, or should not all who work within them share in their ownership and participate in decisions about what is produced, how it is produced, and who profits from production?

Socialism as a Movement

When we move from a socialist critique to consideration of socialism as a movement, political realism casts a heavy shadow. The last significant socialist vote of any magnitude dates back nearly seventy years. What socialist parties and the socialist movement might have gained from the 1960s and early 1970s has been more than offset by an overall national shift toward conservatism.[10] The Democratic Socialist Organizing Committee (DSOC), which works for change within the Democratic Party, has attracted Julian Bond, Gloria Steinem, Doug Fraser, and some other notables, but its membership had reached only 3000 by the end of the 1970s. The New American Movement has about 1000 members; and to these might be added the Socialist Party, the Socialist Labor Party, the Social-Democrats USA, and others. But even the combined forces of both non-Marxist and Marxist socialist groups may well be outweighed by groups on the far right.

Why socialism never developed as a strong political movement in the United States is much debated. In the early 1900s, Werner Sombart proposed an explanation which became very widely accepted. The United States was too affluent, too rich in resources and opportunities, for socialism to take hold. The socialist utopia, said Sombart, foundered upon "roast beef and apple pie."[11] America seemed to offer its own utopia, the idea that everyone could become a capitalist. Populism more often than socialism gave force to this ideal.

Individualism, the non-ideological pragmatism of U.S. politics, ethnic factors which created one set of interests at work and different interests in community, the desire of immigrants to adapt to U.S. ways, the decision of labor leaders to concentrate on union demands rather than build a political party—these and other reasons have been given to explain why socialism did not develop as a major force in U.S. political life.

For a short time in U.S. history, socialism did appear on the rise. In 1912 Eugene Debs won nearly a million votes (6 percent of the total vote) in his bid for the presidency. But splinters within socialist ranks, socialist opposition to World War I, and anti-socialist campaigns because of this after the war, led to the socialist movement's decline. The more radical socialists joined the Communist Party, enthused by the Bolshevik victory in Russia. The Socialist Party seemed to revive on the strength of problems created by the depression. Norman Thomas won 800,000 votes in the 1932 presidential election. But Roosevelt's New Deal programs seemed to embody many socialist ideals and many deserted the Socialist Party to support him.[12]

New conditions might increase the prospects of a socialist movement. Discontent with government spending could shift to discontent with corporate profits, perhaps especially directed at oil companies. Continued inflation, unemployment, and scarcity of resources could lead to a more radical mood. History does bring quite unexpected developments. Few prognoses at the beginning of the 1960s anticipated the radical confrontations of the late 60s. Socialist victories in other countries might certainly also trigger socialist demands in the United States. For the present, socialism can hardly be judged a major force; it remains, in fact, quite marginal. Many socialists recognize this and speak of the need to "put socialism on the agenda" and into the consciousness of people before any socialist movement of any size can develop. The socialist movement can nevertheless serve to raise fundamental questions and draw attention to the serious consequences of monopoly capitalism. The weekly *In These Times,* it might be added, provides an excellent expression of open, critical, independent socialist thought from different perspectives.

Socialism as a Solution

Is socialism the answer? Does socialism provide a solution to contemporary socio-economic problems? For many other countries of the world little else seems to hold much hope. Many are desperately poor. They are not faced with a decision to exchange an already highly developed capitalist economy for a socialist one. Many have neither democracy nor *their own* capitalism even to lose. On purely pragmatic grounds, only the government may have the resources needed to accumulate and invest capital. But the people of the United States face a very different situation. The great majority are not desperately poor; we are an affluent nation. On moral grounds one could argue socialism as a means to end exploitation of other countries; but on political grounds no country has ever undertaken radical, revolutionary change in order to benefit other countries. Part of the reluctance of U.S. citizens to give more of a hearing to socialism can be traced to negative views given by political leaders and the media.[13] Part is due to the pejorative connotations which have become associated with socialism—Communism, government control, welfarism.

The problems created by these connotations will be addressed in the first part of this section. A fourth connotation, however, raises the most serious questions: Is socialism only utopianism? Is it a clear plan or simply an ideal against which capitalism is judged? Perhaps it is because of my own conservative misgivings, as already suggested by comments on Marxist socialism, that I raise this question as the most serious. But it is also the objection I constantly hear whenever a critique of capitalism is given. Usually it takes the form of the question: "Would socialism be any better, or might it not be much worse than we now have?" But before turning to this question let us address the identifications of socialism with Communism, state control, and welfarism.

"Socialism = Communism." For many people this identification proves a stumbling block. Even if the difference is grasped intellectually, some think of Communism and loss of democracy when socialism is mentioned. Some hard-line Marxist-Leninists see revolution and a dictatorship of the proletariat as the only path to socialism in the United States. While democracy is espoused even in this strategy for attaining socialism, I agree with critics who point to the fact that not only in the U.S.S.R. but in all Marxist countries

which began with single-Party rule, democracy as U.S. Americans understand it has never developed. But the great majority of socialists in this
country, including some Marxist groups, are clearly committed to democratic
socialism both as a means of attaining socialism and as fundamental to
socialism itself. The very purpose of socialism is that people should control
their work and their lives. Hence "democratic socialism" is not just a
stratagem to gain support, but expresses a fundamental goal of socialism
itself.

"Socialism = State Control." This view of socialism is quite prevalent, and
indeed it is a form socialism can take. When the papal encyclicals spoke of a
"total collectivity" or contemporary critics speak of "the government running
everything," this is the model of socialism they have in mind. Current feelings
about government spending and waste, and criticisms that government
workers are less energetic and less efficient than workers for private enterprises, tend to reinforce negative views of socialism. But many contemporary
socialists would advocate a decentralized economy, with local groups and
organizations carrying through planning. Some would have in mind a "market
socialism" as in Yugoslavia. Some would see the maintenance of small
businesses and family farms as fully compatible with socialism. A socialism
which contains this kind of "mix" could, I believe, even be an expression of
the traditional Roman Catholic social teachings on "the principle of subsidiarity."

That public ownership would kill initiative is quite disputable. Initiative
depends on a host of factors—ambition, degree of responsibility, pride and
fulfillment in work, and material and social incentives—and not just on
private versus public ownership. Do top government officials work less hard
than top business executives? Do professors at state universities work less
hard than their colleagues at private ones? Examples of initiative are almost
always drawn from the business class, not from the masses of factory workers,
clerks, and the millions whose work consists of routine tasks. A decentralized, democratic socialism in principle, I believe, is quite consistent with
democracy, Christianity, and even traditional Roman Catholic social thought.
But whether it is only an ideal, and how a transition to such an economic
system could occur, remain serious problems.

"Socialism = Welfarism." When some Americans complain that we already
have "creeping socialism," they reflect one of the most common misconcep-
tions about socialism—that it is a system to provide for those who do not feel
like working. Ironically, the issue of work is one point on which most
socialists and staunch conservatives *agree*. The Communist Party Program of
the U.S.S.R. puts it strongly: "He who does not work does not eat." Welfare
is not a product of socialism but of capitalism, at least where unemployed but
able-bodied persons are concerned. One hopes that no society will disavow
responsibility for the sick, the handicapped, and the elderly. The fact that
many view "socialized medicine" as the next step toward socialism only

confirms this misconception. Doctors do not control the chief means of production in American society. Whatever other reasons might be given for socialized medicine, it would not fundamentally alter the basic property relations of society. Ownership and control of production, and not a giant welfare system, are the objectives of democratic socialism.

"Socialism = Utopianism." Any hope or plan for a new social order has to contain some utopian element. Christianity itself is filled with utopian hopes for the coming Kingdom of God. The great American dream of success was a utopian vision that attracted immigrants. But at some point utopian vision must appear concretely realizable or at least able to be approximated. This includes a clear sense of the problems involved and how to meet them.

Let me set down my own position so that my problems with socialism on this score may be clear. My problems are not with the ideals of democratic socialism, but with the assumption that if capitalism is replaced with socialism these ideals will be fulfilled, at least to a significant degree. I don't think it is quite that simple or certain. Socialist enthusiasts point to China, Cuba, and the early years of Allende as example of what can happen positively through socialism. Poor people who had nothing, who were treated as nothing, found new hope in socialism, new pride, new meaning in their lives. I believe this did happen. But I do not believe that the majority of people in the United States are at this starting point. Most have jobs and education; 97 percent even have televisions. Hence a closer parallel would be socialism in Eastern Europe where worker alienation is great, productivity and wages low, and enthusiasm for socialism much less evident. The fact that the United States is already a highly developed industrial nation could create *more* problems for socialism, not less, especially if a significant part of social ownership was in the hands of the state. For as is evident from strikes and protests at present, no group in society feels satisfied, not even sports stars with $200.000-plus salaries. Each contending group in society will continue to make demands for its share whether the economy is socialist or not. Without socialist attitudes, Julius Nyerere has said, true socialism is impossible. But such attitudes will be more difficult to attain in the United States, where individualism has long been stressed.

At the same time I *disagree* with the conclusions which conservatives draw from this kind of argument: "For all its faults capitalism is still the best, so let's stay with it." No social change would ever occur on this basis; the Marxist-socialist critique has convinced me that monopoly capitalism undermines democracy and too often does not promote the common good; hence simply to stay with what we have is for me un-Christian. What I see as a solution of this dilemma is not original; it stresses structural reforms; it embodies my own interpretation of Gramsci's concept of hegemony, and of building on positive steps as opposed to only negative criticisms. But before going to it, let me return to the issue of socialism and utopianism.

Michael Lerner's *The New Socialist Revolution* exemplifies the kind of socialist position I find questionable. For nearly three hundred pages he criticizes U.S. capitalism and discusses at length the need to crush bourgeois hegemony. He devotes a scant four pages to the transition to socialism and then describes in glowing terms the democratic institutions which will flourish under socialism. He makes no attempt to address, or even show an awareness of, the great difficulties which such a radical social transition would entail. What the new society will look like, he says simply, will depend on what we do with it.[14] Though addressing only one of the same points Lerner takes up, Erik Olin Wright is much more candid and honest when he states that in the United States no strategy for socialism is particularly plausible at present.[15] Much more hard, creative thinking is needed, I believe, both about workable forms socialism might take and transitions to socialism, before most people in the United States can begin even to think about opting for socialism.

In a series of articles for *In These Times,* entitled "For a Socialism That Works," Leland Stauber addressed one aspect of the issue we have just been discussing. While noting that the U.S. press and politicians have created an ideological bias against socialism, he accuses socialists of contributing to this bias by not proposing any fresh alternatives. The twentieth century, he contends, has been a graveyard for inadequate socialist ideas. The only socialist alternative which he sees as able to avoid defeat is one that promises as much efficiency as capitalism. He proposes a "market socialism" drawing on both the successes and failures of Yugoslavian socialism. The socialism he envisions includes a public or government sector, a market socialist sector which would not be government-owned but publicly-owned by groups operating along the lines of private firms today, a private sector to include small businesses and family farms, and a cooperative sector.[16]

His proposals triggered numerous rejoinders in subsequent issues of *In These Times,* ranging from support to complete rejection. His effort, I believe, is an example of the kind of creative, long-range thinking needed to make democratic socialism more plausible. The negative responses indicate how little agreement exists on what constitutes a workable but genuine socialism. Perhaps some other proposal would have generated more support. The controversy over Stauber's articles may only confirm the need for "putting socialism on the agenda" so that more creative thinking will be stimulated. But the controversy also indicates why proposing socialism as a solution is to present a very unclear option.

The problem of a transition to socialism is also important. The worst possible transition that I could imagine would be one that counts on "waiting to work it out until we get there" or one that is necessitated by a sudden collapse of capitalism. To try to build up a new society out of the chaos and anarchy left by the collapse of an old one offers the least amount of hope that a truly just and democratic social order will emerge. Hence to promote a strategy of "the worse the better" seems to me even immoral. Some look to the Swedish Social-Democrats and their plans to socialize Sweden as a possible model for democratic transition to socialism. Theoretical work about strategies of transition from capitalism to socialism is needed, but a successful example of such a transition would aid the socialist movement most.

In Michael Harrington's strategy of long-range vision and realistic approximations I found personally the kind of approach I had been looking for. I would express my long range vision as "economic democracy" rather than socialism at this point. But I agree fully with the approach Harrington takes. He calls for a long-range vision of structural, anti-capitalist change, but adds:

> We do not, however, assert this ultimatistically, insisting that America suddenly convert to socialist values *in toto*. We address immediate problems and seek immediate solutions. We join with trade unionists and minority activists and feminists and Democratic Party reformers— and, for that matter, with all women and men of good will. We do not reject increments of change—but we seek to influence them, to design them, to move them, in the direction of the massive transformations which alone can solve the present crisis. [7]

What, as a conclusion to all of this, can socialism contribute and what stance might a Christian take? If socialism cannot claim to have "the" solution, capitalism certainly does not. Socialism points to an important alternative possibility, and offers a needed critique of capitalism. For a Christian to work for a democratic socialism would seem a perfectly justifiable option. The very uncertainties about socialism might be all the more reason for Christians to be part of the movement, to help shape its direction and values.

A Personal Strategy

If Erik Olin Wright is correct that there is no plausible strategy for socialism at the present time in the United States, then it would certainly be pretentious to offer an even broader strategy which might lead to democratic socialism or to economic democracy in some other form. What follows, then, is not an argument for "the" correct strategy Christians in the United States should follow. It is perhaps a "philosophy of social change" which dovetails with Michael Harrington's strategy of long-range vision and immediate tasks. It is a strategy of moving toward a fundamental restructuring of society through "increments of change" and reforms. But underlying this strategy is a conviction that such a process is not just a matter of political realism but the process most apt for achieving the desired results. This brief philosophy of social change is offered in the hope that some other Christians who share the same concerns, values, and misgivings, may be helped in their reflection.

First, I believe that any option taken should be both idealistic and realistic.

Uncompromising idealism in politics leads only to frustration; realism alone offers insufficient vision and hope. The long-range vision and idealism, I have called "economic democracy" (with no intended reference to Tom Hayden's movement in California). It is open to democratic socialism, especially to one that embraces the various kinds of sectors Stauber enumerated: the public sector, a private sector, a cooperative sector. It is open to the kind of vision E. F. Schumacher presented in *Small is Beautiful.*[18] Since Schumacher's model enterprises are still "private" enterprises, some may see this option as contradicting my earlier critique of capitalism. But "economic democracy" means sharing in ownership and participating in decision making, which Schumacher stresses. Like democratic socialism, Schumacher's vision is for the most part an untested ideal and leaves unresolved any political strategy for achieving it. Large corporations would be broken up; owners and executives would have to cede much of their control. But at this point I am speaking only of long-range visions. The ideal economic democracy may be something beyond both socialism and capitalism as we now know them.

All this "openness" to creative alternatives may seem to contradict my criticisms of socialism for not presenting a clear, defined, or tested alternative. But my criticisms were of the assumption that a clear alternative *has been found* and that it can simply be put in place once the right moment arises. I spoke earlier in this chapter of Gramsci's concept of "hegemony," in which control results not primarily from force but from consent. Perhaps more accurately I should say that what is presented here is my own use or adaptation of his concept. Gramsci insists that socialism can succeed only if widespread support has been built up *before* a radical restructuring of society occurs. While part of this development of hegemony consists of breaking down the domination of capitalist ideology and institutions, part of it also consists in building up new attitudes and new institutions, so that people will be prepared to accept and even enthusiastically support a new social order. Tapping the sensitivity and caring attitudes of people, and constructing institutions that develop these, are as important as rousing anger against what is wrong. Building on patriotism and the fulfillment of the "American dream" of equal opportunity should be stressed. This process of moving towards consent and support involves, I believe, being open to new historical developments. If dissatisfaction with the present system mounts, very different alternative directions will emerge, and at *that* point it will be important to decide which option appears realistically to be the one most likely to gain support and idealistically the one which seems most promising to fulfill ideals of justice. With Gandhi I believe that new institutions need to be built up along the way. If some experience of new institutions has already occurred, for example of cooperative enterprises, a greater assurance will be had of their success in a new social order. In short, I am placing great stress on the "transition" to any new social order, and on a democratic process.

A Marxist-Leninist approach, I believe, often fails to distinguish what people are opposed to and what they might want in its place. People may be opposed to the present system which dominates their lives, but that does not mean that they espouse a Party-determined socialism as an alternative. What they want is precisely to shape their own lives, to make their own decisions, to express or develop their own worldviews. It is difficult to arrive at consensus through democratic process. It is certainly unrealistic to think that a majority of U.S. Americans would adopt a Leninist "democratic centralism" in which all agree to a unified course of action once a plan or issue had been debated. And I would greatly fear for a democracy if any vanguard group decided within its own ranks what was best for society and had the power to carry their plan through. I believe that democracy itself, or certainly U.S. democracy, is closely allied to pragmatism and compromise, to testing out proposals on a small scale before attempting them globally, and to accepting approxima- tions rather than holding out for the ideological purity of an ideal. Perhaps through such pragmatism and compromise "true" socialism or "true" economic democracy will not be fully attained, but neither will it be attained without such a process. The means used to achieve a new society will be the means used to maintain it. But when I speak of democratic process I mean a democratic one, not one weighted heavily, as it is at present, with representa- tives of one social class. Working with and mobilizing the efforts of those who now feel powerless in society will be essential to such a process. This, in short, is the philosophy which underlies the strategy I see as best suited to social change in the United States.

But isn't all of this terribly idealistic and utopian? Do I really think such a process will occur? Do I really even think any change will occur in respect to capitalism? My answer is that while I do not know if this model of social change will succeed, it stands the best chance of ultimate success and a very realistic chance of partial success. The objection to this from the far left has been repeated often: reformism has never succeeded in bringing about the radical restructuring of society; reforms only permit the old system to sustain itself. My answer to this is quite simple. There is not a single example of success for a revolutionary strategy of social change in any advanced capitalist country of the world. The objection to reformism has been repeated end- lessly for over 130 years. But revolutionary social change has only occurred in countries which lacked democratic political institutions capable of intro- ducing change in another way. Hence neither a reformist nor a revolutionary strategy can point to any ultimate successes. Reforms have on the other hand, produced important immediate benefits; they have bettered society. Moreover in a democratic country there is a dynamic of "rising expectations" that could lead to fundamental social change. It occurred in the 1960s in the United States, when liberal demands led to more radical ones. It occurred in Chile when Christian-Democratic reforms led to demands for socialism.

There are two kinds of reforms or increments of change that I feel should be given priority: those which affect the very structure of the political-economic system and those which address an urgent and immediate need. The former might include more public control over energy resources, fundamental changes in political representation, legislation affecting multinationals, the encouragement of worker and consumer cooperatives, employee and consumer representation on corporation boards. The latter would include full employment, a guaranteed minimum income, elimination of poverty, legislation affecting food production and trade with other countries, military spending, and minority rights. These are meant only as examples, not as an indication of priorities.

While these are immediate targets, what Harrington added should also be stressed: the need to influence, design, and move reforms in the direction of long-range fundamental goals. Specific issues can be used to raise larger and more fundamental questions. Moreover, since "single issue politics" has become quite dominant in U.S. political life, working from one issue may be the best way to raise more fundamental ones. Tax reform, for example, involves the fundamental issue of who owns, controls, and profits from the present economic system. Reforms to make elective office truly representative of the majority of American people involves the issue of capitalist domination of the state; and I think steps toward a more truly democratic political rule are critically important for establishing economic democracy. Almost any important issue can be used in a way which also allows for raising larger issues and changing consciousness in the direction of more fundamental changes.

One very practical final note might be added. Each person has only so much energy. Most people are not engaged full-time in social and political work. Most find it difficult to find time for additional commitments. One of the reasons for a sense of powerlessness in contemporary society is the overwhelming number of social and political problems that deserve effort—world hunger, racial and sexual discrimination, military spending, etc. It seems to me that an important way of breaking through this sense of powerlessness in the face of so many issues is to choose one issue and one group to work with. It is possible to become knowledgeable in one area and to make a contribution in that area. Together these efforts could help to move society toward a social order which truly benefits all its members and gives them some sense of dignity and control over their destinies.

A Christian Epilogue

This book was written to explore the compatibility or non-compatibility of Marxism and Christianity. The major stress throughout the book has been on Marxism, so that a Christian might better understand Marxism in its origins, its developments, and its variances in the contemporary world. If the book has attempted a reappraisal of Marxism, it has made little effort to reappraise Christianity. Chapter 7 on Marxist atheism, for example, was written with a view to judging whether atheism and materialism are essential or not to Marxism. Another author might have used this occasion to stress much more the validity of many Marxist critiques of religion, to show how the Church and institutionalized Christianity have failed to serve justice and have thus justified the attacks of political atheism.

As for what Christianity might contribute to Marxism, or more importantly what it might bring to the construction of a more just social order, even less has been said. Christian advocates of Marxism appear at times to view the contribution of Christianity in a very limited way: Christians should acknowledge their failures to fight for justice in the past; they can prove themselves just as revolutionary or subversive as Marxists by drawing on biblical inspiration; over and above problems of social change Christianity can contribute a hope and transcendence that goes beyond death itself. It is true that Christians have failed to see and to act upon demands for justice arising from their own biblical tradition. It is also true that there is no specifically Christian socio-economic analysis or plan for society. But Christians do have a precious and important heritage that bears upon Marxism and social change.

The dominant Marxist tradition has made an important contribution in stressing the conditioning and limiting effect of socio-economic conditions on human life. But it has been deficient in overstressing these conditions. Its belief that changed conditions will change human nature and "produce" new persons has led it in practice to overplan society and overcontrol individual lives. Christianity, at its best, brings to the problem of social change a profound sense of the dignity, freedom, and fallibility of every individual. It has failed at times in the past to recognize the impact of socio-economic conditions on the individual. It has overstressed the individual in its appeals for moral and spiritual conversion. Its message has often become entangled in status-quo ideologies. But its message, exemplified both in Jesus' uncompromising resistance to injustice and his compassion for individuals, remains critically important. Christianity has often been charged with "weakness" for its stress on interpersonal love, compassion, and forgiveness. Its recognition of the sinfulness of human nature has been derided as justification for avoiding societal change. But any truly human social order needs to embody these interpersonal virtues and to recognize its own limits and fallibility. No social order will ever "produce" new persons. It can only remove obstacles and create a better environment in which human freedom and dignity can prosper. Christians thus must work not simply for social change, but for a social change that minimizes violence and hostility, that insists on respect for the dignity and freedom of every individual, and that accepts human limitations.

Christianity in recent years has learned, often from Marxism, to become more aware of the historical conditions that shaped and at times misshaped its theory and practice. Christianity may paradoxically now serve to make Marxism more conscious of the conditions that shaped *its* development and hence help it to become more self-critical of its present theory and practice. Neither Christianity nor Marxism exists as a pure ideal. Christianity is embodied in the Church and Marxism in political parties and movements. Only through the Church has the Christian message been kept alive over the centuries, and only through Marxist movements has the message of economic liberation been sustained. Both must acknowledge their failures. In addition many other religious faiths and political-social ideologies have laid claim to their own importance in shaping the future. A respect for pluralism of beliefs is itself an expression of respect for the human dignity of those who hold those beliefs. All religious faiths and political ideologies share in common some vision of a truly just and humane society. My own loyalty to the Church and deep love of my faith give expression to this vision in a Christian way, in work and prayer that looks to "a new heaven and a new earth." At present this vision exists largely in hope, but a hope that God has expressed as promise: "The world of the past is gone. . . . Now I am making the whole of creation new" (Rev. 21:4–5).

Notes

1. Reinhold Niebuhr, *The Nature and Destiny of Man,* Vol. II (London: Nisbet, 1943), p. 229.

2. Robert L. Heilbroner, "Inescapable Marx," in *The New York Review of Books,* June 29, 1978, Vol. XXV., No. 11, p. 33.

3. Charles E. Lindbloom, *Politics and Markets: The World's Political-Economic Systems* (New York: Basic Books, 1977), p. 77.

4. "This Land Is Home to Me," A Pastoral Letter on Powerlessness in Appalachia by the Catholic Bishops of the Region (Prestonburg, Kentucky: Catholic Committee of Appalachia, 1976), pp. 5–8.

5. For a discussion of Marxist groups and parties, see Jim O'Brien, "American Leninism in the 1970s," in *Radical America,* Vol. 11, No. 6, November 1977, and Vol. 12, No. 1, February 1978. See also *The New Left of the Sixties,* ed. Michael Friedman (Berkeley, Calif.: Independent Socialist Press, 1972).

6. *Truth,* Organ of Trotskyist Organization USA Section (Sympathizing) Fourth International, January 12, 1979, No. 86.

7. V.I. Lenin, "Political Report of the Central Committee to the 11th Congress of the R.C.P. (B.), March 27, 1922," in *Selected Works,* Vol. IX (New York International Publishers, 1943), p. 333.

8. Michael Novak, *The American Vision, An Essay on the Future of Democratic Capitalism* (Washington, D.C.: American Enterprise Institute for Public Policy Research, 1978), pp. 9–10. Novak wrote this as a consultor to the Exxon Corporation to suggest a strategy to them for counterattacking anti-capitalist criticisms on the part of a new "adversarial class" of intellectuals. This fact alone could evoke a very cynical response. But he represents a significant neo-conservative trend. While challenging his main thesis I believe some of his reflections about American "values" and also his critique of socialism do merit consideration.

9. Most of the arguments which follow are drawn from Lindbloom, *Politics and Markets,* which I discussed in Chapter 4. The ideas on consumer sovereignty came to me in reading Lappé and Collins, *Food First,* also discussed in Chapter 4.

10. In October 1977, a national Gallup poll was taken to determine where people stand or place themselves in politics. Forty-seven percent called themselves "conservative" and only 32 percent liberal, with 10 percent middle road and 11 percent no opinion. The far right, 4 percent, outnumbered the far left, 3 percent. See *U.S. News and World Report,* Jan. 23, 1978, p. 24. While moods change, historians have long commented on the general conservatism of the U.S. people.

11. Werner Sombart, *Why Is There No Socialism in the United States?,* trans. Patricia M. Hocking and C. T. Husbands (New York: M. E. Sharpe, 1978). Only recently has the first full translation of Sombart appeared in English. See a long, excellent review by Jerome Karabel, in *The New York Review of Books,* February 8, 1979, Vol. XXVI, No. 1, pp. 22–27. See also Michael Harrington, *Socialism* (New York: Bantam, 1971), p. 131.

12. On the history of socialism in the U.S. see Harrington, *Socialism*, Chapter 6; David Shannon, *The Socialist Party of America* (New York: Macmillan, 1955); Donald D. Egbert and Stow Persons, eds., *Socialism and American Life*, Volume I (Princeton, N.J.: Princeton University Press, 1952).

13. *Time* magazine's special feature report on "Socialism," May 13, 1978, and its feature on "Can Capitalism Survive?," July 14, 1975, both conclude, not surprisingly, that capitalism is the best.

14. Michael P. Lerner, *The New Socialist Revolution; An Introduction to its Theory and Strategy* (New York: Delacorte, 1973), pp. 297—322 on transition and description of socialism.

15. Erik Olin Wright, *Class, Crisis and the State*, p. 233, n.11.

16. Leland Stauber, "For a Socialism That Works," in three parts for *In These Times*, May 3-9, May 10-16, May 17-23, 1978. Stauber is a professor of political science at Southern Illinois University. *In These Times*, it is worth adding, carried a series of articles on religion in the August 2-8, 1978 issue.

17. Michael Harrington, "The Socialist Case," in *The Center Magazine* Vol. IX, No. 4, July/August 1976, p. 64.

18. E. F. Schumacher, *Small Is Beautiful* (New York: Harper Torchbooks, 1973).

Index of Names

Index of Subjects

OTHER ORBIS TITLES

THE COMING
OF THE THIRD CHURCH
An Analysis of the Present and Future of the Church

Walbert Buhlmann

"Not a systematic treatment of contemporary ecclesiology but a popular narrative analogous to Alvin Toffler's Future Shock." America

ISBN 0-88344-069-5 CIP

ISBN 0-88344-070-9

Cloth $12.95

Paper $6.95

FREEDOM MADE FLESH

Ignacio Ellacuría

"Ellacuría's main thesis is that God's saving message and revelation are historical, that is, that the proclamation of the gospel message must possess the same historical character that revelation and salvation history do and that, for this reason, it must be carried out in history and in a historical way." Cross and Crown

ISBN 0-88344-140-3

ISBN 0-88344-141-1

Cloth $8.95

Paper $4.95

CHRISTIAN POLITICAL THEOLOGY
A MARXIAN GUIDE

Joseph Petulla

"Petulla presents a fresh look at Marxian thought for the benefit of Catholic theologians in the light of the interest in this subject which was spurred by Vatican II, which saw the need for new relationships with men of all political positions." Journal of Economic Literature

ISBN 0-88344-060-1

Paper $4.95

THE GOSPEL IN SOLENTINAME

Ernesto Cardenal

"Upon reading this book, I want to do so many things—burn all my other books which at best seem like hay, soggy with mildew. I now know who (not what) is the church and how to celebrate church in the eucharist. The dialogues are intense, profound, radical. The Gospel in Solentiname calls us home." Carroll Stuhlmueller, National Catholic Reporter

ISBN 0-88344-168-3 CIP   *Cloth* $6.95

THE CHURCH AND POWER IN BRAZIL

Charles Antoine

"This is a book which should serve as a basis of discussion and further study by all who are interested in the relationship of the Church to contemporary governments, and all who believe that the Church has a vital role to play in the quest for social justice." Worldmission

ISBN 0-88344-062-8   *Paper* $4.95

HISTORY AND
THE THEOLOGY OF LIBERATION

Enrique Dussel

"The book is easy reading. It is a brilliant study of what may well be or should be the future course of theological methodology." Religious Media Today

ISBN 0-88344-179-9   *Cloth* $8.95
ISBN 0-88344-180-2   *Paper* $4.95

LOVE AND STRUGGLE
IN MAO'S THOUGHT

Raymond L. Whitehead

"Mao's thoughts have forced Whitehead to reassess his own philosophy and to find himself more fully as a Christian. His well documented and meticulously expounded philosophy of Mao's love and struggle-thought might do as much for many a searching reader." Prairie Messenger

ISBN 0-88344-289-2 CIP   *Cloth* $8.95
ISBN 0-88344-290-6   *Paper* $3.95

A THEOLOGY OF LIBERATION
Gustavo Gutiérrez

"*The movement's most influential text.*" Time

ISBN 0-88344-477-1

ISBN 0-88344-478-X

Cloth $7.95
Paper $4.95

THE NEW CREATION: MARXIST AND CHRISTIAN?
José María González-Ruiz

"*A worthy book for lively discussion.*" The New Review of Books and Religion

ISBN 0-88344-327-9 CIP

Cloth $6.95

CHRISTIANS AND SOCIALISM
Documentation of the Christians for
Socialism Movement in Latin America

edited by John Eagleson

"*Compelling in its clear presentation of the issue of Christian commitment in a revolutionary world.*" The Review of Books and Religion

ISBN 0-88344-058-X

Paper $4.95

POLYGAMY RECONSIDERED
Eugene Hillman

"*This is by all odds the most careful consideration of polygamy and the attitude of Christian Churches toward it which it has been my privilege to see.*" Missiology

ISBN 0-88344-391-0

ISBN 0-88344-392-9

Cloth $15.00
Paper $7.95

AFRICAN TRADITIONAL RELIGION
E. Bolaji Idowu

"*A great work in the field and closely comparable to Mbiti's African Religions and Philosophy. It is worthwhile reading.*" The Jurist

ISBN 0-88344-005-9

Cloth $6.95